Collins

First published in 2005 by Collins
an imprint of
HarperCollins Publishers
77–85 Fulham Palace Road
London w6 8jb

www.collins.co.uk

© HarperCollinsPublishers, 2005
Maps © Collins Bartholomew Ltd, 2005

The contents of this edition of the Collins Need to
Know The World are believed correct at the time of
printing. Nevertheless, the publisher can accept no
responsibility for errors or omissions, changes in the
detail given or for any expense or loss thereby
caused.

A catalogue record for this book is available from
the British Library

Series design: Mark Thomson

ISBN 0 00 719831 0

RH11881 Imp 001

Printed in Thailand

need to know?

The World

Collins

Introduction

Atlas features

This world atlas provides all you need to know to get a detailed picture of how the world looks today and to get a clear impression of each part of the world. Through detailed maps, descriptive information and key geographical facts, it presents a portrait of the world, its continents, and regions and countries within them. Each map is accompanied by a general description of the area covered, and additional facts. *Geo terms* explain geographical terms which appear within place and feature names in local languages; *Know the ...* panels give insight into important locations, and the history and geography of areas covered by each map; *Discover more* allows further exploration of places and geographical themes through important web sites; and the *Watch out!* feature provides warnings for travellers and highlights interesting aspects of the area to look out for. The atlas is introduced by details of the world's **states and territories**, which include key government and tourist web sites for more information.

Map types

Several types of map are used throughout the atlas to give the best impression of the world and its features. Small-scale **world maps** of countries and physical features provide the overall context, while world **thematic maps** cover major geographical topics of relevance today. **Continental maps** of the physical features and countries within each continent, complemented by key facts about the continent, introduce each atlas section. These are followed by **reference maps** of specific countries and regions which include detailed depiction of mountain ranges, rivers, communications networks, towns and cities, and other important features. Maps of the world's oceans, introduced by facts and statistics, complete the worldwide coverage.

Map symbolization

Maps show information by using symbols which are designed to reflect the features on the earth that they represent. Map symbols can be in the form of **points** – such as those used to show towns and airports; **lines** – used to represent roads and rivers; or **areas** – such as lakes. Variation in **size**, **shape** and **colour** of these types of symbol allow a great range of information to be shown. The symbols used in this atlas are explained opposite. Not all detail can be shown at the small map scales used in this atlas, so information is generalized to allow easy interpretation. This generalization takes the form of **selection** – the inclusion of some features and the omission of others of less importance; and **simplification** – where lines are smoothed, areas combined, or symbols displaced slightly to aid clarity. This is done in such a way that the overall character of the area mapped is retained. The degree of generalization varies with map scale.

Scale

Scale is the relationship between the size of an area, or a distance, on the map and the actual size of the area, or distance, on the ground. It determines the amount of detail shown on a map - larger scales show more, smaller scales show less. The scale of each map is indicated by a **scale bar**, which allows distances to be measured, and a **scale statement** – for example 1: 8 000 000, which means that one unit measured on the map (1 millimetre, for example) represents eight million of those units on the ground (in this case 8 million millimetres, or 8 kilometres).

Geographical names

The spelling of place names on maps is a complex problem as there is no single standard way of converting names from one alphabet, or symbol set, to another. Changes in official languages also have to be taken into account when creating maps and policies need to be established for the spelling of names on individual atlases and maps. Such policies must take account of the local official names, international conventions or traditions, as well as the purpose of the atlas or map. The policy in this atlas is to use **local name forms** which are recognized by the governments of the countries concerned, but with **English conventional names** being used for the most well-known places, country names and international features. In such cases, the local name form is often included in brackets on the map and also appears as a cross-reference in the index.

Boundaries

The status of nations and their boundaries are shown in this atlas as they are at the time of going to press, as far as can be ascertained. Where international boundaries are the subject of disputes, the aim is to take a strictly neutral viewpoint and to represent as accurately as possible the situation on the ground.

Map symbols

Settlements

Population	National Capital		Administrative Capital		City or Town	
over 5 million	▣	BEIJING	◉	Tianjin	◉	New York
1 million – 5 million	▢	MADRID	○	Sydney	○	Madurai
500 000 – 1 million	▫	BANGUI	○	Douala	○	Barranquilla
100 000 – 500 000	▫	WELLINGTON	○	Mansa	○	Yong'an
50 000 – 100 000	▫	PORT OF SPAIN	○	Lubango	○	Puruliya
under 50 000	▫	MALABO	○	Chinhoyi	○	El Tigre

Styles of lettering

Country name	FRANCE	Island	Gran Canaria
Overseas territory / Dependency	Guadaloupe	Lake	Lake Erie
Administrative name	SCOTLAND	Mountain	Mt Blanc
Area name	PATAGONIA	River	Thames

Physical features

- Freshwater lake
- Seasonal freshwater lake
- Salt lake
- Seasonal salt lake
- Dry salt lake
- Ice cap
- River
- Mountain pass (2188)

Other features

- ∴ Site of special interest
- ⌒⌒⌒ Wall

Communications

- ═══ Motorway (selected countries only)
- ─── Main road
- - - - Track
- - - - Railway
- ✈ Main airport
- ⊢⊢⊢ Canal

Relief
Contour intervals and layer colours

metres

6000	
5000	
4000	
3000	
2000	
1000	
500	△ 6960 Summit height in metres
200	-123 Spot height height in metres
0	123 Ocean deep depth in metres
below sea level	
0	
200	
2000	
4000	
6000	

Boundaries

- ━━━ International
- ▪▪▪▪ International disputed
- ━━━ Administrative (selected countries only)
- ●●●●● Ceasefire line

Geo terms

The language and meaning of important non-English geographical terms appearing on each map are explained in the 'Geo terms' box on each spread. Below is a more comprehensive list of such terms for the main languages. Generic terms such as these are commonly used within the names of places and geographical features to describe their nature or origin.

Afrikaans
Berg, -berg, -berge	mountain(s)
Groot	big
-punt	cape, point
-veld	field

Amharic (Ethiopia)
Häyk'	lake
Ras	mountain
Shet'	river
Wenz	river

Arabic
Bahr	river
Buḥayrat	lake
Chott	impermanent lake, salt lake
Erg	sandy desert
Ghubbat	bay
Ḥadabat	plain
Hawr	lake
Jabal, Jebel	mountain(s)
Jazā'ir	islands
Jiddat	desert
Juzur	islands
Khalīj	gulf, bay
Nafūd	desert
Ra's	cape, point
Ramlat	sandy desert
Sebkha	impermanent lake, salt lake
Wāḥāt	oasis
Wādī	watercourse

Bulgarian
Nizina	lowland
Nos	cape, point
Planina	hills, mountains

Chinese
Bandao	peninsula
Feng	mountain
Gaoyuan	plateau
Hai	sea
He	river
Hu	lake
Jiang	river
Ling	mountain range
Nur	lake
Pendi	basin
Shamo	desert
Shan	mountain(s)
Tao	island
Wan	bay
Yunhe	canal

Dutch
Kanaal	canal
-meer	lake
-zee	sea

Farsi (Iran), Dari (Afghanistan)
Daryācheh	lake
Dasht	desert
Hāmūn	marsh, salt pan
Kūh, Kūhha	mountain(s)
Reshteh	mountain range
Rūd	river

French
Baie	bay
Cap	cape, point
Chaîne	mountain range
Étang	lagoon, lake
Golfe	gulf, bay
Grande	big
Île, Îles	island; islands
Lac	lake
Massif	mountains, upland
Mont, Monts	mountain(s)
Petit	small
Pic	peak
Pointe (Pte)	cape, point

German
Alb	mountain range
-berg	hill, mountain
Bucht	gulf, bay
-gebirge	mountains
Heide	heath, moor
Inseln	islands
Kap	cape, point
Wald, -wald	forest (mountains)

Greek
Akra	cape, point
Kolpos	gulf, bay
Nisoi	islands
Pelagos	sea

Indonesian
Bukit	mountain
Gunung	mountain
Kepulauan	islands
Laut	sea
Pegunungan	mountain range
Pulau-pulau	islands
Puncak	mountain
Selat	strait
Semenanjung	peninsula
Tanjung	cape, point
Teluk	gulf, bay

Italian
Capo	cape, point
Golfo	gulf, bay
Isola, Isole	island; islands
Monte, Monti	mountain(s)

Japanese
-dake	mountain
-gang	river
-hantō	peninsula
-jima	island
-kaikyō	strait
-ko	lake
-misaki	cape, point
-nada	gulf, bay
-rettō	islands
-san	mountain
-sanmyaku	mountain range
-shima	island
-shotō	islands
-suidō	strait
-tō	island
-wan	bay
-zaki	cape, point

Korean
-bong	mountain
-do	island
-gang	river
-haehyŏp	strait
-ho	lake
-man	bay
-san	mountain

Malay
Banjaran	mountain range
Gunung	mountain

Norwegian
-dal	valley
-halvøya	peninsula
-kapp	cape, point

Portuguese
Baía	bay
Barragem	dam, reservoir
Cabo	cape, point
Chapada	hills, uplands
Ilha	island
Lago	lake
Lagoa	lagoon
Pico	peak
Planalto	plateau
Ponta	cape, point
Represa	reservoir
Rio	river
São, Santa, Santo	saint
Serra	mountain range

Romanian
Lacul	lake
Meridionali	southern
Pasul	pass
Podişul	plateau
Vârful	mountain

Russian
Bol'shoy	big
Gora	mountain
Gryada	ridge
Guba	gulf, bay
Khrebet	mountain range
Kryazh	hills, ridge
Les	forest
Malyy	small
More	sea
Mys	cape, point
Nizmennost'	lowland
Ostrov, Ostrova	island(s)
Ozero	lake
Peski	desert
Ploskogor'ye	plateau
Poluostrov	peninsula
Proliv	strait
Ravnina	plain
Vodokhranilishche	reservoir
Vozvyshennost'	upland
Zaliv	gulf, bay
Zemlya	land

Spanish
Bahía	bay
Cabo	cape, point
Cayos	islands
Cerro	mountain
Cordillera	mountain range
Costa	coastal area
Embalse	reservoir
Estrecho	strait
Golfo	gulf, bay
Gran, Grande	big
Isla, Islas	island; islands
Lago	lake
Laguna	lagoon
Mar	sea
Montes	mountains
Nevado, Nudo	snow-covered mountain
Picacho, Pico	peak
Presa	reservoir
Punta	cape, point
Río	river
Salar	salt pan
San, Santa, Santo	saint
Sierra	mountain range
Volcán	volcano

Turkish
Burun	cape, point
Dağ, Dağı	mountain
Dağları	mountain range
Denizi	sea
Gölü	lake
Körfezi	gulf, bay

Vietnamese
Cao Nguyên	plateau
Hô	lake
Mui	cape, point
Sông	river

Geo tables

Highest mountains

	metres	feet	Location
Mt Everest	8 848	29 028	China/Nepal
K2	8 611	28 251	China/J & K*
Kangchenjunga	8 586	28 169	India/Nepal
Lhotse	8 516	27 939	China/Nepal
Makalu	8 463	27 765	China/Nepal
Cho Oyu	8 201	26 906	China/Nepal
Dhaulagiri	8 167	26 794	Nepal
Manaslu	8 163	26 781	Nepal
Nanga Parbat	8 126	26 660	Jammu and Kashmir
Annapurna I	8 091	26 545	Nepal

*Jammu and Kashmir

Longest rivers

	km	miles	Continent
Nile	6 695	4 160	Africa
Amazon	6 516	4 049	South America
Yangtze	6 380	3 965	Asia
Mississippi-Missouri	5 969	3 709	North America
Ob'-Irtysh	5 568	3 460	Asia
Yenisey-Angara-Selenga	5 550	3 449	Asia
Yellow River	5 464	3 395	Asia
Congo	4 667	2 900	Africa
Río de la Plata-Paraná	4 500	2 796	South America
Irtysh	4 440	2 759	Asia

Largest lakes

	sq km	sq miles	Continent
Caspian Sea	371 000	143 243	Asia/Europe
Lake Superior	82 100	31 698	North America
Lake Victoria	68 800	26 563	Africa
Lake Huron	59 600	23 011	North America
Lake Michigan	57 800	22 316	North America
Lake Tanganyika	32 900	12 702	Africa
Great Bear Lake	31 328	12 095	North America
Lake Baikal	30 500	11 776	Asia
Lake Nyasa	30 044	11 600	Africa
Aral Sea	28 687	11 076	Asia

Largest islands

	sq km	sq miles	Continent
Greenland	2 175 600	840 004	North America
New Guinea	808 510	312 167	Australasia
Borneo	745 561	287 863	Asia
Madagascar	587 040	266 657	Africa
Baffin Island	507 451	195 927	North America
Sumatra	473 606	182 860	Asia
Honshū	227 414	87 805	Asia
Great Britain	218 476	84 354	Europe
Victoria Island	217 291	83 897	North America
Ellesmere Island	196 236	75 767	North America

Deepest lakes

	Depth metres	feet	Continent
Lake Baikal	1 741	5 712	Asia
Lake Tanganyika	1 471	4 826	Africa
Caspian Sea	1 025	3 363	Europe/Asia
Lake Nyasa	706	2 316	Africa
Ysyk-Köl	702	2 303	Asia

Highest waterfalls

	Height metres	feet	Location
Angel Falls	979	3 212	Venezuela
Tugela	948	3 110	South Africa
Utigård	800	2 625	Norway
Mongfossen	774	2 539	Norway
Mtarazi	762	2 500	Zimbabwe

Largest countries by population

	Population
China	1 289 161 000
India	1 065 462 000
United States of America	294 043 000
Indonesia	219 883 000
Brazil	178 470 000
Pakistan	153 578 000
Bangladesh	146 736 000
Russian Federation	143 246 000
Japan	127 654 000
Nigeria	124 009 000

Largest countries by area

	Area sq km	sq miles
Russian Federation	17 075 400	6 592 849
Canada	9 984 670	3 855 103
United States of America	9 826 635	3 794 085
China	9 584 492	3 700 593
Brazil	8 514 879	3 287 613
Australia	7 692 024	2 969 907
India	3 064 898	1 183 364
Argentina	2 766 889	1 068 302
Kazakhstan	2 717 300	1 049 155
Sudan	2 505 813	967 500

EUROPE COUNTRIES		area sq km	area sq miles	population	capital
ALBANIA		28 748	11 100	3 166 000	Tirana
ANDORRA		465	180	71 000	Andorra la Vella
AUSTRIA		83 855	32 377	8 116 000	Vienna
BELARUS		207 600	80 155	9 895 000	Minsk
BELGIUM		30 520	11 784	10 318 000	Brussels
BOSNIA-HERZEGOVINA		51 130	19 741	4 161 000	Sarajevo
BULGARIA		110 994	42 855	7 897 000	Sofia
CROATIA		56 538	21 829	4 428 000	Zagreb
CZECH REPUBLIC		78 864	30 450	10 236 000	Prague
DENMARK		43 075	16 631	5 364 000	Copenhagen
ESTONIA		45 200	17 452	1 323 000	Tallinn
FINLAND		338 145	130 559	5 207 000	Helsinki
FRANCE		543 965	210 026	60 144 000	Paris
GERMANY		357 022	137 849	82 476 000	Berlin
GREECE		131 957	50 949	10 976 000	Athens
HUNGARY		93 030	35 919	9 877 000	Budapest
ICELAND		102 820	39 699	290 000	Reykjavik
IRELAND, REPUBLIC OF		70 282	27 136	3 956 000	Dublin
ITALY		301 245	116 311	57 423 000	Rome
LATVIA		63 700	24 595	2 307 000	Rīga
LIECHTENSTEIN		160	62	34 000	Vaduz
LITHUANIA		65 200	25 174	3 444 000	Vilnius
LUXEMBOURG		2 586	998	453 000	Luxembourg
MACEDONIA (F.Y.R.O.M.)		25 713	9 928	2 056 000	Skopje
MALTA		316	122	394 000	Valletta
MOLDOVA		33 700	13 012	4 267 000	Chişinău
MONACO		2	1	34 000	Monaco-Ville
NETHERLANDS		41 526	16 033	16 149 000	Amsterdam/The Hague
NORWAY		323 878	125 050	4 533 000	Oslo
POLAND		312 683	120 728	38 587 000	Warsaw
PORTUGAL		88 940	34 340	10 062 000	Lisbon
ROMANIA		237 500	91 699	22 334 000	Bucharest
RUSSIAN FEDERATION		17 075 400	6 592 849	143 246 000	Moscow
SAN MARINO		61	24	28 000	San Marino
SERBIA AND MONTENEGRO		102 173	39 449	10 527 000	Belgrade
SLOVAKIA		49 035	18 933	5 402 000	Bratislava
SLOVENIA		20 251	7 819	1 984 000	Ljubljana
SPAIN		504 782	194 897	41 060 000	Madrid

languages	currency	official website	tourism website
Albanian, Greek	Lek	www.keshilliministrave.al	www.albaniantourism.com
Spanish, Catalan, French	Euro	www.andorra.ad	www.andorra.ad
German, Croatian, Turkish	Euro	www.oesterreich.at	www.austria-tourism.at
Belorussian, Russian	Belarus rouble	www.government.by	www.mst.by
Dutch (Flemish), French (Walloon), German	Euro	www.belgium.be	www.visitflanders.com www.opt.be
Bosnian, Serbian, Croatian	Marka	www.fbihvlada.gov.ba	www.bhtourism.ba
Bulgarian, Turkish, Romany, Macedonian	Lev	www.government.bg	www.bulgariatravel.org
Croatian, Serbian	Kuna	www.vlada.hr	www.croatia.hr
Czech, Moravian, Slovak	Czech koruna	www.czech.cz	www.visitczech.cz
Danish	Danish krone	www.denmark.dk	www.visitdenmark.com
Estonian, Russian	Kroon	www.riik.ee	visitestonia.com
Finnish, Swedish	Euro	www.valtioneuvosto.fi	www.visitfinland.com
French, Arabic	Euro	www.premier-ministre.gouv.fr	www.franceguide.com
German, Turkish	Euro	www.bundesregierung.de	www.germany-tourism.de
Greek	Euro	www.greece.gov.gr	www.gnto.gr
Hungarian	Forint	www.magyarorszag.hu	www.hungarytourism.hu
Icelandic	Icelandic króna	www.eng.stjornarrad.is	www.icetourist.is
English, Irish	Euro	www.irlgov.ie	www.ireland.travel.ie
Italian	Euro	www.governo.it	www.enit.it
Latvian, Russian	Lats	www.saeima.lv	www.latviatourism.lv
German	Swiss franc	www.liechtenstein.li	www.tourismus.li
Lithuanian, Russian, Polish	Litas	www.lrv.lt	www.tourism.lt
Letzeburgish, German, French	Euro	www.gouvernement.lu	www.ont.lu
Macedonian, Albanian, Turkish	Macedonian denar	www.gov.mk	-
Maltese, English	Maltese lira	www.gov.mt	www.visitmalta.com
Romanian, Ukrainian, Gagauz, Russian	Moldovan leu	www.moldova.md	www.turism.md
French, Monegasque, Italian	Euro	www.monaco.gouv.mc	www.monaco-congres.com
Dutch, Frisian	Euro	www.overheid.nl	www.visitholland.com
Norwegian	Norwegian krone	www.norway.no	www.visitnorway.com
Polish, German	Złoty	www.gov.mt	www.poland-tourism.pl
Portuguese	Euro	www.portugal.gov.pt	www.portugalinsite.pt
Romanian, Hungarian	Romanian leu	www.guv.ro	www.romaniatravel.com
Russian, Tatar, Ukrainian, local languages	Russian rouble	www.gov.ru	www.russiatourism.ru
Italian	Euro	www.consigliograndeegenerale.sm	www.visitsanmarino.com
Serbian, Albanian, Hungarian	Serbian dinar, Euro	www.gov.yu	www.visit-montenegro.com www.serbia-tourism.org
Slovak, Hungarian, Czech	Slovakian koruna	www.government.gov.sk	www.slovakiatourism.sk
Slovene, Croatian, Serbian	Tólar	www.sigov.si	www.slovenia-tourism.si
Castilian, Catalan, Galician, Basque	Euro	www.la-moncloa.es	www.spain.info

EUROPE COUNTRIES (continued)		area sq km	area sq miles	population	capital
SWEDEN		449 964	173 732	8 876 000	Stockholm
SWITZERLAND		41 293	15 943	7 169 000	Bern
UKRAINE		603 700	233 090	48 523 000	Kiev
UNITED KINGDOM		243 609	94 058	58 789 194	London
VATICAN CITY		0.5	0.2	472	Vatican City

EUROPE DEPENDENT TERRITORIES			area sq km	area sq miles	population
Azores		Autonomous Region of Portugal	2 300	888	242 073
Faroe Islands		Self-governing Danish Territory	1 399	540	47 000
Gibraltar		United Kingdom Overseas Territory	7	3	27 000
Guernsey		United Kingdom Crown Dependency	78	30	62 701
Isle of Man		United Kingdom Crown Dependency	572	221	75 000
Jersey		United Kingdom Crown Dependency	116	45	87 186

ASIA COUNTRIES		area sq km	area sq miles	population	capital
AFGHANISTAN		652 225	251 825	23 897 000	Kābul
ARMENIA		29 800	11 506	3 061 000	Yerevan
AZERBAIJAN		86 600	33 436	8 370 000	Baku
BAHRAIN		691	267	724 000	Manama
BANGLADESH		143 998	55 598	146 736 000	Dhaka
BHUTAN		46 620	18 000	2 257 000	Thimphu
BRUNEI		5 765	2 226	358 000	Bandar Seri Begawan
CAMBODIA		181 000	69 884	14 144 000	Phnom Penh
CHINA		9 584 492	3 700 593	1 289 161 000	Beijing
CYPRUS		9 251	3 572	802 000	Nicosia
EAST TIMOR		14 874	5 743	778 000	Dili
GEORGIA		69 700	26 911	5 126 000	T'bilisi
INDIA		3 064 898	1 183 364	1 065 462 000	New Delhi
INDONESIA		1 919 445	741 102	219 883 000	Jakarta
IRAN		1 648 000	636 296	68 920 000	Tehrān
IRAQ		438 317	169 235	25 175 000	Baghdād
ISRAEL		20 770	8 019	6 433 000	Jerusalem *(De facto capital. Disputed)*
JAPAN		377 727	145 841	127 654 000	Tōkyō
JORDAN		89 206	34 443	5 473 000	'Ammān
KAZAKHSTAN		2 717 300	1 049 155	15 433 000	Astana
KUWAIT		17 818	6 880	2 521 000	Kuwait
KYRGYZSTAN		198 500	76 641	5 138 000	Bishkek

languages	currency	official website	tourism website
Swedish	Swedish krona	www.sweden.se	www.visit-sweden.com
German, French, Italian, Romansch	Swiss franc	www.admin.ch	myswitzerland.com
Ukrainian, Russian	Hryvnia	www.kmu.gov.ua	www.tourism.gov.ua
English, Welsh, Gaelic	Pound sterling	www.ukonline.gov.uk	www.visitbritain.com
Italian	Euro	www.vatican.va	-

capital	languages	currency	official website	tourism website
Ponta Delgada	Portuguese	Euro	www.azores.gov.pt	www.drtacores.pt
Tórshavn	Faroese, Danish	Danish krone	www.tinganes.fo	www.tourist.fo
Gibraltar	Engllish, Spanish	Gibraltar pound	www.gibraltar.gov.gi	www.gibraltar.gov.gi
St Peter Port	English, French	Pound sterling	www.gov.gg	www.guernseytouristboard.com
Douglas	English	Pound sterling	www.gov.im	www.gov.im/tourism
St Helier	English, French	Pound sterling	www.gov.je	www.jersey.com

languages	currency	official website	tourism website
Dari, Pushtu, Uzbek, Turkmen	Afghani	www.afghanistan-mfa.net	-
Armenian, Azeri	Dram	www.gov.am	www.armeniainfo.am
Azeri, Armenian, Russian, Lezgian	Azerbaijani manat	www.president.az	-
Arabic, English	Bahrain dinar	www.bahrain.gov.bh	www.bahraintourism.com
Bengali, English	Taka	www.bangladesh.gov.bd	www.parjatan.org
Dzongkha, Nepali, Assamese	Ngultrum, Indian rupee	www.bhutan.gov.bt	www.tourism.gov.bt
Malay, English, Chinese	Brunei dollar	www.brunei.gov.bn	www.tourismbrunei.com
Khmer, Vietnamese	Riel	www.cambodia.gov.kh	www.visit-mekong.com/cambodia/mot/
Mandarin, Wu, Cantonese, Hsiang, regional languages	Yuan, Hong Kong dollar, Macau pataca	www.china.org.cn	www.cnta.com/lyen/index.asp
Greek, Turkish, English	Cyprus pound	www.cyprus.gov.cy	www.visitcyprus.org.cy
Portuguese, Tetun, English	US dollar	www.gov.east-timor.org	-
Georgian, Russian, Armenian, Azeri, Ossetian, Abkhaz	Lari	www.parliament.ge	www.parliament.ge/TOURISM/
Hindi, English, many regional languages	Indian rupee	www.goidirectory.nic.in	www.tourismofindia.com
Indonesian, local languages	Rupiah	www.indonesia.go.id	www.budpar.go.id
Farsi, Azeri, Kurdish, regional languages	Iranian rial	www.president.ir	www.itto.org
Arabic, Kurdish, Turkmen	Iraqi dinar	www.iraqmofa.net	-
Hebrew, Arabic	Shekel	www.index.gov.il/FirstGov	www.tourism.gov.il
Japanese	Yen	www.web-japan.org	www.jnto.go.jp
Arabic	Jordanian dinar	www.nic.gov.jo	www.see-jordan.com
Kazakh, Russian, Ukrainian, German, Uzbek, Tatar	Tenge	www.president.kz	www.president.kz
Arabic	Kuwaiti dinar	www.kuwaitmission.com	-
Kyrgyz, Russian, Uzbek	Kyrgyz som	www.gov.kg	-

ASIA
COUNTRIES (continued)

COUNTRIES (continued)	area sq km	area sq miles	population	capital
LAOS	236 800	91 429	5 657 000	Vientiane
LEBANON	10 452	4 036	3 653 000	Beirut
MALAYSIA	332 965	128 559	24 425 000	Kuala Lumpur/Putrajaya
MALDIVES	298	115	318 000	Male
MONGOLIA	1 565 000	604 250	2 594 000	Ulan Bator
MYANMAR	676 577	261 228	49 485 000	Rangoon
NEPAL	147 181	56 827	25 164 000	Kathmandu
NORTH KOREA	120 538	46 540	22 664 000	P'yŏngyang
OMAN	309 500	119 499	2 851 000	Muscat
PAKISTAN	803 940	310 403	153 578 000	Islamabad
PALAU	497	192	20 000	Koror
PHILIPPINES	300 000	115 831	79 999 000	Manila
QATAR	11 437	4 416	610 000	Doha
RUSSIAN FEDERATION	17 075 400	6 592 849	143 246 000	Moscow
SAUDI ARABIA	2 200 000	849 425	24 217 000	Riyadh
SINGAPORE	639	247	4 253 000	Singapore
SOUTH KOREA	99 274	38 330	47 700 000	Seoul
SRI LANKA	65 610	25 332	19 065 000	Sri Jayewardenepura Kotte
SYRIA	185 180	71 498	17 800 000	Damascus
TAIWAN	36 179	13 969	22 548 000	T'aipei
TAJIKISTAN	143 100	55 251	6 245 000	Dushanbe
THAILAND	513 115	198 115	62 833 000	Bangkok
TURKEY	779 452	300 948	71 325 000	Ankara
TURKMENISTAN	488 100	188 456	4 867 000	Ashgabat
UNITED ARAB EMIRATES	77 700	30 000	2 995 000	Abu Dhabi
UZBEKISTAN	447 400	172 742	26 093 000	Tashkent
VIETNAM	329 565	127 246	81 377 000	Ha Nôi
YEMEN	527 968	203 850	20 010 000	San'ā'

ASIA
DEPENDENT AND DISPUTED TERRITORIES

DEPENDENT AND DISPUTED TERRITORIES		area sq km	area sq miles	population
Christmas Island	Australian External Territory	135	52	1 560
Cocos Islands	Australian External Territory	14	5	632
Gaza	Semi-autonomous region	363	140	1 203 591
Jammu and Kashmir	Disputed territory (India/Pakistan)	222 236	85 806	13 000 000
West Bank	Disputed territory	5 860	2 263	2 303 660

languages	currency	official website	tourism website
Lao, local languages	Kip	www.un.int/lao	mekongcenter.com
Arabic, Armenian, French	Lebanese pound	www.presidency.gov.lb	www.destinationlebanon.com
Malay, English, Chinese, Tamil, local languages	Ringgit	www.mcsl.mampu.gov.my	tourism.gov.my/
Divehi (Maldivian)	Rufiyaa	www.maldivesinfo.gov.mv	-
Khalka (Mongolian), Kazakh, local languages	Tugrik (tögrög)	www.pmis.gov.mn	www.mongoliatourism.gov.mn
Burmese, Shan, Karen, local languages	Kyat	www.myanmar.com	www.myanmar-tourism.com
Nepali, Maithili, Bhojpuri, English, local languages	Nepalese rupee	www.nepalhmg.gov.np	www.welcomenepal.com
Korean	North Korean won	www.korea-dpr.com	-
Arabic, Baluchi, Indian languages	Omani riyal	www.moneoman.gov.om	www.omantourism.gov.om
Urdu, Punjabi, Sindhi, Pushtu, English	Pakistani rupee	www.infopak.gov.pk	www.tourism.gov.pk
Palauan, English	US dollar	www.palauembassy.com	visit-palau.com
English, Pilipino, Cebuano, local languages	Philippine peso	www.gov.ph	www.tourism.gov.ph
Arabic	Qatari riyal	www.english.mofa.gov.qa	www.experienceqatar.com
Russian, Tatar, Ukrainian, local languages	Russian rouble	www.gov.ru	www.russiatourism.ru/eng
Arabic	Saudi Arabian riyal	www.saudinf.com	www.sauditourism.gov.sa
Chinese, English, Malay, Tamil	Singapore dollar	www.gov.sg	www.visitsingapore.com
Korean	South Korean won	www.korea.net	english.tour2korea.com
Sinhalese, Tamil, English	Sri Lankan rupee	www.priu.gov.lk	www.srilankatourism.org
Arabic, Kurdish, Armenian	Syrian pound	www.moi-syria.com	www.syriatourism.org
Mandarin, Min, Hakka, local languages	Taiwan dollar	www.gov.tw	www.tbroc.gov.tw
Tajik, Uzbek, Russian	Somoni	www.tjus.org	www.tajiktour.tajnet.com
Thai, Lao, Chinese, Malay, Mon-Khmer languages	Baht	www.thaigov.go.th	www.tourismthailand.org
Turkish, Kurdish	Turkish lira	www.mfa.gov.tr	www.turizm.gov.tr
Turkmen, Uzbek, Russian	Turkmen manat	www.turkmenistanembassy.org	www.turkmenistanembassy.org
Arabic, English	United Arab Emirates dirham	www.uae.gov.ae	-
Uzbek, Russian, Tajik, Kazakh	Uzbek som	www.gov.uz	www.uzbektourism.uz
Vietnamese, Thai, Khmer, Chinese, local languages	Dong	www.na.gov.vn	www.vietnamtourism.com
Arabic	Yemeni rial	www.nic.gov.ye	www.yementourism.com

capital	languages	currency	official website	tourism website
The Settlement	English	Australian dollar	-	www.tourism.org.cx
West Island	English	Australian dollar	-	www.cocos-tourism.cc
Gaza	Arabic	Israeli shekel	www.pna.gov.ps	www.visit-palestine.com
Srinagar			-	-
	Arabic, Hebrew	Jordanian dinar, Israeli shekel	www.pna.gov.ps	www.visit-palestine.com

AFRICA COUNTRIES		area sq km	area sq miles	population	capital
ALGERIA		2 381 741	919 595	31 800 000	Algiers
ANGOLA		1 246 700	481 354	13 625 000	Luanda
BENIN		112 620	43 483	6 736 000	Porto-Novo
BOTSWANA		581 370	224 468	1 785 000	Gaborone
BURKINA		274 200	105 869	13 002 000	Ouagadougou
BURUNDI		27 835	10 747	6 825 000	Bujumbura
CAMEROON		475 442	183 569	16 018 000	Yaoundé
CAPE VERDE		4 033	1 557	463 000	Praia
CENTRAL AFRICAN REPUBLIC		622 436	240 324	3 865 000	Bangui
CHAD		1 284 000	495 755	8 598 000	Ndjamena
COMOROS		1 862	719	768 000	Moroni
CONGO		342 000	132 047	3 724 000	Brazzaville
CONGO, DEMOCRATIC REP. OF		2 345 410	905 568	52 771 000	Kinshasa
CÔTE D'IVOIRE		322 463	124 504	16 631 000	Yamoussoukro
DJIBOUTI		23 200	8 958	703 000	Djibouti
EGYPT		1 000 250	386 199	71 931 000	Cairo
EQUATORIAL GUINEA		28 051	10 831	494 000	Malabo
ERITREA		117 400	45 328	4 141 000	Asmara
ETHIOPIA		1 133 880	437 794	70 678 000	Addis Ababa
GABON		267 667	103 347	1 329 000	Libreville
THE GAMBIA		11 295	4 361	1 426 000	Banjul
GHANA		238 537	92 100	20 922 000	Accra
GUINEA		245 857	94 926	8 480 000	Conakry
GUINEA-BISSAU		36 125	13 948	1 493 000	Bissau
KENYA		582 646	224 961	31 987 000	Nairobi
LESOTHO		30 355	11 720	1 802 000	Maseru
LIBERIA		111 369	43 000	3 367 000	Monrovia
LIBYA		1 759 540	679 362	5 551 000	Tripoli
MADAGASCAR		587 041	226 658	17 404 000	Antananarivo
MALAWI		118 484	45 747	12 105 000	Lilongwe
MALI		1 240 140	478 821	13 007 000	Bamako
MAURITANIA		1 030 700	397 955	2 893 000	Nouakchott
MAURITIUS		2 040	788	1 221 000	Port Louis
MOROCCO		446 550	172 414	30 566 000	Rabat
MOZAMBIQUE		799 380	308 642	18 863 000	Maputo
NAMIBIA		824 292	318 261	1 987 000	Windhoek
NIGER		1 267 000	489 191	11 972 000	Niamey
NIGERIA		923 768	356 669	124 009 000	Abuja

languages	currency	official website	tourism website
Arabic, French, Berber	Algerian dinar	www.el-mouradia.dz	www.mta.gov.dz
Portuguese, Bantu, local languages	Kwanza	www.angola.org	www.angola.org.uk/prov_tourism.htm
French, Fon, Yoruba, Adja, local languages	CFA franc*	www.gouv.bj	www.benintourisme.com
English, Setswana, Shona, local languages	Pula	www.gov.bw	www.gov.bw/tourism
French, Moore (Mossi), Fulani, local languages	CFA franc*	www.primature.gov.bf	www.culture.gov.bf
Kirundi (Hutu, Tutsi), French	Burundian franc	www.burundi.gov.bi	www.burundi.gov.bi/tour.htm
French, English, Fang, Bamileke, local languages	CFA franc*	www.spm.gov.cm	www.camnet.cm/mintour/tourisme
Portuguese, creole	Cape Verde escudo	www.governo.cv	-
French, Sango, Banda, Baya, local languages	CFA franc*	-	-
Arabic, French, Sara, local languages	CFA franc*	www.tit.td	-
Comorian, French, Arabic	Comoros franc	www.presidence-uniondescomores.com	-
French, Kongo, Monokutuba, local languages	CFA franc*	www.congo-site.com	-
French, Lingala, Swahili, Kongo, local languages	Congolese franc	www.un.int/drcongo	-
French, creole, Akan, local languages	CFA franc*	www.pr.ci	-
Somali, Afar, French, Arabic	Djibouti franc	-	www.office-tourisme.dj
Arabic	Egyptian pound	www.sis.gov.eg	www.egypttreasures.gov.eg
Spanish, French, Fang	CFA franc*	www.ceiba-equatorial-guinea.org	-
Tigrinya, Tigre	Nakfa	www.shabait.com	-
Oromo, Amharic, Tigrinya, local languages	Birr	www.ethiopar.net	www.tourismethiopia.org
French, Fang, local languages	CFA franc*	www.un.int/gabon	www.tourisme-gabon.com
English, Malinke, Fulani, Wolof	Dalasi	www.statehouse.gm	www.visitthegambia.qm
English, Hausa, Akan, local languages	Cedi	www.ghana.gov.gh	www.ghanatourism.gov.gh
French, Fulani, Malinke, local languages	Guinea franc	www.guinee.gov.gn	www.mirinet.net.gn/ont/
Portuguese, crioulo, local languages	CFA franc*	-	-
Swahili, English, local languages	Kenyan shilling	www.kenya.go.ke	www.magicalkenya.com
Sesotho, English, Zulu	Loti, S. African rand	www.lesotho.gov.ls	www.lesotho.gov.ls/lstourism.htm
English, creole, local languages	Liberian dollar	www.liberiaemb.org	-
Arabic, Berber	Libyan dinar	www.libya-un.org	-
Malagasy, French	Malagasy franc	www.madagascar-diplomatie.ch	-
Chichewa, English, local languages	Malawian kwacha	www.malawi.gov.mw	www.tourismmalawi.com
French, Bambara, local languages	CFA franc*	www.maliensdelexterieur.gov.ml	www.malitourisme.com
Arabic, French, local languages	Ouguiya	www.mauritania.mr	-
English, creole, Hindi, Bhojpuri, French	Mauritius rupee	www.gov.mu	www.mauritius.net
Arabic, Berber, French	Moroccan dirham	www.mincom.gov.ma	www.tourism-in-morocco.com
Portuguese, Makua, Tsonga, local languages	Metical	www.mozambique.mz	www.mozambique.mz/turismo/topics.htm
English, Afrikaans, German, Ovambo, local languages	Namibian dollar	www.grnnet.gov.na	www.namibiatourism.com.na
French, Hausa, Fulani, local languages	CFA franc*	www.delgi.ne/presidence	-
English, Hausa, Yoruba, Ibo, Fulani, local languages	Naira	www.nigeria.gov.ng	www.nigeriatourism.net

*Communauté Financière Africaine franc

AFRICA
COUNTRIES (continued)

		area sq km	area sq miles	population	capital
RWANDA		26 338	10 169	8 387 000	Kigali
SÃO TOMÉ AND PRÍNCIPE		964	372	161 000	São Tomé
SENEGAL		196 720	75 954	10 095 000	Dakar
SEYCHELLES		455	176	81 000	Victoria
SIERRA LEONE		71 740	27 699	4 971 000	Freetown
SOMALIA		637 657	246 201	9 890 000	Mogadishu
SOUTH AFRICA, REPUBLIC OF		1 219 090	470 693	45 026 000	Pretoria/Cape Town
SUDAN		2 505 813	967 500	33 610 000	Khartoum
SWAZILAND		17 364	6 704	1 077 000	Mbabane
TANZANIA		945 087	364 900	36 977 000	Dodoma
TOGO		56 785	21 925	4 909 000	Lomé
TUNISIA		164 150	63 379	9 832 000	Tunis
UGANDA		241 038	93 065	25 827 000	Kampala
ZAMBIA		752 614	290 586	10 812 000	Lusaka
ZIMBABWE		390 759	150 873	12 891 000	Harare

AFRICA
DEPENDENT AND DISPUTED TERRITORIES

			area sq km	area sq miles	population
Canary Islands		Autonomous Community of Spain	7 447	2 875	1 694 477
Madeira		Autonomous Region of Portugal	779	301	242 603
Mayotte		French Territorial Collectivity	373	144	171 000
Réunion		French Overseas Department	2 551	985	756 000
St Helena and Dependencies		United Kingdom Overseas Territory	121	47	5 644
Western Sahara		Disputed territory (Morocco)	266 000	102 703	308 000

OCEANIA
COUNTRIES

		area sq km	area sq miles	population	capital
AUSTRALIA		7 692 024	2 969 907	19 731 000	Canberra
FIJI		18 330	7 077	839 000	Suva
KIRIBATI		717	277	88 000	Bairiki
MARSHALL ISLANDS		181	70	53 000	Delap-Uliga-Djarrit
MICRONESIA, FED. STATES OF		701	271	109 000	Palikir
NAURU		21	8	13 000	Yaren
NEW ZEALAND		270 534	104 454	3 875 000	Wellington
PAPUA NEW GUINEA		462 840	178 704	5 711 000	Port Moresby
SAMOA		2 831	1 093	178 000	Apia
SOLOMON ISLANDS		28 370	10 954	477 000	Honiara
TONGA		748	289	104 000	Nuku'alofa
TUVALU		25	10	11 000	Vaiaku
VANUATU		12 190	4 707	212 000	Port Vila

languages	currency	official website	tourism website
Kinyarwanda, French, English	Rwandan franc	www.rwanda1.com	www.rwandatourism.com
Portuguese, creole	Dobra	www.uns.st	www.saotome.st
French, Wolof, Fulani, local languages	CFA franc*	www.gouv.sn	www.senegal-tourism.com
English, French, creole	Seychelles rupee	www.virtualseychelles.sc	www.virtualseychelles.sc
English, creole, Mende, Temne, local languages	Leone	www.statehouse-sl.org	-
Somali, Arabic	Somali shilling	-	-
Afrikaans, English, nine official local languages	Rand	www.gov.za	www.southafrica.net
Arabic, Dinka, Nubian, Beja, Nuer, local languages	Sudanese dinar	www.sudan.gov.sd	-
Swazi, English	Emalangeni, S. African rand	www.gov.sz	www.mintour.gov.sz
Swahili, English, Nyamwezi, local languages	Tanzanian shilling	www.tanzania.go.tz	www.tanzaniatouristboard.com
French, Ewe, Kabre, local languages	CFA franc*	www.republicoftogo.com	-
Arabic, French	Tunisian dinar	www.tunisiaonline.com	www.tourismtunisia.com
English, Swahili, Luganda, local languages	Ugandan shilling	www.government.go.ug	www.visituganda.com
English, Bemba, Nyanja, Tonga, local languages	Zambian kwacha	www.zambiatourism.com	www.zambiatourism.com
English, Shona, Ndebele	Zimbabwean dollar	www.zim.gov.zw	www.zimbabwetourism.co.zw

capital	languages	currency	official website	tourism website
Santa Cruz de Tenerife, Las Palmas	Spanish	Euro	www.gobcan.es	www.gobcan.es/turismo
Funchal	Portuguese	Euro	www.gov-madeira.pt/madeira	www.madeiratourism.org
Dzaoudzi	French, Mahorian	Euro	-	-
St-Denis	French, creole	Euro	-	www.la-reunion-tourisme.com
Jamestown	English	St Helena pound	www.sainthelena.gov.sh	www.sthelenatourism.com
Laâyoune	Arabic	Moroccan dirham	-	-

*Communauté Financière Africaine franc

languages	currency	official website	tourism website
English, Italian, Greek	Australian dollar	www.gov.au	www.australia.com
English, Fijian, Hindi	Fiji dollar	www.fiji.gov.fj	www.bulafiji.com
Gilbertese, English	Australian dollar	-	-
English, Marshallese	US dollar	www.rmiembassyus.org	www.visitmarshallislands.com
English, Chuukese, Pohnpeian, local languages	US dollar	www.fsmgov.org	visit-fsm.org
Nauruan, English	Australian dollar	www.un.int/nauru	-
English, Maori	New Zealand dollar	www.govt.nz	www.newzealand.com
English, Tok Pisin (creole), local languages	Kina	www.pngonline.gov.pg	www.pngtourism.org.pg/
Samoan, English	Tala	www.govt.ws	www.visitsamoa.ws
English, creole, local languages	Solomon Islands dollar	www.commerce.gov.sb	www.commerce.gov.sb/Tourism
Tongan, English	Pa'anga	www.pmo.gov.to	www.tongaholiday.com
Tuvaluan, English	Australian dollar	-	www.timelesstuvalu.com
English, Bislama (creole), French	Vatu	www.vanuatugovernment.gov.vu	www.vanuatutourism.com

OCEANIA
DEPENDENT TERRITORIES

			area sq km	area sq miles	population
American Samoa		United States Unincorporated Territory	197	76	67 000
Cook Islands		Self-governing New Zealand Territory	293	113	18 000
French Polynesia		French Overseas Territory	3 265	1 261	244 000
Guam		United States Unincorporated Territory	541	209	163 000
New Caledonia		French Overseas Territory	19 058	7 358	228 000
Niue		Self-governing New Zealand Territory	258	100	2 000
Norfolk Island		Australian External Territory	35	14	2 037
Northern Mariana Islands		United States Commonwealth	477	184	79 000
Pitcairn Islands		United Kingdom Overseas Territory	45	17	51
Tokelau		New Zealand Overseas Territory	10	4	2 000
Wallis and Futuna Islands		French Overseas Territory	274	106	15 000

NORTH AMERICA
COUNTRIES

		area sq km	area sq miles	population	capital
ANTIGUA AND BARBUDA		442	171	73 000	St John's
THE BAHAMAS		13 939	5 382	314 000	Nassau
BARBADOS		430	166	270 000	Bridgetown
BELIZE		22 965	8 867	256 000	Belmopan
CANADA		9 984 670	3 855 103	31 510 000	Ottawa
COSTA RICA		51 100	19 730	4 173 000	San José
CUBA		110 860	42 803	11 300 000	Havana
DOMINICA		750	290	79 000	Roseau
DOMINICAN REPUBLIC		48 442	18 704	8 745 000	Santo Domingo
EL SALVADOR		21 041	8 124	6 515 000	San Salvador
GRENADA		378	146	80 000	St George's
GUATEMALA		108 890	42 043	12 347 000	Guatemala City
HAITI		27 750	10 714	8 326 000	Port-au-Prince
HONDURAS		112 088	43 277	6 941 000	Tegucigalpa
JAMAICA		10 991	4 244	2 651 000	Kingston
MEXICO		1 972 545	761 604	103 457 000	Mexico City
NICARAGUA		130 000	50 193	5 466 000	Managua
PANAMA		77 082	29 762	3 120 000	Panama City
ST KITTS AND NEVIS		261	101	42 000	Basseterre
ST LUCIA		616	238	149 000	Castries
ST VINCENT AND THE GRENADINES		389	150	120 000	Kingstown
TRINIDAD AND TOBAGO		5 130	1 981	1 303 000	Port of Spain
UNITED STATES OF AMERICA		9 826 635	3 794 085	294 043 000	Washington DC

capital	languages	currency	official website	tourism website
Fagotogo	Samoan, English	US dollar	www.government.as	www.amsamoa.com/tourism
Avarua	English, Maori	New Zealand dollar	www.cook-islands.gov.ck	www.cook-islands.com
Papeete	French, Tahitian, Polynesian languages	CFP franc*	www.presidence.pf	www.tahiti-tourisme.pf
Hagåtña	Chamorro, English, Tapalog	US dollar	www.ns.gov.gu	www.visitguam.org
Nouméa	French, local languages	CFP franc*	www.gouv.nc	-
Alofi	English, Polynesian	New Zealand dollar	www.niuegov.com	www.niueisland.com
Kingston	English	Australian dollar	www.norfolk.gov.nf	www.norfolkisland.nf
Capitol Hill	English, Chamorro, local languages	US dollar	www.gov.mp	www.mymarianas.com
Adamstown	English	New Zealand dollar	www.government.pn	www.government.pn/tourist.htm
	English, Tokelauan	New Zealand dollar	www.tokelau.org.nz	-
Matā'utu	French, Wallisian, Futunian	CFP franc*	www.wallis.co.nc/assemblee.ter	-

*Franc des Comptoirs Français du Pacifique

languages	currency	official website	tourism website
English, creole	East Caribbean dollar	www.un.int/antigua	www.antigua-barbuda.org
English, creole	Bahamian dollar	www.bahamas.gov.bs	www.bahamas.com
English, creole	Barbados dollar	www.barbados.gov.bb	www.barbados.org/bta.htm
English, Spanish, Mayan, creole	Belize dollar	www.belize.gov.bz	www.travelbelize.org
English, French	Canadian dollar	www.canada.gc.ca	www.travelcanada.ca
Spanish	Costa Rican colón	www.casapres.go.cr	www.visitcostarica.com
Spanish	Cuban peso	www.cubagob.gov.cu	www.cubatravel.cu
English, creole	East Caribbean dollar	www.dominica.co.uk	www.ndcdominica.dm
Spanish, creole	Dominican peso	www.presidencia.gov.do	www.dominicanrepublic.com/Tourism
Spanish	El Salvador colón, US dollar	www.casapres.gob.sv	www.elsalvadorturismo.gob.sv
English, creole	East Caribbean dollar	www.grenadaconsulate.org	grenadagrenadines.com
Spanish, Mayan languages	Quetzal, US dollar	www.congreso.gob.gt	www.mayaspirit.com.gt
French, creole	Gourde	www.haiti.org	www.haititourisme.org
Spanish, Amerindian languages	Lempira	www.congreso.gob.hn	www.letsgohonduras.com
English, creole	Jamaican dollar	www.jis.gov.jm	www.visitjamaica.com
Spanish, Amerindian languages	Mexican peso	www.presidencia.gob.mx	www.visitmexico.com
Spanish, Amerindian languages	Córdoba	www.asamblea.gob.ni	www.visit-nicaragua.com
Spanish, English, Amerindian languages	Balboa	www.pa	www.visitpanama.com
English, creole	East Caribbean dollar	www.stkittsnevis.net	www.stkitts-tourism.com
English, creole	East Caribbean dollar	www.stlucia.gov.lc	www.stlucia.org
English, creole	East Caribbean dollar	-	www.svgtourism.com
English, creole, Hindi	Trinidad and Tobago dollar	www.gov.tt	www.visittnt.com
English, Spanish	US dollar	www.firstgov.gov	www.tourstates.com

NORTH AMERICA DEPENDENT TERRITORIES			area sq km	area sq miles	population
Anguilla		United Kingdom Overseas Territory	155	60	12 000
Aruba		Self-governing Netherlands Territory	193	75	100 000
Bermuda		United Kingdom Overseas Territory	54	21	82 000
Cayman Islands		United Kingdom Overseas Territory	259	100	40 000
Greenland		Self-governing Danish Territory	2 175 600	840 004	57 000
Guadeloupe		French Overseas Department	1 780	687	440 000
Martinique		French Overseas Department	1 079	417	393 000
Montserrat		United Kingdom Overseas Territory	100	39	4 000
Netherlands Antilles		Self-governing Netherlands Territory	800	309	221 000
Puerto Rico		United States Commonwealth	9 104	3 515	3 879 000
St Pierre and Miquelon		French Territorial Collectivity	242	93	6 000
Turks and Caicos Islands		United Kingdom Overseas Territory	430	166	21 000
Virgin Islands (U.K.)		United Kingdom Overseas Territory	153	59	21 000
Virgin Islands (U.S.A.)		United States Unincorporated Territory	352	136	111 000

SOUTH AMERICA COUNTRIES		area sq km	area sq miles	population	capital
ARGENTINA		2 766 889	1 068 302	38 428 000	Buenos Aires
BOLIVIA		1 098 581	424 164	8 808 000	La Paz/Sucre
BRAZIL		8 514 879	3 287 613	178 470 000	Brasília
CHILE		756 945	292 258	15 805 000	Santiago
COLOMBIA		1 141 748	440 831	44 222 000	Bogotá
ECUADOR		272 045	105 037	13 003 000	Quito
GUYANA		214 969	83 000	765 000	Georgetown
PARAGUAY		406 752	157 048	5 878 000	Asunción
PERU		1 285 216	496 225	27 167 000	Lima
SURINAME		163 820	63 251	436 000	Paramaribo
URUGUAY		176 215	68 037	3 415 000	Montevideo
VENEZUELA		912 050	352 144	25 699 000	Caracas

SOUTH AMERICA DEPENDENT TERRITORIES			area sq km	area sq miles	population
Falkland Islands		United Kingdom Overseas Territory	12 170	4 699	3 000
French Guiana		French Overseas Department	90 000	34 749	178 000

capital	languages	currency	official website	tourism website
The Valley	English	East Caribbean dollar	www.gov.ai	www.anguilla-vacation.com
Oranjestad	Papiamento, Dutch, English	Arubian florin	www.aruba.com	www.aruba.com
Hamilton	English	Bermuda dollar	www.gov.bm	www.bermudatourism.com
George Town	English	Cayman Islands dollar	www.gov.ky	www.caymanislands.ky
Nuuk	Greenlandic, Danish	Danish krone	www.nanoq.gl	www.greenland.com
Basse-Terre	French, creole	Euro	www.cr-guadeloupe.fr	www.antilles-info-tourisme.com/guadeloupe
Fort-de-France	French, creole	Euro	www.cr-martinique.fr	www.martinique.org
Plymouth	English	East Caribbean dollar	-	www.visitmontserrat.com
Willemstad	Dutch, Papiamento, English	Netherlands guilder	www.gov.an	-
San Juan	Spanish, English	US dollar	www.gobierno.pr	www.gotopuertorico.com
St-Pierre	French	Euro	-	-
Grand Turk	English	US dollar	-	www.turksandcaicostourism.com
Road Town	English	US dollar	-	www.bvitouristboard.com
Charlotte Amalie	English, Spanish		www.usvi.org	www.usvitourism.vi

languages	currency	official website	tourism website
Spanish, Italian, Amerindian languages	Argentinian peso	www.info.gov.ar	www.turismo.gov.ar
Spanish, Quechua, Aymara	Boliviano	www.bolivia.gov.bo	.
Portuguese	Real	www.brazil.gov.br	www.embratur.gov.br
Spanish, Amerindian languages	Chilean peso	www.gobiernodechile.cl	www.visit-chile.org
Spanish, Amerindian languages	Colombian peso	www.gobiernoenlinea.gov.co	www.idct.gov.co
Spanish, Quechua, other Amerindian languages	US dollar	www.ec-gov.net	www.vivecuador.com
English, creole, Amerindian languages	Guyana dollar	www.gina.gov.gy	www.guyana-tourism.com
Spanish, Guaraní	Guaraní	www.presidencia.gov.py	www.senatur.gov.py
Spanish, Quechua, Aymara	Sol	www.peru.gob.pe	www.peru.org.pe
Dutch, Surinamese, English, Hindi	Suriname guilder	www.kabinet.sr.org	www.mintct.sr
Spanish	Uruguayan peso	www.presidencia.gub.uy	www.turismo.gub.uy
Spanish, Amerindian languages	Bolivar	www.gobiernoenlinea.ve	-

capital	languages	currency	officail website	tourism website
Stanley	English	Falkland Islands pound	www.falklands.gov.fk	www.tourism.org.fk
Cayenne	French, creole	Euro	www.guyane.pref.gouv.fr	www.tourisme-guyane.gf

The present picture of the political world is the result of a long history of exploration, colonialism, conflict and negotiation. In 1950 there were eighty-two independent countries. Since then there has been a significant trend away from colonial influences and although many dependent territories still exist, there are now 193 independent countries. The newest country is East Timor which gained independence from Indonesia in May 2002. The shapes of countries reflect a combination of natural features, such as mountain ranges, and political agreements. There are still areas of the world where boundaries are disputed or only temporarily settled as ceasefire lines.

World extremes – capitals		
Largest national capital (population)	Tōkyō, Japan	26 849 000
Smallest national capital (population)	Vatican City	472
Most northerly national capital	Reykjavík, Iceland	64° 08'N
Most southerly national capital	Wellington, New Zealand	41° 18'S
Highest capital	La Paz, Bolivia	3 630 m 11 909 ft

A.	ANDORRA		
AL.	ALBANIA	JOR.	JORDAN
ARM.	ARMENIA	K.	KUWAIT
AUS.	AUSTRIA	KYR.	KYRGYZSTAN
AZ.	AZERBAIJAN	LEB.	LEBANON
B.	BURUNDI	LITH.	LITHUANIA
BE.	BENIN	LUX.	LUXEMBOURG
BEL.	BELGIUM	M.	MACEDONIA
B.H.	BOSNIA–HERZEGOVINA	MO.	MOLDOVA
BN.	BAHRAIN	NETH.	NETHERLANDS
BUR.	BURKINA	NI.	NIGERIA
CAM.	CAMEROON	POL.	POLAND
C.A.R.	CENTRAL AFRICAN REPUBLIC	Q.	QATAR
C.D'I.	CÔTE D'IVOIRE	R.	RWANDA
CR.	CROATIA	SL.	SLOVENIA
CYP.	CYPRUS	SLA.	SLOVAKIA
CZ.R.	CZECH REPUBLIC	S.M.	SERBIA AND
DEN.	DENMARK		MONTENEGRO
EQ.G.	EQUATORIAL GUINEA	SUR.	SURINAME
FR.G.	FRENCH GUIANA	SW.	SWITZERLAND
GEOR.	GEORGIA	T.	TOGO
GER.	GERMANY	TAJIK.	TAJIKISTAN
GH.	GHANA	TURKM.	TURKMENISTAN
GUY.	GUYANA	U.A.E.	UNITED ARAB
HUN.	HUNGARY		EMIRATES
ISR.	ISRAEL	UZBEK.	UZBEKISTAN

Go to →

Country facts and flags
pages 10–22
World physical features
page 26
World time zones
page 34

KNOW THE WORLD

* The break up of the Soviet Union (or the U.S.S.R. – Union of Soviet Socialist Republics) in 1991 created fifteen new countries including the Russian Federation.

* The Maldives in the Indian Ocean consist of approximately 1 200 low-lying islands, all under 2 metres in height.

* The Commonwealth, first defined in 1926, has evolved from communities within the British Empire, to a free association of fifty-four member countries.

* Both China and the Russian Federation have borders with fourteen different countries.

* All countries of the world are members of the United Nations except Taiwan and the Vatican City.

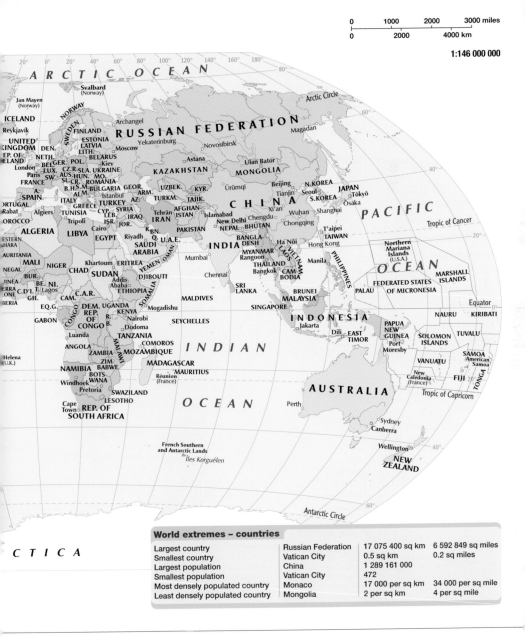

1:146 000 000

World extremes – countries

Largest country	Russian Federation	17 075 400 sq km	6 592 849 sq miles
Smallest country	Vatican City	0.5 sq km	0.2 sq miles
Largest population	China	1 289 161 000	
Smallest population	Vatican City	472	
Most densely populated country	Monaco	17 000 per sq km	34 000 per sq mile
Least densely populated country	Mongolia	2 per sq km	4 per sq mile

DISCOVER MORE

- United Nations www.un.org
- UK Foreign Office www.fco.gov.uk
- European Union Europa.eu.int
- International boundaries www-ibru.dur.ac.uk
- Place names www.pcgn.org.uk and geonames.usgs.gov
- Country profiles www.odci.gov/cia/publications/factbook

WATCH OUT!

- Travelling as a tourist to some countries or travelling within certain areas can be dangerous because of wars and political unrest. Check with the UK Foreign Office for their latest travel advice and security warnings.

- Some areas of the world, particularly tropical regions in the developing world, carry many risks of disease. Before you travel, seek advice on precautions to take and medications required.

The shapes of the continents and oceans have evolved over millions of years. Movement of the tectonic plates which make up the earth's crust has created some of the best known land features. From the highest point Mount Everest to the deepest in the Mariana Trench is a height of almost 20 000 metres. Earthquakes, volcanoes, erosion, climatic variations and man's intervention all continue to affect the earth's landscapes. Different landscapes reflect great variations in climate from deserts such as the Sahara, to the frozen ice cap of Antarctica.

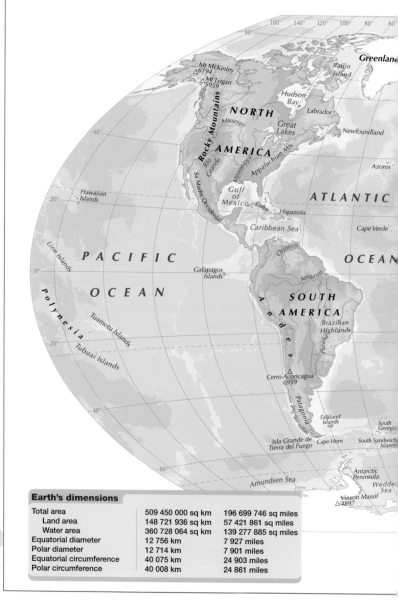

Earth's dimensions

Total area	509 450 000 sq km	196 699 746 sq miles
Land area	148 721 936 sq km	57 421 861 sq miles
Water area	360 728 064 sq km	139 277 885 sq miles
Equatorial diameter	12 756 km	7 927 miles
Polar diameter	12 714 km	7 901 miles
Equatorial circumference	40 075 km	24 903 miles
Polar circumference	40 008 km	24 861 miles

Go to →

Geo tables page 9
World land cover page 30
The oceans page 156

KNOW THE WORLD

- The Pacific Ocean is larger than the continents' land areas combined.
- Over 900 earthquakes of magnitude 5.0 or greater occur every year.
- The average height of the earth's land surface is 840 metres (2 756 feet) above sea level and 52 per cent of the land is below 500 metres (1 640 feet). Approximately 10 per cent of the surface is permanently covered by ice.
- The Ural Mountains define part of the boundary between Europe and Asia.
- The collision of two tectonic plates – the Indo-Australia and the Eurasian Plates – formed the Himalaya mountains which are still rising at a rate of approximately 5 millimetres (0.2 inches) a year

0 1000 2000 3000 miles
0 2000 4000 km

1:146 000 000

ARCTIC OCEAN

40° 20° 0° 20° 40° 60° 80° 100° 120° 140° 160° 180°

80°

Iceland

Arctic Circle

Central Siberia
Siberian
Plateau

West
Siberian
Plain

Scandinavia

Ural Mountains

Yenisey
Lena
Ob
Irtysh
Amur

Sea of
Okhotsk

Bering
Sea

60°

British
Isles

North European
Plain

EUROPE

Alps

Danube

Volga

Black Sea

El'brus
5642

Caspian
Sea

Aral
Sea

Tien Shan

Gobi

ASIA

40°

Sea
of
Japan

Honshū

Lake
Baikal

Mediterranean Sea

Canary
Islands

Atlas Mountains

Zagros Mts

The Gulf

Kunlun Shan

Yellow

Yangtze

East
China
Sea

PACIFIC

Tropic of Cancer

Arabian

Indus

Himalaya

Mt Everest
8848

Ganges

Nile

Red Sea

Arabian
Peninsula

Deccan

Arabian
Sea

Bay
of
Bengal

Mekong

South
China
Sea

Philippines

Challenger
Deep
10920

OCEAN

20°

Micronesia

Equator 0°

Sahara

AFRICA

Niger

Gulf
of Guinea

Congo

Congo
Basin

Ethiopian
Highlands

Great Rift Valley

Lake
Victoria

Kilimanjaro
5892

Zambezi

Ascension

St Helena

Seychelles

Maldives

Sri Lanka

INDIAN

Sumatra

Java

Borneo

Celebes

Puncak Jaya
5030

New
Guinea

Arafura
Sea

Coral
Sea

Melanesia

Madagascar

OCEAN

AUSTRALIA

Great
Victoria
Desert

Great
Australian
Bight

Darling

Great Dividing Ra.

Tropic of Capricorn

20°

Tristan da Cunha

Cape of
Good Hope

Kalahari
Desert

Îles Kerguélen

Tasman
Sea

Tasmania

New Zealand

40°

Davis Sea

Antarctic Circle

ANTARCTICA

World extremes			
Highest mountain	Mt Everest, China/Nepal	8 848 metres	29 028 feet
Longest river	Nile, Africa	6 695 km	4 160 miles
Largest lake	Caspian Sea, Asia/Europe	371 000 sq km	143 244 sq miles
Largest island	Greenland, North America	2 175 600 sq km	840 004 sq miles
Largest drainage basin	Amazon, South America	7 050 000 sq km	2 722 005 sq miles
Lowest point	Dead Sea, Asia	-398 miles	-1 306 feet
Deepest water	Challenger Deep, Pacific Ocean	10 920 metres	35 826 feet

DISCOVER MORE

* Search for satellite images visibleearth.nasa.gov
* Observing the earth earthobservatory.nasa.gov
* The earth's environment www.unep.org
* Monitor earthquakes neic.usgs.gov
* Volcanic activity Volcanoes.usgs.gov and volcano.und.nodak.ed
* Learn about geology www.bgs.ac.uk

WATCH OUT!

* Indonesia has more than 120 volcanoes and over 30 per cent of the world's active volcanoes. Volcanic activity is still largely unpredictable.
* Climate change and man's intervention have reduced the size of the Aral Sea by 40 000 square kilometres (15 444 square miles) and Lake Chad is almost 20 per cent of the size it was in 1970. The Dead Sea also has seen a 16 metre (53 feet) drop in its surface level in that time.

Climate is defined by the long-term weather conditions prevalent in any part of the world. The classification of climate types is based on the relationship between temperature and humidity and also on how these are affected by latitude, altitude, ocean currents and wind. Weather is how climatic conditions affect local areas. Weather stations collect data on temperature and rainfall, which can be plotted on graphs as shown here – based on average monthly figures over a minimum period of thirty years – and which help to monitor climate change.

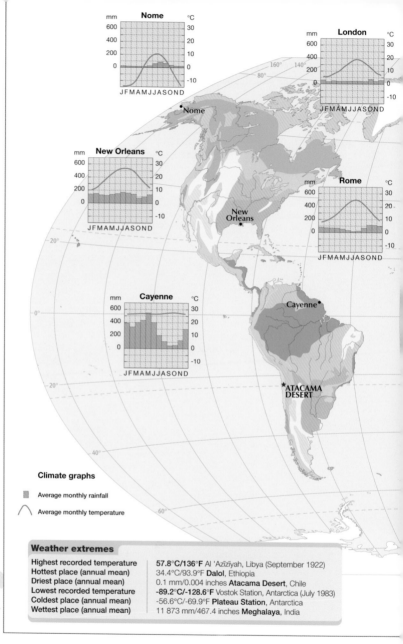

Climate graphs

Average monthly rainfall

Average monthly temperature

Weather extremes

Highest recorded temperature	**57.8°C/136°F** Al 'Azīzīyah, Libya (September 1922)
Hottest place (annual mean)	34.4°C/93.9°F **Dalol**, Ethiopia
Driest place (annual mean)	0.1 mm/0.004 inches **Atacama Desert**, Chile
Lowest recorded temperature	**-89.2°C/-128.6°F** Vostok Station, Antarctica (July 1983)
Coldest place (annual mean)	-56.6°C/-69.9°F **Plateau Station**, Antarctica
Wettest place (annual mean)	11 873 mm/467.4 inches **Meghalaya**, India

Go to →

Antarctica *page 119*
World land cover
page 130
Arctic Ocean *page 162*

KNOW THE WORLD

- Meghalaya, the wettest place in the world, is affected by the tropical monsoon season which causes very heavy rainfall between June and October each year.

- In 2001 the global mean temperature was 0.63 degrees centigrade higher than at the end of the 19th century.

- Climate change is detected through indicators such as the number of frost-free days, length of growing season, heat wave frequency, number of wet days and frequency of extreme weather conditions.

- The ice thickness in the Arctic Ocean has decreased by 4 per cent in the last forty years.

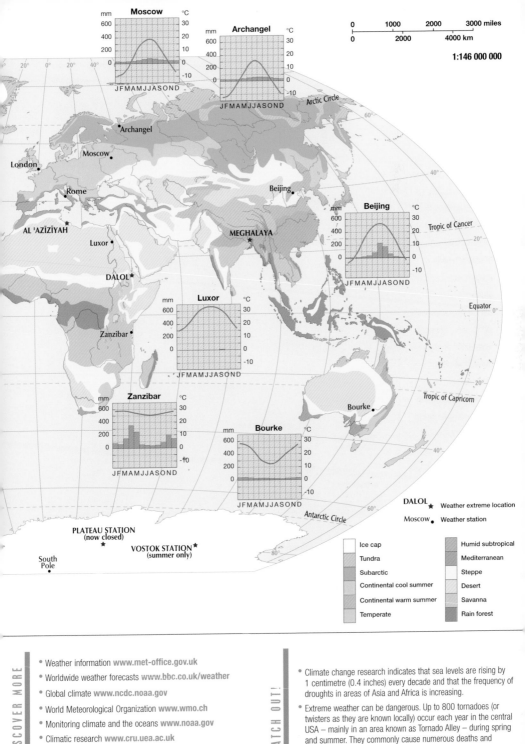

Moscow

Archangel

Beijing

Luxor

Zanzibar

Bourke

1:146 000 000

| 0 | 1000 | 2000 | 3000 miles |
| 0 | 2000 | | 4000 km |

Arctic Circle

Archangel

Moscow

London

Rome

AL 'AZĪZĪYAH

Luxor

DALOL

Zanzibar

MEGHALAYA

Beijing

Tropic of Cancer

Equator

Tropic of Capricorn

Bourke

Antarctic Circle

PLATEAU STATION
(now closed)

VOSTOK STATION
(summer only)

South
Pole

DALOL ★ Weather extreme location

Moscow ● Weather station

	Ice cap		Humid subtropical
	Tundra		Mediterranean
	Subarctic		Steppe
	Continental cool summer		Desert
	Continental warm summer		Savanna
	Temperate		Rain forest

DISCOVER MORE

- Weather information www.met-office.gov.uk
- Worldwide weather forecasts www.bbc.co.uk/weather
- Global climate www.ncdc.noaa.gov
- World Meteorological Organization www.wmo.ch
- Monitoring climate and the oceans www.noaa.gov
- Climatic research www.cru.uea.ac.uk
- Research the oceans www.soc.soton.ac.uk

WATCH OUT!

- Climate change research indicates that sea levels are rising by 1 centimetre (0.4 inches) every decade and that the frequency of droughts in areas of Asia and Africa is increasing.

- Extreme weather can be dangerous. Up to 800 tornadoes (or twisters as they are known locally) occur each year in the central USA – mainly in an area known as Tornado Alley – during spring and summer. They commonly cause numerous deaths and widespread destruction.

The earth has a rich environment which has helped create a wide range of habitats. Forest and woodland form the predominant natural land cover. Tropical rain forests are believed to be home to most of the world's bird, animal and plant species and are part of a delicate land-atmosphere relationship disturbed by changes in land use. Grassland, shrub land and deserts cover most of the unwooded areas with low-growing tundra in the far northern latitudes. Grassland and shrubland regions have been altered greatly by man through agricuture, livestock grazing and settlements.

North America
Land cover composition

South America
Land cover composition

Global land cover composition

Forest/Woodland	27.5%	
Shrubland	14.2%	
Grass/Savanna	14.0%	
Wetland	0.9%	
Crops/Mosaic	19.2%	
Urban	0.2%	
Snow/Ice	11.4%	
Barren	12.6%	

Evergreen needleleaf forest

Evergreen broadleaf forest

Deciduous needleleaf forest

Deciduous broadleaf forest

Mixed forest

Closed shrubland

Open shrubland

Woody savanna

Savanna

Go to →

World physical features
page 26
World climate page 28
The oceans page 156

KNOW THE WORLD

* Land covers less than one-third of the total surface of the planet.

* Slash and burn is one method of deforestation which has led to over 1 per cent (1.23 million square kilometres/470 000 square miles) of tropical forest being lost every year, mainly for food production.

* Climate change and mis-management of land areas by man can lead to soils becoming degraded and semi-arid grasslands becoming arid deserts – a process known as desertification.

* Approximately 10 per cent of the earth's land surface is protected as conservation areas or national parks. The largest single protected area – covering 972 000 square kilometres (375 290 square miles) – is in Greenland.

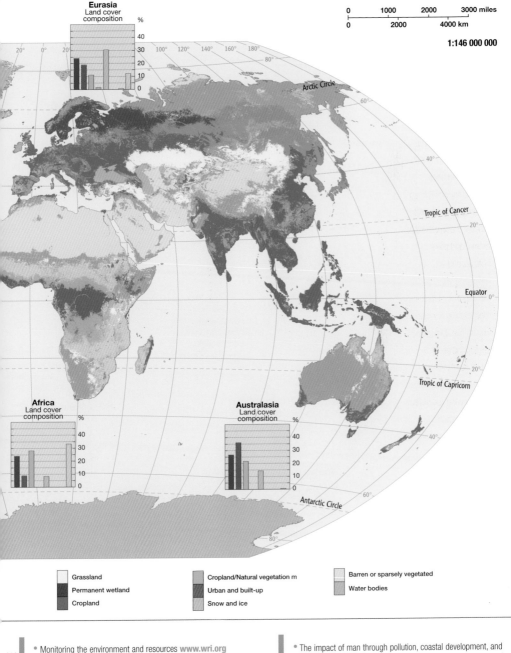

Eurasia
Land cover composition %

40
30
20
10
0

1000   2000   3000 miles
2000   4000 km

1:146 000 000

Arctic Circle

Tropic of Cancer

Equator

Tropic of Capricorn

Africa
Land cover composition %

40
30
20
10
0

Australasia
Land cover composition %

40
30
20
10
0

Antarctic Circle

	Grassland		Cropland/Natural vegetation m		Barren or sparsely vegetated
	Permanent wetland		Urban and built-up		Water bodies
	Cropland		Snow and ice		

The world's population reached 6 billion in 1999. Rates of population growth vary between continents, but overall, the rate of growth has been increasing and it is predicted that by 2050 another 3 billion people will inhabit the planet. The process of urbanization, in particular migration from countryside to city, has led to the rapid growth of many cities. It is estimated that by 2007, more people will be living in urban areas than in rural areas. There are now 387 cities with over 1 million inhabitants and twenty with over 10 million.

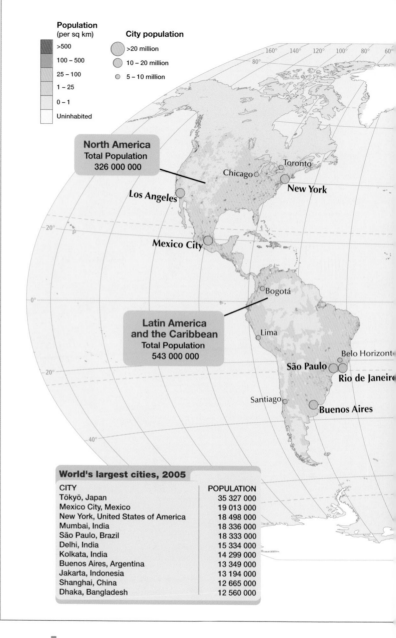

Population
(per sq km)

	>500
	100 – 500
	25 – 100
	1 – 25
	0 – 1
	Uninhabited

City population

- >20 million
- 10 – 20 million
- 5 – 10 million

North America
Total Population
326 000 000

Chicago
Toronto
New York
Los Angeles
Mexico City

Latin America and the Caribbean
Total Population
543 000 000

Bogotá
Lima
Belo Horizonte
São Paulo
Rio de Janeiro
Santiago
Buenos Aires

World's largest cities, 2005

CITY	POPULATION
Tōkyō, Japan	35 327 000
Mexico City, Mexico	19 013 000
New York, United States of America	18 498 000
Mumbai, India	18 336 000
São Paulo, Brazil	18 333 000
Delhi, India	15 334 000
Kolkata, India	14 299 000
Buenos Aires, Argentina	13 349 000
Jakarta, Indonesia	13 194 000
Shanghai, China	12 665 000
Dhaka, Bangladesh	12 560 000

Go to →

Country populations
pages 10–22
World countries map
page 24
World climate page 28

KNOW THE WORLD

- Although urbanization is increasing, with almost half of the world's population living in urban areas, cities take up less than 2 per cent of the earth's land surface.

- It is estimated that 1.2 billion people live below the poverty line which is measured at US$1 a day. In countries such as Ethiopia, Uganda and Nicaragua 80 per cent of the population live on less than that.

- The world's population is growing by 77 million people per year.

- Environmental conditions dictate that 90 per cent of the 70 million inhabitants of Egypt live along the River Nile.

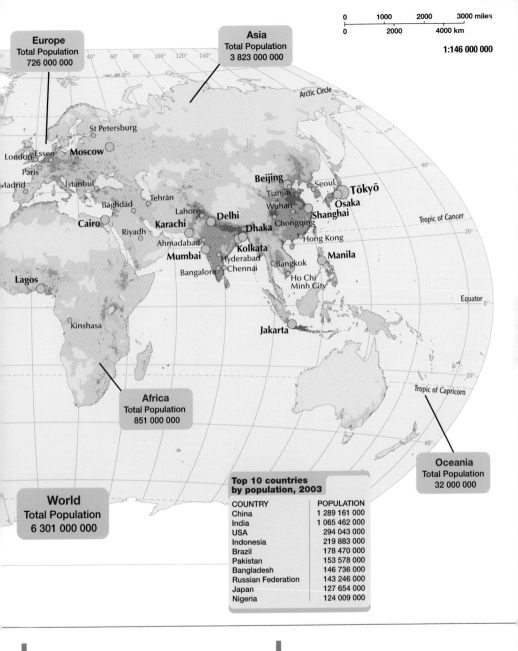

Europe
Total Population
726 000 000

Asia
Total Population
3 823 000 000

| 0 | 1000 | 2000 | 3000 miles |
| 0 | 2000 | 4000 km |

1:146 000 000

Arctic Circle

St Petersburg

London Essen **Moscow**
Paris
Madrid İstanbul
                Tehrān
        Baghdād
                Lahore **Delhi**
Cairo   **Karachi**   **Wuhan**
        Riyadh   **Dhaka** Chongqing
        Ahmadabad   **Kolkata**
Mumbai   Hyderabad   Bangkok
        Bangalore Chennai   Ho Chi
                        Minh City
Lagos
        Kinshasa   **Jakarta**

Beijing
Tianjin
        Seoul **Tōkyō**
                Osaka
        Shanghai
Hong Kong
                Manila

Tropic of Cancer

Equator

Tropic of Capricorn

Africa
Total Population
851 000 000

Oceania
Total Population
32 000 000

World
Total Population
6 301 000 000

**Top 10 countries
by population, 2003**

COUNTRY	POPULATION
China	1 289 161 000
India	1 065 462 000
USA	294 043 000
Indonesia	219 883 000
Brazil	178 470 000
Pakistan	153 578 000
Bangladesh	146 736 000
Russian Federation	143 246 000
Japan	127 654 000
Nigeria	124 009 000

The system of time-keeping throughout the world is based on twenty-four time zones, each stretching over fifteen degrees of longitude – the distance equivalent to a time difference of one hour. The Prime, or Greenwich Meridian (0 degrees west), is the basis for Greenwich Mean Time (GMT), by which other time zones are measured. This universal reference point was agreed at an international conference in 1884. The International Dateline is based on longitude 180 degrees. This imaginary line marks the difference between one day and the next.

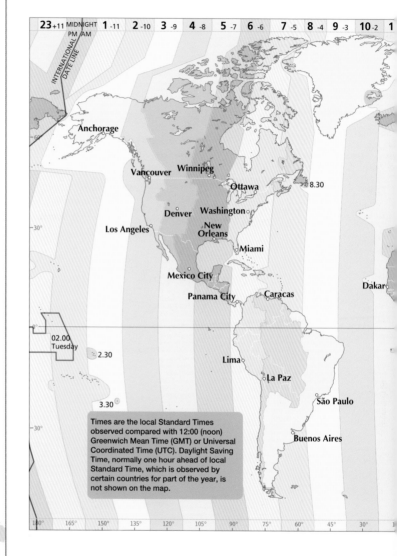

Times are the local Standard Times observed compared with 12:00 (noon) Greenwich Mean Time (GMT) or Universal Coordinated Time (UTC). Daylight Saving Time, normally one hour ahead of local Standard Time, which is observed by certain countries for part of the year, is not shown on the map.

Go to →

World countries map
page 24
World population and
cities page 32
Pacific Ocean page 158

KNOW THE WORLD

- China uses only one time zone although it should theoretically have five, while the Russian Federation stretches over eleven zones.

- Time zones boundaries can be altered to suit international or internal boundaries. The International Dateline was amended so that Caroline Island, in Kiribati, would be the first land area to greet the year 2000. The island was renamed Millennium Island in recognition of this.

- Daylight Saving Time allows nations to adjust their clocks to extend daylight during the working day. It was first introduced to the UK during the First World War to reduce the demand for artificial heating and lighting.

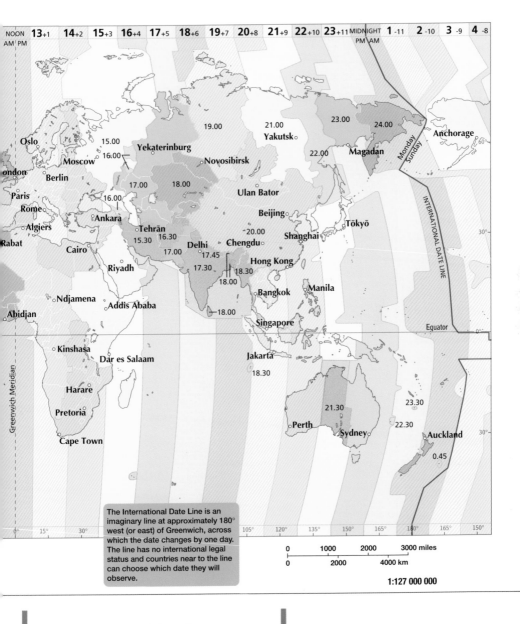

NOON	13 +1	14 +2	15 +3	16 +4	17 +5	18 +6	19 +7	20 +8	21 +9	22 +10	23 +11	MIDNIGHT	1 -11	2 -10	3 -9	4 -8
AM PM												PM AM				

Oslo

15.00

ondon

Moscow 16.00

Yekaterinburg

19.00

21.00

Yakutsk

23.00

24.00

Anchorage

60

Berlin

Novosibirsk

22.00

Magadan

Monday
Sunday

Paris

17.00

18.00

Ulan Bator

Rome

16.00

Algiers

Ankara

Beijing

20.00

Tōkyō

30°

Rabat

Tehrān 16.30

Shanghai

INTERNATIONAL DATE LINE

Cairo

15.30

Delhi

Chengdu

Riyadh

17.00

17.45

Hong Kong

Ndjamena

Addis Ababa

17.30

18.30

Manila

Abidjan

18.00

Bangkok

Equator

Singapore

Kinshasa

Dar es Salaam

Jakarta

Greenwich Meridian

18.30

Harare

21.30

23.30

Pretoria

Perth

Sydney

22.30

Auckland

30°

Cape Town

0.45

The International Date Line is an imaginary line at approximately 180° west (or east) of Greenwich, across which the date changes by one day. The line has no international legal status and countries near to the line can choose which date they will observe.

| 15° | 30° | 105° | 120° | 135° | 150° | 165° | 180° | 165° | 150° |

| 0 | 1000 | 2000 | 3000 miles |
| 0 | 2000 | 4000 km |

1:127 000 000

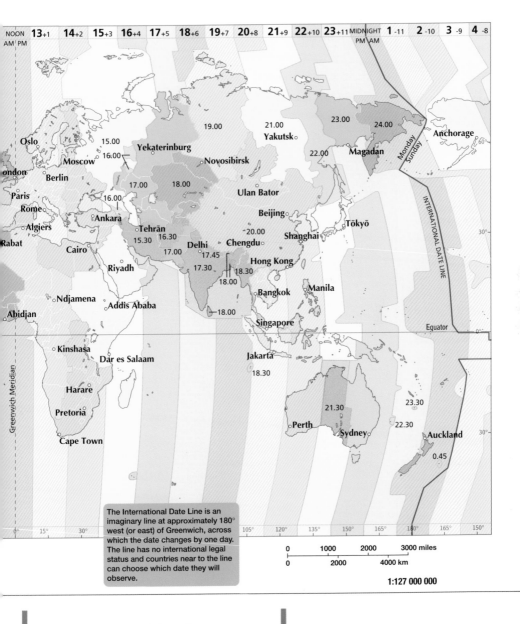

Europe's extremes

Total land area		9 908 599 sq km	3 825 710 sq miles
Largest lake	Caspian Sea	371 000 sq km	143 243 sq miles
Largest Island	Great Britain, United Kingdom	218 476 sq km	84 354 sq miles
Largest drainage basin	Volga, Russian Federation	1 380 000 sq km	532 818 sq miles
Lowest point	Caspian Sea	-28 metres	-92 feet

The continent consists of a complex, irregular arrangement of extensive plains, plateaus, and mountain ranges. There are several significant island groups – notably the British Isles and Iceland in the Atlantic, and in the Mediterranean the Balearic Islands, Corsica and Sardinia, Sicily, and Crete. The general outline of the continent is complicated further by a number of prominent peninsulas, among which are the Balkan Peninsula (principally occupied by Greece), Italy, Iberia (Spain and Portugal), Denmark, and the Scandinavian peninsula consisting of Norway and Sweden.

Geo terms

French
Golfe gulf, bay
German
Wald forest, mountains
Portuguese
Cabo cape, point
Russian
Ostrov island
Vozvyshennost' upland
Spanish
Golfo gulf, bay

Go to →

Geo terms *page 8*
World physical features *page 26*
Europe countries map *page 38*

36

Map labels:
Horn
Faxaflói **Iceland** Fontur
Vestmannaeyjar Snæfell 1833
Vatnajökull
Norwegian Sea
Faroe Islands
Galdhøpigge 247
ATLANTIC OCEAN
Shetland
Cape Wrath Orkney
Outer Hebrides
British Isles Grampian Mountains
North Sea
Skagerra
Jutlan
Pennines
Irish Sea
Ireland
Great Britain
Weser
Rhine
Thames
Ardennes
English Channel
Channel Islands
Seine
Loire
Vosges
Jura Lake Geneva
Bay of Biscay
Massif Central
Rhône
Mont Blanc 4808
Liguria
Azores
Cape Finisterre
Gulf of Gascony
Pyrenees Aneto 3404
Golfe du Lion
Ligurian Sea
Cordillera Cantábrica
Douro
Iberian
Ebro
Balearic Islands
Corsic
Tagus
Peninsula
Golfo de Valencia
Minorca
Sardini
1:28 500 000
0 150 300 450 miles
0 300 600 km
Cabo de São Vicente
Sierra Morena
Mulhacén 3482
Ibiza Majorca
Sierra Nevada
Medite
Madeira
Strait of Gibraltar
AFRICA

KNOW THE REGION

- The Danube flows through seven countries and has six different local names – Donau (Austria and Germany), Dunaj (Slovakia), Duna (Hungary), Dunav (Serbia and Montenegro), Dunarea (Romania) and Dunay (Ukraine). 'Danube' is the conventional English name.

- All the seas on this map (except the Caspian) are in effect branches of the Atlantic Ocean.

- Europe's four highest mountains – El'brus, Gora Dykh-Tau, Shkhara and Kazbek – are in the Caucasus. Mont Blanc, the highest mountain in the Alps, is fifth highest.

- By stretching north–south over more than 45 degrees of latitude, Europe has a greatly varied climate, from the hot Mediterranean to the frozen Arctic.

Europe's longest rivers

Volga	3 688 km	2 291 miles
Danube	2 850 km	1 770 miles
Dnieper	2 285 km	1 419 miles
Kama	2 028 km	1 260 miles
Don	1 931 km	1 199 miles

Europe's highest mountains

El'brus, Russian Federation	5 642 m	18 510 ft
Gora Dykh-Tau, Russian Federation	5 204 m	17 073 ft
Shkhara, Georgia/Russian Federation	5 201 m	17 063 ft
Kazbek, Georgia/Russian Federation	5 047 m	16 558 ft
Mont Blanc, France/Italy	4 808 m	15 774 ft

DISCOVER MORE

- Explore Europe's environment www.eea.eu.int
- Search for satellite images of Europe www.visibleearth.nasa.gov
- Nature conservation issues in Europe www.ecnc.nl
- European weather forecasts www.metoffice.com/weather/wxforecast.html
- Heritage sites in Europe whc.unesco.org

WATCH OUT!

- Iceland is growing. Due to its situation straddling two of the earth's tectonic plates, volcanic activity means that over an average human's life the island grows by about the length of a car.
- Pollution in the Mediterranean Sea is a growing problem. It is made worse by the fact that both the tidal range and the rate of water exchange to and from the Atlantic are low. Full turnover is estimated to take 150 years.

Europe's countries

Largest country	Russian Federation	17 075 400 sq km	6 592 812 sq miles
Smallest country	Vatican City	0.5 sq km	0.2 sq miles
Largest population	Russian Federation	143 246 000	
Smallest population	Vatican City	472	
Most densely populated country	Monaco	17 000 per sq km	34 000 per sq mile
Least densely populated country	Iceland	3 per sq km	7 per sq mile

Europe's dense jigsaw of countries reflects the complex history of its many national groupings. The political map was redrawn significantly after the First and Second World Wars, and changes have continued since – Germany reunified in 1990, Yugoslavia and the former Soviet Union broke up in 1991, and Czechoslovakia was divided into two in 1993. Many European countries are small by world standards – some are among the world's smallest – but European Russia is part of the largest country in the world.

AL.   ALBANIA
B.H.   BOSNIA-HERZEGOVINA
CR.   CROATIA
CZ.R.   CZECH REPUBLIC
HUN.   HUNGARY
LIE.   LIECHTENSTEIN
LUX.   LUXEMBOURG
M.   MACEDONIA
NETH. NETHERLANDS
S.M.   SERBIA AND MONTENEGRO
SW.   SWITZERLAND

1:28 500 000

0	150	300	450 miles
0	300		600 km

Reykjavík ICELAND

Norwegian Sea

Tórshavn Faroe Islands (Denmark)

ATLANTIC OCEAN

Bergen

Glasgow Edinburgh
Belfast UNITED *North Sea* DE
REPUBLIC KINGDOM
OF Dublin
IRELAND   Manchester NETH.
Birmingham The Hague Amsterdam
Cardiff London Brussels Esser
English Channel BELGIUM Frankfurt
Channel Islands Paris LUX. am Main
(U.K.)   Luxembourg
Nantes   Orléans Strasbourg
Bay of Loire Zürich
Biscay FRANCE Bern SW.
Bordeaux Lyon Geneva Vadu
Milan
Turin
Azores (Portugal)
Marseille MONAC
Andorra ANDORRA
la Vella Vatica
Oporto Corsica
Lisbon Madrid Barcelona
Tagus SPAIN Palma Sardini
de Mallorca
Valencia *Balearic*
Seville *Islands*
Cádiz Cartagena *M e d i t*
Madeira (Portugal)
Gibraltar (U.K.)

AFRICA

Go to →

World countries *page 24*
World time zones
page 34
Europe physical features
page 36

KNOW THE REGION

• The European Union increased its membership from fifteen to twenty-five members in 2004, with several other countries keen to join. It now includes Malta and Cyprus, and some eastern European countries, but not Norway, Switzerland or Iceland.

• Iceland and the Faroe Islands belong culturally and linguistically to Scandinavia.

• Europe has the two smallest independent countries in the world – Vatican City and Monaco.

• Serbia and Montenegro is the new name (since 2003) for what was previously called Yugoslavia. There are moves for Montenegro to secede from this union and become an independent country.

Novaya Zemlya

Barents Sea

Ostrov Kolguyev

Vorkuta

Pechora

Kola Peninsula

Lappland

White Sea

Archangel

R U S S I A N

Severnaya Dvina

FINLAND

Lake Ladoga

Perm'

N O R W A Y

F E D E R A T I O N

Oslo

Helsinki

St Petersburg

Izhevsk

Ufa

S W E D E N

Gulf of Bothnia

Stockholm

Gulf of Finland

Tallinn

ESTONIA

Yaroslavl'

Nizhniy Novgorod

Kazan'

Volga

A S I A

alborg

LATVIA

Riga

Moscow

Ul'yanovsk

Samara

MARK

Malmö

Baltic Sea

Orenburg

openhagen

LITHUANIA

RUS. FED.

Vilnius

Tula

Saratov

Hamburg

Kaliningrad

Minsk

Voronezh

Volgograd

Volga

Berlin

BELARUS

Homyel'

Warsaw

Dnieper

Poznan

Łódź

Brest

Kiev

Kharkiv

Don

Astrakhan'

MANY

POLAND

Rivne

U K R A I N E

Donets'k

Rostov-na-Donu

Caspian Sea

Prague

Katowice

L'viv

Dnipropetrovs'k

Danube

CZ.R.

Dniester

Krasnodar

SLOVAKIA

Munich

Vienna

MOLDOVA

Groznyy

Bratislava

Budapest

Chişinău

Odesa

C a u c a s u s

AUSTRIA

HUN.

SLOVENIA

ROMANIA

Ljubljana

Zagreb

Belgrade

Bucharest

Constanța

SAN MARINO

CR.

B. H.

Sarajevo

Danube

B l a c k   S e a

ty

Split

S.M.

Niš

BULGARIA

Rome

Podgorica

Sofia

Naples

Tirana

M.

Skopje

İstanbul

Tyrrhenian Sea

AL.

Thessaloniki

T U R K E Y

alermo

GREECE

Aegean Sea

Sicily

Ionian Sea

Athens

ranean Sea

Valletta

MALTA

Crete

A d r i a t i c   S e a

I T A L Y

Europe's capitals		
Largest capital (population)	Paris, France	9 753 000
Smallest capital (population)	Vatican City	472
Most northerly capital	Reykjavík, Iceland	64° 39'N
Most southerly capital	Valletta, Malta	35° 54'N
Highest capital	Andorra la Vella, Andorra	1 029 metres 3 376 feet

DISCOVER MORE

• Get EU facts and statistics europa.eu.int
• Explore the European parliament www.europarl.eu.int
• Country profiles www.odci.gov/cia/publications/factbook
• Visiting Europe www.visiteurope.com
• Travel advice www.fco.gov.uk
• International boundaries www.ibru.dur.ac.uk

WATCH OUT!

• The Baltic Sea borders on nine countries and is important for shipping. In winter, the northern parts of the sea are icebound for almost 6 months when navigation is suspended. Southern areas can be frozen for 2 to 3 weeks.

• Be wary of using Global Positioning System (GPS) devices in the Russian Federation. You could be seen as a security threat and arrested if deemed to be using GPS in suspicious circumstances.

European Russia is conventionally defined as ending at the Ural Mountains, the Caspian Sea and the Caucasus mountains. The rest of the Russian Federation lies within Asia. A large section of Kazakhstan also falls into this map area, although all or most of it is traditionally regarded as Asian. In the south of the map are the extensive water areas of the Caspian Sea, the largest lake in the world, and the Black Sea. In the north is the Barents Sea, part of the Arctic Ocean.

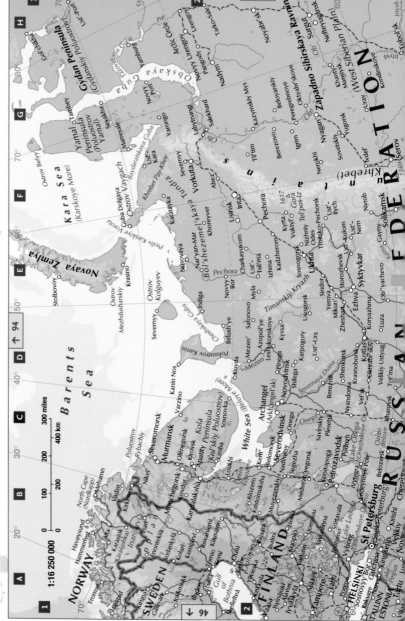

Geo terms

Russian
Guba gulf, bay
Khrebet mountain range
Nizmennost' lowland
Ozero lake
Poluostrov peninsula
Ravnina plain

40

Go to →

Map symbols *page 6*
Geo terms *page 8*
Europe physical features *page 36*

KNOW THE REGION

* The Russian Federation is often referred to as Russia. However, although the majority of its population are ethnic Russians, it encompasses many other ethnic groups including Tatars, Ukrainians and Chechens.

* The northeastern area of European Russia, bordering the Arctic Ocean, forms part of the enormous physical region known as Siberia (Sibir' in Russian).

* A small section of the Russian Federation – Kaliningrad – lies off this map to the west (see page 42).

* Mount El'brus, Europe's highest mountain (5 642 metres/18 510 feet), lies on the southern edge of the Russian Federation near the Georgian border.

KAZAKHSTAN

UZBEKISTAN

TURKMENISTAN

IRAN

TURKEY

GEORGIA

AZERBAIJAN

UKRAINE

BELARUS

LATVIA

RUSSIAN

Kyzylkum Desert

Karakum Desert (Peski Karakumy)

Aral Sea

Caspian Sea

Black Sea

Sea of Azov

Caucasus

MOSCOW

KIEV

MINSK

BAKU

ANKARA

T'BILISI

YEREVAN

ASHGABAT

Central Russian Upland

Caspian Lowland (Prikaspiyskaya Nizmennost')

↑ 88
↓ 92
93 →

The map focuses on the states of Estonia, Latvia and Lithuania, known as the Baltic states. To their south lies Belarus, formerly known as Belorussia or White Russia. The eastern half of the map covers a large part of European Russia, centred on Moscow, the capital of the Russian Federation. All of these countries were parts of the former Soviet Union until it broke up in 1991. A small, separate enclave of the Russian Federation, centred on the city of Kaliningrad, is sandwiched between Lithuania and Poland.

Geo terms

Russian

Les forest
Mys cape, point
Ozero lake
Vodokhranilishche reservoir
Vozvyshennost' upland

Go to →

Map symbols *page 6*
Geo terms *page 8*
European countries
pages 10–12

KNOW THE REGION

• The Baltic Sea is truly international – the islands of Öland and Gotland belong to Sweden, the Åland Islands to Finland, and Hiiumaa and Saaremaa to Estonia.

• Much of this area consists of the North European Plain. As a result, many of the major roads and railways run straight for great distances, and the map shows how Moscow in particular, is a focus for these routes.

• The Russian city of St Petersburg, founded by the Tsar Peter the Great, was first renamed Petrograd in 1914, then Leningrad, after the communist leader, in 1924. It reverted to its original name in 1991.

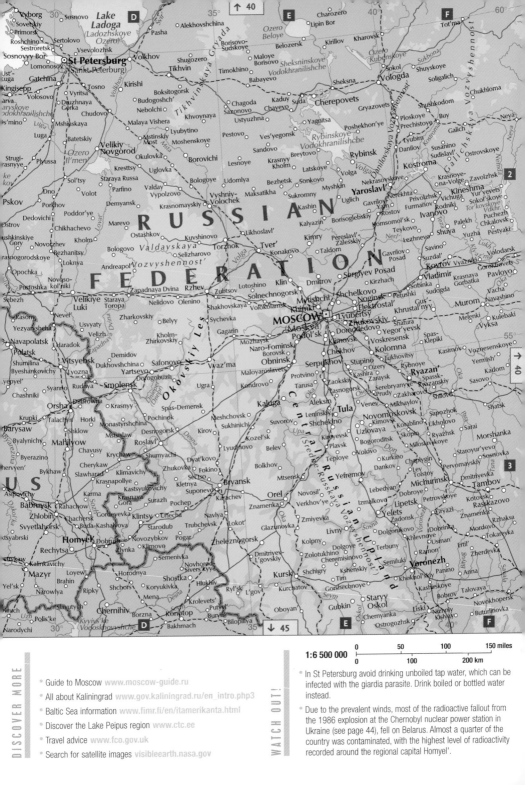

The map is focused on the Ukraine, along with its smaller neighbour, Moldova, which used to be called Moldavia. Both were republics within the former Soviet Union until its demise in 1991. The map also covers the whole of Romania. A small section of the Ukraine extends along the Black Sea coast until it meets with Romania at the delta of the river Danube, which up to this point has flowed through seven countries from its source in southwest Germany.

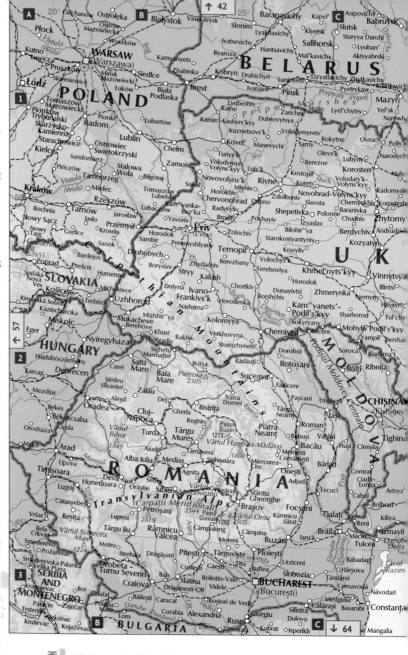

Geo terms

Romanian
Lacul lake
Podişul plateau
Russian
Bol'shoy big
Kryazh hills, ridge
Ukrainian
Vodoskhovyshche reservoir
Zatoka gulf, bay

44

Go to →

Map symbols *page 6*
Geo terms *page 8*
European countries *pages 10–12*

KNOW THE REGION

- Moldova and the Ukraine both opted to give their own languages precedence in the early 1990s, before which Russian had been dominant. Ukrainian is closely related to Russian, written in the Cyrillic alphabet. Moldova and Romania both mainly speak Romanian, which is written in the Roman alphabet.

- The Crimea, a large peninsula in the Ukraine, was the scene of the Crimean War in the 1850s, when the famous Charge of the Light Brigade took place.

- In the north of the Ukraine lies the now abandoned town of Chernobyl, notorious for a disastrous explosion at its nuclear power station in 1986.

↑ 43

→ 41

↓ 92

1:6 500 000

| | 50 | 100 | 150 miles |

| | 100 | 200 km |

DISCOVER MORE

- The River Danube www.danube-river.org
- Danube delta details www.romaniatourism.com/delta.html
- Crimea facts and figures www.crimea-portal.gov.ua
- Chernobyl nuclear incident www.chernobyl.info
- Heritage sites in this region whc.unesco.org
- Search for satellite images visibleearth.nasa.gov

WATCH OUT!

- The Chernobyl nuclear accident in 1986 resulted in the world's largest accidental release of radioactive materials and caused high levels of radioactive ground contamination within a 30 kilometre (19 mile) radius of the plant.
- There is a risk of rabies infection in Romania from dogs, cats, bats and monkeys. Avoid contact with stray dogs – of which there is a significant number in and around Bucharest – and other animals.

The main countries on this map fall into two broad groups: Scandinavia; and the Baltic states of Estonia, Latvia and Lithuania. The latter three used to be parts of the former Soviet Union. Norway, Sweden, Denmark and Iceland speak languages that are very closely related to each other, while Finland, also regarded as part of Scandinavia, speaks quite a different language whose only close relative in the region is Estonian. Sami (Lappish) is spoken in parts of the north, an area known as Lappland.

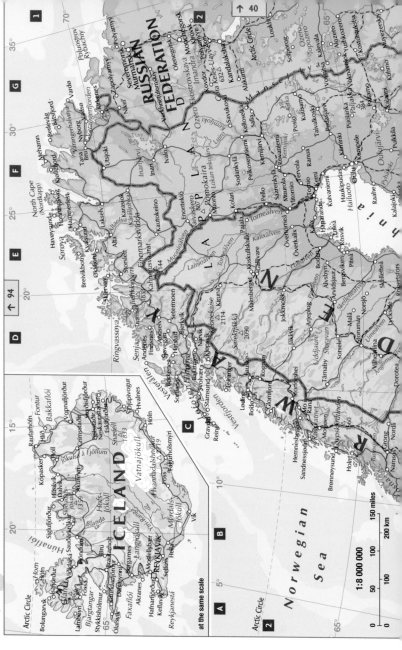

Geo terms

Finnish
-*järvi* lake
tekojärvi reservoir
Icelandic
-*flói* gulf, bay
Norwegian
-*dal* valley
-*halvøya* peninsula
Swedish
-*älven* river
-*bukten* gulf, bay

Go to →
Map symbols *page 6*
Geo terms *page 8*
European countries
pages 10–12

KNOW THE REGION

- Denmark and Sweden have been linked since 2000 by a major bridge over the Öresund strait. Denmark has also built long bridges between its main islands, notably over the Great Belt sea channel.

- The Åland Islands, although part of Finland, are Swedish-speaking and enjoy a considerable degree of autonomy. Swedish is also spoken widely in the southwestern coastal areas of Finland.

- Iceland is physically isolated in the North Atlantic, and is far closer to Greenland than to mainland Europe. Its capital, Reykjavík, is the world's northernmost national capital.

- Lakes cover almost 10 per cent of the total land area of Finland.

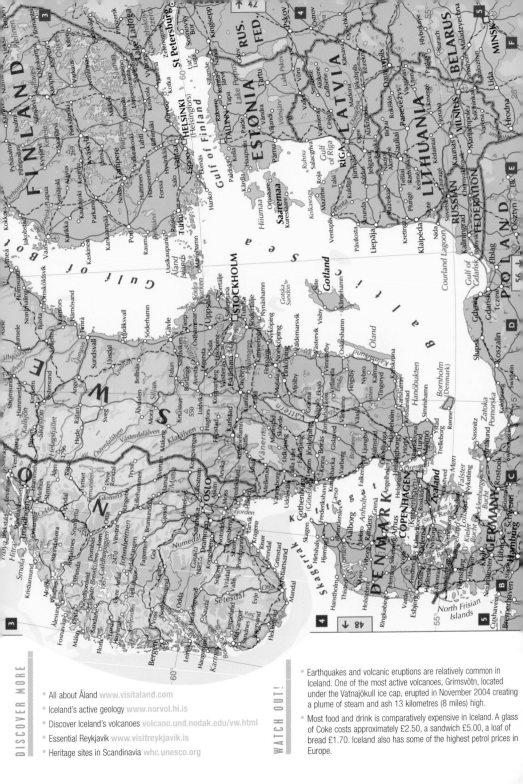

↑ 42

↓ 48

DISCOVER MORE

* All about Åland www.visitaland.com
* Iceland's active geology www.norvol.hi.is
* Discover Iceland's volcanoes volcano.und.nodak.edu/vw.html
* Essential Reykjavik www.visitreykjavik.is
* Heritage sites in Scandinavia whc.unesco.org

WATCH OUT!

* Earthquakes and volcanic eruptions are relatively common in Iceland. One of the most active volcanoes, Grímsvötn, located under the Vatnajökull ice cap, erupted in November 2004 creating a plume of steam and ash 13 kilometres (8 miles) high.

* Most food and drink is comparatively expensive in Iceland. A glass of Coke costs approximately £2.50, a sandwich £5.00, a loaf of bread £1.70. Iceland also has some of the highest petrol prices in Europe.

The British Isles are the largest islands in Europe, and are separated from the continental mainland by only about 35 kilometres (21 miles) across the Strait of Dover. The Isle of Man and the Channel Islands do not form part of the United Kingdom, but are Crown Dependencies of the UK, with three separate administrations. The Faroe Islands, which also come within the area of this map, are a dependency of Denmark. They are also sometimes referred to as the Faeroes.

48

Geo terms

Faroese
-oy island
French
Baie bay
Golfe gulf, bay
Île island

Go to →

Map symbols *page 6*
Geo terms *page 8*
Europe physical features *page 36*

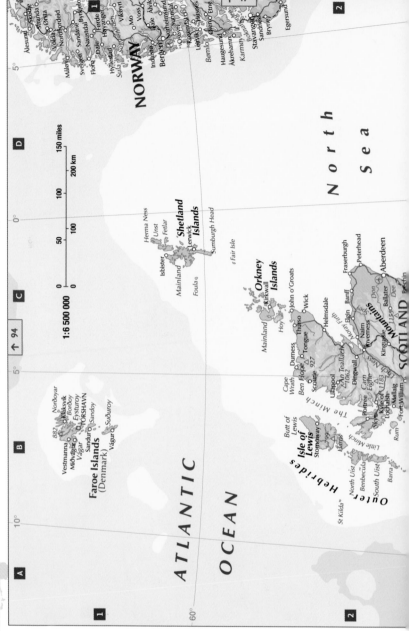

1:6 500 000

* The term 'British Isles' signifies the group of islands of which Great Britain is the major component. The term 'Britain' refers only to the main island, although the terms 'Britain' and 'British' are commonly used when referring to the UK as a whole.

* The Republic of Ireland (sometimes shortened simply to 'Ireland') does not cover the whole of the island of Ireland, since Northern Ireland remains part of the UK.

* The Shetland Islands, Orkney Islands and Outer Hebrides have many cultural features (including place names) which are a result of strong historical Scandinavian influences.

54

58

DISCOVER MORE

- Statistical Britain www.statistics.gov.uk
- Check the weather www.metoffice.com
- Unearth Britain's landscape www.bgs.ac.uk
- Britain's transport www.dft.gov.uk
- Royal Britain www.royal.gov.uk
- Britain abroad www.fco.gov.uk

WATCH OUT!

- Many rural areas of the British Isles, particularly western Scotland, Wales, the Lake District and the West Country have single track roads which demand careful driving. Use marked passing places to allow on-coming traffic to pass and to allow overtaking.

- Although Britain's mountains are not high by world standards, they can be dangerous places. Their weather can be very severe and can change quickly. Be prepared by carrying the right equipment and checking weather forecasts. It is also advisable to let somebody know you're planned route before you leave.

Scotland forms the northernmost part of the United Kingdom. It includes many islands, among which are the Inner and Outer Hebrides to the west, and the Shetland Islands, located well to the north of the Orkney Islands. Ireland, which is the second largest island in the British Isles after Great Britain, is politically divided into two parts: the Republic of Ireland occupies most of the south and the northwest, while Northern Ireland in the northeast is part of the United Kingdom.

Geo terms

Gaelic
Ben mountain
Loch lake
Irish
Lough lake
Slieve hill, mountain

50

Go to →

Map symbols *page 6*
Geo terms *page 8*
British Isles *page 48*

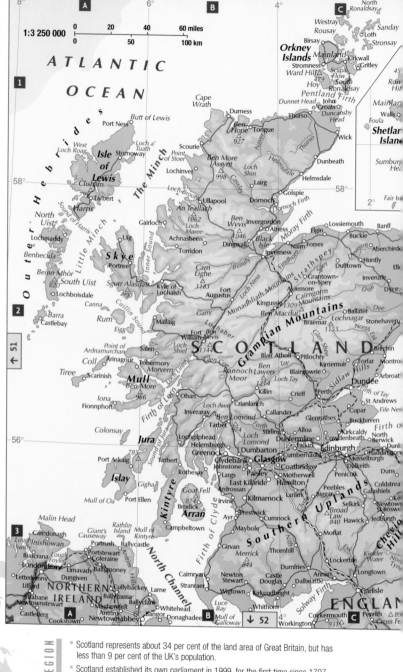

KNOW THE REGION

- Scotland represents about 34 per cent of the land area of Great Britain, but has less than 9 per cent of the UK's population.
- Scotland established its own parliament in 1999, for the first time since 1707.
- Ireland is separated from the closest point in Great Britain (the Mull of Kintyre) by only 20 kilometres (12 miles).
- The island of Ireland is traditionally divided into four provinces – Connaught, Leinster, Munster and Ulster. Northern Ireland consists of the majority of Ulster.
- Different forms of Gaelic, a Celtic language related to Welsh and Breton, are spoken, and actively encouraged, in parts of both Scotland and Ireland.

ATLANTIC OCEAN

1:3 250 000

0   20   40   60 miles
0   50   100 km

SCOTLAND

Herma Ness
Unst
ell
bister
Ulsta Fetlar
Toft Whalsay
Lerwick
Bressay
Sumburgh

raserburgh
Rattray
Head
Peterhead

Aberdeen

North Sea

orth

t Abb's Head
Berwick-upon-Tweed
(Holy Island
Lindisfarne)
he Cheviot
15
Rothbury
Ashington
Morpeth
Newcastle upon Tyne
xham
Blaydon Gateshead
Consett 0
Durham,
Wear
Spennymoor
2'

Colonsay
Jura
Lochgilphead Helensburgh
Port Askaig
Gigha
Greenock
Rothesay
Largs
Islay
SCOTLAND
Goat Fell
Ardrossan
Mull of Oa
Port Ellen
Kintyre
Brodick
Arran
Irvine
Prestwick
Ayr
Firth of Clyde

Malin Head
Giant's Causeway
Mull of Kintyre
Campbeltown
Girvan
52
West Town Tory Island
Inishowen
Portrush
Ballycastle
Rathlin Island
Cairnryan
Bloody Foreland
Carndonagh
Portstewart
Antrim Mts
Stranraer
Gweedore
Errigal
752
Buncrana
Coleraine
Luce Bay
Aran Island
Londonderry
Limavady
Ballymoney
Burtonport
Lough Foyle
Cullybackey
Ballymena
Larne
Gweebarra Bay
Letterkenny
Dungiven
ULSTER
Whitehead
Glenties
Lifford
Strabane
Magherafelt
Antrim
Ballyclare
Bangor
Isle of Man (U.K.)
Malin More
Donegal
676
Blue Stack Mts
Castlederg
NORTHERN
Newtownstewart
Cookstown
Newtownabbey
Newtownards
Peel
Rossan Point
Killybegs
Ballyshannon
Omagh
Lough Neagh
Belfast
Dunmurry
Lisburn
Strangford Lough
Donaghadee
Port Erin
Donegal Bay
Bundoran
IRELAND
Portadown
Dromore
Ballynahinch
Portaferry
Calf of Man
Benwee Head
Erris Head
Killala
Sligo Bay
Lower Lough Erne
Upper Lough Erne
Banbridge
Slieve Donard 852
Downpatrick
Belmullet
Ballycastle
Bay
Enniskillen
Armagh
Keady
Mourne Mts
Newcastle
Dundrum Bay
Ballina
Sligo
Lisnaskea
Monaghan
Newry
Kilkeel
Blacksod Bay
Nephin
806
Slieve Gamph
Colloney
Clones
Castleblayney
Warrenpoint
Achill Island
Nephin Beg Range
Lough Allen
Carrick-on-Shannon
Cavan
Carrickmacross
Dundalk
Carlingford Lough
Clare Island
Croagh Patrick
765
Westport
Castlebar
Boyle
Lough Sheelin
Kells
Drogheda
Irish Sea
Inishbofin
Louisburgh
Ballaghaderreen
Longford
Balbriggan
Skerries
Slyne Head
Claremorris
Roscommon
Lough Ree
Navan
Trim
Swords
Connemara
Ballinrobe
Tuam
Mullingar
Boyne
DUBLIN
(Baile Átha Cliath)
Clifden
Lough Mask
Lough Corrib
Athlone
Edenderry
Lough Derg
Bog of Allen
Leixlip
Lucan
Dún Laoghaire
Gorumna Island
Galway
Ballinasloe
Liffey
Naas
Bray
Inishmore
Aran Islands
Galway Bay
Burren
Loughrea
Tullamore
Newbridge
Lungnaquilla Mountain 926
Greystones
Hag's Head
Liscannor Bay
Ennistymon
Portumna
Lough Derg
Birr
Portlaoise
Athy
Wicklow
Wicklow Head
Spanish Point
Ennis
Killaloe
Nenagh
Roscrea
Carlow
Muine Bheag
Arklow
Kilkee
Kilrush
Limerick
Templemore
Kilkenny
Thomastown
Gorey
Enniscorthy
Loop Head
Mouth of the Shannon
Golden Vale
Thurles
Cashel
New Ross
Cahore Point
Listowel
Newcastle West
Tipperary
Clonmel
Wexford
Brandon Mountain 953
Glanaruddery Mts
Galtymore 920
Cahir
Comeragh Mountains
Carrick-on-Suir
Rosslare
Sleea Head
Dingle
Tralee
Castleisland
Newtown
Mitchelstown
Fermoy
Blackwater
Waterford
Tramore
Carnsore Point
Dingle Bay
Kanturk
Mallow
Dungarvan
Helvick Head
Carrantuohill 1041
Lough Leane
Killarney
Boggeragh Mts
Macroom
Midleton
Youghal
Waterford Harbour
St David's Head
Fishguard
WALES
Macgillycuddy's Reeks
Kenmare
Cork
Cobh
Haverfordwest
Cahersiveen
Sneem
Bandon
Kinsale
St George's Channel
Dursey Island
Cahermore
Bantry
Clonakilty
Old Head of Kinsale
Skibbereen
Caha Mts
Bantry Bay
Mizen Head
Cape Clear

REPUBLIC OF IRELAND

CONNAUGHT

LEINSTER

MUNSTER

→ 50
→ 52
→ 53

DISCOVER MORE

- Statistical Scotland www.scotland.gov.uk
- Visit Scotland www.visitscotland.com
- The new Scottish Parliament www.scottish.parliament.uk
- Discover Northern Ireland www.discovernorthernireland.com
- Visit Dublin www.visitdublin.com
- Gaelic language and culture www.pobail.ie/en/AnGhaeltacht

WATCH OUT!

- Parts of the west of Ireland can average 225 days of rain per year. Many mountainous areas have over 2 000 millimetres (79 inches) per year, with the wettest months being December and January.
- Scottish midges – Colicoides Impunctatus – are a major pest in summer in the west highlands of Scotland. These tiny, swarming, biting (only the females bite) insects like damp, cool conditions and can make outdoor life very uncomfortable. Use insect repellant and keep your skin covered.

England and Wales together form the southern part of Great Britain, or about two-thirds of the island. England is separated from France by the English Channel; from the rest of mainland Europe by the North Sea; and from the island of Ireland by the Irish Sea. The backbone of Wales is the broad range of the Cambrian Mountains, while northern England has the Pennines as its main chain of hills, with a rugged, mountainous offshoot in the Lake District of Cumbria.

Go to →

Map symbols *page 6*
Geo terms *page 8*
British Isles *page 48*

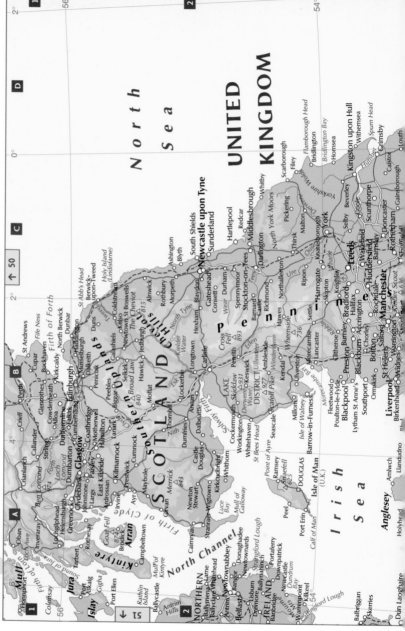

KNOW THE REGION

- The Isle of Man is a separate entity from the United Kingdom, and has a parliament (the Tynwald) which is much older than that of the UK – over 1000 years old.

- The Channel Islands consist of two separate dependencies of the UK – the Bailiwicks of Jersey and Guernsey. UK ownership of the islands is the last remnant of England's historical connections with France.

- The English Channel is known in French as 'La Manche', meaning 'the sleeve'.

- The Channel Tunnel, which provides a rail link between England and France, was opened in 1994 – almost 200 years after the idea was first proposed in 1806.

↑ 54

58 →

1:3 250 000

0   20   40   60 miles
0   50   100 km

DISCOVER MORE

- Visit England www.visitengland.com
- London guide www.london.gov.uk
- Explore the Lake District National Park
  www.lake-district.gov.uk
- Delve into the Channel Tunnel www.eurotunnel.com
- Visit Wales www.visitwales.com
- Governing Wales www.wales.gov.uk

WATCH OUT!

- Britain's motorways and main roads can become extremely congested, particularly on public holidays. Routes to and from the southeast of England are usually the worst affected. Try to avoid the main routes and choose your time of travel carefully if travelling to major tourist areas. Listen to local radio stations for traffic reports.

- Large areas of the countryside in parts of England and Wales are military training areas and firing ranges and have restricted public access. Check local maps and watch out for signs and indications that firing is taking place.

Almost all of the eastern half of the map covers Germany, the largest country in western and central Europe. The western part of the map covers the three Benelux countries, Belgium, the Netherlands and Luxembourg, which are also commonly known as the Low Countries. In the Netherlands, a prominent feature is the artificially-dammed Ijsselmeer, which was formerly an inlet of the North Sea called the Zuider Zee. Southern Germany in particular is characterized by a series of major hill regions prominently named on the map.

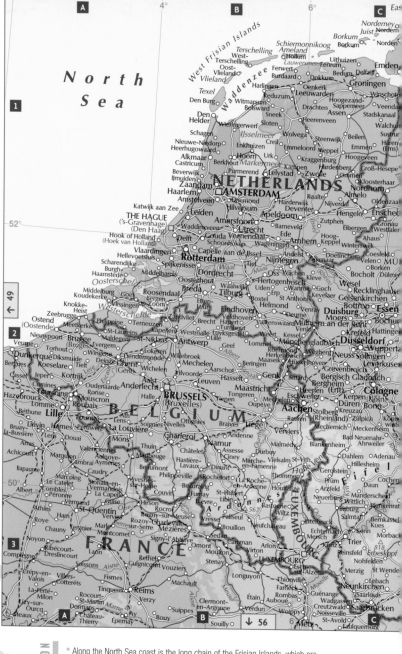

Geo terms

Czech
Hory hills, mountains

Dutch
-meer lake
-zee sea

German
-berg hill, mountain
Heide heath, moor
-wald forest, mountains

54

Go to →

Map symbols *page 6*
Geo terms *page 8*
European countries
pages 10–12

Map symbols *page 6*
Geo terms *page 8*
European countries
pages 10–12

KNOW THE REGION

- Along the North Sea coast is the long chain of the Frisian Islands, which are divided between the Netherlands, Germany and Denmark (see page 56) to the north.

- Significant parts of the Netherlands were reclaimed from the sea over several centuries. The largest of the resultant polders are to the east of Amsterdam, where the new town of Lelystad is shown on the map.

- Luxembourg was one of the original six members of the European Economic Community, now the European Union. It is predominantly French-speaking, but Luxembourg's own language (Letzeburgish), and German, are also in use.

↑ 56

1 : 3 250 000

0   20   40   60 miles
0   50   100 km

DISCOVER MORE

* Visit Berlin www.berlin.de
* Discover Amsterdam www.amsterdam.nl
* See Brussels www.bruxelles.irisnet.be
* Drive the German autobahns www.autobahn-online.de
* Heritage sites in northwest Europe whc.unesco.org

WATCH OUT!

* Some parts of the German autobahn (motorway) network have no speed limits. In recent years sections with 100–130 kilometres per hour (62–80 miles per hour) limits have been introduced to improve safety and reduce noise levels.

* Gentlemen be careful if you wear a tie in Germany on Weiberfastnacht (Women's Day) – the Thursday before Ash Wednesday. Women have the right to cut off men's ties on that day!

Central Europe consists of an extensive plain bordered in the south by the Alps (principally in Switzerland and Austria); in the east by the Carpathian and Tatra Mountains; in the west by the Low Countries (Belgium, the Netherlands and Luxembourg); and in the north by the North and Baltic Seas. Germany and Austria are at the core of Central Europe, together with some of the countries traditionally identified as being in Eastern Europe, such as Poland, Hungary, Slovakia and the Czech Republic.

Geo terms

German
Alb mountain region
Bucht gulf, bay
-gebirge mountains
Wald forest, mountains

Polish
Zatoka gulf, bay

Slovak
Malé small
štit peak

Go to →

Map symbols *page 6*
Geo terms *page 8*
European countries *pages 10–12*

KNOW THE REGION

- The Rhine and Danube rivers both have a wide variety of local names, including Rhin and Rhein (the Rhine in France and Germany), and Duna and Dunaj (the Danube in Hungary and Slovakia).

- Following the reunification of East and West Germany in 1990, Berlin was designated again as the capital of Germany, a title it relinquished at the end of World War II.

- The map shows the Slavic-speaking countries of Poland, the Czech Republic, Slovakia, Slovenia, the Ukraine, Belarus and Lithuania. Romanian is a Latin-based language related to French and Italian, while Hungarian is unique and largely unrelated to any of its neighbouring languages.

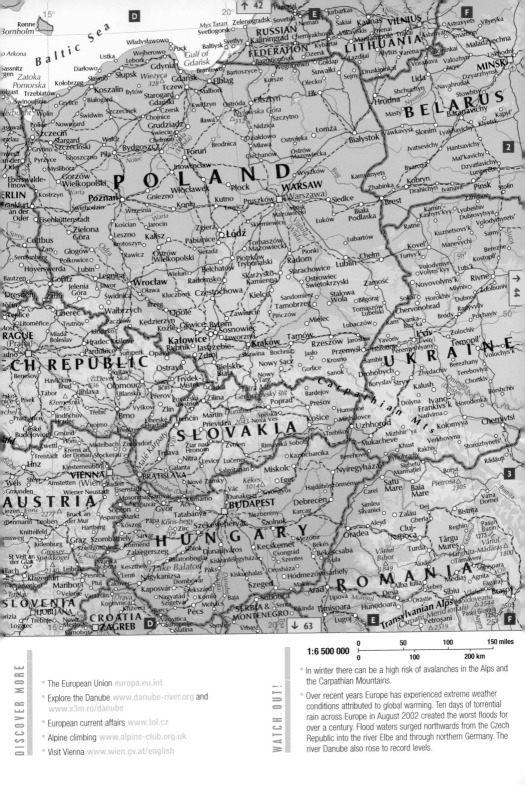

The map focuses on the position of France and Switzerland and their immediate neighbours. Spain lies across the Pyrenees in the south and Italy, which with France divides the western end of the Alps, lies to the southeast. Switzerland shares Lake Geneva with France, and borders Austria in the east. Germany is an important neighbour of France and Switzerland in the northeast, with Belgium lying to the north. The United Kingdom lies only a short distance from France across the English Channel.

Geo terms

French

Baie bay

Étang lagoon, lake

Golfe gulf, bay

Île, Îles island, islands

Massif mountains, upland

Pointe (Pte) cape, point

Go to →

Map symbols *page 6*
Geo terms *page 8*
Europe physical features *page 36*

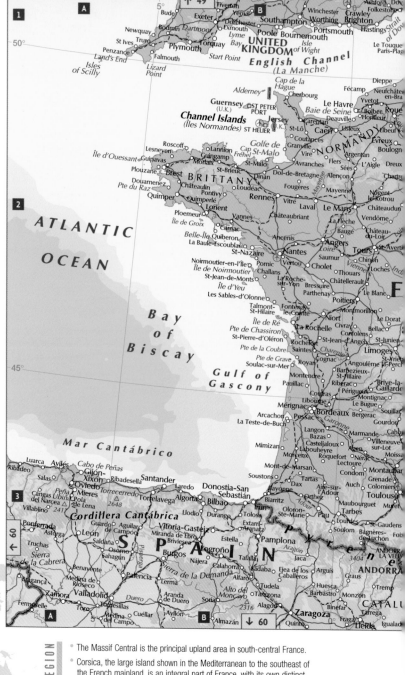

- The Massif Central is the principal upland area in south-central France.

- Corsica, the large island shown in the Mediterranean to the southeast of the French mainland, is an integral part of France, with its own distinct culture and dialect.

- The spectacular mountain range of the Alps is the source for several of Europe's major rivers including the Rhine, the Rhône and the Po.

- Monaco is set on the Mediterranean coast close to the Italian border. It is the second smallest country in the world. Its chief town, Monte Carlo, is renowned for its casinos.

Spain and Portugal virtually cover the Iberian Peninsula in southwest Europe. Gibraltar, a tiny enclave in the far south, remains a UK Overseas Territory. The small nation of Andorra is located high in the Pyrenees between Spain and France. The Balearic Islands, the chief of which are known to English-speakers as Majorca, Minorca and Ibiza, are a part of Spain lying in the Mediterranean Sea. Spain is also in possession of several small enclaves on the Moroccan coast, chief among which are Ceuta and Melilla.

Geo terms

Catalan
Golf gulf, bay
Portuguese
Baía bay
Serra mountain range
Spanish
Cordillera mountain range
Embalse reservoir
Mar sea
Sierra mountain range

Go to →

Map symbols *page 6*
European countries *pages 10–12*
Europe physical features *page 36*

KNOW THE REGION

- Andorra's government is subject to a special arrangement between France and Spain. Since 1278, the two joint rulers have been the President of France and the Bishop of Le Seu d'Urgell in Spain.

- Gibraltar has been a possession of the UK since the early 18th century, although ownership is disputed by Spain.

- The narrowness of the Strait of Gibraltar is mainly responsible for the low tidal range found throughout the Mediterranean.

- The Mediterranean coast of Spain is well known to holidaymakers, being divided mainly into the Costa Brava, the Costa Blanca, and the Costa del Sol.

This is a map showing the Mediterranean coast of Spain, southern France, the Balearic Islands, and northern Algeria.

Grid references: C, D, E (top); 1, 2 (right side); ↑ 58, → 62, → 100, ↓ 100 (directional page references)

Gulf of Gascony

FRANCE — PROVENCE, MONTE-CARLO, Cévennes

Selected place names (France): Arcachon, La Teste-de-Buch, Mimizan, Morcenx, Mont-de-Marsan, Soustons, Dax, Tartas, Bayonne, Biarritz, Orthez, Pau, Lourdes, St-Gaudens, Foix, Quillan, Limoux, Carcassonne, Narbonne, Béziers, Agde, Montpellier, Nîmes, Arles, Avignon, Aix-en-Provence, Marseille, La Ciotat, Toulon, Hyères, Cannes, Antibes, Nice, San Remo, Grasse, Marmande, Agen, Toulouse, Castres, Albi, Rodez, Millau, Mende, Orange, Digne-les-Bains, Sisteron, Figeac, Cahors, Montauban

SPAIN — MADRID, CATALUNA

Selected place names: Donostia-San Sebastián, Bilbao, Pamplona, Logroño, Zaragoza, Lleida, Barcelona, Sabadell, Tarragona, Tortosa, Castelló de la Plana, Valencia, Teruel, Cuenca, Albacete, Alicante, Murcia, Cartagena, Lorca, Granada, Almería, Motril, Aguilas, Benidorm, Elche-Elx, Orihuela

ANDORRA — ANDORRA LA VELLA

Costa Brava, Costa Blanca

Balearic Islands (Islas Baleares) (Spain)

Minorca (Menorca), Mahón, Ciutadella de Menorca, Majorca (Mallorca), Palma de Mallorca, Manacor, Felanitx, Alcúdia, Cabrera, Ibiza (Eivissa), Formentera, San Antonio Abad, San Francisco Javier

Mediterranean Sea

ALGERIA — ALGIERS (Alger)

Selected place names: Oran, Mostaganem, Tipasa, Blida, Médéa, Miliana, Sétif, Béjaïa, Bou Saâda, Batna, Biskra, Tiaret, Mascara, Sidi Bel Abbès, Tlemcen, Ghazaouet, Relizane

40° (latitude line)

Scale 1:6 500 000

| 0 | 50 | 100 | 150 miles |
| 0 | 100 | 200 km |

DISCOVER MORE
- Balearic Islands www.illesbalears.es
- Explore Madrid www.munimadrid.es
- Visit Lisbon www.tourismlisbon.com
- The Mediterranean region www.planbleu.org
- Explore the Pyrenees National Park www.parc-pyrenees.com

WATCH OUT!
- When driving in Portugal you must carry a red warning triangle for use in case of a breakdown or accident. Spanish legislation requires that you must carry two red warning triangles and a reflective jacket.
- Protect yourself from sunburn, particularly in the south of the region, by using high factor sunscreen, and covering up with clothing and hats.

The western half of this map area is occupied by the familiar leg-like peninsula of Italy, culminating in a 'boot' pointing to a 'football' in the shape of Sicily, which along with the other large island of Sardinia is an integral part of the Italian Republic. Corsica, to the north of Sardinia, is an administrative region of France. In the east, the patchwork of countries on the modern map has been made more complex in recent years by the dissolution of the former Yugoslavia into five separate republics.

Geo terms

Croatian
Rt cape, point
Italian
Arcipelago archipelago
Capo cape, point
Golfo gulf, bay
Isola, Isole island, islands
Monte mountain
Monti mountains

Go to →

Map symbols *page 6*
Geo terms *page 8*
European countries *pages 10–12*

KNOW THE REGION

- The Balkans are usually regarded as consisting of mainland Greece, Albania, Bulgaria, the countries of the former Yugoslavia and southern Romania.

- Yugoslavia is now divided into the independent nations of Slovenia, Croatia, Bosnia-Herzegovina, Macedonia, and Serbia and Montenegro.

- The Vatican City is the world's smallest independent nation. It was formed by agreement with the Italian government in the 1920s from part of central Rome.

- San Marino, another tiny independent nation within the borders of Italy, is unique in having survived the unification of Italy as a single country in the 19th century.

1:6 500 000

| 0 | 50 | 100 | 150 miles |

| 0 | 100 | 200 km |

The principal focus of the map is the Balkan Peninsula (see also page 62). The map covers the whole of Greece, with its many islands in the Aegean Sea extending to Crete in the south. Greece's mainland neighbours are shown in full – Albania, Macedonia (also known by its more formal name the Former Yugoslav Republic of Macedonia or F.Y.R.O.M.), Bulgaria and the western part of Turkey. Also covered by the map are the eastern European countries of Romania and Moldova.

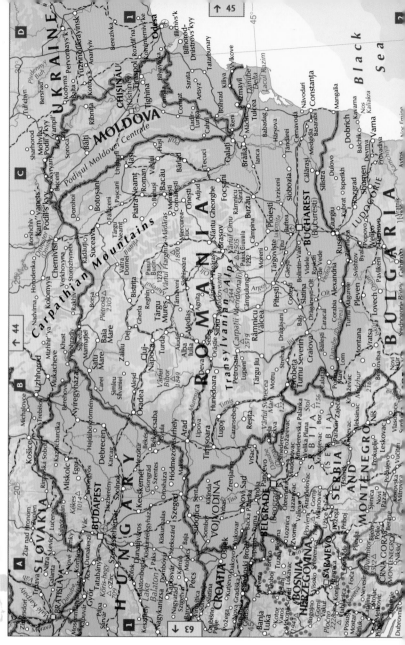

Geo terms

Bulgarian
Nos cape, point
Planina hills, mountains
Greek
Kolpos gulf, bay
Pelagos sea
Romanian
Lacul lake
Vârful mountain

Go to →

Map symbols *page 6*
Geo terms *page 8*
European countries *pages 10–12*

KNOW THE REGION

- For historical reasons and Greek cultural influences in Asia Minor (modern-day Turkey), most of the islands off the Turkish coast remain Greek.

- The Sea of Marmara links the Mediterranean with the Black Sea via the Bosporus, on which stands Istanbul, and the Dardanelles, adjacent to Gallipoli, scene of fierce fighting during the First World War.

- Corfu, a popular Greek island resort, is located much closer to the Albanian coast than to the Greek mainland.

- The Cyclades island group got its name from a word meaning a 'circle' of islands, while 'Dodecanese' means a group of twelve islands.

WATCH OUT!

- Greece has one of the highest motorcycle death rates in Europe. Accidents involving locally hired mopeds, scooters and motorbikes are common, often causing serious and sometimes fatal injury.

- In Albania and Bulgaria an up/down nod of the head means no, and a shake from side to side means yes.

- Some areas of southern Serbia and Kosovo have unexploded land mines left over from the Balkan wars of the early 1990s.

The map highlights the many major mountain ranges – in particular the Himalaya – and plateaus which make up much of Asia. These contrast with enormous low-lying plains, especially in the far north (Siberia) and on the Yellow Sea coast of China. The Ganges and Indus rivers on the Indian subcontinent also occupy extensive lowlands. Indonesia represents by far the most complex island chain, although there are many other large and important islands, in particular Sri Lanka (formerly Ceylon), the Philippines, Taiwan, Japan, and the various island groups in the Arctic Ocean.

Geo terms

Chinese
Shan mountain, mountains

Indonesian
Kepulauan islands
Laut sea
Puncak mountain

Mongolian
Nur lake

Russian
Khrebet mountain range

Go to →

Geo terms *page 8*
World physical features *page 26*
Asia countries map *page 68*

Asia's extremes

Total land area		45 036 492 sq km	17 388 589 sq miles
Largest lake	Caspian Sea	371 000 sq km	143 243 sq miles
Largest island	Borneo	745 561 sq km	287 861 sq miles
Largest drainage basin	Ob'-Irtysh, Kazakhstan/Rus. Fed.	2 990 000 sq km	1 154 439 sq miles
Lowest point	Dead Sea	-398 metres	-1 306 feet

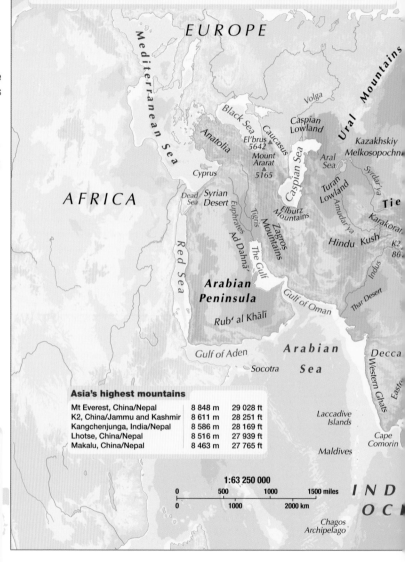

EUROPE

Mediterranean Sea

Black Sea

Volga

Caspian Lowland

Ural Mountains

Anatolia

Caucasus

El'brus 5642

Mount Ararat 5165

Aral Sea

Kazakhskiy Melkosopochn

Cyprus

Caspian Sea

Syrdar'ya

AFRICA

Dead Sea

Syrian Desert

Euphrates

Tigris

Elburz Mountains

Turan Lowland

Amudar'ya

Tie

Zagros Mountains

Karakoram

Red Sea

Ad Dahna

The Gulf

Hindu Kush

K2 86

Indus

Arabian Peninsula

Gulf of Oman

Thar Desert

Rub' al Khālī

Decca

Gulf of Aden

Arabian Sea

Western Ghats

Easte

Socotra

Laccadive Islands

Cape Comorin

Maldives

Asia's highest mountains

Mt Everest, China/Nepal	8 848 m	29 028 ft
K2, China/Jammu and Kashmir	8 611 m	28 251 ft
Kangchenjunga, India/Nepal	8 586 m	28 169 ft
Lhotse, China/Nepal	8 516 m	27 939 ft
Makalu, China/Nepal	8 463 m	27 765 ft

1:63 250 000

0	500	1000	1500 miles
0	1000	2000 km	

IND OCI

Chagos Archipelago

KNOW THE REGION

- The outline of Asia is characterised by a number of major peninsulas, including Arabia, the Indian subcontinent, Indo-China and its offshoot Peninsular Malaysia, Korea and the highly volcanic Kamchatka peninsula.

- Ninety of the world's one hundred highest mountains are in Asia. Many lie in the Himalayan kingdom of Nepal where the height of the land ranges from 60 to 8 848 metres (197 to 29 028 feet).

- The Indonesian archipelago is made up of more than 13 000 islands.

- The deepest lake in the world is Lake Baikal in the Russian Federation, which is over 1 700 metres (5 577 feet) deep.

ARCTIC OCEAN

Zemlya
Frantsa-Iosifa

Novaya
Zemlya

Kara Sea

West
Siberian
Plain

Severnaya
Zemlya

New Siberia
Islands

Wrangel
Island

Chukchi
Sea

Bering Strait

East
Siberian
Sea

Laptev
Sea

Taymyr
Peninsula

S i b e r i a

Central
Siberian
Plateau

Nizhnyaya
Tunguska

Yenisey

Ob'

Irtysh

Lake
Balkhash

Altai
Mountains

Vostochnyy
Sayan

Hangayn
Nuruu

Selenga

Lena

Vilyuy

Angara

Stanovoye
Nagor'ye

Lena

Indigirka

Kolyma

Verkhoyanskiy
Khrebet

Khrebet
Dzhugdzhur

Khrebet
Kolymskiy

Sredinnyy Khrebet

Kamchatka
Peninsula

Bering
Sea

Sea
of
Okhotsk

Sakhalin

Kuril Islands

PACIFIC

OCEAN

Lake
Baikal

Hulun
Nur

Da Hinggan Ling

Manchurian
Plain

Amur

Lake
Khanka

Sikhote-Alin'

Hokkaidō

Sea
of
Japan
(East Sea)

Honshū

▲7439
peda
eak

Tarim
Basin

Qilian Shan

Yellow River

Ningjing Shan

Qin Ling

Yellow
Sea

Korea Strait

Shikoku

Kyūshū

ange

unlun Shan

Plateau
of Tibet

imalaya

Mount
Everest
8848

Kangchenjunga
8586

Qionglai
Shan

▲7514
Gongga
Shan

Yangtze

Wuyi
Shan

East
China
Sea

Ryukyu Islands

Taiwan Strait

Taiwan

Luzon Strait

Asia's longest rivers

Yangtze	6 380 km	3 964 miles
Ob'-Irtysh	5 568 km	3 459 miles
Yenisey-Angara-Selenga	5 550 km	3 448 miles
Yellow	5 464 km	3 395 miles
Irtysh	4 440 km	2 759 miles

Ganges

Brahmaputra

Irrawaddy

Salween

Bay
of
Bengal

hats

ri

anka

Andaman
Islands
Andaman
Sea

Tonle
Sap

Gulf
of
Thailand

Mekong

Hainan

South
China
Sea

Palawan

Sulu
Sea

Philippine
Sea

Luzon

Mindanao

Philippines

Palau Islands

Nicobar
Islands

Strait of Malacca

Peninsular
Malaysia

Kepulauan
Mentawai

Sumatra

Greater Sunda Islands

Java

Borneo

Celebes
Sea

Selat Makassar

Celebes
▲3074

Laut Maluku

Moluccas

Seram

Laut Banda

Puncak
Jaya
▲5030

New
Guinea

Arafura Sea

Timor

Laut Jawa

Laut Flores

Lesser Sunda Islands

OCEANIA

N

N

DISCOVER MORE

• Search for satellite images www.visibleearth.nasa.gov
• Asian weather forecasts
  www.metoffice.com/weather/wxforecast.html
• Heritage sites in Asia whc.unesco.org
• Climb mountains in Asia www.peakware.com
• Severe Acute Respiratory Syndrome (SARS) www.who.int/csr
• Search for volcano information www.volcano.si.edu

WATCH OUT!

• Although over 1 000 people have succeeded in climbing Mount Everest, more than 170 have been killed trying to reach the summit.

• Lake Balkhash, Asia's fourth largest lake, is highly susceptible to changes in climate and human activity. The western half of the lake is fresh water, the other half is salt water. If the flow of fresh water from rivers were reduced, then the salinity would increase and a major fresh water resource would be under threat.

Asia's countries

Largest country	Russian Federation	17 075 400 sq km	6 592 812 sq miles
Smallest country	Maldives	298 sq km	115 sq miles
Largest population	China	1 289 161 000	
Smallest population	Palau	20 000	
Most densely populated country	Singapore	6 656 per sq km	17 219 per sq mile
Least densely populated country	Mongolia	2 per sq km	4 per sq mile

With approximately 60 per cent of the world's population, Asia is home to numerous cultures and lifestyles. It also has a great variety of geographical regions which can be defined by the cultural, economic and political systems they support. The main divisions are: the arid, oil-rich, mainly Islamic southwest; southern Asia, isolated from the rest of Asia by major mountain ranges; Southeast Asia including Indo-China; the mainly Chinese-influenced industrialized areas of eastern Asia; and north-central Asia, made up of most of the former Soviet Union.

EUROPE

Mediterranean Sea

AFRICA

Moscow
Nizhniy Novgorod
Volga Samara Yekaterinburg
Ural'sk
Ural Mountains
Black Sea
Ankara
TURKEY GEORGIA
Adana T'bilisi
Nicosia ARMENIA
CYPRUS Yerevan
LEBANON SYRIA AZERBAIJAN
Beirut Damascus Baku
Jerusalem Amman
ISRAEL JORDAN
Baghdād Tehrān Ashgabat
IRAQ
KUWAIT IRAN
Kuwait The Gulf Herāt Kābul
Shīrāz AFGHANISTAN Islamabad
Jeddah BAHRAIN Kandahar Lahore
Riyadh QATAR Manama PAKISTAN Delhi
Mecca Doha Dubai New Delhi
SAUDI U.A.E. Abu Dhabi Hyderabad Agra
ARABIA Muscat Karachi
OMAN Ahmadabad
Saṇ'ā' Arabian Mumbai
YEMEN Sea
Aden
Socotra
Caspian Sea
Aral Sea
KAZAKHSTAN
Astana
UZBEKISTAN
TURKMENISTAN Tashkent Bishkek
Dushanbe Tie
TAJIKISTAN
Hyderabad
Bangalore
Chennai
Laccadive Madurai
Islands
Sri Jayewardenepura
Kotte
Colombo
MALDIVES Male
British Indian
Ocean Territory
IND
IND
OC

Asia's capitals

Largest capital (population)	Tōkyō, Japan	26 849 000	
Smallest capital (population)	Koror, Palau	14 000	
Most northerly capital	Astana, Kazakhstan	51° 10'N	
Most southerly capital	Dili, East Timor	8° 35'S	
Highest capital	Thimphu, Bhutan	2 423 metres	7 949 feet

Go to →

Asian countries
pages 12–14
World time zones
page 34
Asia physical features
page 66

KNOW THE REGION

- The line dividing Asia from Oceania is generally taken to separate Indonesia and Papua New Guinea. This results in the island of New Guinea being divided between the two continents.

- The break-up of the former Soviet Union in 1991 created two groups of countries in Asia: Kazakhstan, Uzbekistan, Turkmenistan, Tajikistan and Kyrgyzstan on the one hand and Georgia, Armenia and Azerbaijan on the other. This still left the Russian Federation as by far the largest country in the world.

- Cyprus, although now part of the European Union and having long-standing cultural links with Europe, is classed as being within Asia.

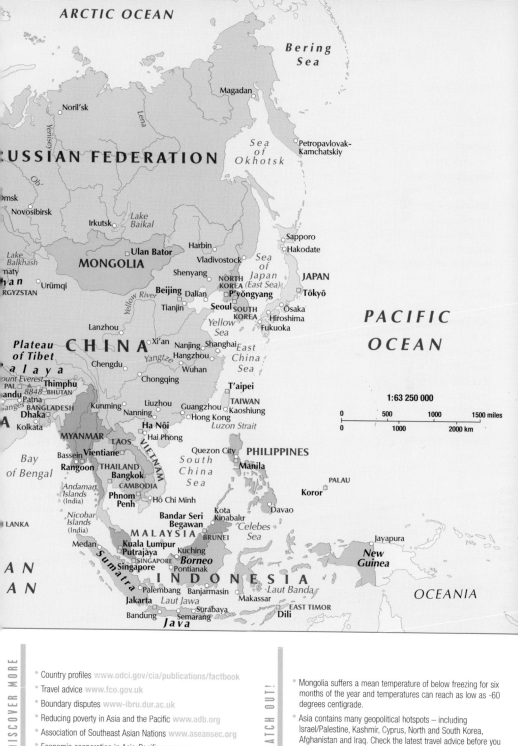

ARCTIC OCEAN

Bering
Sea

Noril'sk

Magadan

Lena

RUSSIAN FEDERATION

Sea
of
Okhotsk

Petropavlovak-
Kamchatskiy

Yenisey

Ob'

Omsk

Novosibirsk

Irkutsk

Lake
Baikal

Sapporo

Hakodate

Lake
Balkhash

Ulan Bator

Harbin

Vladivostock

Sea
of
Japan
(East Sea)

JAPAN

maty

Urümqi

MONGOLIA

Shenyang

NORTH
KOREA

Tōkyō

han

RGYZSTAN

Yellow River

Beijing

Dalian

P'yŏngyang

Ōsaka

Lanzhou

Tianjin

Seoul

SOUTH
KOREA

Hiroshima
Fukuoka

PACIFIC
OCEAN

Plateau
of Tibet

CHINA

Xi'an

Nanjing

Shanghai

Yellow
Sea

alaya

Yangtze

Hangzhou

East
China
Sea

ount Everest

Chengdu

Wuhan

PAL

8848

Thimphu

BHUTAN

Chongqing

1:63 250 000

andu

Patna

T'aipei

0   500   1000   1500 miles

Ganges

Dhaka

BANGLADESH

Kunming

Liuzhou

Guangzhou

Kaoshiung

TAIWAN

0   1000   2000 km

A

Kolkata

Nanning

Hong Kong

Luzon Strait

MYANMAR

LAOS

Ha Nôi

Hai Phong

Bay
of Bengal

Bassein

Vientiane

VIETNAM

Quezon City

PHILIPPINES

Rangoon

THAILAND

South
China
Sea

Manila

Andaman
Islands
(India)

Bangkok

CAMBODIA

PALAU

Nicobar
Islands
(India)

Phnom
Penh

Hồ Chí Minh

Koror

LANKA

Bandar Seri
Begawan

Kota
Kinabalu

Davao

Celebes
Sea

Jayapura

MALAYSIA

BRUNEI

Medan

Kuala Lumpur

Kuching

New
Guinea

Sumatra

Putrajaya

SINGAPORE

Singapore

Borneo

Pontianak

OCEANIA

INDONESIA

AN

Palembang

Banjarmasin

Laut Banda

EAST TIMOR

AN

Jakarta

Laut Jawa

Makassar

Dili

Bandung

Surabaya
Semarang

Java

Southeast Asia is physically divided into two parts. The mainland section consists largely of two very prominent peninsulas: Indo-China, covering Vietnam, Laos and Cambodia; and the Malay Peninsula, occupied by Malaysia and by the southerly extensions of Thailand and Myanmar (Burma) at its narrower, mainland end. Almost all of the rest of the region consists of large groups of islands: chiefly Indonesia, stretching from east to west across the map for almost 4 500 km (3 000 miles), and the Philippines to the north.

Geo terms

Indonesian
Kepulauan islands
Laut sea
Pegunungan mountain range
Selat strait
Tanjung cape, point

Go to →

Map symbols *page 6*
Geo terms *page 8*
Pacific Ocean *page 158*

Map symbols *page 6*
Geo terms *page 8*
Pacific Ocean *page 158*

KNOW THE REGION

- The Indonesian archipelago is made up of over 13 000 islands, approximately 6 000 of which are inhabited.
- East Timor, part of the island of Timor in the southeast of the map, was a Portuguese possession (Portuguese Timor), but was absorbed by Indonesia in the 1970s. It gained its independence as a new member of the United Nations in 2002, using its Portuguese-based name Timor-Leste.
- Indonesia has the fourth biggest population of any country – only exceeded by China, India and the United States. Java is one of the most densely populated parts of the globe.

PACIFIC OCEAN

TAIWAN
Luzon Strait
Philippine Sea
PHILIPPINES
Northern Mariana Islands (U.S.A.)
Guam (U.S.A.)
FEDERATED STATES OF MICRONESIA
Caroline Islands
PALAU
KOROR
Celebes Sea
Halmahera
Seram
Laut Banda (Banda Sea)
New Guinea
PAPUA NEW GUINEA
PORT MORESBY
Gulf of Papua
Bismarck Archipelago
EAST TIMOR
OCUSSI
Timor
Arafura Sea
AUSTRALIA
Gulf of Carpentaria
Timor Sea

1:24 250 000

| 0 | 150 | 300 | 450 miles |
| 0 | 300 | 600 km |

↓ 114

DISCOVER MORE

- Volcanoes www.volcano.si.edu
- Search for earthquake information neic.usgs.gov
- See tropical storm tracks www.solar.ifa.hawaii.edu/Tropical
- Stay healthy while travelling www.cdc.gov/travel
- Climbing Puncak Jaya www.peakware.com
- Travel advice www.fco.gov.uk
- Heritage sites in southeast Asia whc.unesco.org

WATCH OUT!

- This region has a high incidence of earthquakes, volcanoes, typhoons, flash floods and landslides. Watch out for warnings of such events.
- Insect borne diseases, prevalent in many parts of southeast Asia, include malaria (mosquito), Dengue fever (mosquito), Japanese encephalitis (mainly mosquito) and plague (infection usually by the bite of rodent fleas). Protection against insect bites will help to prevent these diseases.

The map concentrates on Malaysia and the major islands of Indonesia. Malaysia is divided into two parts – Peninsular Malaysia on the Asian mainland, and East Malaysia – the two states of Sabah and Sarawak on the (mainly Indonesian) island of Borneo, and Labuan, just off the coast of Sabah. The very wealthy, independent sultanate of Brunei also lies on the north coast of Borneo. At the southernmost tip of Peninsular Malaysia lies the independent city state of Singapore.

Geo terms

Indonesian
Bukit mountain
Gunung mountain
Pulau-pulau islands
Semenanjung peninsula
Teluk gulf, bay
Malay
Banjaran mountain range
Gunung mountain

Go to →

Map symbols *page 6*
Geo terms *page 8*
Asian countries *pages 12–14*

KNOW THE REGION

- The devastating tsunami of December 2004 was triggered by a major earthquake off the northwest coast of Sumatra. It devastated parts of Sumatra and caused over 150 000 deaths and widespread destruction in several countries around the Indian Ocean.

- The islands of Sumatra, Java, Borneo and Celebes are known as the Greater Sunda Islands. The islands east of Java form part of the Lesser Sundas.

- The small island of Krakatau (more well known as Krakatoa) exploded in a devastating volcanic eruption in 1883. Rather than being 'east of Java', as in the film title, it is located between Java and Sumatra.

South China Sea

LAYSIA

Natuna Besar
Panarik

epulauan
Natuna

Balabac Strait

Kudat
Kota Belud
Banggi
Mapin
Gunung
Kinabalu
4095
Kota
Kinabalu
Ranau
Beaufort
Labuan
BANDAR SERI
BEGAWAN
Kuala Belait
Lutong
Miri
Seria
BRUNEI
Lawas
Lamag
Kuamut
Pensiangan
Lumbis

Sulu Sea
Zamboanga D Moro Gulf
Basilan
Isabela
Jolo Jolo PHILIPPINES
Sulu
Archipelago

Sandakan
SABAH
Lahad
Datu
Tawitawi
Tumindao
Semporna
Tawau

C e l e b e s
S e a

Long
Akah
Kubuang
Tarakan
Tanjungselor

1

Bintulu
Igan Mukah
Belaga
Sarikei
Sibu
Rajang
Kapit
Debak
Saratok
Kuching
Sematan
Liku
Sambas
Pemangkat
ngkawang
Bengkayang
Sanggau
Ngabang
Pontianak
Balaiberkuak
Telukbatang
Sukadana
Ketapang
Kendawangan
Manggar
elitung
Pangkalanbuun

SARAWAK
Datadian
2988
Putusibau
Sri Aman
Lubok
Antu
Semitau
Sintang
Nangahpinoh
Rantaupanjang
Nangatayap
Palangkaraya
Sampit
Sukaraja
Kualapembuang
Tanjung
Puting
Tanjung
Selatan

Tanjungredeb

B o r n e o
K A L I M A N T A N

Longiram
Muaralaung
Muarateweh
Samarinda
Tenggarong
Balikpapan
Tanahgrogot
Amuntai
Kandangan
Kotabaru
Martapura
Banjarmasin
Pagatan
Laut

Sepinang
Sangkulirang
Bontang

Semenanjung Minahasa
Tolitoli
Kwandang
Moutong Gorontalo
Sidoan
Teluk Tomini
Donggala
Palu
Mapane Poso
Tenteno
Bukit
Gandadiwata
Polewali
Majene
Parepare
Singkang
Makassar
G. Lompobattang
2871
Bulukumba
Bontosunggu
Benteng

C e l e b e s
(Sulawesi)
Malili
Rantepao
Palopo
Makale
Malamala
Kolonedale
Luwuk
Uekuli
Togian Kepulauan
Togian
Batudaka
Peleng
Tataba Banggai
Kepulauan
Banggai
Kendari
Manui
Wowoni
Anabanua
Kolaka
Watampone
Raha
Muna
Buton
Sinjai
Baubau
Kabaena
Salayar

INDONESIA

L a u t J a w a
(J a v a S e a)

Pulau-pulau
Karimunjawa
Kemujan
Bawean

Kepulauan
Laut Kecil

2

Tanjung
Indramayu
Cirebon
andung
Garut
Tegal Semarang
Pekalongan
Kudus
Ciamis
Kebumen
Temanggung
Java
(Jawa)
Cilacap
Yogyakarta
Surakarta
Madiun
Malang
Lumajang
Jember
Barung
Semeru
3676
G. Raung
3142
Banyuwangi

Madura
Sumenep
Bangkalan
Tuban
Surabaya
Jombang
Pasuruan
Situbondo

Kepulauan
Kangean
Sabalana
Raas
Selat Madura
Bali
Denpasar
Lombok
Singaraja
Gianyar
Mataram
Praya
Taliwang

L a u t B a l i
(Bali Sea)
Kepulauan
Tengah

S u m b a w a
Alas
Sumbawabesar
Dompu
Raba
Labuhanbajo

Tanahjampea
Kalao
Kalaotoa
Kepulauan
Bonerate

L a u t F l o r e s
(Flores Sea)
Reo
Ruteng
Bajawa
Ende
Larantuka
Flores
Maumere

3

Waikabubak
Memboro
Waingapu
Sumba

L a u t S a w u
(Savu Sea)
Savu

10°

→ 71

DISCOVER MORE

* Visiting Sabah www.sabahtourism.com
* Visiting Sarawak www.sarawaktourism.com
* Discover Kuala Lumpur www.kualalumpur.gov.my
* Explore Malaysian Wildlife and National Parks
  www.wildlife.gov.my
* Visit Borneo www.visitborneo.com
* Get details of Indonesia's volcanoes volcano.und.nodak.edu
* Travel advice www.fco.gov.uk

1:12 250 000

| 0 | 100 | 200 | 300 miles |
| 0 | 150 | 300 | 450 km |

WATCH OUT!

* Dengue fever, a major health risk in Malaysia, is transmitted by a mosquito which is mainly found in areas of human habitation. Protect yourself from bites.

* In recent years Indonesia has seen tension and violence as a result of separatist struggles, religious and racial differences and migration of ethnic groups from overpopulated areas. It has also suffered terrorist attacks, including the Bali bombing in 2002 which killed more than 200 people.

The map concentrates on Indo-China, Thailand, Myanmar (or Burma) and southwestern China. The name Indo-China relates to former influences from India and China, and the area consists of Laos, Vietnam and Cambodia. Cambodia was known during the 1970s as Kampuchea, and the Khmer Republic. The Andaman and Nicobar Islands, stretching northwards from the tip of Sumatra in Indonesia form part of India. Four major world rivers appear on the map – the Brahmaputra, the Irrawaddy, the Mekong and the Yangtze.

Geo terms

Burmese
Kyun island
Yoma mountain range
Malay
Gunung mountain
Thai
Ko island
Vietnamese
Hô lake
Mui cape, point
Sông river

74

Go to →

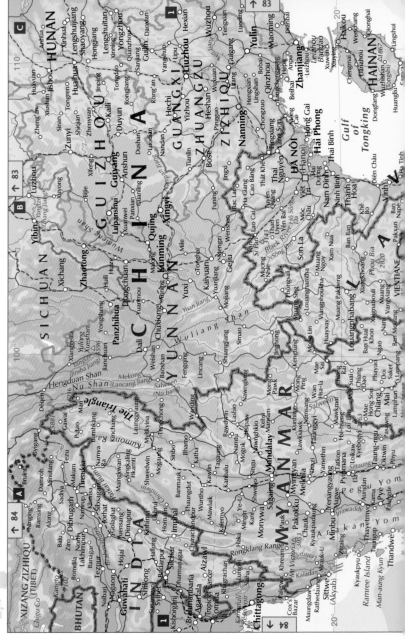

KNOW THE REGION

* Country names change: Cambodia used to be Kampuchea; Myanmar was officially adopted in the 1980s and is now used in place of Burma; Thailand used to be called Siam.

* Cambodia suffered huge problems, including widespread massacres, under the Khmer Rouge régime in the late 1970s. It now once again attracts many visitors to its notable historic sites such as Angkor.

* Thailand is unique among its neighbours in never having been a dependency of a European power.

* There have been ideas to build a canal through the Malay Peninsula for sea traffic which currently has to pass through the busy Strait of Malacca.

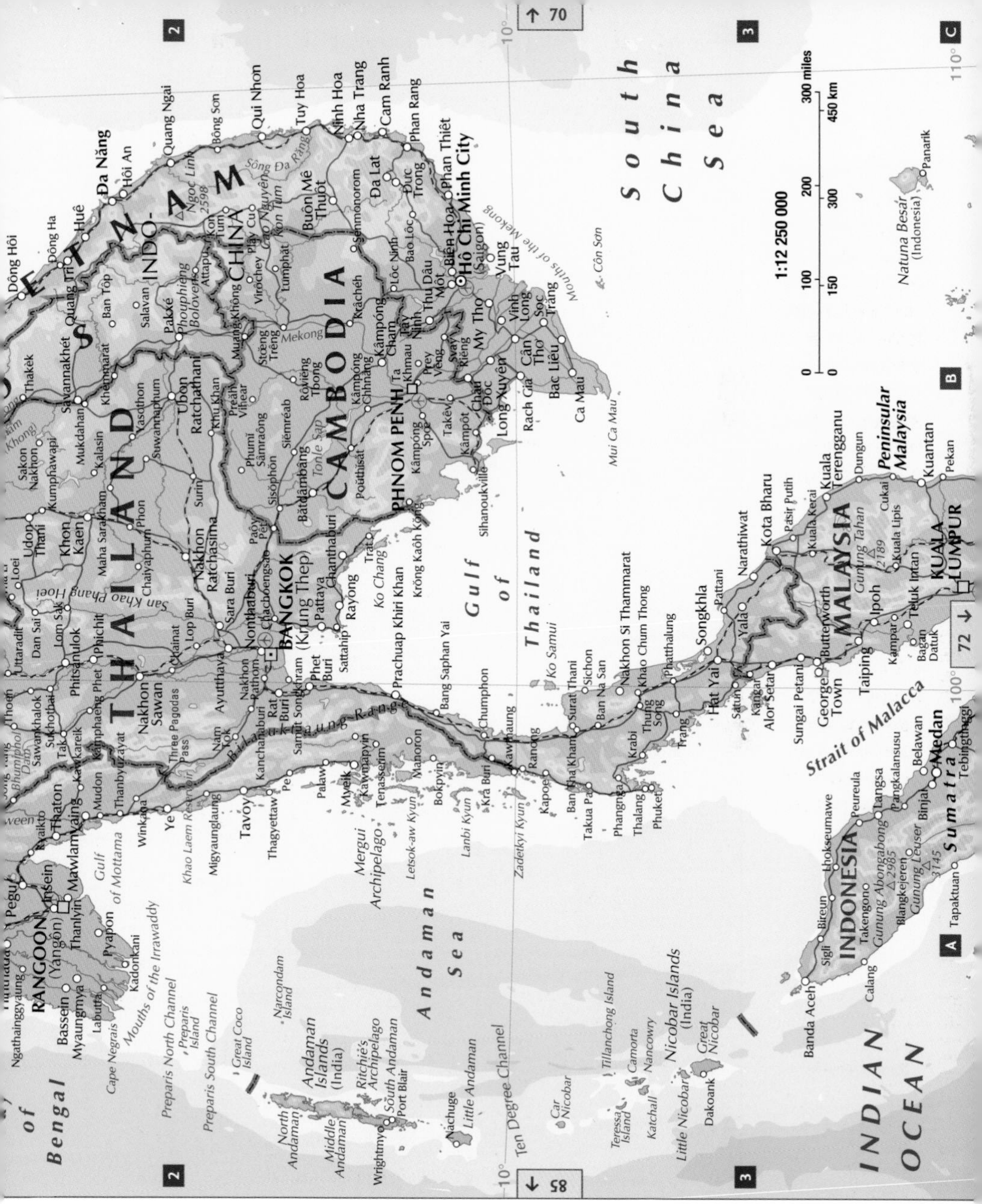

THAILAND
CAMBODIA
VIETNAM
MALAYSIA
INDONESIA
South China Sea
Gulf of Thailand
Andaman Sea
Bay of Bengal
INDIAN OCEAN
Strait of Malacca
Gulf of Mottama
BANGKOK (Krung Thep)
PHNOM PENH
Hô Chi Minh City (Saigon)
RANGOON (Yangôn)
KUALA LUMPUR
Đa Năng
Huê
Hôi An
Quang Ngai
Qui Nhon
Tuy Hoa
Ninh Hoa
Nha Trang
Cam Ranh
Phan Rang
Đa Lat
Buôn Mê Thuôt
Phan Thiêt
Biên Hoa
Vung Tau
My Tho
Cân Tho
Long Xuyên
Rach Gia
Ca Mau
Bac Liêu
Sihanoukville
Kâmpôt
Bătdâmbâng
Siĕmréab
Tonle Sap
Mekong
Mouths of the Mekong
Côn Sơn
Chiang Mai
Nakhon Sawan
Phitsanulok
Ayutthaya
Nakhon Ratchasima
Khon Kaen
Udon Thani
Ubon Ratchathani
Pattaya
Rayong
Chanthaburi
Trat
Ko Chang
Prachuap Khiri Khan
Chumphon
Surat Thani
Ko Samui
Nakhon Si Thammarat
Phuket
Krabi
Hat Yai
Songkhla
Pattani
Narathiwat
Kota Bharu
Kuala Terengganu
Kuantan
George Town
Butterworth
Ipoh
Taiping
Medan
Banda Aceh
Sumatra
Peninsular Malaysia
Mawlamyaing
Tavoy
Mergui Archipelago
Andaman Islands (India)
Nicobar Islands (India)
Port Blair
Ten Degree Channel
Natuna Besar (Indonesia)
1:12 250 000
0 100 200 300 miles
0 150 300 450 km
↑ 70
72 →
← 85

DISCOVER MORE

- Travel advice www.fco.gov.uk
- Visit Bangkok www.bma.go.th
- Angkor and other heritage sites whc.unesco.org
- Landmine clearance in Cambodia www.cmac.org.kh
- Health advice for travellers www.dh.gov.uk
- Protect against Avian flu www.who.int/csr
- Country profiles www.odci.gov/cia/publications/factbook

WATCH OUT!

- Outbreaks of avian influenza (bird flu) in 2004 were reported in many southeast Asian countries, causing around thirty fatalities in Vietnam and Thailand. The virus, spread through contact with infected poultry, is unlikely to be transmitted to travellers, although suitable precautions should be observed.
- Thirty years of conflicts have left Cambodia as one of the most heavily land-mined countries in the world.
- When entering religious sites, it is important to dress in appropriate clothing and to remove shoes and socks.

← 70

The Philippines is a single country consisting of a large group of islands which separates the South China Sea from the Pacific Ocean and which lies between Taiwan and East Malaysia. The two island arcs almost connect with the Malaysian part of Borneo. The map of Korea shows how the two separate countries of North and South Korea occupy a large peninsula between China and Japan, separating the Yellow Sea from the Sea of Japan (known to the Koreans as the East Sea).

ASIA PHILIPPINES, NORTH KOREA AND SOUTH KOREA

Geo terms

Korean
-*bong* mountain
-*do* island
-*gang* river
-*haehyŏp* strait
-*ho* lake
-*man* bay
-*san* mountain

76

Go to →

Map symbols *page 6*
Geo terms *page 8*
Asia countries map
page 68

KNOW THE REGION

- The Philippines is largely English-speaking, but also has an official language known as Filipino (or Pilipino), derived from the native Tagalog language.

- Mount Pinatubo on the island of Luzon erupted violently in 1991, the second largest volcanic eruption of the 20th century. The resulting cloud of volcanic ash was hundreds of miles wide.

- The Korean peninsula was divided into North Korea and South Korea in 1948, approximately along the thirty-eighth parallel.

- North Korea retains one of the world's few remaining communist governments, under Kim Jong-Il – the son of the original president, and known officially as the 'Dear Leader'.

DISCOVER MORE

- Search for volcano information www.volcano.si.edu and vulcan.wr.usgs.gov/volcanoes
- Visit Manila www.cityofmanila.com.ph
- Heritage sites in the Philippines and the Korean peninsula whc.unesco.org
- See Seoul english.seoul.go.kr
- Search for satellite images visibleearth.nasa.gov
- Travel advice www.fco.gov.uk

WATCH OUT!

- There is a high risk of terrorism, kidnapping and piracy throughout the Philippines and in the surrounding seas.
- The Philippines is in an earthquake zone, has many active volcanoes and is commonly hit by typhoons during the rainy season. In late 2004, two powerful storms caused devastating flash floods and mudslides to the east of Manila, killing over 1 000 people.
- Travel in North Korea is restricted and visitors must be accompanied by a guide.

The main islands of Japan form a large, curving archipelago lying off the east coast of Asia. By far the biggest island is Honshū; to the south are Kyūshū and Shikoku (separated from Honshū by the now-bridged Inland Sea). To the north is Hokkaidō, connected by a long rail tunnel. The islands are volcanic and the region is prone to earthquakes. Japan also controls a far-flung spread of much smaller islands across a large area of the northwest Pacific Ocean.

ASIA **JAPAN**

78

Geo terms

Japanese
-*dake* mountain
-*jima* island
-*misaki* cape, point
-*san* mountain
-*sanmyaku* mountain range
-*shima* island
-*shotō* islands

Go to →

Map symbols *page 6*
Asian countries *pages 12–14*
Pacific Ocean *page 158*

KNOW THE REGION

* The Japanese name for Japan, which can be spelt either Nippon or Nihon, means 'Land of the Rising Sun'. The national flag symbolises this, with a red disc on a white background.

* Japan has a long-standing territorial dispute with the Russian Federation since the former Soviet Union occupied several previously Japanese-controlled islands at the end of the Kuril island chain, including Kunashir, shown on this map.

* The Japanese language is written using three different sets of characters, one of which is derived from Chinese.

* Japanese food, in all its exciting forms, is an increasingly popular cultural export of Japan.

↓ 81

DISCOVER MORE

- Visit Tōkyō www.tcvb.or.jp
- Mount Fuji www.mt-fuji.co.jp
- Japanese food www.eat-japan.com
- Tourist guide to Hokkaidō
  kanko.pref.hokkaido.jp/kankodb/foreign
- Travel by train www.japanrail.com
- News on Japan news.bbc.co.uk
- Heritage sites in Japan whc.unesco.org

WATCH OUT!

- Watch your manners: excessive eye contact when talking is considered to be rather aggressive; it is impolite to drink or eat while walking down the street; make plenty of slurping sounds when eating noodles!
- Some fish are poisonous and can be fatal if not prepared properly before eating.

This map centres on China – the world's most populous country – and the wider region known as the Far East. The density of settlements in the eastern half of China contrasts sharply with the relatively sparsely inhabited western areas of Tibet and Xinjiang, and the north of the country adjacent to Mongolia. There are great physical contrasts within this region, from the Himalaya, the highest mountains in the world, and the vast, high Plateau of Tibet, to the Gobi and the deserts of western China.

Geo terms

Chinese
Hai sea
He river
Hu lake
Shan mountain, mountains
Mongolian
Nuruu mountain range
Nuur lake

Go to →

Map symbols *page 6*
Geo terms *page 8*
Asia physical features *page 66*

KNOW THE REGION

- Mongolia was traditionally referred to as Outer Mongolia while a large zone of northern China is still known as Inner Mongolia. China actually extends further north than any part of Mongolia.

- Tibet, formerly an independent nation, was taken over by China in the 1950s, and its spiritual ruler, the Dalai Lama, has lived abroad since then.

- The system now used for converting Chinese characters into our alphabet, called Pinyin, involves frequent use of the letters q, x and z, which gives some spellings still relatively unfamiliar in the West (e.g. Xinjiang, Guangzhou). Other Pinyin spellings, such as Beijing, are more well known.

1:24 250 000

0   150   300   450 miles
0   300   600 km

This is the most heavily populated part of China, as shown by the numerous cities and the dense network of roads and railways. The relative sparseness of population in the north (Inner Mongolia) stands out. The island of Hainan, in the south, is a province of China in its own right. The other large island shown, Taiwan, functions as an independent nation. Two of China's great rivers are in this region: the Yangtze (or Chang Jiang) and the Yellow River (Huang He).

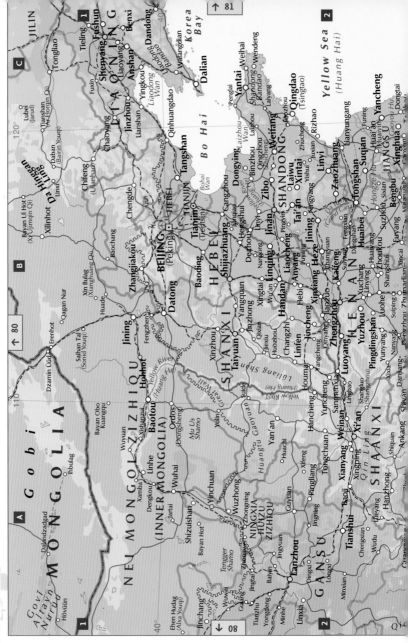

Geo terms

Chinese

Bandao peninsula

He river

Hu lake

Ling mountain range

Shan mountain, mountains

Wan bay

Go to →

Map symbols *page 6*
Geo terms *page 8*
Asian countries *pages 12–14*

Map symbols *page 6*
Geo terms *page 8*
Asian countries *pages 12–14*

KNOW THE REGION

- Taiwan (Republic of China), has been claimed by China since the People's Republic was established in 1949. It is not a member of the United Nations – now the only *de facto* independent country in the world not to be so, other than the Vatican City.

- Hong Kong, formerly a UK possession, was returned to China in 1997 as a Special Administrative Region. Macau (formerly Portuguese) was similarly returned in 1999.

- The Three-Gorges Dam project on the Yangtze river is the largest of its kind. Millions of people were relocated and over 100 towns and villages were destroyed during its construction.

DISCOVER MORE

* Hong Kong www.info.gov.hk
* Macau www.macau.gov.mo
* News on China and Taiwan news.bbc.co.uk
* Visit Beijing www.ebeijing.gov.cn
* Fly to the new Hong Kong International Airport www.hongkongairport.com
* The Three Gorges Dam project civcal.media.hku.hk/threegorges

WATCH OUT!

* Be clean in Hong Kong. You can attract on-the-spot fines for littering or spitting.
* Between May and November there is an average of five typhoons per year in this region. Coastal areas are most at risk. Local flooding and landslides can result from these severe storms.
* China considers Taiwan as an additional province of the People's Republic. Also within the region, off the map to the south, are the Spratly Islands which are disputed between Brunei, China, Malaysia, the Philippines, Taiwan and Vietnam.

The focus of the map is
the Indian subcontinent.
India is the largest and
most populous country
in the subcontinent, but
the map also shows
parts of western China,
including the vast
Himalaya and the
Plateau of Tibet.
Pakistan is shown
almost in its entirety
here, but for its full
extent at a larger scale
see page 86. Sri Lanka
occupies the teardrop-
shaped island off the
southern coast of India.
The other countries
fully covered are
Bangladesh, Nepal and
Bhutan.

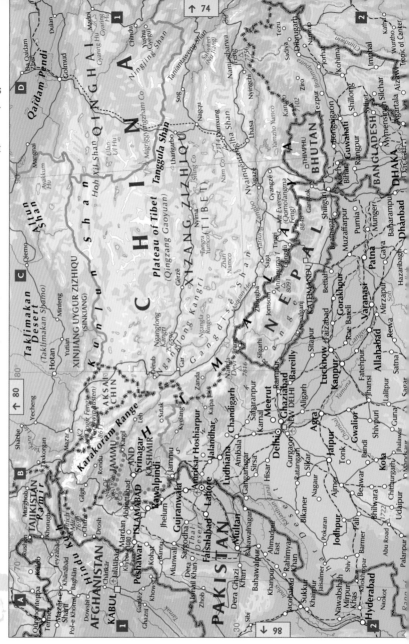

Go to →

Map symbols *page 6*
Asian countries *pages
12–14*
Asia physical features
page 66

KNOW THE REGION

- India is the world's second most populous country after China, although its population is
  increasing at a faster rate than China's – it grows by nearly 16 million people each year.

- The country name Sri Lanka is phonetically related to the country's earlier name, Ceylon.
  Ceylon is still sometimes used to refer to the island itself.

- Sri Lanka has designated a new national capital adjacent to Colombo: Sri
  Jayewardenepura Kotte.

- Bangladesh was originally part of Pakistan, and was referred to as East Pakistan until it
  gained its independence in 1971. After independence its capital, Dacca, was re-spelt as
  Dhaka.

↑ 75

1:16 250 000

0 100 200 300 miles
0 100 200 300 400 km

DISCOVER MORE

- Andaman and Nicobar Islands www.andaman.nic.in
- Dengue fever information www.who.int/csr
- India's population issues www.unfpa.org.in
- Visit Mumbai and its region www.maharashtratourism.gov.in
- Travel advice www.fco.gov.uk
- Search for satellite images visibleearth.nasa.gov
- Heritage sites in southern Asia whc.unesco.org

WATCH OUT!

- In Sri Lanka and southern India take precautions against the extreme heat. Only eat thoroughly cooked food and drink boiled or bottled water to prevent dysentery and diarrhoea.
- Large areas of north and east Sri Lanka remain heavily mined due to the recent civil war.
- The islands of the Maldives are at the mercy of rising sea levels – their highest point is only 2.4 metres (8 feet) and most of the 1 200 islands are less than 1 metre (3 feet) above sea level.

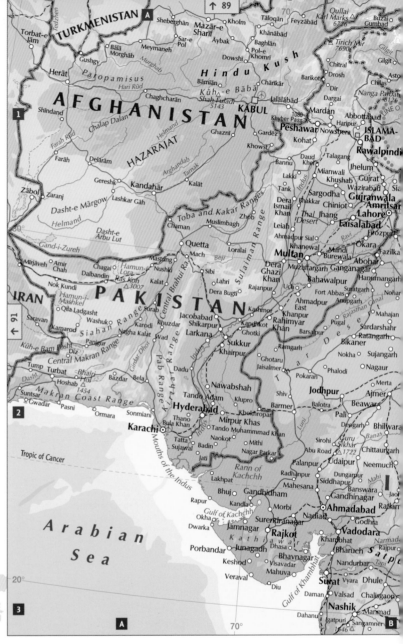

ASIA PAKISTAN, NORTHERN INDIA, NEPAL AND BANGLADESH

The map shows in detail the densely-populated areas of northern India, along with the whole of Pakistan, Nepal and Bhutan, and virtually all of Afghanistan and Bangladesh. This is a volatile region. Jammu and Kashmir, in the north, has long been the basis of a major territorial dispute between India and Pakistan, and the Line of Control named on the map represents the present *de facto* boundary between the countries. The nearby zone called the Aksai Chin is disputed between China and India.

Geo terms

Farsi (Iran), Dari (Afghanistan)

Dasht desert

Kūh mountain, mountains

Rūd river

Tajik

Qullai mountain

86

Go to →

Map symbols *page 6*
Geo terms *page 8*
Indian subcontinent *page 84*

KNOW THE REGION

• India's capital can be regarded as Delhi or New Delhi. The latter is an area within Delhi itself, containing most of the government buildings.

• The area between Nepal and Bhutan, known as Sikkim (capital Gangtok shown on the map) was independent until it became an Indian state in 1975.

• Darjiling, in the far northeast of India, is famous as a tea-growing area whose traditional spelling of Darjeeling is more familiar.

• Mount Everest, the highest mountain in the world and first climbed in 1953, lies in the great Himalaya mountain range on the border between China and Nepal.

1:12 250 000

0   100   200   300 miles
0   150   300   450 km

The centre of attention on this map is the extensive region between China and the Caspian Sea which used to be known as Soviet Central Asia, in the days before the Soviet Union (the USSR) was dissolved in 1991. The five now-independent republics of Kazakhstan, Uzbekistan, Turkmenistan, Tajikistan and Kyrgyzstan were formerly under direct Soviet control. On the border of Kazakhstan and Uzbekistan is the Aral Sea, in its own drainage basin. Much of the region is either semi-desert or mountainous.

ASIA CENTRAL ASIA

Geo terms

Farsi (Iran), Dari (Afghanistan)

Dasht desert

Kūh, Kūhha mountain, mountains

Reshteh mountain range

Russian

Ozero lake

Zaliv gulf, bay

88

Go to →

Map symbols *page 6*
Asian countries *pages 12–14*
Asia physical features *page 66*

KNOW THE REGION

- The Aral Sea has shrunk by almost 40 000 square kilometres (15 450 square miles) as a result of climate change and water extraction for agriculture. This has led to various ecological, economic and health problems.

- The Kazak, Uzbek, Turkmen and Kyrgyz (Kirghiz) languages are all closely linked to Turkish, while Tajik is a relative of Farsi (or Persian), the language of Iran.

- Kazakhstan moved its capital in recent years from the traditional Alma-Ata in the southeast (now spelt Almaty) to Astana. Astana itself has been renamed several times over the years, most recently being changed from Akmola.

1:16 250 000

0   100   200   300 miles
0   200   400 km

The Arabian Peninsula is a largely desert area of southwest Asia, framed by the Red Sea on the west, the Arabian Sea (a section of the Indian Ocean) on the south, and The Gulf (also often referred to as the Persian Gulf) on the east. The southernmost point of the peninsula, in Yemen, is only narrowly separated from Africa. The Strait of Hormuz, a busy shipping channel, joins The Gulf with the Indian Ocean in the Gulf of Oman.

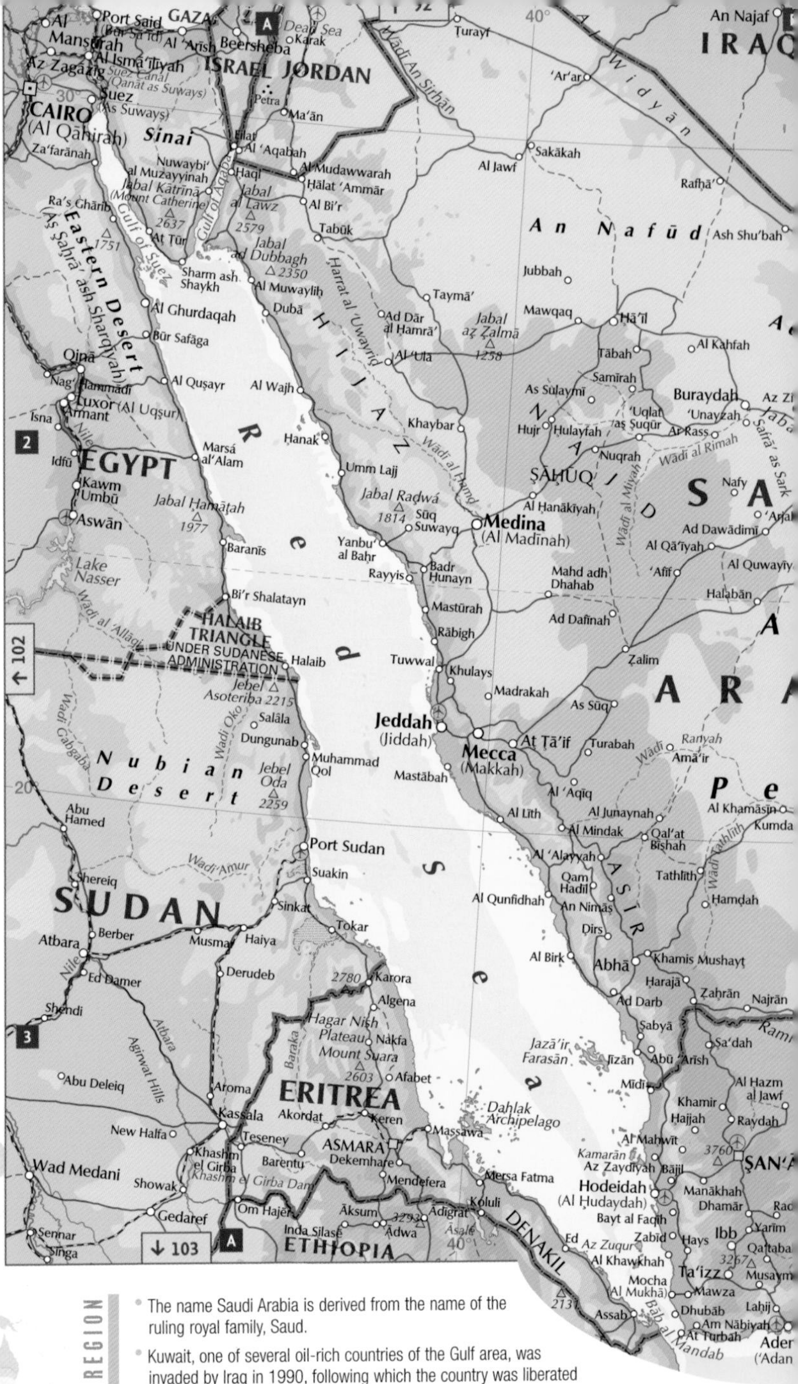

Geo terms

Arabic

Ghubbat bay

Jabal mountain, mountains

Jaza'ir islands

Ramlat sandy desert

Ra's cape, point

Wādī watercourse

Go to →

Map symbols *page 6*
Geo terms *page 8*
Asian countries *pages 12–14*

↑ 102

↓ 103

KNOW THE REGION

- The name Saudi Arabia is derived from the name of the ruling royal family, Saud.

- Kuwait, one of several oil-rich countries of the Gulf area, was invaded by Iraq in 1990, following which the country was liberated by a US-led international force in Operation Desert Storm.

- Bahrain, an independent island kingdom in The Gulf, is connected by a causeway to the Saudi Arabian mainland.

- Mecca was the birthplace of the prophet Mohammed and is the holiest city of Islam. Over one million pilgrims visit the Great Mosque each year – a journey known as the *Hajj*.

WATCH OUT!

• The countries of the Arabian Peninsula are Muslim states which follow Islamic law. Dress modestly and avoid offending local customs. During the month of Ramadan (the ninth month of the Muslim year) you should not eat, drink or smoke in public from sunrise to sunset each day.

• Over the last few years there have been numerous terrorist incidents directed at Western targets across the region. In May and November 2003 foreign residential compounds were attacked in Riyadh, Saudi Arabia, killing 48 people.

The map includes the area of the eastern shore of the Mediterranean Sea traditionally known as the Levant. This area contains the West Bank (between Israel and Jordan) and Gaza (between Israel and Egypt), the two zones which are the scene of the long-running conflict between Israel and the Palestinians. The map covers several other geopolitical hot spots including the Caucasus region between the Black and Caspian Seas (which contains the Russian republic of Chechnia), Iraq and Cyprus.

Geo terms

Arabic

Buḥayrat lake

Hawr lake

Farsi (Iran)

Daryācheh lake

Dasht desert

Turkish

Dağ, Dağı mountain

Dağları mountain range

Körfezi gulf, bay

Go to →

Map symbols *page 6*
Asian countries *pages 12–14*
Asia countries map *page 68*

KNOW THE REGION

- The name West Bank refers to the territory's location on the west bank of the river Jordan. It was part of Jordan until the country relinquished its claim to the area in 1988.

- The whole of Jerusalem is treated by Israel as its national capital, but this is not recognized by the international community. Palestinians share a direct interest in the city and claim it as theirs.

- The level of the Caspian Sea can fluctuate by several metres over periods of several years due to climatic change and irrigation schemes. As a result, the Kara Bogaz Gol inlet can be left almost dry.

↑ 41

↓ 91

1:12 250 000

| 0 | 100 | 200 | 300 mile |
| 0 | 150 | 300 | 450 km |

DISCOVER MORE

* Explore Istanbul www.icvb.org
* The Arab League www.arableagueonline.org
* Middle East Network Information Center
  menic.utexas.edu/menic.html
* News and background information news.bbc.co.uk
* Travel advice www.fco.gov.uk
* International boundary disputes www.ibru.dur.ac.uk
* Search for satellite images visibleearth.nasa.gov

WATCH OUT!

* The Georgian and Armenian languages use special alphabets which are quite unlike the Roman alphabet. Azerbaijan uses the Roman alphabet, but with one addition: an upside-down 'e' or ə.

* The Abşeron peninsula in Azerbaijan is thought to be one of the most environmentally devastated areas in the world due to pollution from industrial plants and intensive farming methods.

* Check travel advice regularly because of the frequency of conflict in this region.

The Russian Federation is split between Asia and Europe, primarily along the Ural Mountains (see also page 40), and is easily the largest country in the world – almost twice the size of Canada, the second largest. The country stretches almost halfway around the globe and has borders with fourteen different countries – a record shared with China. There is a marked contrast between the densely populated west and the sparser north and east.

Geo terms

Russian

Khrebet mountain range

Mys cape, point

Ostrov island

Ostrova islands

Ozero lake

Ploskogor'ye plateau

Zaliv gulf, bay

94

Go to →

Map symbols *page 6*
Geo terms *page 8*
Western Russian Federation *page 40*

KNOW THE REGION

- Some of Russia's Arctic islands are named after famous people – for example, Zemlya Frantsa-Iosifa (after the emperor Franz Josef), Ostrov Greem-Bell (Scottish-born scientist and inventor Alexander Graham Bell) and Ostrova De-Longa (de Long, an American).

- The emptiness of huge areas of Siberia is emphasised here by the lack of settlements, roads and railways. Two important rail routes join east with west – the Trans-Siberian and Baikal-Amur Railways.

- Svalbard, a Norwegian territory in the Arctic Ocean whose main island is Spitsbergen, has no permanent population, but is inhabited by a temporary population of miners and researchers, many of them Russian.

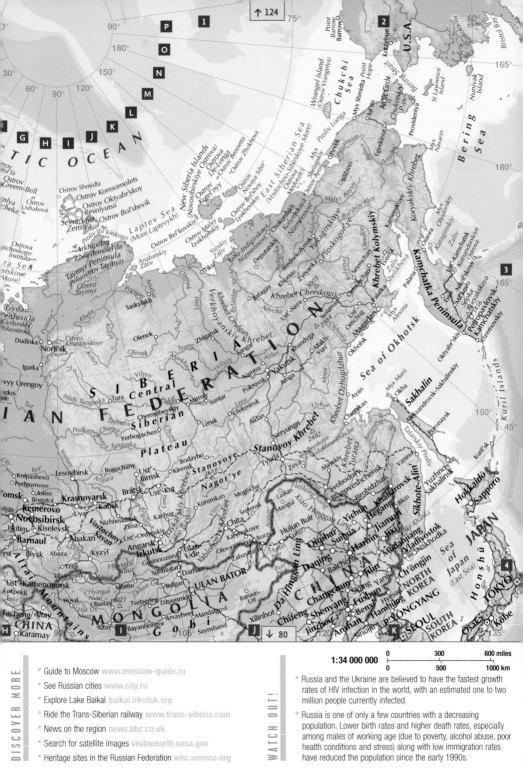

↑ 124

↓ 80

1:34 000 000

0 — 300 — 600 miles
0 — 500 — 1000 km

WATCH OUT!

- Russia and the Ukraine are believed to have the fastest growth rates of HIV infection in the world, with an estimated one to two million people currently infected.

- Russia is one of only a few countries with a decreasing population. Lower birth rates and higher death rates, especially among males of working age (due to poverty, alcohol abuse, poor health conditions and stress) along with low immigration rates have reduced the population since the early 1990s.

Africa is connected to Asia at the narrow Sinai peninsula. It is also separated narrowly from Europe at the Strait of Gibraltar.

It contains some of the world's greatest physical features. The north is dominated by the Sahara Desert and the semi-arid Sahel region, while the mountainous zone of the Great Rift Valley runs down much of the east. The chief feature of central Africa is the vast Congo Basin, while the Kalahari and Namib deserts occupy large parts of the southwest.

Geo terms

Arabic
Ḥamādah plateau
Erg (or `Erg) sandy desert
Jebel mountain, mountains

Berber (Algeria, Morocco)
Adrar hills, mountains

French
Massif mountains, upland

Malagasy (Madagascar)
Tanjona cape, point

Go to →

Geo terms *page 8*
World climate *page 28*
Africa countries map *page 98*

Africa's longest rivers

Nile	6 695 km	4 160 miles
Congo	4 667 km	2 900 miles
Niger	4 184 km	2 599 miles
Zambezi	2 736 km	1 700 miles
Webi Shabeelle	2 490 km	1 547 miles

Africa's highest mountains

Kilimanjaro, Tanzania	5 892 m	19 331 ft
Mt Kenya, Kenya	5 199 m	17 057 ft
Margherita Peak, Dem. Rep. of Congo/Uganda	5 110 m	16 765 ft
Meru, Tanzania	4 565 m	14 977 ft
Ras Dejen, Ethiopia	4 533 m	14 872 ft

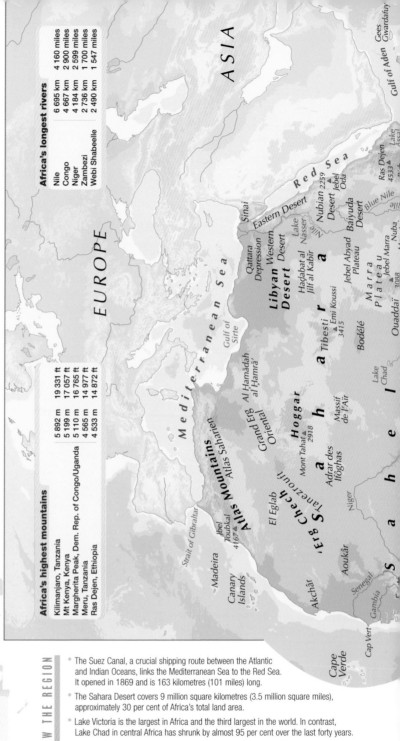

• The Suez Canal, a crucial shipping route between the Atlantic and Indian Oceans, links the Mediterranean Sea to the Red Sea. It opened in 1869 and is 163 kilometres (101 miles) long.

• The Sahara Desert covers 9 million square kilometres (3.5 million square miles), approximately 30 per cent of Africa's total land area.

• Lake Victoria is the largest in Africa and the third largest in the world. In contrast, Lake Chad in central Africa has shrunk by almost 95 per cent over the last forty years.

• The floor of the Great Rift Valley varies from nearly 400 metres (1 312 feet) below sea level to over 1 800 metres (5 900 feet) above sea level.

Map labels

Seychelles

Mauritius
Réunion

Haud
Webi Shabeelle

Ethiopian Highlands

Tanjona Bobaomby
Tanjona Maromokotro
2876

Boby
2658

Madagascar

INDIAN OCEAN

Aldabra Islands
Cabo Delgado
Pemba Island
Zanzibar Island
Mafia Island

Comoro Islands

Mozambique Channel

Tanjona Vohimena

Lake Turkana
Mount Kenya 5199
Kilimanjaro 5892
Meru 4565
Mount Mulanje 3002

Great Rift Valley

Lake Albert
Lake Victoria
Lake Tanganyika

Great Rift Valley

Lake Mweru
Lake Mwumba
Lake Bangweulu
Lake Nyasa
Lake Kariba

Sudd

Massif des Bongo

Margherita Peak 5110
Chaîne des Mitumba
Great Rift Valley

Congo Basin

Congo

Zambezi

Victoria Falls

Okavango Delta

Kalahari Desert

Limpopo

Thabana-Ntlenyana 3482
Drakensberg

Huila Plateau

Cubango

Namib Desert

Cango

Orange

Great Karoo

Cape Agulhas

Cape of Good Hope

Plateau
Benue
Mont Cameroun 4100
Cameroun Dorsale

Niger
Bight of Benin
Gulf of Guinea
Principe
São Tomé
Bioco

Lake Volta

Cape Palmas

ATLANTIC OCEAN

St Helena

Ascension

1:48 750 000

| | | 500 | | 1000 miles |
| 0 | 500 | 1000 | 1500 km | |

Africa's extremes

Total land area	30 343 578 sq km	11 715 655 sq miles
Largest lake	Lake Victoria	68 800 sq km	26 564 sq miles
Largest island	Madagascar	587 040 sq km	226 656 sq miles
Largest drainage basin	Congo, Congo/Dem. Rep. Congo	3 700 000 sq km	1 428 570 sq miles
Lowest point	Lake Assal, Djibouti	-152 metres	-499 feet

DISCOVER MORE

• Combating desertification www.unccd.int

• Health advice www.cdc.gov/travel

• Environmental change in Africa
  edcwww.cr.usgs.gov/earthshots/slow/tableofcontents

• African weather www.metoffice.com/weather

• Search for satellite images visibleearth.nasa.gov

• Water resources www.africanwater.org

WATCH OUT!

• The Cape of Good Hope, known by early navigators as the Cape of Storms, is one of the most dangerous nautical passages in the world and has been the site of frequent shipwrecks. There are gale force winds on an average of 200 days per year.

• The dangerous parasitic infection schistosomiasis (bilharzia) is prevalent in the fresh water throughout most of this region. Diseases such as malaria and sleeping sickness are carried by insects. It is recommended to always use an insect repellent that contains DEET (diethylmetatoluamide).

The political patchwork of Africa is a result of a complex history and of boundaries formed largely during the colonial era, which saw European control of the majority of the continent from the 15th century until widespread moves to independence began in the 1950s. The colonial era effectively came to an end in the 1970s. The status of Western Sahara, formerly Spanish but now effectively under Moroccan control, remains to be agreed internationally. Today there are once again two countries called Congo, since Zaire reverted to the name Democratic Republic of Congo in 1997.

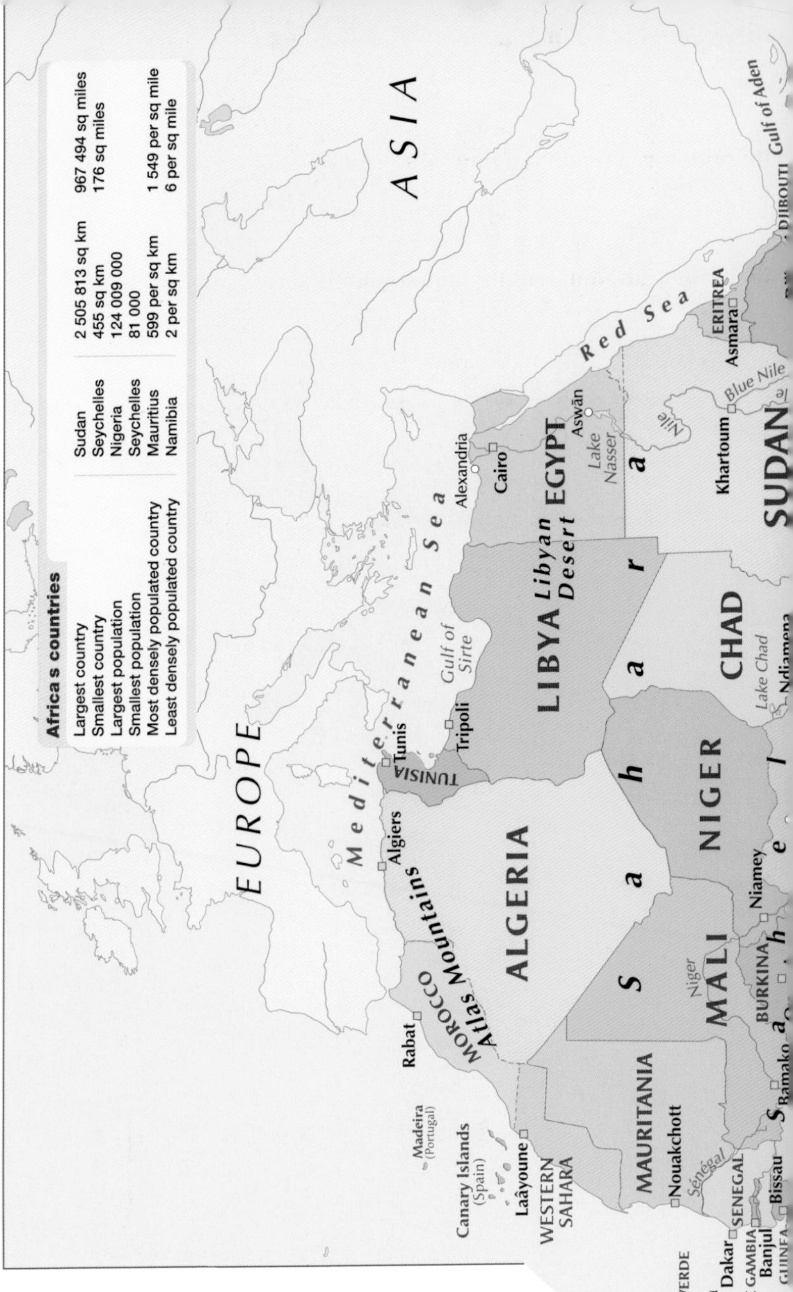

Africa's countries

Largest country	Sudan	2 505 813 sq km	967 494 sq miles
Smallest country	Seychelles	455 sq km	176 sq miles
Largest population	Nigeria	124 009 000	
Smallest population	Seychelles	81 000	
Most densely populated country	Mauritius	599 per sq km	1 549 per sq mile
Least densely populated country	Namibia	2 per sq km	6 per sq mile

KNOW THE REGION

- Many languages are spoken in different parts of Africa, although Arabic is the main native language all across the north. In most other areas, the languages of European powers (mainly English, French, Portuguese and Spanish, along with Afrikaans) remain in common use.
- Only Liberia and Ethiopia have remained free from colonial rule throughout their history.
- UN figures estimate that 258 million people throughout the African continent have no access to clean water.
- Of the ten countries in the world with under-five mortality rates of more than 200 per 1000 live births, nine are in Africa.

Go to →
Asian countries *pages 12–14*
World countries map *page 24*
Asia physical features *page 66*

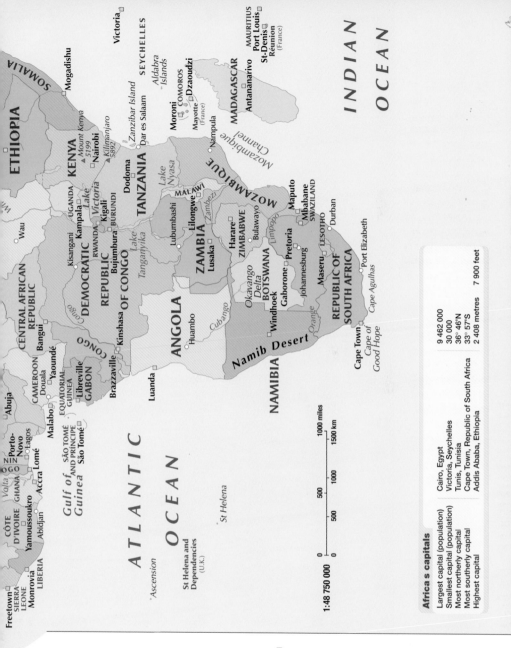

INDIAN OCEAN

ATLANTIC OCEAN

SOMALIA
ETHIOPIA
KENYA
Mogadishu
Nairobi
Mount Kenya 5199
Kilimanjaro 5892
Victoria
SEYCHELLES
Aldabra Islands
COMOROS
Moroni
Mayotte (France)
Dzaoudzi
MADAGASCAR
Antananarivo
Zanzibar Island
Dar es Salaam
TANZANIA
Dodoma
Lake Victoria
UGANDA
Kampala
RWANDA
Kigali
BURUNDI
Bujumbura
Lake Tanganyika
DEMOCRATIC REPUBLIC OF CONGO
Kisangani
Kinshasa
Lubumbashi
Lake Nyasa
MALAWI
Lilongwe
ZAMBIA
Lusaka
Zambezi
Nampula
MOZAMBIQUE
Mozambique Channel
Maputo
Mbabane
SWAZILAND
ZIMBABWE
Harare
Bulawayo
Limpopo
Okavango Delta
BOTSWANA
Gaborone
Pretoria
Johannesburg
Maseru
LESOTHO
Durban
Port Elizabeth
REPUBLIC OF SOUTH AFRICA
Cape Town
Cape of Good Hope
Cape Agulhas
ANGOLA
Huambo
Luanda
CONGO
Brazzaville
Congo
GABON
Libreville
Yaoundé
CAMEROON
Douala
EQUATORIAL GUINEA
Malabo
SÃO TOMÉ AND PRINCIPE
São Tomé
Gulf of Guinea
CENTRAL AFRICAN REPUBLIC
Bangui
Wau
Cubango
Orange
NAMIBIA
Windhoek
Namib Desert

Abuja
BENIN
Porto-Novo
Lagos
TOGO
Lomé
GHANA
Accra
Volta
CÔTE D'IVOIRE
Yamoussoukro
Abidjan
LIBERIA
Monrovia
SIERRA LEONE
Freetown

St Helena
Ascension
St Helena and Dependencies (U.K.)

MAURITIUS
Port Louis
St-Denis
Réunion (France)

1000 miles
1500 km
1000
500
500
0
0

1:48 750 000

DISCOVER MORE

* International relations www.africa-union.org
* Africa's economy www.uneca.org
* Resolving conflicts www.unrec.org
* Boundary disputes www.ibru.dur.ac.uk
* The AIDS crisis www.unaids.org
* Travel advice www.fco.gov.uk
* Country profiles www.odci.gov/cia/publications/factbook

WATCH OUT!

* While sub-Saharan Africa (the south of the continent) has just over 10 per cent of the world's population, it is home to 70 per cent of the world's population infected with HIV/AIDS.
* As a result of landmines, one in every 356 people in Angola is an amputee – one of the highest ratios in the world.
* Be prepared to see extreme poverty and hardship throughout Africa. The twenty-seven countries with the lowest Human Development Index – a United Nations measure of wealth, education provision and life expectancy – are all in Africa.

The Sahara Desert occupies much of the north of the map area, and the countries covering it are accordingly vast. Hoggar and Tibesti are major rocky uplands within it, and the Ergs are large sand deserts. The countries along the southern coast are more densely populated and significantly smaller. In the north, the Atlas Mountains are the chief physical feature. The Spanish-owned Canary Islands and the Portuguese island of Madeira lie off the northwest coast. Lake Chad, formerly huge, is now a relatively insignificant feature.

Geo terms

Arabic

Jebel mountain, mountains

Sebkha impermanent lake, salt lake

Wāḥāt oasis

Berber (Algeria, Morocco)

Adrar hills, mountains

French

Lac lake

Monts mountains

Go to →

Map symbols *page 6*
Geo terms *page 8*
African countries *pages 16–18*

• Names of parts of the West African coast relate to former trading connections dating from the colonial era. For example, the Gold Coast (also the former name of Ghana), Ivory Coast (which gave its name to the country now known as Côte d'Ivoire) and the Slave Coast.

• Long, straight boundaries are usually an indication that the territory involved is largely flat, empty desert.

The map gives a view of the northeast of the African continent, concentrating on Egypt (the country linking Africa to Asia), the Sudan (the largest country in Africa) and mountainous Ethiopia. Somalia occupies the sharply angled corner of the continent – the so-called Horn of Africa – facing Arabia across the Gulf of Aden. Eritrea and the small enclave of Djibouti are also shown. The configuration of the map shows the close proximity of these countries to the Middle East and Arabia.

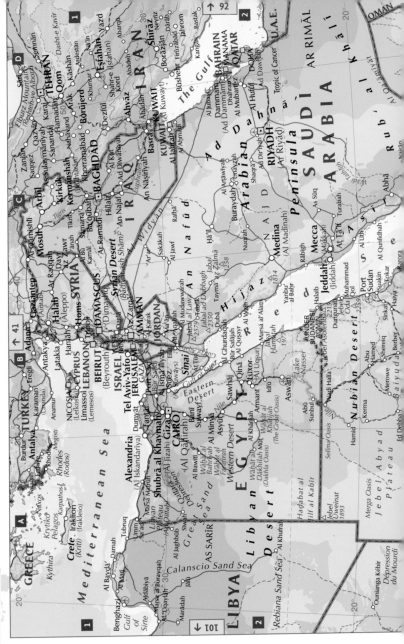

Geo terms

Amharic (Ethiopia)

Wenz river

Arabic

Bahr river

Jabal, Jebel mountain, mountains

Wāḥāt oasis

Wadi watercourse

102

Go to →

Map symbols *page 6*
Geo terms *page 8*
Africa countries map
page 98

KNOW THE REGION

- Ethnic conflict has dogged the modern history of Sudan, with black-African tribal groups in the south seeking autonomy from the largely Arab north. Most recently, ethnic cleansing in the western region of Darfur led to widespread disruption and international concern, and a major refugee problem which also affected neighbouring Chad.

- Somalia has suffered for many years from an absence of effective central government, following years of civil war. Parts of the north are operating in practice as if they were separate countries.

- More than 90 per cent of the 70 million inhabitants of Egypt are located around the River Nile.

Map of northeast Africa including Sudan, Ethiopia, Somalia, Kenya, Tanzania, Uganda, the Democratic Republic of Congo, Yemen, Eritrea and the Indian Ocean. Scale 1:21 000 000.

DISCOVER MORE

* Managing the Nile www.nilebasin.org
* Lakes in northeast Africa
  www.worldlakes.org/searchlakes.asp
* Heritage sites in Africa whc.unesco.org
* The Temple of Philae www.philae.nu/philae/landing.html
* Travel advice www.fco.gov.uk
* Search for satellite images visibleearth.nasa.gov
* Follow the news news.bbc.co.uk

WATCH OUT!

* The site of the ancient Temple of Philae at Aswan has moved! When the High Dam was built, it was taken down and reassembled stone by stone on higher ground on the nearby Agilika Island.

* The Denakil Depression between Ethiopia and Eritrea is one of earth's hottest and most inhospitable places. It sinks to -125 metres (410 feet) below sea level and is covered by salt pans and sulphur fields.

In the centre of this map is the large central African country now called the Democratic Republic of Congo, formerly known as Zaire and earlier the Belgian Congo. The map also covers the East African countries of Kenya, Uganda and Tanzania, along with Rwanda and Burundi in the mountainous centre. To the west is the Congo, a separate country from the Democratic Republic. The African Great Lakes feature prominently in the east, in particular Lake Victoria, the world's third largest lake and the largest in Africa.

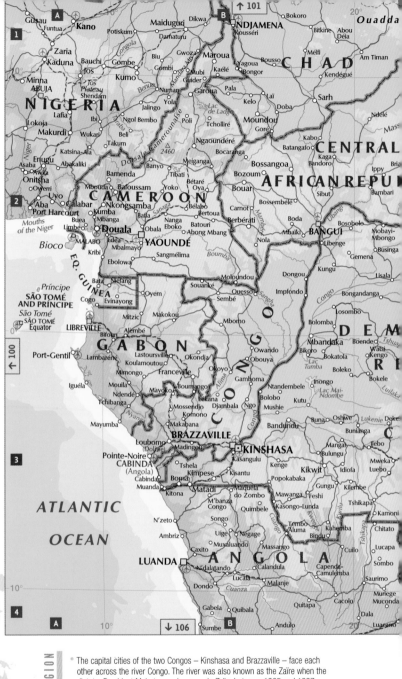

Geo terms

Arabic

Bahr river

Jebel mountain, mountains

French

Chaîne mountain range

Lac lake

Portuguese

Cabo cape, point

104

Go to →

Map symbols *page 6*
Geo terms *page 8*
Africa physical features *page 96*

KNOW THE REGION

- The capital cities of the two Congos – Kinshasa and Brazzaville – face each other across the river Congo. The river was also known as the Zaïre when the dictator President Mobutu was in power in Zaïre between 1965 and 1997.

- Zanzibar was one of the main ports of Tanzania involved in the slave trade. It is estimated that about 600 000 slaves were sold through the Zanzibar market between 1830 and 1873.

- The term Great Rift Valley refers to a dramatic and extensive zone of geological faulting, mountain-building and volcanic activity stretching much of the way up eastern Africa and into the Red Sea and beyond.

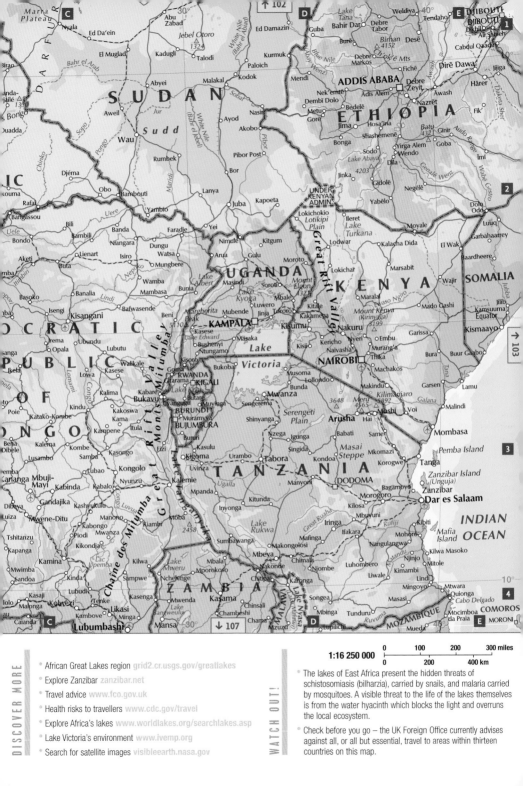

DISCOVER MORE

- African Great Lakes region grid2.cr.usgs.gov/greatlakes
- Explore Zanzibar zanzibar.net
- Travel advice www.fco.gov.uk
- Health risks to travellers www.cdc.gov/travel
- Explore Africa's lakes www.worldlakes.org/searchlakes.asp
- Lake Victoria's environment www.ivemp.org
- Search for satellite images visibleearth.nasa.gov

WATCH OUT!

- The lakes of East Africa present the hidden threats of schistosomiasis (bilharzia), carried by snails, and malaria carried by mosquitoes. A visible threat to the life of the lakes themselves is from the water hyacinth which blocks the light and overruns the local ecosystem.

- Check before you go – the UK Foreign Office currently advises against all, or all but essential, travel to areas within thirteen countries on this map.

1:16 250 000

The chief physical features of this southern part of Africa are Lake Nyasa (also known as Lake Malawi) in the northeast, the Kalahari and Namib deserts in the southwest, and the extensive wetlands of the Makgadikgadi salt flats and the Okavango Delta in the centre. The uplands of the Great Karoo and Drakensberg mountains dominate South Africa (see page 108). The inset shows the island of Madagascar, in the Indian Ocean – the fourth largest island in the world and renowned for its unique flora and fauna.

Geo terms

Afrikaans

-berg mountain, mountains

Groot big

Malagasy (Madagascar)

Nosy island

Tanjona cape, point

Go to →

Map symbols page 6
African countries pages 16–18
Republic of South Africa page 108

AFRICA · SOUTHERN AFRICA

KNOW THE REGION

- The islands known as the Comoros (or Comoro Islands) are split between the country of the Comoros and Mayotte, a French dependency.

- Madagascar, separated from mainland Africa by the Mozambique Channel, speaks a language unique to itself known as Malagasy. For some years the country was known as the Malagasy Republic.

- On the border between Zambia and Zimbabwe is the large reservoir known as Lake Kariba. Further down the Zambezi river is a second major reservoir, Lake Cabora Bassa.

- Zambia used to be called Northern Rhodesia, and Zimbabwe was originally Southern Rhodesia. Malawi was Nyasaland; Botswana was Bechuanaland; and Lesotho was Basutoland.

↑ 105

DEM. REP.
wezi **CONGO** Minga **Mansa** Lake Bangweulu Chambeshi Chama Mbinga **C** **TANZANIA** 40 **D** **COMOROS** MORONI Njazidja (Grande Comore)

Solwezi **Lubumbashi** Chililabombwe Mpika Mzuzu Mzimba Lupilichi Macaloge Salimo Mueda Mocimboa da Praia DZAOUDZI **Mayotte** (France)

Chingola Mufulira Chitambo Nkhotakota Lichinga Marrupa Montepuez Pemba

Kitwe **Ndola** Mfuwe Kasungu **1**

sempa Lunga Kapiri Mposhi **Chipata** Katete Mangochi Mutuali Nacala

Mumbwa **LUSAKA** Songo **Blantyre** Zomba Alto Molócuè Ribauè **Nampula** Moçambique

MOZAMBIQUE

ZIMBABWE

HARARE Chitungwiza

Bulawayo

MADAGASCAR

ANTANANARIVO

INDIAN OCEAN

Mozambique Channel

Tropic of Capricorn

1:16 250 000

DISCOVER MORE

Development of southern African www.sadc.int

Floods and drought www.sadc-hazards.net

Okavango Delta www.africanwater.org/okavango.htm

Explore the Namib region www.met.gov.na/namib.html

Malaria risk www.malaria.org.za

Tourist guide to Mayotte www.mayotte-tourisme.com

Explore protected areas www.peaceparks.org

WATCH OUT!

About 80 per cent of Botswana is desert with no surface water. However, it has two unusual water features – the Makgadikgadi salt flats and the wildlife-rich Okavango river delta, which empties into the desert.

The economy of Zimbabwe is in crisis with massive inflation, growing unemployment and food shortages. In February 2000 the country ran out of petrol due to unpaid bills. Poverty and failing health systems have fuelled the spread of famine and HIV/AIDS.

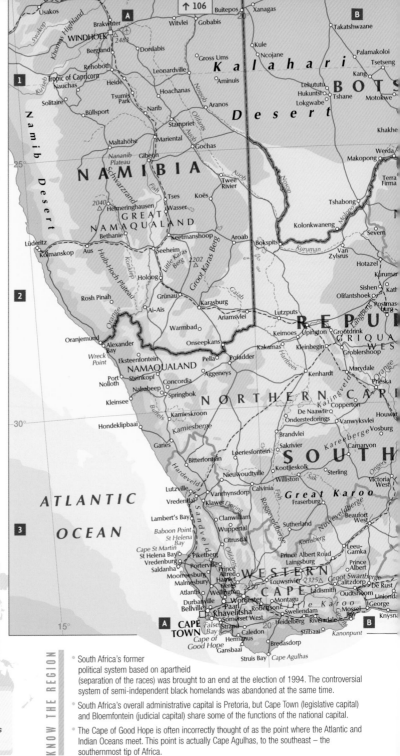

The map focuses on the Republic of South Africa – an important country in the politics and economy of the African continent. The country consists of nine provinces, which replaced the long-established four provinces in 1994. The independent kingdom of Lesotho is entirely enclosed within the Republic of South Africa, while another kingdom, Swaziland, is almost so, located against the border with Mozambique. Dense urban areas, especially around Johannesburg, contrast with the sparsely-populated areas in the northwest towards the Kalahari and Namib deserts.

AFRICA ▸ REPUBLIC OF SOUTH AFRICA

108

Geo terms

Afrikaans

-berg, -berge mountain, mountains

Groot big

-punt cape, point

-veld field

Portuguese

Cabo cape, point

Go to →

Map symbols *page 6*
Geo terms *page 8*
African countries *pages 16–18*

Map symbols *page 6*
Geo terms *page 8*
African countries *pages 16–18*

KNOW THE REGION

- South Africa's former political system based on apartheid (separation of the races) was brought to an end at the election of 1994. The controversial system of semi-independent black homelands was abandoned at the same time.

- South Africa's overall administrative capital is Pretoria, but Cape Town (legislative capital) and Bloemfontein (judicial capital) share some of the functions of the national capital.

- The Cape of Good Hope is often incorrectly thought of as the point where the Atlantic and Indian Oceans meet. This point is actually Cape Agulhas, to the southeast – the southernmost tip of Africa.

↑ 107

→ 107

1:8 000 000

| 0 | 50 | 100 | 150 miles |

| 0 | 100 | 200 km |

DISCOVER MORE

- Explore South Africa's National Parks www.parks-sa.co.za
- Travel advice www.fco.gov.uk
- Health advice www.who.int/csr
- HIV/AIDS facts and figures www.unaids.org
- Water resources in Lesotho www.lhwp.org.ls
- Search for satellite images visibleearth.nasa.gov
- Follow the news news.bbc.co.uk

WATCH OUT!

- AIDS has had a devasting effect on life expectancy figures in this region. In Swaziland life expectancy has dropped from fifty-eight to thirty-seven. In South Africa in 2001, male life expectancy was forty-eight but is forecast to be only thirty-eight by 2010.
- Urban crime has become a problem as South Africa's cities have grown. Some areas have become dangerous to visit or pass through at night and care is needed at all times.

The map highlights the three major island groups traditionally used to categorize the enormously extensive Pacific island chains and their people: Micronesia in the northwest, covering chiefly the Marianas, Marshall and Caroline Islands; Melanesia in the middle, mainly consisting of the Solomon Islands and Papua New Guinea; and Polynesia, encompassing all the remaining islands across the Pacific. The Great Dividing Range, on the eastern side of Australia, is prominent, as is the mountainous ridge forming the backbone of New Guinea.

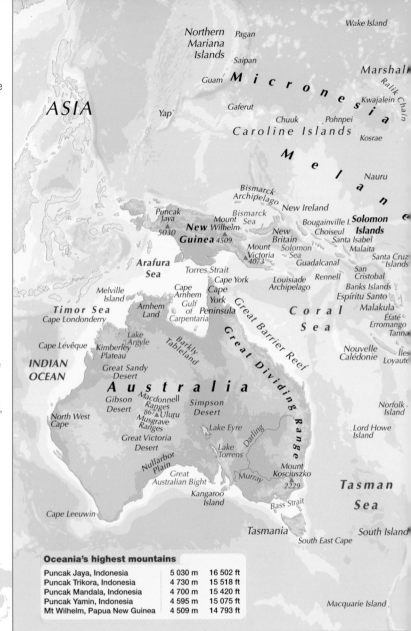

Oceania's highest mountains

Puncak Jaya, Indonesia	5 030 m	16 502 ft
Puncak Trikora, Indonesia	4 730 m	15 518 ft
Puncak Mandala, Indonesia	4 700 m	15 420 ft
Puncak Yamin, Indonesia	4 595 m	15 075 ft
Mt Wilhelm, Papua New Guinea	4 509 m	14 793 ft

Go to →

World physical features
page 26
Oceania countries map
page 112
Pacific Ocean page 158

KNOW THE REGION

* Tasmania is named after Abel Tasman, a 17th-century Dutch explorer. It was originally called Van Diemen's Land (after the admiral who sent Tasman on his voyage). The Cook Islands, in Polynesia, are named after the 18th century British sea captain, James Cook.

* Genetic research shows that the Pacific islands were originally populated by seafarers from Asia, although the Norwegian Thor Heyerdahl's *Kon-Tiki* expedition of the 1950s had suggested that the people originally came from the Americas.

* Pitcairn Island was first occupied by mutineers from the 18th-century British ship *HMS Bounty*. The present-day inhabitants are descended from them.

Hawaiian
Islands

PACIFIC OCEAN

Islands

k
Chain

Majuro

Gilbert
Islands

Tarawa

Beru

Onotoa
Kingsmill
Group
Nanumea

Tuvalu

Funafuti
Nukulaelae

Rotuma

Îles
Wallis

Îles
de Hoorn

Fiji

Viti Levu
Kadavu

Hunter
Island

Palmyra Atoll

Howland Island
Baker Island

Phoenix
Islands

Kanton

Orona

Tokelau
Nukunono

Pukapuka

Savai'i
Upolu
Samoan
Islands

Vanua Levu

Tofua

Vava'u
Group
Niue

Tonga

Tongatapu
Group

Kiritimati

Jarvis Island

Malden
Island

Penrhyn   Caroline Island
(Millennium
Manihiki   Island)

Suwarrow

Palmerston

Cook
Islands   Atiu
Rarotonga

Motu One

Îles
Palliser

Tahiti

Society Islands

Ruruta
Tubuai

Tubuai Islands

Marquesas
Islands

Nuku Hiva   Hiva Oa

Îles du
Désappointement

Fakarava

Hao

Mururoa

Îles Gambier

Groupe
Actéon

Pitcairn Island

Ducie Island

Raoul Island

Kermadec
Islands

Rapa
Marotiri

North
Cape

North
Island

oraki
3754

New
Zealand

Chatham
Islands

Stewart Island

Antipodes
Islands

Auckland Islands

Campbell Island

Oceania's longest rivers

Murray-Darling	3 750 km	2 330 miles
Darling	2 739 km	1 702 miles
Murray	2 589 km	1 608 miles
Murrumbidgee	1 690 km	1 050 miles
Lachlan	1 480 km	919 miles

1:52 750 000

0	500	1000		1500 miles
0	500	1000	1500	2000 km

Oceania's extremes

Total land area		8 844 516 sq km	3 414 868 sq miles
Largest lake	Lake Eyre, Australia	0–8 900 sq km	0–3 436 sq miles
Largest island	New Guinea, Indonesia/Papua New Guinea	808 510 sq km	312 166 sq miles
Largest drainage basin	Murray-Darling, Australia	1 058 000 sq km	408 494 sq miles
Lowest point	Lake Eyre, Australia	-16 metres	-53 feet

DISCOVER MORE

- Search for satellite images visibleearth.nasa.gov
- Heritage sites in Oceania whc.unesco.org
- Oceania's climate and weather www.metoffice.com/weather
- Climbing Oceania's mountains www.peakbagger.com
- Volcanic activity www.volcano.si.edu
- Search for lakes in Oceania
  www.worldlakes.org/searchlakes.asp

WATCH OUT!

- Many Melanesian and Polynesian islands are coral atolls which are under threat from exploitation, pollution and rising sea levels.
- Tropical storms in the western Pacific are called typhoons. They are most frequent between August and December. Winds reach an average speed of 120 kilometres per hour (75 miles per hour) but supertyphoons can reach 240 kilometres per hour (149 miles per hour).
- Beware of venomous fish such as stonefish, lionfish and the cone shell. Jellyfish and flame coral can also cause great pain.

Oceania is defined here as covering Australia, New Zealand, the independent nations of the Pacific Ocean, and various islands in the southwestern Pacific which remain as dependent territories. The whole of Papua New Guinea is included, following a common convention which divides New Guinea between Asia (Indonesia) and Oceania (Papua New Guinea). The political boundaries shown on this map are intended to clarify the physical coverage of island countries and dependencies rather than actually defining strict territorial limits, which are very much more complex and sometimes as yet unsettled.

Wake Island (U.S.A.)

MARSHALL ISLANDS

Pagan
Northern Mariana Islands (U.S.A.)
Saipan **Capitol Hill**
Guam (U.S.A.) **Hagåtña**

Yap
Gaferut
Chuuk Pohnpei **Palikir**
Caroline Islands
Kosrae
FEDERATED STATES OF MICRONESIA

ASIA

Yaren
NAURU

New Ireland
Rabaul
Mount Wilhelm **PAPUA**
New Wilhelm **PAPUA**
Guinea 4509 **NEW**
New Britain
Bougainville I.
SOLOMON ISLANDS
Solomon Sea **Honiara**
Malaita
Santa Cruz Islands

Arafura Sea
Torres Strait **Port Moresby**
GUINEA

Banks Islands
VANUATU
Espíritu Santo
Malakula
Éfaté
Port Vila
Îles Loyauté
New Caledonia (France)
Nouméa

Timor Sea
Darwin
Gulf of Carpentaria
Cairns
Coral Sea Islands Territory (Australia)
Coral Sea

Cape Lévêque
Lake Argyle
Townsville

INDIAN OCEAN
Broome

North West Cape
Uluru 867
Alice Springs
AUSTRALIA
Brisbane
Norfolk Island (Australia)
Lord Howe Island (Australia)

Kalgoorlie
Lake Eyre
Lake Torrens
Darling
Sydney
Canberra
Tasman Sea

Perth
Great Australian Bight
Adelaide
Murray
Mount Kosciuszko 2229
Melbourne
Kangaroo Island

Cape Leeuwin
Bass Strait
Tasmania
Hobart
South Island

Macquarie Island (Australia)

Oceania's capitals

Largest capital (population)	Canberra, Australia	387 000
Smallest capital (population)	Vaiaku, Tuvalu	5 100
Most northerly capital	Delap-Uliga-Djarrit, Marshall Islands	7° 7'N
Most southerly capital	Wellington, New Zealand	41° 18'S
Highest capital	Canberra, Australia	581 metres 1 906 feet

Go to →

World countries map page 24
Oceania countries pages 18–20
Oceania physical features page 110

KNOW THE REGION

- The former UN Trust Territory of the Pacific Islands, administered by the USA, was divided during the 1980s to form the independent nations of Micronesia, the Marshall Islands, and Palau, and the US dependencies of Guam and the Northern Marianas.

- Several small uninhabited islands across the Pacific are also under US control. These include Wake, Howland, Baker, Jarvis and Palmyra. Hawaii has been a state of the USA since the late 1950s.

- Kiribati (pronounced 'Kiribass') was formerly known as the Gilbert Islands. Tuvalu used to be a UK dependency known as the Ellice Islands and Vanuatu was once a UK/French territory, the New Hebrides.

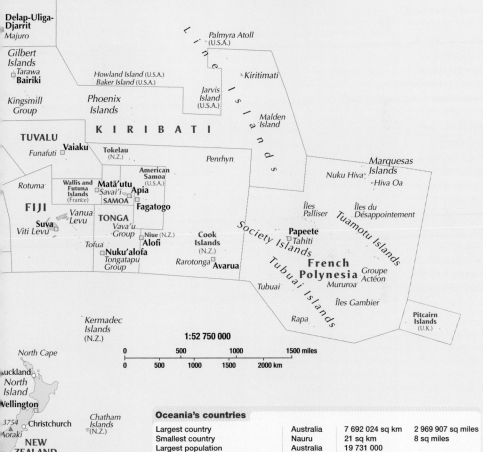

PACIFIC OCEAN

Hawaiian
Islands
(U.S.A.)

Delap-Uliga-
Djarrit
Majuro

Gilbert
Islands
Tarawa
Bairiki

Kingsmill
Group

Palmyra Atoll
(U.S.A.)

Howland Island (U.S.A.)
Baker Island (U.S.A.)

Kiritimati

Jarvis
Island
(U.S.A.)

Phoenix
Islands

Malden
Island

Line Islands

K I R I B A T I

TUVALU Vaiaku
Funafuti

Tokelau
(N.Z.)

Penrhyn

Marquesas
Islands
Nuku Hiva Hiva Oa

Rotuma

Wallis and
Futuna
Islands
(France)

American
Samoa
(U.S.A.)
Savai'i

Matā'utu

Apia
SAMOA
Fagatogo

Îles
Palliser

Îles du
Désappointement

FIJI
Vanua
Levu
Suva
Viti Levu

TONGA
Vava'u
Group

Niue (N.Z.)
Alofi

Cook
Islands
(N.Z.)

Papeete
Tahiti

Society Islands

Tuamotu Islands

French
Polynesia

Groupe
Actéon

Tofua
Nuku'alofa
Tongatapu
Group

Rarotonga
Avarua

Tubuai Islands

Mururoa

Îles Gambier

Tubuai

Pitcairn
Islands
(U.K.)

Kermadec
Islands
(N.Z.)

Rapa

1:52 750 000

| 0 | 500 | 1000 | 1500 miles |

| 0 | 500 | 1000 | 1500 | 2000 km |

North Cape

Auckland
North
Island

Wellington

3754 Christchurch
Aoraki

NEW
ZEALAND

Stewart Island

Chatham
Islands
(N.Z.)

Antipodes
Islands
(N.Z.)

Auckland Islands
(N.Z.)

Campbell Island
(N.Z.)

Oceania's countries

Largest country	Australia	7 692 024 sq km	2 969 907 sq miles
Smallest country	Nauru	21 sq km	8 sq miles
Largest population	Australia	19 731 000	
Smallest population	Tuvalu	11 000	
Most densely populated country	Nauru	619 per sq km	1 625 per sq mile
Least densely populated country	Australia	3 per sq km	7 per sq mile

DISCOVER MORE

- Economic cooperation in the region www.apecsec.org.sg
- The Pacific Community www.spc.int
- Country profiles www.odci.gov/cia/publications/factbook
- Boundary disputes www-ibru.dur.ac.uk
- Travel advice www.fco.gov.uk
- Oceania travel health guide www.who.int/csr

WATCH OUT!

- New Caledonia, with a population of just over 20 000, has twenty-nine vernacular Melanesian languages, six of which are taught in schools.
- Parts of Papua New Guinea, Vanuatu and the Solomon Islands carry a risk of malaria. Other islands in the south Pacific are malaria-free.
- On Samoa and some other Pacific Islands, Sunday is deemed a quiet day when excessive noise and activity are considered bad manners.

Australia is often regarded as a continent in its own right, but here it is classified as part of the wider continent of Oceania. Australia's western half consists of a low plateau, broken in places by mountain ranges, with few permanent rivers or lakes. The narrow, fertile coastal plain of the east coast is separated from the interior by the Great Dividing Range which includes Mount Kosciuszko, the highest mountain in Australia. The Great Barrier Reef, off the northeast coast, is the largest coral reef in the world.

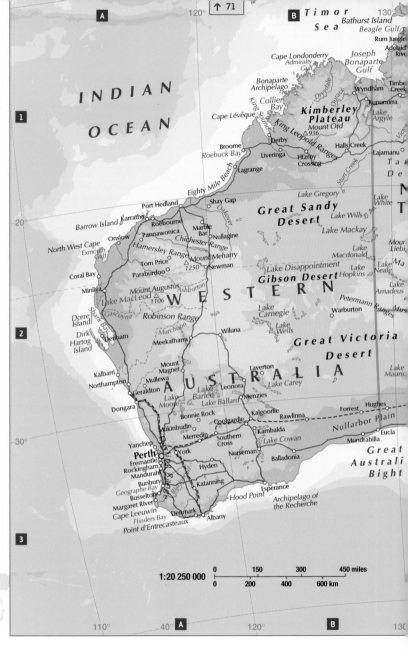

1:20 250 000

OCEANIA   AUSTRALIA

114

Go to →

Map symbols *page 6*
Oceania countries
pages 18–20
Oceania physical
features *page 110*

KNOW THE REGION

• Australia is divided into large states or territories. Western Australia is the biggest, with Queensland second. The island of Tasmania ranks as a state in its own right. The Northern Territory occupies most of the north-central area of the country. The small area around Canberra is designated as the Australian Capital Territory (A.C.T.).

• Large areas of the interior, or outback, are desert. Most of Australia's lakes are impermanent, and their size and outline – and even their existence – may change from year to year owing to climatic changes.

• The longest straight railway line in the world crosses the Nullarbor Plain (meaning treeless), between South Australia and Western Australia.

WATCH OUT!

- Take care if you make the popular ascent of Uluru (Ayers Rock). Apart from upsetting the local Anangu people who consider it a sacred spiritual place, it is very steep, hot and prone to strong winds across the summit.
- Travelling inland is better during the cooler winter months; the desert temperature is less harsh but it is still vital to be well prepared. Check weather and road conditions with the local police or Automobile Association.

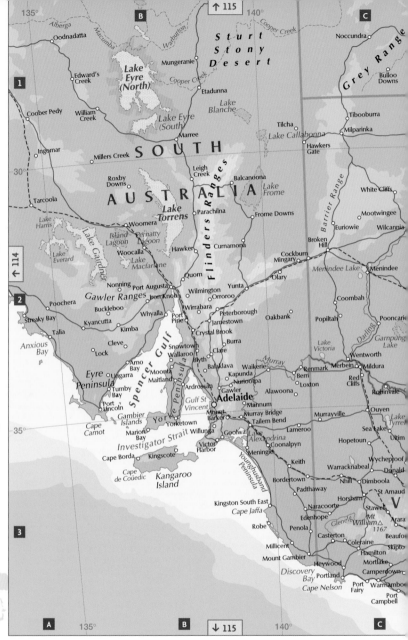

The map shows Australia's most densely populated states, on the southeastern mainland – New South Wales (capital Sydney, the largest city in Australia and in Oceania), and the smaller Victoria (capital Melbourne). All along the eastern coast lies the Great Dividing Range, the highest and most extensive mountain range in Australia with the country's highest point, Mount Kosciuszko. In the northwest the most prominent map features are several major salt lakes, the largest of which is Lake Eyre, divided into two parts whose sizes vary throughout the year and according to rainfall.

Go to →

Map symbols page 6
Oceania countries
pages 18–20
Oceania countries map
page 112

KNOW THE REGION

• Brisbane, the capital of Queensland, lies on the coast almost at the southern boundary of the state – a distance of well over 2 000 kilometres (1 243 miles) from Cape York, the state's northernmost point.

• The Australian Capital Territory, around Canberra, has an offshoot in the Jervis Bay Territory on the coast.

• The straight administrative boundaries on the map indicate the relative emptiness of the interior. Where boundaries are more sinuous they often follow rivers, as between New South Wales and Victoria where the boundary follows the Murray river which, with its tributary the Darling, is the longest river in Australia.

↑ 115
↓ 115

1 : 8 000 000

| 0 | 50 | 100 | 150 miles |

| 0 | 100 | 200 km |

DISCOVER MORE

- Visit Sydney www.sydneyaustralia.com/
- Canberra – Australia's capital www.canberratourism.com.au
- Climbing the Great Dividing Range www.peakbagger.com
- Explore Lake Eyre www.lakeeyrebasin.org.au
- The Murray-Darling river basin www.mdbc.gov.au
- Search for satellite images visibleearth.nasa.gov
- Travel health guide to Australia www.who.int/csr

WATCH OUT!

- Red back and funnel-web are two types of spiders to avoid. Funnel-web spiders, confined to Sydney and its surrounding area, are the most toxic in the world.

- The beaches are inviting but be aware of the red and yellow flags which indicate safe swimming areas. Also beware of the risk of sunburn which poses a more common threat than sharks. Always wear a hat and liberally apply sunscreen.

New Zealand is divided into two main islands, known simply as North Island and South Island, separated by the Cook Strait. The capital, Wellington, is situated on the North Island facing the Cook Strait. Dominating the South Island are the Southern Alps, famous for their scenery, glaciers and notable mountains. North Island is notable for its volcanic activity. Antarctica occupies the area around the South Pole. It has always been uninhabited apart from temporary research staff. The permanent Antarctic ice cap reaches a maximum thickness of over 4 kilometres (2.5 miles).

Go to →

Map symbols *page 6*
Oceania countries
pages 18–20
Oceania physical
features *page 110*

1:8 000 000

° Before its discovery by Europeans, New Zealand had long been populated by Maoris, of Polynesian origin. In recent years there has been an increased trend for Maori place names to be recognized officially. Aoraki (cloud-piercer) is the Maori name for Mount Cook, the country's highest mountain.

° New Zealand has benefited from a tourist boom resulting from J.R.R. Tolkien's *Lord of the Rings*, the films of which were filmed there.

° All territorial claims to parts of Antarctica are suspended, under the Antarctic Treaty of 1959.

° Global warming has recently led to significant reductions in the ice shelves around Antarctica.

KNOW THE REGION

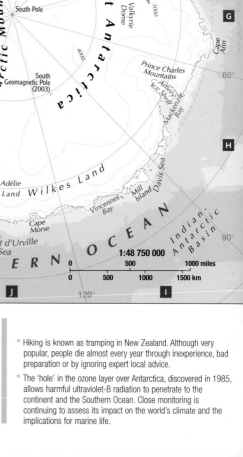

1

O SOUTH AMERICA
Falkland Islands
60°
35°
D
30°
South Georgia
South Sandwich Is.
E
50°

Cape Horn
4
Scotia Sea

Drake Passage
South Orkney Islands
Scotia Ridge
SOUTHERN OCEAN Atlantic-Indian-
American-Antarctic Ridge
0°
90°

South Shetland Is.
3
Antarctic Basin

2
Hicks Bay
Raukumara Range
Hikurangi
1754
Matawai
Gisborne

Graham Land
Larsen Ice Shelf
Weddell Sea
Cape Norvegia
70°
Riiser-Larsen Ice Shelf
Fimbull Ice Shelf

N
Peter I Island
Palmer Land
Alexander Island

120°
Bellingshausen Sea
Abbot Ice Shelf
Ronne Ice Shelf
Berkner Island
Filchner Ice Shelf
Coats Land
Queen Maud Land
Thorshavnheiane
F
Antarctic Circle
30°

Vinson Massif
4897
Ellsworth Mountains
Shackleton Range
80°
Valkyrie Dome
3000
2000

M
Amundsen Ridge
Amundsen Sea
Carney Island
Siple Island
West Antarctica
Marie Byrd Land
Pensacola Mts.
Queen Maud Mts.
South Pole
East Antarctica
1000
Cape Ann
G
60°

Ross Ice Shelf
Roosevelt Island
Mount Erebus 3794
South Geomagnetic Pole (2003)
4000
Prince Charles Mountains
Amery Ice Shelf
Mackenzie Bay

3
Antarctic Circle
150°
Ross Sea
Transantarctic Mountains

L
Victoria Land
George V Land
Adélie Land
Wilkes Land
Vincennes Bay
Mill Island
Davis Sea
H

Balleny Islands
South Magnetic Pole (2003)
Cape Morse
Indian-Antarctic Ridge

45°
180°
Dumont d'Urville Sea
SOUTHERN OCEAN
Indian-Antarctic Basin
90°

4
Campbell Islands
1:48 750 000
0   500   1000 miles
0   500   1000   1500 km

K
150°
J
120°
I

DISCOVER MORE

° Maori culture www.maori.org.nz
° New Zealand's National Parks www.doc.govt.nz
° Climb Aoraki and other mountains www.peakbagger.com
° Explore Wellington www.wellingtonnz.com
° The British Antarctic Survey www.antarctica.ac.uk
° All about Antarctica www.aad.gov.au
° Polar research www.spri.cam.ac.uk

WATCH OUT!

° Hiking is known as tramping in New Zealand. Although very popular, people die almost every year through inexperience, bad preparation or by ignoring expert local advice.

° The 'hole' in the ozone layer over Antarctica, discovered in 1985, allows harmful ultraviolet-B radiation to penetrate to the continent and the Southern Ocean. Close monitoring is continuing to assess its impact on the world's climate and the implications for marine life.

The continent of North America is taken to include Mexico, Central America and the Caribbean. Mexico is physically part of the continent, but since it is Spanish-speaking its cultural and linguistic links connect it closely with South and Central America. The mostly ice-covered island of Greenland – a dependency of Denmark – lies to the northeast. The continent contains a wide range of landscapes, from the Arctic north to sub-tropical Central America, and from the high mountains of the west, to the central Great Plains.

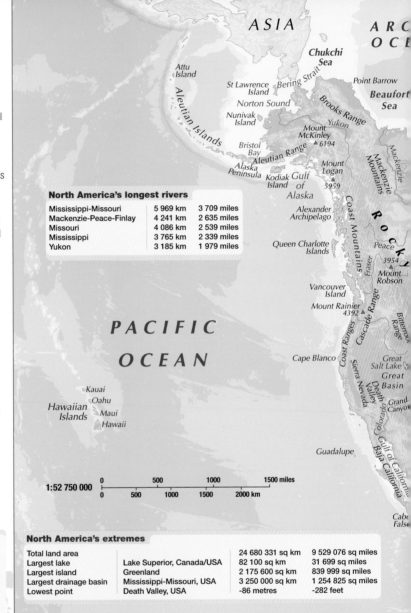

ASIA

ARC
OCE

Chukchi
Sea

Attu
Island

St Lawrence   Bering Strait   Point Barrow
Island   Beaufort
Norton Sound   Brooks Range   Sea
Nunivak   Yukon
Island   Mount
Bristol   McKinley
Bay   ▲ 6194   Mackenzie
                  Mount   Mountains   Mackenzie
Alaska   Aleutian Range Logan
Peninsula Kodiak Gulf   5959
           Island   of   Coast
                    Alaska   Mountains   Rocky
                         Alexander
                         Archipelago   Peace
                                                  3954
Queen Charlotte   Fraser   ▲
        Islands   Mount
                                                 Robson
Vancouver
Island

Mount Rainier   Bitterroot
▲ 4392   Range

PACIFIC   Cape Blanco   Great
                                                   Salt Lake
OCEAN   Great
                                                   Basin
Kauai
Oahu   Grand
Hawaiian   Maui   Canyon
Islands   Hawaii

                                                   Guadalupe

                                                   Cabo
                                                   False

North America's longest rivers

Mississippi-Missouri	5 969 km	3 709 miles
Mackenzie-Peace-Finlay	4 241 km	2 635 miles
Missouri	4 086 km	2 539 miles
Mississippi	3 765 km	2 339 miles
Yukon	3 185 km	1 979 miles

1:52 750 000

0	500	1000	1500 miles
0	500	1000	1500	2000 km

North America's extremes

Total land area		24 680 331 sq km	9 529 076 sq miles
Largest lake	Lake Superior, Canada/USA	82 100 sq km	31 699 sq miles
Largest island	Greenland	2 175 600 sq km	839 999 sq miles
Largest drainage basin	Mississippi-Missouri, USA	3 250 000 sq km	1 254 825 sq miles
Lowest point	Death Valley, USA	-86 metres	-282 feet

Geo terms

French
Île island
Péninsule peninsula

Spanish
Bahía bay
Cabo cape, point
Sierra mountain range
Volcán volcano

Go to →

World physical features
page 26
North America physical
features page 120
North America countries
map page 122

KNOW THE REGION

- The term Rocky Mountains is often applied to the whole mountain zone in the west. This area does, however, include many other significant mountain ranges and extensive plateaus.
- The Aleutian Islands, stretching in an arc across the northern Pacific, are part of Alaska.
- Lake Superior is the world's largest freshwater lake.
- Over 320 000 square kilometres (124 000 square miles) of the USA is protected for conservation purposes.
- The inlet of the Pacific Ocean known as the Gulf of California is entirely within Mexico. The peninsula which defines it is known as Baja California, meaning Lower California.

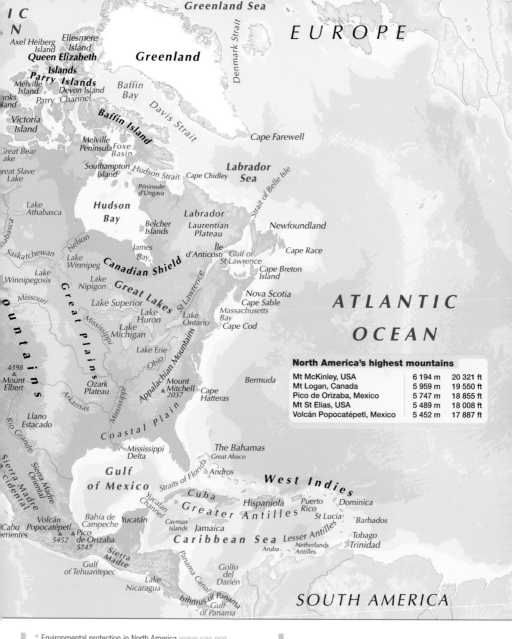

North America's highest mountains		
Mt McKinley, USA	6 194 m	20 321 ft
Mt Logan, Canada	5 959 m	19 550 ft
Pico de Orizaba, Mexico	5 747 m	18 855 ft
Mt St Elias, USA	5 489 m	18 008 ft
Volcán Popocatépetl, Mexico	5 452 m	17 887 ft

The United States of America consists of the states south of the '49th Parallel', plus Hawaii, far out in the Pacific Ocean, and Alaska, the large peninsula in the northwest of the continent. Alaska lies partly within the Arctic Circle, and faces the Russian Federation across the narrow Bering Strait. Canada, formerly a dominion of the UK, occupies the north of the Continent. The region includes numerous overseas territories, from enormous Greenland to tiny islands in the Caribbean Sea.

North America's capitals

Largest capital (population)	Mexico City, Mexico	18 934 000
Smallest capital (population)	Belmopan, Belize	9 000
Most northerly capital	Ottawa, Canada	45° 25'N
Most southerly capital	Panama City, Panama	8° 56'N
Highest capital	Mexico City, Mexico	2 300 metres 7 546 feet

North America's countries

Largest country	Canada	9 984 670 sq km	3 855 103 sq miles
Smallest country	St Kitts and Nevis	261 sq km	101 sq miles
Largest population	United States of America	294 043 000	
Smallest population	St Kitts and Nevis	42 000	
Most densely populated country	Barbados	628 per sq km	1 627 per sq mile
Least densely populated country	Canada	3 per sq km	8 per sq mile

Go to →

North American countries *pages 20–22*
World countries map *page 24*
North America physical features *page 120*

KNOW THE REGION

- St Pierre and Miquelon is a small French dependent territory off the coast of Newfoundland and Labrador.

- The Caribbean Sea is defined as the area between the mainland of South America and the two major island arcs of the Greater Antilles (Cuba, Jamaica, Hispaniola, Puerto Rico) and the Lesser Antilles, which between them form the West Indies.

- Some islands of the West Indies remain as overseas dependencies of France, the Netherlands, the UK and the USA.

- The world's longest single continuous land border stretches for 6 416 kilometres (3 987 miles) between Canada and the USA.

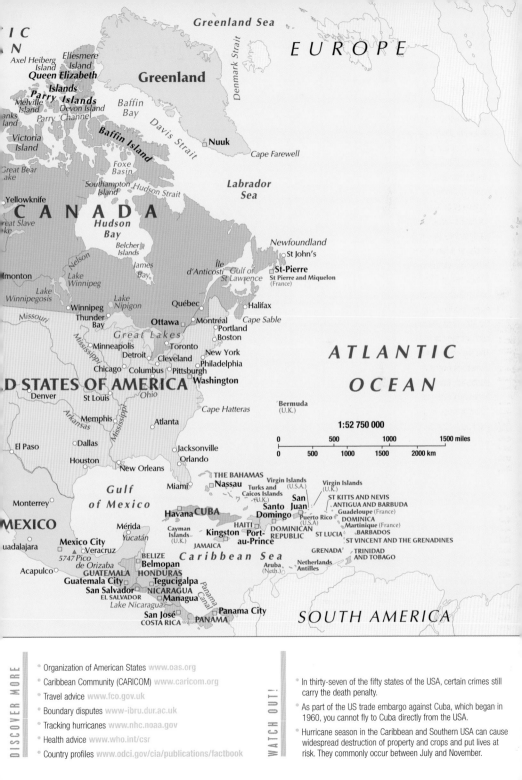

Greenland Sea

EUROPE

IC
AN

Axel Heiberg *Ellesmere*
Island *Island*
Queen Elizabeth
Islands
Parry Islands
Melville *Devon Island*
Island
anks *Parry Channel*
land

Greenland

Baffin
Bay

Denmark Strait

Davis Strait

Victoria
Island

Baffin Island

Nuuk

Cape Farewell

Great Bear
Lake

Foxe
Basin

**Labrador
Sea**

Yellowknife

Southampton *Hudson Strait*
Island

eat Slave
ke

C A N A D A

Hudson
Bay

Belcher
Islands

Newfoundland

St John's

Nelson

James
Bay

Île
d'Anticosti Gulf of
St Lawrence

St-Pierre
St Pierre and Miquelon
(France)

monton

Lake
Winnipeg

Québec

Halifax

Lake
Winnipegosis

Lake
Nipigon

Winnipeg
Thunder
Bay

Ottawa

Montréal
Portland

Cape Sable

Missouri

Great Lakes

Minneapolis
Detroit
Chicago Columbus

Toronto
Cleveland
Pittsburgh

Boston
New York
Philadelphia

A T L A N T I C

O C E A N

D STATES OF AMERICA Washington

Denver

St Louis

Ohio

Bermuda
(U.K.)

1:52 750 000

El Paso

Memphis

Atlanta

Cape Hatteras

0   500   1000   1500 miles

Dallas

Mississippi

Jacksonville

0   500   1000   1500   2000 km

Houston

New Orleans

Orlando

Gulf

Miami

THE BAHAMAS

Monterrey

of Mexico

Nassau

Turks and
Caicos Islands
(U.K.)

Virgin Islands
(U.S.A.)

Virgin Islands
(U.K.)

**San
Juan**

ST KITTS AND NEVIS
ANTIGUA AND BARBUDA

Mérida

Havana CUBA

Cayman
Islands
(U.K.)

**Santo
Domingo**

Puerto Rico
(U.S.A)

Guadeloupe (France)
DOMINICA

uadalajara

Mexico City
5747 Pico
de Orizaba

Veracruz
Yucatán

Kingston

HAITI

**Port-
au-Prince**

**DOMINICAN
REPUBLIC**

Martinique (France)
BARBADOS

ST LUCIA

MEXICO

Acapulco

BELIZE
Belmopan

JAMAICA

Caribbean Sea

GRENADA

ST VINCENT AND THE GRENADINES

TRINIDAD
AND TOBAGO

GUATEMALA HONDURAS
Guatemala City Tegucigalpa
San Salvador NICARAGUA
EL SALVADOR **Managua**
Lake Nicaragua

Netherlands
Antilles

Aruba
(Neth.)

South America

San José
COSTA RICA

Panama Canal

Panama City
PANAMA

SOUTH AMERICA

Canada and Alaska occupy the northern half of North America. The Arctic north consists of a vast group of islands, the largest of which is Baffin Island. Hudson Bay forms a huge inlet in the east, while the west is dominated by major mountain ranges, particularly the Rocky Mountains. Much of the rest is lowland or plateau, dotted by thousands of lakes. Part of the boundary with the USA passes through the Great Lakes, west of which it runs along the 49th parallel.

Geo terms

Danish
Kyst coastal area
French
Île, Îles island, islands
Péninsule peninsula

Go to →

Map symbols *page 6*
Geo terms *page 8*
North America physical features *page 120*

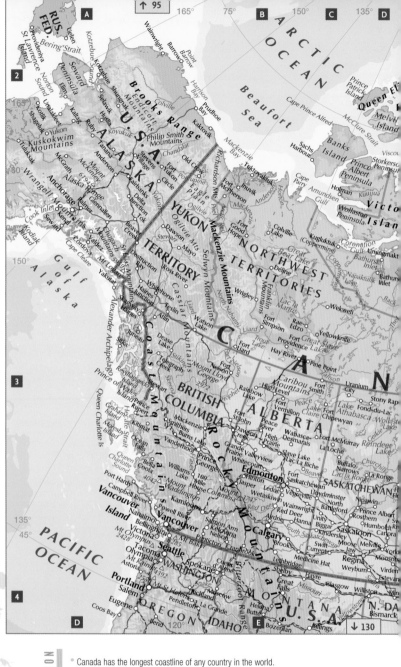

KNOW THE REGION

- Canada has the longest coastline of any country in the world.
- The territory of Nunavut is Canada's newest administrative division, created in 1999 from the eastern part of the Northwest Territories.
- The term Inuit is now used to refer to the Arctic people formerly called Eskimos. An individual is called an Inuk, and the language of the Inuit, with its own special alphabet, is Inuktitut.
- The Canadian province of Québec is largely French-speaking, a legacy of its French ownership in the 18th century.
- The state of Alaska was bought by the USA from Russia in 1867.

DISCOVER MORE

- Visit Alaska state.ak.us
- Canada's natural resources www.nrcan-rncan.gc.ca
- Canada's Provinces and Territories canada.gc.ca/othergov/prov_e.html
- Natural heritage of Canada www.pc.gc.ca

WATCH OUT!

- The Canadian wilderness is a great attraction to hikers and campers but bears are attracted to the smell of food for an easy meal. Don't keep food in your tent or leave it lying around.

- There are about 9 000 forest fires recorded annually in Canada. An average of 2.1 million hectares is burned every year. Lightning accounts for about 85 per cent of the area burned annually – people cause the rest.

Scale 1:24 250 000

0 — 150 — 300 — 450 miles
0 — 300 — 600 km

This map shows the western half of Canada (with the exception of the extreme north), concentrating on the large provinces of British Columbia, Alberta, Saskatchewan and Manitoba. British Columbia includes Vancouver Island and the Queen Charlotte Islands. Manitoba contains numerous lakes, notably lakes Winnipeg and Winnipegosis, while in the Northwest Territories are the Great Slave and Great Bear Lake. The broad chain of the Rocky Mountains dominates the west. In contrast Manitoba, Saskatchewan and eastern Alberta cover the extensive, flat plains known as the Prairies.

Go to →

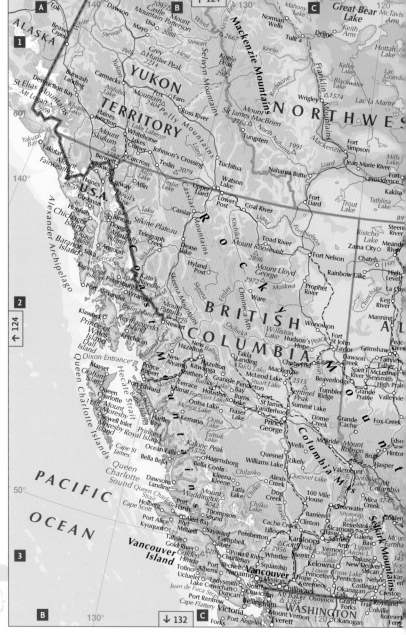

KNOW THE REGION

- The Prairies of Canada and the USA are among the world's most productive agricultural lands, famous for wheat production.

- While Vancouver is the largest city in British Columbia it is not the capital. This is Victoria, which is on Vancouver Island.

- Straight-line boundaries often indicate vast stretches of plain or very sparsely populated territory. The boundaries of Saskatchewan are entirely straight lines which follow lines of latitude and longitude.

- The map highlights the great profusion of lakes in central and western Canada. In the three Prairie provinces alone there are well over 5 000.

1:12 250 000

| 0 | 100 | 200 | 300 miles |
| 0 | 150 | 300 | 450 km |

WATCH OUT!

- Smoking in public buildings such as bars and restaurants is banned in British Columbia.

- Accommodation in and around Calgary is hard to find during the ten days of the Calgary Stampede starting on the second week of July. Plan ahead!

- Watch out at the end of April until mid-May for the thousands of garter snakes that emerge from snake pits in Manitoba to mate. They form huge entwined masses but are not dangerous

The large eastern provinces of Ontario and Québec are the chief focus of this map. Also shown are Newfoundland and Labrador, and the much smaller Nova Scotia, New Brunswick and Prince Edward Island – Canada's Maritime Provinces. Ontario borders the USA along the Great Lakes which form the dominant physical feature of this map and are one of the most prominent features of the whole North American continent. Canada's national capital, Ottawa, is located within Ontario but is on the border with Québec.

Geo terms

French
Île, Îles island, islands
Lac lake
Mont mountain
Rivière river

128

Go to →

Map symbols *page 6*
North America physical features *page 120*
Canada map *page 124*

- French spellings are used throughout Québec. Indian languages and Inuktitut (formerly Eskimo) are also spoken here, particularly in the north.

- The province of Newfoundland and Labrador was officially renamed (from just Newfoundland) in 2001. It has always, however, included the large mainland region of Labrador, adjoining Québec.

- All the islands in Hudson Bay, even those very close against the Québec shore, belong to the northern province of Nunavut (see page 124).

- Nova Scotia means 'New Scotland' in Latin. Scots Gaelic language and culture are still prevalent in some areas of the province.

↑ 125

↓ 137

1:12 250 000

| 0 | | 100 | | 200 | | 300 miles |
| 0 | 150 | | 300 | | 450 km | |

DISCOVER MORE

- Explore Ontario www.ontariotravel.net
- See Canada's capital www.city.ottawa.on.ca
- Québec province www.gouv.qc.ca
- Visit Newfoundland and Labrador www.gov.nf.ca
- Native culture and languages www.native-languages.org
- See the Great Lakes www.on.ec.gc.ca/greatlakes
- Toronto's Tower www.cntower.ca

WATCH OUT!

- In the height of summer and if the weather is good, allow up to two hours queueing to get up the CN Tower in Toronto and another two hours queueing to come back down.
- There is a high risk of collision with moose on some Canadian highways. A collision is twice as likely to happen between dusk and dawn, compared to daytime – moose are obviously difficult to see at night.

This map shows the forty-nine 'contiguous states' of the USA (including District of Columbia). The remaining states are Alaska (see page 124) and Hawaii (see page 122). Squeezing the USA onto a single map like this gives a 'snapshot' of the country and the locations of the individual states. It also shows the extents within the country of some of the world's most notable physical features, from the Rocky Mountains to the Mississippi-Missouri river – together the fourth longest in the world.

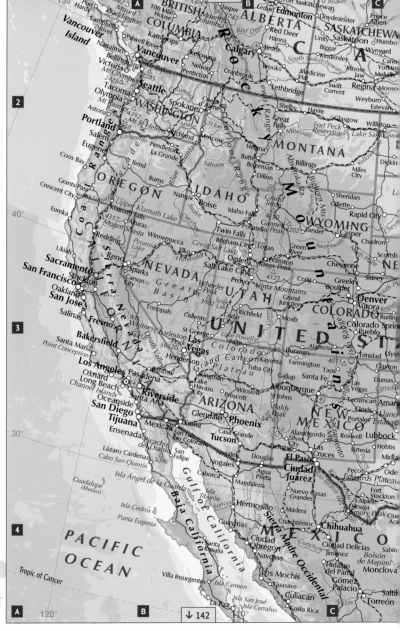

Go to →

Map symbols *page 6*
World time zones
page 34
North America physical
features *page 120*

KNOW THE REGION

- The Great Lakes, all shared with Canada apart from Lake Michigan, include the three biggest lakes in North America. Lake Superior is also the second biggest lake in the world, Lake Huron fourth, and Lake Michigan fifth.

- All the administrative divisions of the USA are designated as States except the area immediately surrounding the national capital, Washington, which is known as the District of Columbia – hence the expression 'Washington, D.C.'.

- Washington is not only the name of the capital, but also of one of the states - on the opposite side of the country, in the far northwest.

↑ 125
↓ 144

1:20 250 000

0   150   300   450 miles
0 200 400 600 km

WATCH OUT!

- The USA has increased security on entering the country. Check visa regulations and at airports, expect more checks and even if you have an onward flight you will have to check in your luggage. Biometric passports are being introduced with digital photos and scans of index fingers.

- There are four, one hour timezones covering the continental USA. Alaska is then one hour beyond Pacific Time and Hawaii-Aleutian Time is a further hour on.

The area of the country covered here is the zone west of the Rocky Mountains, consisting of various mountain ranges separated by extensive plains and plateaus. The most important mountains apart from the Rockies themselves are the Sierra Nevada and the Coast Ranges. One large basin is occupied by the Great Salt Lake, next to which is Salt Lake City. The world famous Grand Canyon lies in the southeast of the map. Death Valley, notorious for its harsh climate lies to its west.

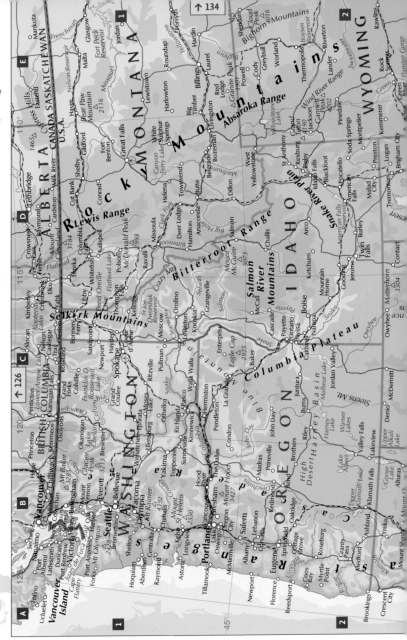

Go to →

Map symbols *page 6*
North America physical
features *page 120*
Pacific Ocean *page 158*

KNOW THE REGION

- California the most populous state of the USA. Its population exceeded 35 million in 2002. Next in rank is Texas, with about 22 million and New York is third with 19 million.

- Spanish place names (such as Los Angeles and San Francisco) derive from early colonial times when Spain controlled large parts of what is now the western USA. The Spanish language is still widely spoken today.

- The huge western extension of the Great Salt Lake is an area of desert which is allowed to flood when the main lake becomes particularly full – known as the Newfoundland Evaporation Basin.

DISCOVER MORE

- Climbing in the Rockies www.peakbagger.com
- About Great Salt Lake ut.water.usgs.gov/greatsaltlake
- Explore the National Parks nps.gov/grca
- Visit California
  gocalif.ca.gov/state/tourism/tour_homepage.jsp
- Viva Las Vegas www.vegasfreedom.com
- Weather in the western United States www.nws.noaa.gov

WATCH OUT!

- Las Vegas can seriously damage your wallet! In the casinos, all gambling apart from poker, is against the house. The best odds are always with the house.

- California's deserts are dangerous places, with extremely hot days and freezing nights. The only water there is what you can carry. However, camping in the winter season is very popular.

- California is not just a sunny place. In 1911 Tamarac recorded the greatest ever depth of snow of 11.5 metres (37 feet). At Mount Shasta Ski Bowl, 4.8 metres (16 feet) of snow fell in a single blizzard in 1959.

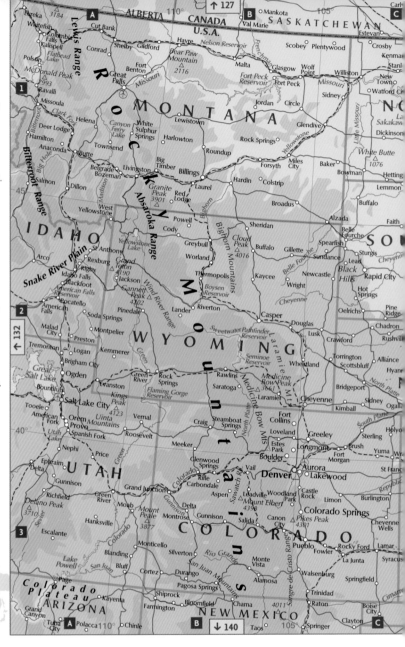

The map focuses on the northern half of the Great Plains – the extensive grassland zone in the centre of the USA, stretching from Canada to Mexico. The plains rise gently from the valleys of the Mississippi and Missouri rivers to the Rocky Mountains. Denver is the only major city in this area, and is located where the mountains begin to give way to the plains. Lake Superior, the highest of the Great Lakes, comes onto the corner of the map area.

134

Go to →

Map symbols *page 6*
North America physical
features *page 120*
United States map
page 130

KNOW THE REGION

• The Mississippi-Missouri is the longest river in North America – at nearly 6 000 km (3 700 miles) – and the fourth longest in the world. (This includes lengthy headstreams which have other names).

• Kansas City is divided by the Missouri river between Kansas and Missouri. By far the larger of the two cities is in Missouri.

• Colorado and Wyoming are the only states of the USA to be bounded entirely by four straight lines.

• The eastern half of this map and the western part of the following map, cover what is known as the American 'Midwest'.

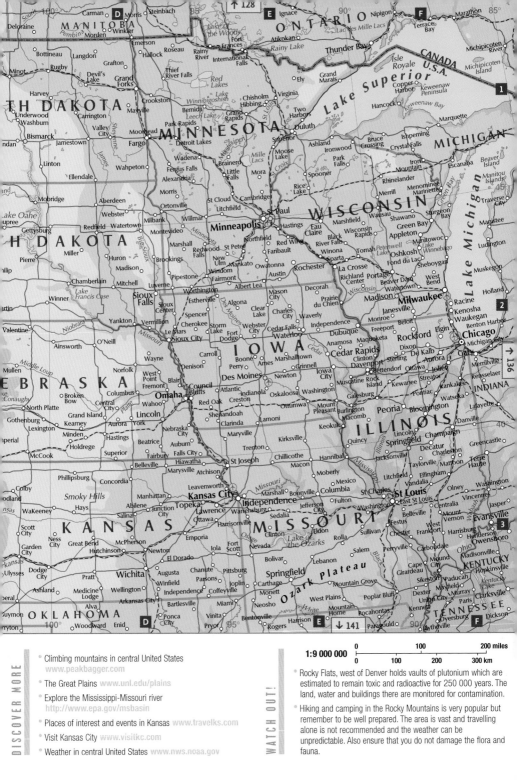

DISCOVER MORE

- Climbing mountains in central United States
  www.peakbagger.com
- The Great Plains www.unl.edu/plains
- Explore the Mississippi-Missouri river
  http://www.epa.gov/msbasin
- Places of interest and events in Kansas www.travelks.com
- Visit Kansas City www.visitkc.com
- Weather in central United States www.nws.noaa.gov

WATCH OUT!

1:9 000 000

| 0 | 100 | 200 miles |

- Rocky Flats, west of Denver holds vaults of plutonium which are estimated to remain toxic and radioactive for 250 000 years. The land, water and buildings there are monitored for contamination.
- Hiking and camping in the Rocky Mountains is very popular but remember to be well prepared. The area is vast and travelling alone is not recommended and the weather can be unpredictable. Also ensure that you do not damage the flora and fauna.

This map brings the densely-populated northeastern USA, along with the important Great Lakes region, into focus. The great cities of the northeast are covered here, from Chicago (on Lake Michigan, in the centre-west) via Detroit (between Lakes Huron and Erie), to Boston, New York, Philadelphia, Baltimore and the capital, Washington, ranged in a line down the east coast. The northeastern part of the map is New England, a region consisting of the states Connecticut, Rhode Island, Massachusetts, Vermont, New Hampshire and Maine.

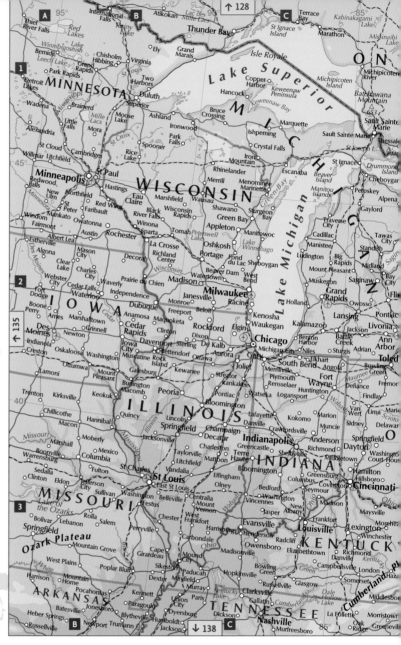

Go to →

Map symbols *page 6*
North America physical
features *page 120*
United States map
page 130

- New York, although the biggest city in the USA, is not the capital of New York state – this is the more central town of Albany.

- The USA's smallest state, Rhode Island, is not an island. The name is a shortening of a historic title which includes the small offshore island of that name.

- Niagara Falls, on the US/Canadian border, is commonly regarded as the second biggest waterfall in the world, by volume of water, after Khone falls on the Mekong river in Asia.

- The term 'Megalopolis' was first used to describe the large, adjoining cities in the northeast USA.

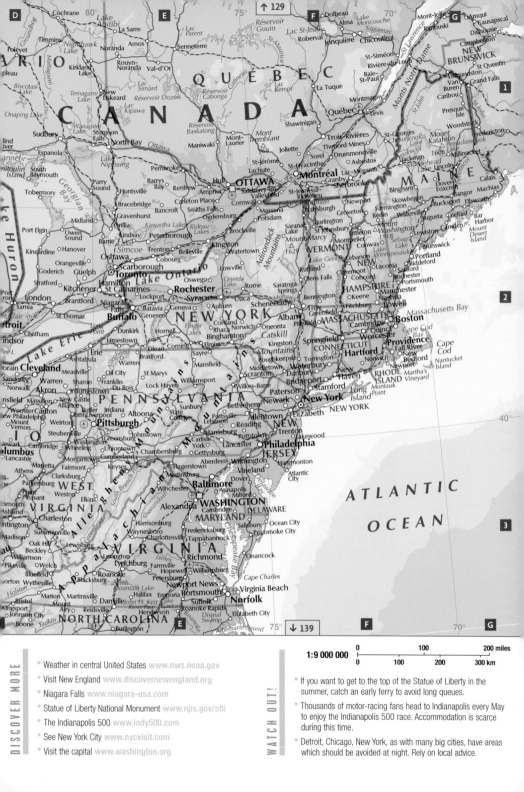

↑ 129

↓ 139

1:9 000 000

| | 0 | 100 | 200 miles |
| | 0 | 100 | 200 | 300 km |

DISCOVER MORE

- Weather in central United States www.nws.noaa.gov
- Visit New England www.discovernewengland.org
- Niagara Falls www.niagara-usa.com
- Statue of Liberty National Monument www.nps.gov/stli
- The Indianapolis 500 www.indy500.com
- See New York City www.nycvisit.com
- Visit the capital www.washington.org

WATCH OUT!

- If you want to get to the top of the Statue of Liberty in the summer, catch an early ferry to avoid long queues.
- Thousands of motor-racing fans head to Indianapolis every May to enjoy the Indianapolis 500 race. Accommodation is scarce during this time.
- Detroit, Chicago, New York, as with many big cities, have areas which should be avoided at night. Rely on local advice.

The map is dominated by the peninsula of Florida, which defines the eastern side of the Gulf of Mexico. Not far offshore, the Bahamas form an independent country which used to be a possession of the United Kingdom. The historic city of New Orleans lies on the delta of the Mississippi river. At the far west side is Houston, famous as the home of NASA space-exploration. The map also shows the southern end of the Appalachians, the main mountain range of the eastern United States.

Go to →

Map symbols *page 6*
North America physical
features *page 120*
Atlantic Ocean
page 160

KNOW THE REGION

- Florida is one of the world's major holiday destinations, most notably the cities of Orlando (of Disney World fame), Miami and West Palm Beach, and the wildlife-rich wetlands known as the Everglades.

- Western Florida is nicknamed the Panhandle because of its shape.

- The Mississippi/Missouri is the longest river system in North America. The lower Mississippi is a classic case of an old river meandering across a wide floodplain.

- The coasts of Florida and North Carolina have long chains of narrow reefs or islands, often referred to as keys or cays.

C Elizabethtown 85 Danville ↑ 137 **D** WEST VIRGINIA 80 Petersburg **E** Cape Charles 75
Madisonville Campbellsville Green Pikeville Welch Blacksburg Roanoke Lynchburg Smith Mountain Lake Newport News Portsmouth Virginia Beach
Hopkinsville Russellville Bowling Green Somerset London Hazard Norton Bluefield Wytheville Marion Bristol Martinsville Danville Halifax Emporia Suffolk Norfolk
Clarksville Glasgow Cumberland Dale Hollow Lake Cookeville Middlesboro La Follette Kingsport Johnson City Mount Airy Reidsville Henderson High Point Chapel Hill Burlington Durham Roanoke Rapids Dismal Swamp Elizabeth City **1**
NNESSEE Nashville Murfreesboro McMinnville Crossville Oak Ridge Knoxville Morristown Morganton Winston-Salem Statesville Raleigh Smithfield Wilson Greenville Washington Pamlico Sound Cape Hatteras 35
Columbia Shelbyville Tullahoma Maryville Waynesville Asheville Hendersonville NORTH CAROLINA Southern Pines Goldsboro Kinston New Bern Morehead City Cape Lookout
wrenceburg Fayetteville Athens Cleveland Murphy Gastonia Gaffney Rock Hill Charlotte Albemarle Fayetteville Whiteville Onslow Bay
Florence Huntsville Chattanooga Dalton Oglethorpe Greenville Chester Lancaster Lumberton Wilmington
ussellville Decatur La Fayette Mount 2037 Spartanburg SOUTH Florence Green Swamp Southport
Hamilton Cullman Fort Payne Rome Gainesville Toccoa Anderson Greenwood Newberry CAROLINA Marion Myrtle Beach Cape Fear
Gadsden Lake Sidney Lanier Elberton Saluda Columbia Sumter Lake City Long Bay
Birmingham Marietta Athens Clark Hill Reservoir Aiken Orangeburg Lake Marion Georgetown Cape Romain
mbus Bessemer Sylacauga La Grange Griffin Milledgeville Waynesboro Barnwell Walterboro Charleston **2**
Tuscaloosa Alexander City Auburn Opelika GEORGIA Swainsboro Beaufort
Selma Tuskegee Phenix City Warner Robins Dublin Statesboro Hilton Head Island
mopolis Montgomery Eufaula Americus Cordele Eastman Savannah
ALABAMA Troy Dawson Albany Tifton Douglas Jesup Hinesville
Monroeville Greenville Ozark Moultrie Waycross Brunswick
kson Andalusia Enterprise Dothan Blakely Bainbridge Okefenokee Swamp Folkston Fernandina Beach
tmore Crestview Marianna Thomasville Valdosta
nsacola Fort Walton Beach Tallahassee Perry Lake City Jacksonville
Panama City Port St Joe Apalachee Bay Cross City FLORIDA Gainesville St Augustine 30
Cape San Blas St George Island Waccasassa Bay Ocala Palatka ATLANTIC
Lake George Daytona Beach
Leesburg Sanford OCEAN
Brooksville Lake Apopka Orlando Titusville Cape Canaveral
Spring Hill Lakeland Winter Haven Melbourne Little Abaco
Clearwater Kissimmee Lake Kissimmee Marsh Harbour
St Petersburg Tampa Bartow Sebring Vero Beach Freeport Grand Bahama Great Abaco **3**
Tampa Bradenton Fort Pierce THE BAHAMAS
Sarasota Arcadia Lake Okeechobee West Palm Beach Berry Islands Eleuthera
Venice Port Charlotte Clewiston Belle Glade Lake Worth Bimini Islands Governor's Harbour
Charlotte Harbor Fort Myers Naples FLORIDA Fort Lauderdale Hollywood Miami Everglades Miami Beach New Providence NASSAU Andros Town Exuma Cays Arthur's Town 25
Cape Sable Homestead Andros Cat Island **4**
Key West Florida Keys Key Largo Marathon Straits of Florida **E**
C 85 **D** ↓ 144 80

1:9 000 000
0 100 200 miles
0 100 200 300 km

DISCOVER MORE

• Visit Florida www.flausa.com
• See the Everglades www.nps.gov/ever
• Guide to New Orleans www.neworleanscvb.com
• Preserving the Mississippi www.fmr.org
• Conservation in the Gulf of Mexico www.gulfmex.or
• Visit Houston www.visithoustontexas.com
• The Bahamas www.bahamas.com

WATCH OUT!

• Look out for jellyfish off the Atlantic coast. Stings can be very sore. The most dangerous is the Portuguese man-of-war whose sting produces a feeling comparable to being stung by a swarm of bees.

• Choose your viewing point early in the day to see the Madi Gras parade in New Orleans. It happens on the day before Ash Wednesday.

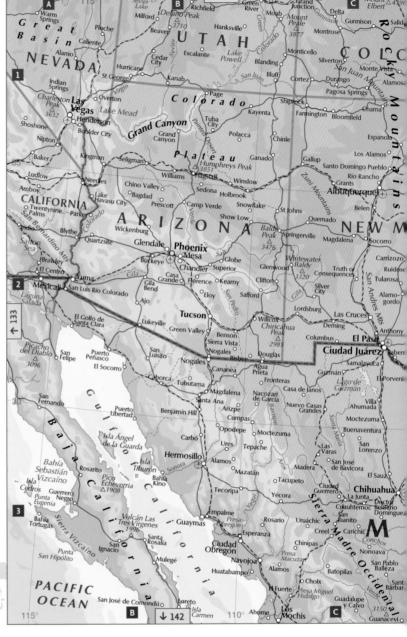

The map shows almost the whole of the border area between Mexico and the USA, including all of Texas, New Mexico, Arizona, and Oklahoma. A large part of the US/Mexico border follows the Rio Grande river. The central area is the southern end of the Great Plains, which extend northwards to the prairies of Canada. The southern end of the Rocky Mountains in New Mexico is also shown. In the west is the Gulf of California – an inlet of the Pacific Ocean.

Go to →

Map symbols page 6
North America physical features page 120
Canada and Alaska page 124

KNOW THE REGION

• Texas is the largest of the USA's contiguous states, but is only 40 per cent of the size of Alaska.

• As in California, there is considerable Spanish influence on this part of the USA resulting from its proximity to Mexico. The cross-border relationship has given rise to a culture and cuisine commonly referred to as Tex-Mex.

• The Grand Canyon, which cuts through the Colorado Plateau in Arizona, is the world's largest and most spectacular canyon, and one of the best-known World Heritage Sites. It was established as a National Park in 1919.

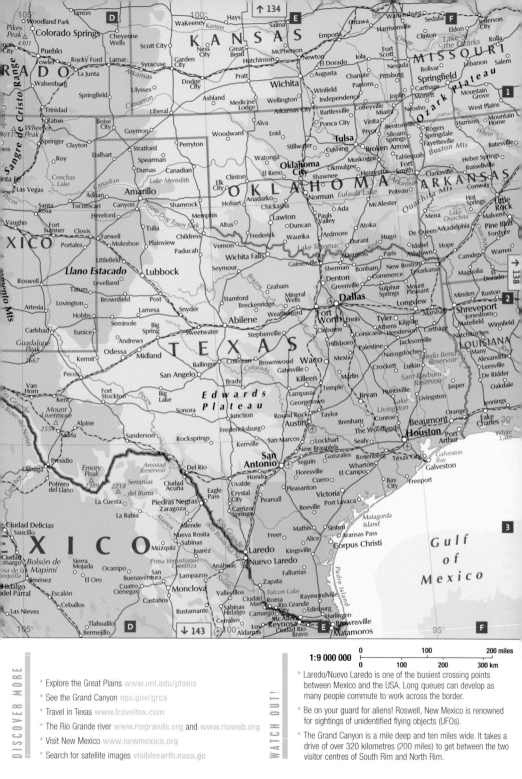

1:9 000 000

0   100   200 miles

0   100   200   300 km

↑ 134

→ 138

→ 2

↓ 143

DISCOVER MORE

- Explore the Great Plains www.unl.edu/plains
- See the Grand Canyon nps.gov/grca
- Travel in Texas www.traveltex.com
- The Rio Grande river www.riogrande.org and www.rioweb.org
- Visit New Mexico www.newmexico.org
- Search for satellite images visibleearth.nasa.go

WATCH OUT!

- Laredo/Nuevo Laredo is one of the busiest crossing points between Mexico and the USA. Long queues can develop as many people commute to work across the border.
- Be on your guard for aliens! Roswell, New Mexico is renowned for sightings of unidentified flying objects (UFOs).
- The Grand Canyon is a mile deep and ten miles wide. It takes a drive of over 320 kilometres (200 miles) to get between the two visitor centres of South Rim and North Rim.

This map covers the whole of Mexico, sandwiched between the USA and Guatemala. It stretches from Tijuana in the far northwest, along the Rio Grande river and the border with the USA, to the Gulf of Mexico, and southeastwards to the narrow isthmus of Central America. The Yucatán is the large peninsula which extends northwards into the Gulf of Mexico, forming the large bay Bahía de Campeche. The Pacific Ocean lies to the west and southwest, with some small isolated islands belonging to Mexico.

Geo terms

Spanish

Bahía bay
Cerro mountain
Isla, Islas island, islands
Laguna lagoon
Presa reservoir
Sierra mountain range
Volcán volcano

142

Go to →

Map symbols *page 6*
Geo terms *page 8*
North American countries *pages 20–22*

KNOW THE REGION

- Mexico was colonized by the Spanish in the 16th century, and gained independence in 1821.

- Mexico City, located in the south-centre of the country, is currently classed as the world's second biggest city, after Tōkyō, with a population of over 19 million.

- Several historic native cultures in Mexico are represented by important archaeological remains, some involving pyramids and evidence of bloodthirsty religious practices – including Chichén Itzá, near Pisté, a major Maya site in the Yucatán peninsula.

- Mexico City was founded on the site of the Aztec city of Tenochtitlán. It is amongst many major world tourist destinations throughout the country.

The map shows the whole chain of islands constituting the West Indies, including all the islands of the Greater and Lesser Antilles, and the countries of mainland Central America. With the southern coast of the USA and the northern coast of South America, these encircle the Caribbean Sea and the Gulf of Mexico – both branches of the Atlantic Ocean. Central America's countries take up the narrow neck of land linking North and South America together via the Isthmus of Panama.

Geo terms

Spanish
Bahía bay
Cayos islands
Golfo gulf, bay
Isla island
Islas islands
Punta cape, point
San, Santa saint

144

Go to →

Map symbols page 6
North American countries pages 20–22
Pacific Ocean page 158

KNOW THE REGION

- Cuba is the largest island in the region. For several decades, it was seen as a security threat to the USA, owing to its extreme proximity and its close alliance with the former Soviet Union.

- The USA maintains a military base on the coast of Cuba, at Guantánamo Bay – well-known in recent years as a detention camp for suspected terrorists.

- Guadeloupe and Martinique are governed as integral parts of France, rather than as dependent overeseas territories in the usual sense.

- The narrowness of Panama has been taken advantage of by the Panama Canal – a vital shipping route opened in 1914.

↓ 150

DISCOVER MORE

- Island countries islands.unep.ch
- The Caribbean Community (CARICOM) www.caricom.org
- Association of Caribbean States http://www.acs-aec.org
- Explore the Panama Canal www.pancanal.com
- Travel advice www.fco.gov.uk
- Caribbean weather forecasts www.metoffice.com/weather/wxpast.html
- Health advice www.who.int/csr

1:16 250 000

0 — 100 — 200 — 300 miles
0 — 200 — 400 km

WATCH OUT!

- Be careful of the souvenirs you buy which could be made illegally from protected animals – watch out particularly for tropical bird feathers, turtle shell and black coral. Trading in such items is banned.
- Robbery from tourists is common in poor countries such as Haiti and Dominican Republic. Care should be taken not to cause offence or flaunt your wealth. Harassment of visitors in these and other Caribbean countries can be an annoyance.

South America stretches from north of the Equator to a point less than 1 000 kilometres (621 miles) away from Antarctica at Cape Horn. The most dominant physical features are the Andes, stretching down the western side, and the enormous Amazon Basin. Vast plains occupy much of the south and southeast – in the Pampas grasslands and the region of Patagonia in southern Argentina. Much of the rest of the continent consists of dissected plateaus, undulating lowlands and lesser mountain ranges.

Geo terms

Portuguese

Chapada hills, uplands

Ilha island

Planalto plateau

Spanish

Cerro mountain

Cordillera mountain range

Isla, Islas Island, islands

Islas islands

Punta cape, point

Go to →

World physical features page 26

World land cover page 30

South America countries map page 148

South America's highest mountains

Cerro Aconcagua, Argentina	6 959 m	22 831 ft
Nevado Ojos del Salado, Argentina/Chile	6 908 m	22 664 ft
Cerro Bonete, Argentina	6 872 m	22 546 ft
Cerro Pissis, Argentina	6 858 m	22 500 ft
Cerro Tupungato, Argentina/Chile	6 800 m	22 211 ft

South America's longest rivers

Amazon	6 516 km	4 049 miles
Río de la Plata-Paraná	4 500 km	2 796 miles
Purus	3 218 km	1 999 miles
Madeira	3 200 km	1 988 miles
São Francisco	2 900 km	1 802 miles

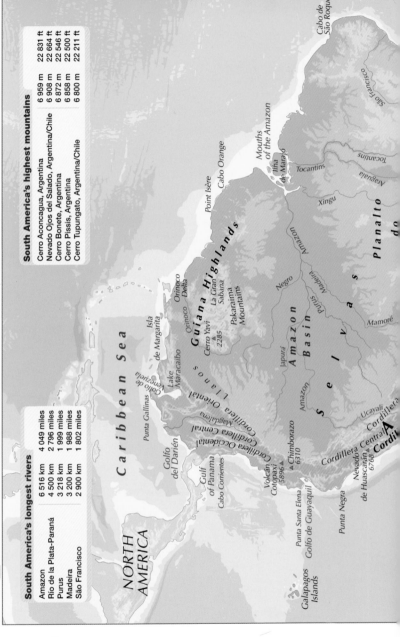

- The Galapagos Islands, made famous by research by Charles Darwin and renowned for its wildlife and biodiversity, are a far-flung part of Ecuador, situated about 750 kilometres (466 miles) out in the Pacific Ocean.

- Cerro Aconcagua, at 6 959 metres (22 832 feet), is the highest point in the western hemisphere.

- South Georgia and the South Sandwich Islands, lying between South America and Antarctica, are collectively a UK dependency, with no permanent population.

- The world's driest desert is the Atacama, where only 1 millimetre of rain may fall as infrequently as once every five to twenty years.

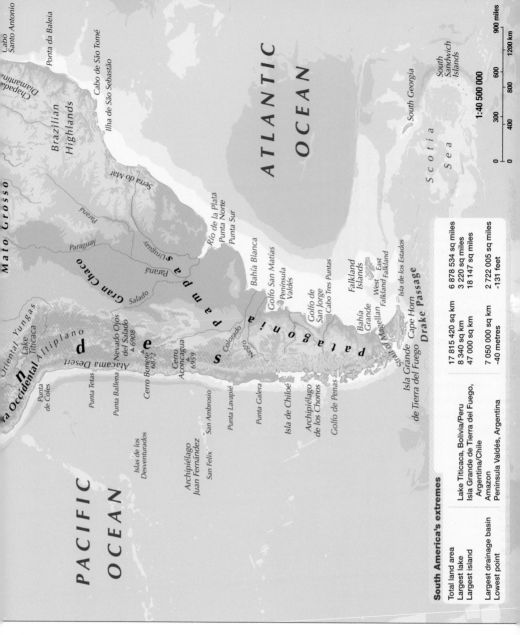

ATLANTIC OCEAN

PACIFIC OCEAN

Scotia Sea

Drake Passage

Cape Horn

South Georgia

South Sandwich Islands

1:40 500 000

| 0 | 300 | 600 | 900 miles |
| 0 | 400 | 800 | 1200 km |

South America's extremes

Total land area		17 815 420 sq km	6 878 534 sq miles
Largest lake	Lake Titicaca, Bolivia/Peru	8 340 sq km	3 220 sq miles
Largest island	Isla Grande de Tierra del Fuego, Argentina/Chile	47 000 sq km	18 147 sq miles
Largest drainage basin	Amazon	7 050 000 sq km	2 722 005 sq miles
Lowest point	Península Valdés, Argentina	-40 metres	-131 feet

Cabo Santo Antonio
Ponta da Baleia
Chapada Diamantina
Brazilian Highlands
Cabo de São Tomé
Ilha de São Sebastião
Mato Grosso
Serra do Mar
Paraná
Gran Chaco
Paraguay
Salado
Paraná
Uruguay
Río de la Plata
Punta Norte
Punta Sur
Bahía Blanca
P a m p a s
Oriental
Yungas
Lake Titicaca
Altiplano
Cordillera Occidental
Atacama Desert
Nevado Ojos del Salado ▲ 6908
Cerro Bonete
Cerro Aconcagua ▲ 6959
▲ 6872
Colorado
Negro
Golfo San Matías
Península Valdés
Golfo de San Jorge
Cabo Tres Puntas
Punta de Coles
Punta Tetas
Punta Ballena
A n d e s
San Ambrosio
Punta Lavapié
Punta Galera
Isla de Chiloé
Archipiélago de los Chonos
Golfo de Penas
P a t a g o n i a
Bahía Grande
Falkland Islands
West Falkland
East Falkland
Isla de los Estados
Strait of Magellan
Isla Grande de Tierra del Fuego
Islas de los Desventurados
Archipiélago Juan Fernández
San Félix

DISCOVER MORE

* Rainforest Information www.rainforestweb.org
* Conservation in South America www.unep-wcmc.or
* South American weather forecasts www.metoffice.com/weather/wxpast.html
* Heritage sites in South America whc.unesco.org
* Climbing the Andes www.peakbagger.com
* Health advice www.cdc.gov/travel
* Search for satellite images visibleearth.nasa.gov

WATCH OUT!

* The Amazon rainforest is thought to be home to about half of the world's species. Damage to the forests and the process of deforestation – South America loses over 37 000 square kilometres (14 286 square miles) of forest each year – put this great diversity at risk. Once forest is cleared it is almost impossible for it to regenerate.

* Travelling in the Andes may bring on altitude sickness at heights above 2 500 metres (8 200 feet). This can result in headaches, sleeplessness, nausea and breathlessness. Ascend slowly to minimize the effects.

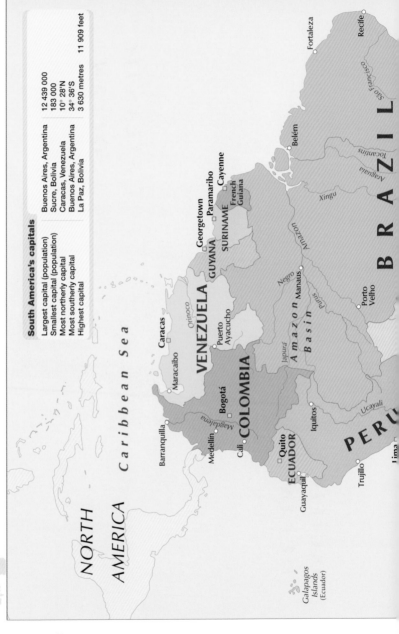

Brazil fills most of the north of the continent, while Argentina is the largest country in the narrower south. Chile consists of a long, narrow strip along the Pacific coast. French Guyana is the only remaining territory under overseas control, on a continent which has a long colonial history. Spanish is the language of the majority of the continent, although Brazil is largely Portuguese-speaking. There has been a steady process of urbanization and the majority of South America's population live in the major cities and close to the coast.

South America's capitals

Largest capital (population)	Buenos Aires, Argentina	12 439 000
Smallest capital (population)	Sucre, Bolivia	183 000
Most northerly capital	Caracas, Venezuela	10° 28'N
Most southerly capital	Buenos Aires, Argentina	34° 36'S
Highest capital	La Paz, Bolivia	3 630 metres 11 909 feet

Go to →

South American countries page 22

World countries map page 24

South America physical features page 146

KNOW THE REGION

* South America is often referred to as Latin America, reflecting the historic influences of Spain and Portugal.

* Bolivia and Paraguay are the only landlocked countries on the continent.

* The Falkland Islands were first settled by the British, although Argentina retains a claim over them and calls them the Malvinas Islands (Islas Malvinas in Spanish). This claim resulted in a war in 1982 between Argentina and the UK.

* The Juan Fernandez Islands (Archipiélago Juan Fernández), a group of Chilean islands in the Pacific, are known for having been the location of the famous 'castaway' novel, Robinson Crusoe.

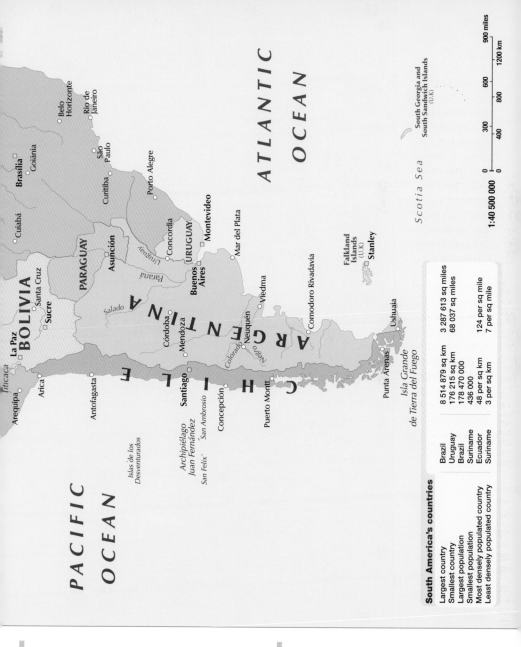

PACIFIC OCEAN

ATLANTIC OCEAN

Scotia Sea

South America's countries

Largest country	Brazil	8 514 879 sq km	3 287 613 sq miles
Smallest country	Uruguay	176 215 sq km	68 037 sq miles
Largest population	Brazil	178 470 000	
Smallest population	Suriname	436 000	
Most densely populated country	Ecuador	48 per sq km	124 per sq mile
Least densely populated country	Suriname	3 per sq km	7 per sq mile

1:40 500 000

0   300   600   900 miles
0   400   800   1200 km

Titicaca · Arequipa · Arica · Antofagasta · Islas de los Desventurados · Archipiélago Juan Fernández · San Félix · San Ambrosio · Concepción · Puerto Montt · Santiago · Mendoza · Córdoba · Salado · Sucre · Santa Cruz · La Paz · BOLIVIA · PARAGUAY · Asunción · Cuiabá · Brasília · Goiânia · Belo Horizonte · Rio de Janeiro · São Paulo · Curitiba · Porto Alegre · Paraná · Uruguay · Concordia · URUGUAY · Montevideo · Mar del Plata · Buenos Aires · Colorado · Negro · Neuquén · Viedma · ARGENTINA · CHILE · Comodoro Rivadavia · Falkland Islands (U.K.) · Stanley · Punta Arenas · Isla Grande de Tierra del Fuego · Ushuaia · South Georgia and South Sandwich Islands (U.K.)

DISCOVER MORE

* Organization of American States www.oas.org
* Learn about Latin American lanic.utexas.edu
* Travel advice www.fco.gov.uk
* Health advice www.who.int/csr
* International boundaries www-ibru.dur.ac.uk
* Place names www.pcgn.org.uk and geonames.usgs.gov
* Country profiles www.odci.gov/cia/publications/factbook

WATCH OUT!

* Colombia, Peru and parts of Brazil have serious problems of robbery and armed robbery. Some parts of Peru are also subject to guerrilla activity. Venezuela and Guyana are also known for attacks on visitors. Always be vigilant, never let go of your possessions unless you are seriously threatened. Check the latest travel advice before you go.
* Do not carry items onto flights for anybody else. Carrying illegal drugs is a serious crime and carries heavy sentences in many South American countries.

This wide, northern section of the continent is dominated by Brazil, the greater part of which consists of the tropical rain forest zone of the Amazon river basin. Ecuador is named after its position straddling the equator. The northern part of Bolivia also comes into the map area, with Lake Titicaca – the largest in South America – featuring prominently on the border with Peru. The sprawling delta of the Amazon, along with the mouth of the nearby river Tocantins, is a notable feature of the northeast coast.

Geo terms

Portuguese
Baía bay
Chapada hills, uplands
Represa reservoir
São, Santa, Santo saint
Serra mountain range

Spanish
Cordillera mountain range
Embalse reservoir

150

Go to →

Map symbols *page 6*
Geo terms *page 8*
Geo tables *page 9*

↑ 145
↑ 144
↓ 152

KNOW THE REGION

- The mountains collectively known as the Andes, contain a number of major active volcanoes, including Cotopaxi and Chimborazo in Ecuador.

- Machu Picchu, located near Cusco in Peru, is one of the world's most famous archaeological sites. It is a former capital of the Inca empire.

- Colombia is a major producer of illegal drugs and the world's largest producer of cocaine.

- Bolivia is named after an anti-colonial fighter of the 19th century, Simón Bolívar.

- Water flow along the Amazon is over 1 500 times that of the River Thames.

ST GEORGE'S
Scarborough
Tobago
Trinidad
San Fernando
TRINIDAD AND TOBAGO

Orinoco Delta

ayana Mabaruma
Callao
Anna Regina
mereng **GEORGETOWN**
Linden New Amsterdam
Nieuw PARAMARIBO
Nickerie St-Laurent-du-Maroni
Mahdia Kourou CAYENNE
Roraima Professor van
2810 Blommestein Meer **French**
A N D S **SURINAME** **Guiana**
Lethem Olapoque
Boa Pontoetoe
Vista Lourenço Calçoene
Nova Paraiso Amapá *Ilha de Maracá*

Represa de Balbina
Trombetas Arere Pau Macapá Porto Santana Mazagão *Cabo Maguarinho*
Oriximiná Óbidos Almeirim Chaves *Baía de Marajó*
Urucara Breves Salinópolis
Manaus Parintins Monte Alegre PorteIO Viseu Bragança
Urucurituba Santarém Portel **Belém** Castanhal
Manacapuru Itacoatiara Altamira Cametá Acará Curuçú Pinheiro **São Luís**
Itaituba Tucuruí Bacabal Viana Parnaíba Camocim
Borba Tapajós Jacunda Itapicuru Luzilândia **Fortaleza**
Novo Maraba Pedreiras Mirim Tianguá Caucaia
Aripuanã Jacareacanga Imperatriz Grajaú Codó Campo Maior Sobral Caucaia
anicoré Tocantinópolis Pres. Dutra Caxias Timon **Teresina** Crateús Quixadá
Araras São Barra Buriti Bravo Palmeiras Aracati
Aripuanã Manuelzinho Félix do Corda Floriano Taua Mossoró Macau Touros
Barra do **Araguaína** Balsas Jerumenha Poti Picos Iguatu **Natal**
São Manuel Porto Franco Oeiras Spusa João
menta Bueno Peixoto de Carolina Canto do Buriti Crato Juàzeiro Pessoa
Azevedo Conceição Paulistana do Norte Olinda
do Araguaia São Raimundo Nonato Floresta Caruaru **Recife**
Vilhena Santa Maria Pedro Caracol Salgueiro Garanhuns **Maceió**
das Barreiras Afonso Petrolina Paulo Arapiraca
menta Bueno **Palmas** São Juàzeiro Afonso Monte Santo
Porto dos Porto Senhor do Bonfim Jacobina Aracaju
Gaúchos Óbidos Diamantino Nacional Xique Feira de Estância
Peixoto de *Ilha do* Dianópolis Corrente Xique Serrinha Santana Alagoinhas
Azevedo *Bananal* Natividade Ibotirama Itaberaba Santo Antônio **Salvador**
Porto São Félix Barreiras Irecê de Jesus
Artur **Diamantino** Bom Jesus Itabuna Ubaitaba
menta Bueno Rosário Oeste da Lapa Brumado Jequié Ilhéus
Porto Barra do Garças Santana Correntina Guanambi Itabuna Una
Esperidião Cáceres Niquelândia Posse Januária Espinosa Vitória Itapetinga
Puerto Cuiabá Formosa Montes da Conquista Itapetinga
Isabel Rondonópolis **BRASÍLIA** Unaí Janaúba Claros Salinas Almenara Porto Seguro
ierto Frey Diamantino Alto Garças Iporá Anápolis Vianópolis Jequitaí Teófilo Alcobaça
Mato Grosso Serra do **Goiânia** Paracatu Otoni
Pontes-e- Caiapó Unaí Patos de
Lacerda Porto Ipameri Itumbiara Minas ↓ 154
Esperidião Jataí **Rio Verde** Paraúna **Araguari**
ados Coxim Rio Verde de Mato Grosso
Izozog Puerto Tucavaca
Isabel

ATLANTIC OCEAN

Equator 0°

B R A Z I L

Pantanal

1:20 250 000

| 0 | 150 | 300 | 450 miles |

| 0 | 200 | 400 | 600 km |

W • The northern tropical areas of South America carry a serious
A risks of malaria and yellow fever. Both are transmitted by
T mosquito. Some countries require travellers to carry a yellow
C fever certificate.
H
  • Angel Falls in Venezuela – the highest in the world – are very
O remote and are not much easier to get to now than in the days
U of James Angel who discovered them in 1937. Visits must be by
T light aircraft or motorised canoe.
!

This map highlights the broad southern section of Brazil, stretching, the continent tapering down through Argentina to Cape Horn, which is in fact on a small island. The map covers the whole of Bolivia; Paraguay (sandwiched between Brazil and Argentina in the great plain known as the Gran Chaco); Chile, along the west coast; Uruguay, a smaller country located on the inlet of the river Plate (Río de la Plata) opposite Buenos Aires; and the UK dependency of the Falkland Islands in the far south.

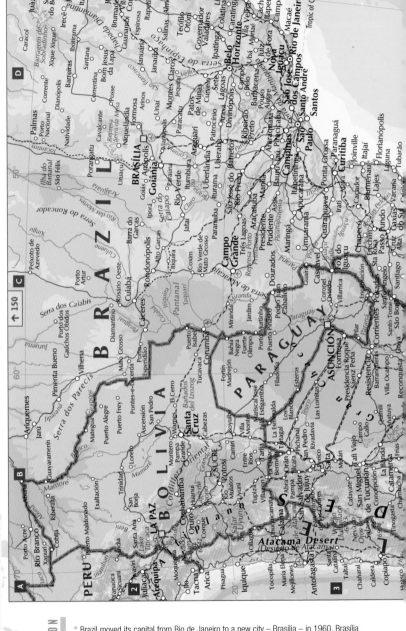

Geo terms

Portuguese
Lagoa lagoon
Represa reservoir
Rio river

Spanish
Estrecho strait
Nevado snow-covered mountain
Salar salt pan
Volcán volcano

152

Go to →

Map symbols *page 6*
Geo terms *page 8*
South American countries *page 22*

KNOW THE REGION

* Brazil moved its capital from Rio de Janeiro to a new city – Brasília – in 1960. Brasília now has a population of over three million.

* Bolivia shares the functions of its national capital between two cities – La Paz and Sucre.

* Cape Horn (Cabo de Hornos in Spanish) was notorious for centuries as a particularly dangerous passage for ocean-going vessels. There is no other land between here and Antarctica.

* Patagonia, the southern part of Argentina, has a long history of Welsh settlement.

* The Pantanal, in western Brazil, is the largest area of wetland in the world.

4 **5** **6**

E

D

C

B

A

South Georgia (U.K.)

Grytviken

Cape Disappointment

450 miles

600 km

0 150 300

0 200 400

1:20 250 000

ATLANTIC

OCEAN

Falkland Islands (U.K.)
STANLEY
East Falkland

West Falkland

Porto Alegre

Mostardas

Lagoa dos Patos

Rio Grande

Pelotas

Lagoa Mirim

Canguçu

Bagé

São Gabriel

Rivera

Tacuarembó

Melo

Florida

Punta del Este

MONTEVIDEO

Rocha

URUGUAY

Río de la Plata

Bahía Samborombón

Mar del Plata

Pinamar

Necochea

Tres Arroyos

Bahía Blanca

Punta Alta

Río Colorado

Viedma

Punta Rasa

Península Valdés

Golfo San Matías

Puerto Madryn

Trelew

Rawson

Cabo Dos Bahías

Golfo de San Jorge

Cabo Tres Puntas

Comodoro Rivadavia

Caleta Olivia

Deseado

Puerto Deseado

Punta Medanosa

Bahía Grande

Río Gallegos

Puerto Santa Cruz

Puerto San Julián

BUENOS AIRES

ARGENTINA

PATAGONIA

Isla de los Estados

Estrecho de Le Maire

Río Grande

Ushuaia

Isla Navarino

Cape Horn

Tierra del Fuego

Punta Arenas

Puerto Natales

Reina Adelaida

Archipiélago de la

Isla Wellington

Isla Campana

Península de Taitao

Golfo de Penas

Chonos

Archipiélago de los

Puerto Aisén

Puerto Montt

Osorno

Valdivia

Temuco

Concepción

Chillán

Los Ángeles

Talca

Curicó

SANTIAGO

Valparaíso

Viña del Mar

Mendoza

San Rafael

Aconcagua 6959

Coquimbo

La Serena

Córdoba

Rosario

Santa Fe

Paraná

CHILE

Isla de Chiloé

Castro

DISCOVER MORE

- Visit Buenos Aires www.bue.gov.ar
- Climb Cerro Aconcagua www.aconcagua.org
- Explore Patagonia www.patagoniaaustral.net
- Heritage sites in South America whc.unesco.org
- Country profiles www.odci.gov/cia/publications/factbook
- Travel advice www.fco.gov.uk
- Search for satellite images visibleearth.nasa.gov

WATCH OUT!

- The Andes are growing in height. Due to tectonic and volcanic activity, the mountain range is gaining height at a rate of 30.5 centimetres (12 inches) every 300 years. They form part of the highly volatile Ring of Fire around the Pacific Ocean. They also contain the Atacama Desert – the driest place on earth.

- Be careful when visiting the Iguaçu Falls which straddle the Argentine-Brazilian border. The falls at their peak are very fast and be aware of pickpockets who commonly target tourists watching the falls.

The map concentrates on the most densely populated part of Brazil which includes the major cities of São Paulo and Rio de Janeiro. The southeast region consists of approximately 11 per cent of Brazil's area but contains over 40 per cent of its population. The interior of the region is characterized by an array of enormous reservoirs, most notably on the Paraná river. Virtually all of the area of the map falls outside the enormous Amazon drainage basin, emphasizing the sheer size of Brazil.

Geo terms

Portuguese

Baía bay
Cabo cape, point
Lago lake
Lagoa lagoon
Ponta cape, point
Represa reservoir
Serra mountain range

154

Go to →

Map symbols *page 6*
Geo terms *page 8*
South America
countries map *page 148*

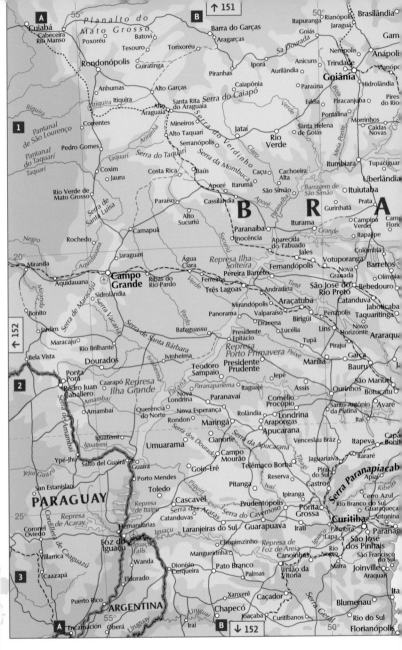

KNOW THE REGION

- São Paulo has a population of over 18 million. It was the first city in South America to exceed the 10 million mark. Rio de Janeiro, the former national capital (before Brasília), has over 11 million inhabitants.

- Numerous large dams lie along the course of the Paraná river. They generate huge amounts of hydro-electricity for the cities of the region.

- Rio de Janeiro is one of the world's most attractive cities, with dramatic hills and bays. Corcovado peak is topped by the famous statue of Christ *Cristo Redentor* which overlooks the wide inlet of Guanabara Bay.

- Guide to Rio www.therioguide.com
- Visit São Paulo anhembi.terra.com.br/turismo/eng
- Lakes in South America
  www.worldlakes.org/searchlakes.asp
- Explore the Pantanal www.parqueregionaldopantanal.org.br
- Travel advice www.fco.gov.uk
- Heritage sites in Brazil whc.unesco.org
- Search for satellite images visibleearth.nasa.gov

WATCH OUT!

1:8 000 000

| 0 | 50 | 100 | 150 miles |
| 0 | 100 | 200 km | |

- Robberies from tourists, often by gangs, is common in Brazil's cities and on Rio de Janeiro's beaches. Look after your possessions and be on your guard at night.
- Rio de Janeiro's Carnaval is a huge attraction in the spring of each year. Prices in the city escalate and accommodation can be difficult to find.

Between them, the world's oceans cover approximately 70 per cent of the earth's surface. The oceans contain 96 per cent of the earth's water and a vast range of flora and fauna. They are a major influence on the world's climate, particularly through ocean currents – the circulation of water within and between the oceans. Our understanding of the oceans has increased enormously over the last twenty years through the development of new technologies, including that of satellite images, which can generate vast amounts of data relating to the sea floor, ocean currents and sea surface temperatures.

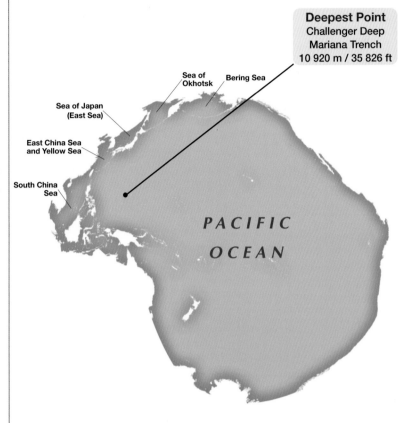

Deepest Point
Challenger Deep
Mariana Trench
10 920 m / 35 826 ft

Sea of Okhotsk

Bering Sea

Sea of Japan (East Sea)

East China Sea and Yellow Sea

South China Sea

PACIFIC OCEAN

Pacific Ocean

	AREA		MAXIMUM DEPTH	
	sq km	sq miles	metres	feet
Extent	166 241 000	64 186 000	10 920	35 826
Bering Sea	2 261 000	873 000	4 150	13 615
Sea of Okhotsk	1 392 000	537 000	3 363	11 033
Sea of Japan (East Sea)	1 013 000	391 000	3 743	12 280
East China Sea and Yellow Sea	1 202 000	464 000	2 717	8 913
South China Sea	2 590 000	1 000 000	5 514	18 090

Go to →

World climate *page 28*
Antarctica *page 119*
World physical features *page 26*

KNOW THE REGION

* Global warming threatens to raise sea level, endangering many low-lying coastal regions. If all of Antarctica's ice melted, world sea level would rise by more than 60 metres (197 feet).

* Approximately three-quarters of waste products and pollutants released into the environment will end up in the sea.

* The Circumpolar current in the Southern Ocean, which stretches around the whole of Antarctica, carries 125 million cubic metres (4 413 million cubic feet) of water per second.

* Ocean currents redistribute enormous amounts of heat around the globe. The northward flow in the Atlantic carries up to 1.4 petawatts of heat – over eighty times the global consumption of energy.

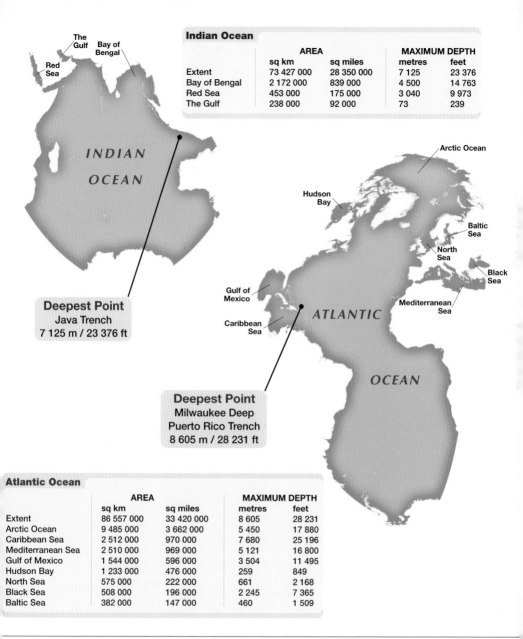

Indian Ocean

	AREA		MAXIMUM DEPTH	
	sq km	sq miles	metres	feet
Extent	73 427 000	28 350 000	7 125	23 376
Bay of Bengal	2 172 000	839 000	4 500	14 763
Red Sea	453 000	175 000	3 040	9 973
The Gulf	238 000	92 000	73	239

The Gulf • Bay of Bengal • Red Sea

INDIAN OCEAN

Arctic Ocean • Hudson Bay • Baltic Sea • North Sea • Black Sea • Mediterranean Sea • Gulf of Mexico • Caribbean Sea

ATLANTIC OCEAN

Deepest Point
Java Trench
7 125 m / 23 376 ft

Deepest Point
Milwaukee Deep
Puerto Rico Trench
8 605 m / 28 231 ft

Atlantic Ocean

	AREA		MAXIMUM DEPTH	
	sq km	sq miles	metres	feet
Extent	86 557 000	33 420 000	8 605	28 231
Arctic Ocean	9 485 000	3 662 000	5 450	17 880
Caribbean Sea	2 512 000	970 000	7 680	25 196
Mediterranean Sea	2 510 000	969 000	5 121	16 800
Gulf of Mexico	1 544 000	596 000	3 504	11 495
Hudson Bay	1 233 000	476 000	259	849
North Sea	575 000	222 000	661	2 168
Black Sea	508 000	196 000	2 245	7 365
Baltic Sea	382 000	147 000	460	1 509

DISCOVER MORE

* Research the oceans www.soc.soton.ac.uk
* Observe the oceans www.noaa.gov
* The world's climate www.wmo.ch
* Ocean exploration sio.ucsd.edu
* Hydrographic charts www.hydro.gov.uk
* Mapping the oceans www.ngdc.noaa.gov/mgg/gebco

WATCH OUT!

* Watch the tides. Tidal range – the difference between high and low tide – varies throughout the oceans, with the greatest range of 21 metres (69 feet) occurring in the Bay of Fundy in Canada.
* Don't get caught in the doldrums! This is the name given to the zone along the equator where two sets of trade winds meet, causing great calms in which sailing boats can be stuck for days on end.

Stretching half way around the globe, the Pacific is the world's largest ocean and contains 45 per cent of the earth's water area. It is larger than the earth's continents combined and contains the earth's deepest point – Challenger Deep in the Mariana Trench. It includes hundreds of islands, including the main Pacific island groups of Polynesia (meaning many islands), Micronesia (small islands) and Melanesia (black islands). The ocean has an enormous effect on the world's climate, as a breeding ground for tropical storms and as the source of the climatic phenomenon El Niño.

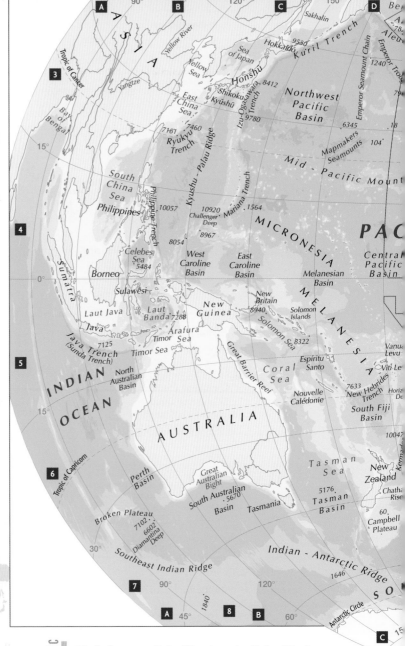

KNOW THE PACIFIC

- The Pacific was named by the 16th-century explorer Ferdinand Magellan after the calm waters he experienced there.

- The Panama Canal, 65 kilometres (40 miles) long and opened in 1914, carries over 12 000 ships each year between the Pacific and Atlantic Oceans. It saves a journey of over 12 000 kilometres (7 457 miles) around the hazardous Cape Horn.

- The Pacific is estimated to contain over 315 million cubic kilometres (76 million cubic miles) of water and has an average depth of over 4 000 metres (13 123 feet).

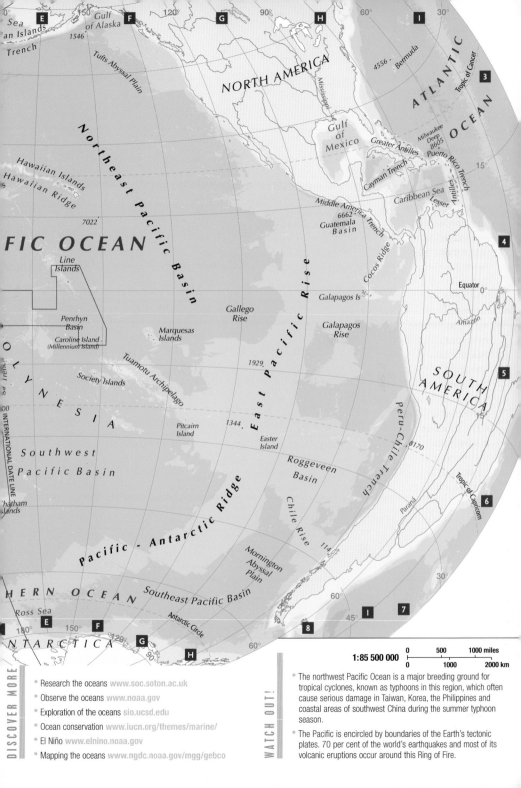

1:85 500 000

WATCH OUT!

• The northwest Pacific Ocean is a major breeding ground for tropical cyclones, known as typhoons in this region, which often cause serious damage in Taiwan, Korea, the Philippines and coastal areas of southwest China during the summer typhoon season.

• The Pacific is encircled by boundaries of the Earth's tectonic plates. 70 per cent of the world's earthquakes and most of its volcanic eruptions occur around this Ring of Fire.

The Atlantic Ocean is the warmest and saltiest of the world's oceans. The Mediterranean Sea, the Gulf of Mexico, the Caribbean Sea and the Arctic Ocean are generally described as parts of the Atlantic. It joins the Indian Ocean, which contains the Arabian Sea, the Bay of Bengal, the Red Sea and The Gulf, south of Cape Agulhas, the southernmost tip of Africa and also through the Suez Canal between the Mediterranean Sea and the Red Sea. Combined together, these two oceans are still smaller than the Pacific.

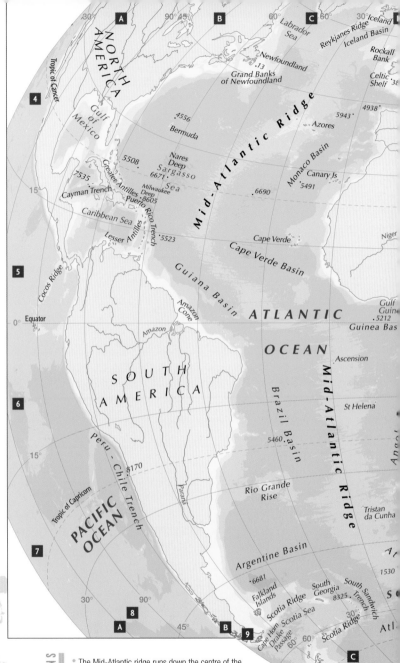

Go to →

World physical features
page 26
Antarctica *page 119*
Ocean features
page 156-157

160

- The Mid-Atlantic ridge runs down the centre of the Atlantic. It marks the boundary between two of the Earth's tectonic plates and is an active volcanic zone which is pulling Europe and America apart at a rate of over 2 centimetres (almost one inch) per year.

- The major tsunami of December 2004 originated just off the coast of Sumatra and travelled the whole width of the Indian Ocean, hitting north Africa over six hours later.

- The North Atlantic Drift is an ocean current originating in the Gulf of Mexico. It carries warm water towards the Arctic Ocean and modifies the climate of northwest Europe.

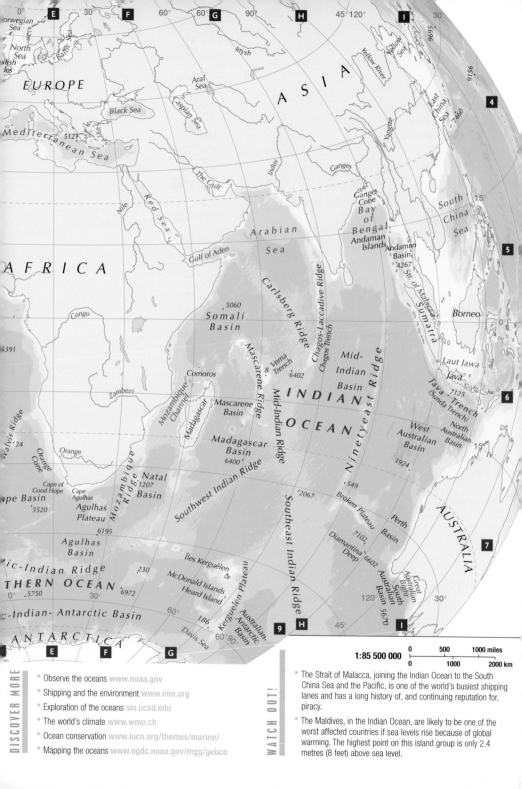

WATCH OUT!

- The Strait of Malacca, joining the Indian Ocean to the South China Sea and the Pacific, is one of the world's busiest shipping lanes and has a long history of, and continuing reputation for, piracy.

- The Maldives, in the Indian Ocean, are likely to be one of the worst affected countries if sea levels rise because of global warming. The highest point on this island group is only 2.4 metres (8 feet) above sea level.

1:85 500 000

0 500 1000 miles

0 1000 2000 km

Lying entirely within the Arctic Circle, a large proportion of the Arctic Ocean is permanently covered in sea ice, which in some places reaches a thickness of over 4 metres (13 feet). It generates up to 50 000 icebergs per year. The ocean is almost landlocked, and is connected to the Pacific Ocean only by the narrow Bering Strait – an important shipping route for Russian merchant ships. It's main connection with the Atlantic Ocean is the Greenland Sea. It is the smallest and shallowest of the oceans, and is often considered to be an extension of the Atlantic Ocean.

162

Go to →

World climate *page 28*
Antarctica *page 119*
World physical features
page 26

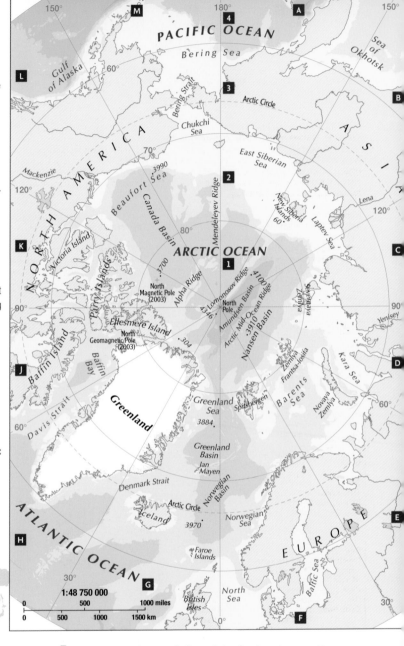

1:48 750 000

KNOW THE ARCTIC

- Sea ice extent varies seasonally. For monitoring of sea ice go to www.nsidc.org
- Many features in the Arctic are named after early explorers, including the Englishman John Davis, the Dutchman Willem Barents, Vitus Bering from Denmark and the Norwegian Fridtjof Nansen.
- The North Pole is believed to have been first visited by the American Robert Peary in 1909. The Magnetic Pole – north on a compass – lies approximately 900 kilometres (560 miles) to the south, towards Canada.
- Because of the number of major rivers flowing into it and its low evaporation rate, the Arctic is the least salty of all the oceans. For details on polar research visit www.spri.cam.ac.uk

INTRODUCTION TO THE INDEX

The index includes all names shown on the reference maps in the atlas. Names are referenced by the left hand page number and by a grid reference. The grid reference relates to the alphanumeric values along the edges of each map which reflect the lines of latitude and longitude. Names are generally referenced to the largest scale map on which they appear. Each entry also includes the country or geographical area in which the feature is located. Where relevant, the index clearly indicates □ if a feature appears on an inset map.

Name forms are as they appear on the maps, with additional alternative names or name forms included as cross-references which refer the user to the entry for the map form of the name. Names beginning with Mc or Mac are alphabetized exactly as they appear. The terms Saint, Sainte, etc, are abbreviated to St, Ste, etc, but alphabetized as if in the full form.

Names of physical features beginning with generic geographical terms are permuted – the descriptive term is placed after the main part of the name. For example, Lake Superior is indexed as Superior, Lake; Mount Everest as Everest, Mount. This policy is applied to all languages.

Entries, other than those for towns and cities, include a descriptor indicating the type of geographical feature. Descriptors are not included where the type of feature is implicit in the name itself.

Administrative divisions are included to differentiate entries of the same name and feature type within the one country. Additional qualifiers are also included for names within selected geographical areas. Selected entries include additional gazetteer-style information. Important geographical facts which relate specifically to the entry are included within the entry.

INDEX ABBREVIATIONS

admin. div.	administrative division	**Ger.**	Germany	**Port.**	Portugal
Afgh.	Afghanistan	**Guat.**	Guatemala	**prov.**	province
Alg.	Algeria	**h.**	hill	**pt.**	point
Arg.	Argentina	**hd**	headland	**r.**	river
Austr.	Australia	**Hond.**	Honduras	**reg.**	region
aut. reg.	autonomous region	**i.**	island	**Rep.**	Republic
aut. rep.	autonomous republic	**imp. l.**	impermanent lake	**resr**	reservoir
		Indon.	Indonesia	**rf**	reef
Azer.	Azerbaijan	**is**	islands	**Rus. Fed.**	Russian Federation
b.	bay	**isth.**	isthmus		
Bangl.	Bangladesh	**Kazakh.**	Kazakhstan	**S.**	South
B.I.O.T.	British Indian Ocean Territory	**Kyrg.**	Kyrgyzstan	**Serb. and Mont.**	Serbia and Montenegro
		l.	lake		
Bol.	Bolivia	**lag.**	lagoon	**str.**	strait
Bos.-Herz.	Bosnia-Herzegovina	**Lith.**	Lithuania	**Switz.**	Switzerland
Bulg.	Bulgaria	**Lux.**	Luxembourg	**Tajik.**	Tajikistan
c.	cape	**Madag.**	Madagascar	**Tanz.**	Tanzania
Can.	Canada	**Maur.**	Mauritania	**terr.**	territory
C.A.R.	Central African Republic	**Mex.**	Mexico	**Thai.**	Thailand
		Moz.	Mozambique	**Trin. and Tob.**	Trinidad and Tobago
Col.	Colombia	**mt.**	mountain		
Czech Rep.	Czech Republic	**mts**	mountains	**Turkm.**	Turkmenistan
Dem. Rep. Congo	Democratic Republic of Congo	**mun.**	municipality	**U.A.E.**	United Arab Emirates
		N.	North		
depr.	depression	**Neth.**	Netherlands	**U.K.**	United Kingdom
des.	desert	**Nic.**	Nicaragua	**Ukr.**	Ukraine
Dom. Rep.	Dominican Republic	**N.Z.**	New Zealand	**Uru.**	Uruguay
		Pak.	Pakistan	**U.S.A.**	United States of America
esc.	escarpment	**Para.**	Paraguay		
est.	estuary	**pen.**	peninsula	**Uzbek.**	Uzbekistan
Eth.	Ethiopia	**Phil.**	Philippines	**val.**	valley
Fin.	Finland	**plat.**	plateau	**Venez.**	Venezuela
for.	forest	**P.N.G.**	Papua New Guinea	**vol.**	volcano
g.	gulf	**Pol.**	Poland		

Aizkraukle Latvia **42** C2
Aizu-wakamatsu Japan **78** C3
Ajaccio France **58** D3
Ajdābiyā Libya **100** E1
Ajmer India **86** B2
Ajo U.S.A. **140** B2
Akbulak Rus. Fed. **40** E3
Akçakale Turkey **92** B2
Akchâr *reg.* Maur. **96**
Akdağmadeni Turkey **92** B2
Åkersberga Sweden **42** A2
Aketi Dem. Rep. Congo **104** C2
Akhalk'alak'i Georgia **40** D4
Akhḍar, Jabal *mts* Oman **90** C2
Akhisar Turkey **64** C3
Akhtubinsk Rus. Fed. **40** D4
Akimiski Island Can. **124** G3
Akita Japan **78** B4
Akjoujt Maur. **100** A3
Akkol' Kazakh. **88** E1
Akmeṇrags *pt* Latvia **42** B2
Akmola Kazakh. *see* Astana
Akobo Sudan **102** B4
Akola India **86** B2
Akordat Eritrea **90** A3
Akpatok Island Can. **124** H2
Akranes Iceland **46**□
Akrathos, Akra *pt* Greece **64** B2
Åkrehamn Norway **48** E2
Akron U.S.A. **136** D2
Aksai Chin *terr.* Asia **86** B1
  Disputed territory (China/India).
Aksaray Turkey **92** B2
Aksay Kazakh. **88** C1
Aksay Rus. Fed. **44** E2
Akşehir Turkey **92** B2
Akshiganak Kazakh. **88** D2
Aksu China **88** F2
Āksum Eth. **90** A3
Aktau Kazakh. **88** C2
Aktobe Kazakh. **88** C1
Aktogay Kazakh. **88** E2
Aktsyabrski Belarus **42** C3
Akure Nigeria **100** C4
Akureyri Iceland **46**□
Akyab Myanmar *see* Sittwe
Alabama *r.* U.S.A. **138** C2
Alabama *state* U.S.A. **138** C2
Alacant Spain *see* Alicante
Alaçatı Turkey **64** C3
Alagir Rus. Fed. **92** C1
Alagoinhas Brazil **150** F4
Alagón Spain **60** C1
Al Aḥmadī Kuwait **90** B2
Alakol', Ozero *salt l.* Kazakh. **88** F2
Alakurtti Rus. Fed. **46** G2
Al 'Alayyah Saudi Arabia **90** B3
Al 'Amādīyah Iraq **92** C2
Al 'Āmirīyah Egypt **92** A2
Alamo U.S.A. **132** C3
Alamogordo U.S.A. **140** C2
Alamos Sonora Mex. **142** A2
Alamos Sonora Mex. **142** B2
Alamos *r.* Mex. **142** B2
Alamosa U.S.A. **134** B3
Åland Islands Fin. **46** D3
Alanya Turkey **92** B2
Al 'Aqabah Jordan **92** B3
Al 'Aqīq Saudi Arabia **90** B2
Alarcón, Embalse de *resr* Spain **60** C2
Al 'Arīsh Egypt **92** B2
Al Arṭāwīyah Saudi Arabia **90** B2
Alas Indon. **72** C2
Alaşehir Turkey **64** C3
Alaska *state* U.S.A. **124** C2
Alaska, Gulf of U.S.A. **124** C3
Alaska Peninsula U.S.A. **120**
Alaska Range *mts* U.S.A. **124** C2
Älät Azer. **92** C1
Alatyr' Rus. Fed. **40** D3
Alausí Ecuador **150** B3

Alavus Fin. **46** E3
Alawoona Austr. **116** C2
Alba Italy **62** A2
Albacete Spain **60** C2
Alba Iulia Romania **44** B2
Albania *country* Europe **64** A2
Albany Austr. **114** A3
Albany *r.* Can. **128** B1
Albany *GA* U.S.A. **138** D2
Albany *NY* U.S.A. **136** F2
  Capital of New York state.
Albany *OR* U.S.A. **132** B2
Albatross Bay Austr. **114** D1
Al Bawīṭī Egypt **102** A2
Al Bayḍā' Libya **100** E1
Al Bayḍā' Yemen **90** B3
Albemarle U.S.A. **138** D1
Albemarle Sound *sea chan.* U.S.A.
  138 E1
Albenga Italy **62** A2
Alberga *watercourse* Austr. **116** B1
Albert France **54** A3
Albert, Lake Dem. Rep. Congo/Uganda
  104 D2
Alberta *prov.* Can. **126** D2
Albert Kanaal *canal* Belgium **54** B2
Albert Lea U.S.A. **134** E2
Albi France **58** C3
Al Bi'r Saudi Arabia **90** A2
Al Birk Saudi Arabia **90** B3
Al Biyāḍh *reg.* Saudi Arabia **90** B2
Alborz, Reshteh-ye *mts* Iran *see*
  Elburz Mountains
Albufeira Port. **60** B2
Albuquerque U.S.A. **140** C1
Al Buraymī Oman **90** C2
Albury Austr. **116** D3
Alcácer do Sal Port. **60** B2
Alcalá de Henares Spain **60** C1
Alcalá la Real Spain **60** C2
Alcamo Italy **62** B3
Alcañiz Spain **60** C1
Alcántara Spain **60** B2
Alcaraz Spain **60** C2
Alcaraz, Sierra de *mts* Spain **60** C2
Alcaudete Spain **60** C2
Alcázar de San Juan Spain **60** C2
Alchevs'k Ukr. **44** E2
Alcobaça Brazil **154** E1
Alcora Spain **60** C1
Alcoy-Alcoi Spain **60** C2
Alcúdia Spain **60** D2
Aldabra Islands Seychelles **102** C5
Aldama Mex. **142** C2
Aldan Rus. Fed. **94** K3
Aldan *r.* Rus. Fed. **94** K2
Alderney *i.* Channel Is **52** B5
Aleg Maur. **100** A3
Alegre Brazil **154** D2
Alegrete Brazil **152** C3
Alekhovshchina Rus. Fed. **42** D1
Aleksandrovsk-Sakhalinskiy Rus. Fed.
  94 L3
Aleksandry, Zemlya *i.* Rus. Fed. **94** F1
Alekseyevka *Belgorodskaya Oblast'*
  Rus. Fed. **44** E1
Alekseyevka *Belgorodskaya Oblast'*
  Rus. Fed. **44** E1
Aleksin Rus. Fed. **42** E3
Aleksinac S.M. **64** B2
Alèmbè Gabon **104** B3
Além Paraíba Brazil **154** D2
Ålen Norway **46** C3
Alençon France **58** C2
Aleppo Syria **92** B2
Alerta Peru **150** B4
Alert Bay Can. **126** C2
Alès France **58** C3
Aleşd Romania **44** B2
Alessandria Italy **62** A2
Ålesund Norway **46** B3

Aleutian Islands U.S.A. **158** E1
Aleutian Range *mts* U.S.A. **120**
Alevina, Mys *c.* Rus. Fed. **94** M3
Alexander Archipelago *is* U.S.A. **126** B2
Alexander Bay S. Africa **108** A2
Alexander City U.S.A. **138** C2
Alexander Island Antarctica **118** N2
Alexandra Austr. **116** D3
Alexandra N.Z. **118** A4
Alexandreia Greece **64** B2
Alexandria Egypt **102** A1
  4th most populous city in Africa.
Alexandria Romania **44** C3
Alexandria S. Africa **108** C3
Alexandria *LA* U.S.A. **138** B2
Alexandria *MN* U.S.A. **134** D1
Alexandria *VA* U.S.A. **136** E3
Alexandrina, Lake Austr. **116** B3
Alexandroupoli Greece **64** C2
Alexis *r.* Can. **128** E1
Alexis Creek Can. **126** C2
Aleysk Rus. Fed. **88** F1
Alfaro Spain **60** C1
Al Fāw Iraq **92** C3
Al Fayyūm Egypt **92** B3
Alfeld (Leine) Ger. **54** D2
Alfenas Brazil **154** C2
Al Fujayrah U.A.E. *see* Fujairah
Algeciras Spain **60** B2
Algemesí Spain **60** C2
Algena Eritrea **90** A3
Alger Alg. *see* Algiers
Algeria *country* Africa **100** C2
  2nd largest country in Africa.
Al Ghaydah Yemen **90** C3
Alghero Italy **62** A2
Al Ghurdaqah Egypt **102** B2
Al Ghwaybiyah Saudi Arabia **90** B2
Algiers Alg. **100** C1
  Capital of Algeria.
Algoa Bay S. Africa **108** C3
Algona U.S.A. **134** E2
Algorta Spain **60** C1
Al Ḥadīthah Iraq **92** C2
Al Ḥajar al Gharbī *mts* Oman **90** C2
Al Ḥamādah al Ḥamrā' *plat.* Libya
  100 D2
Alhama de Murcia Spain **60** C2
Al Ḥammām Egypt **92** A2
Al Ḥanākīyah Saudi Arabia **90** B2
Al Ḥasakah Syria **92** C2
Al Ḥayy Iraq **92** C2
Al Ḥazm al Jawf Yemen **90** B3
Al Ḥibāk *des.* Saudi Arabia **90** C3
Al Ḥillah Saudi Arabia **90** B2
Al Ḥinnāh Saudi Arabia **90** B2
Al Hoceima Morocco **60** C2
Al Ḥudaydah Yemen *see* Hodeidah
Al Ḥufūf Saudi Arabia **90** B2
Al Ḥulayq al Kabīr *hills* Libya **100** D2
'Alīābād Iran **92** D3
Aliağa Turkey **64** C3
Aliakmonas *r.* Greece **64** B2
Alicante Spain **60** C2
Alice U.S.A. **140** E3
Alice, Punta *pt* Italy **62** C3
Alice Springs Austr. **114** C2
Aligarh India **86** B2
Alīgūdarz Iran **92** C2
Alihe China **80** E1
Alima *r.* Congo **104** B3
Aliova *r.* Turkey **64** C3
Ali Sabieh Djibouti **102** C3
Al Iskandarīya Egypt *see* Alexandria
Al Ismā'īlīyah Egypt **102** B1
Aliwal North S. Africa **108** C3
Al Jaghbūb Libya **100** E2
Al Jahrah Kuwait **90** B2
Al Jamalīyah Qatar **90** C2
Al Jawf Libya **100** E2
Al Jawf Saudi Arabia **90** A2

Anabanua Indon. **72** D2
Anabar *r.* Rus. Fed. **94** J2
Anabarskiy Zaliv *b.* Rus. Fed. **94** J2
Anaconda U.S.A. **132** D1
Anadarko U.S.A. **140** E1
Anadolu Dağları *mts* Turkey **92** B1
Anadyr' *r.* Rus. Fed. **94** N2
'Ānah Iraq **92** C2
Anáhuac Mex. **142** B2
Anambas, Kepulauan *is* Indon. **72** B1
Anamosa U.S.A. **134** E2
Anamur Turkey **92** B2
Anan Japan **78** B4
Anantapur India **84** B3
Anantnag India **86** B1
Anan'yiv Ukr. **44** C2
Anapa Rus. Fed. **44** E3
Anápolis Brazil **154** C1
Anatolia *reg.* Turkey **66**
Añatuya Arg. **152** B3
Anbyon N. Korea **76** D2
Ancenis France **58** B2
Anchorage U.S.A. **124** C2
Ancona Italy **62** B2
Ancud Chile **152** A5
Åndalsnes Norway **46** B3
Andalucía *aut. comm.* Spain **60** C2
Andalusia U.S.A. **138** C2
Andaman Islands India **84** D3
Andaman Sea Indian Ocean **74** A2
Andapa Madag. **106**◻ D1
Andelst Neth. **54** B2
Andenes Norway **46** D2
Andenne Belgium **54** B2
Anderlecht Belgium **54** B2
Anderson *r.* Can. **124** D2
Anderson *AK* U.S.A. **124** C2
Anderson *IN* U.S.A. **136** C2
Anderson *SC* U.S.A. **138** D2
Andes *mts* S. America **152** A1
Andijon Uzbek. **88** E2
Andilamena Madag. **106**◻ D1
Andilanatoby Madag. **106**◻ D1
Andizhan Uzbek. *see* Andijon
Andoany Madag. **106**◻ D1
Andong S. Korea **76** D2
Andorra *country* Europe **58** C3
Andorra la Vella Andorra **58** C3
Capital of Andorra.
Andover U.K. **52** C4
Andradina Brazil **154** B2
Andreapol' Rus. Fed. **42** D2
Andrelândia Brazil **154** D1
Andrews U.S.A. **140** D2
Andria Italy **62** C2
Androka Madag. **106**◻ D2
Andros *i.* Bahamas **144** C2
Andros *i.* Greece **64** B3
Andros Town Bahamas **138** E4
Andrott *i.* India **84** B3
Andrushivka Ukr. **44** C1
Andselv Norway **46** D2
Andújar Spain **60** C2
Andulo Angola **106** A1
Anéfis Mali **100** C3
Aneto *mt.* Spain **36**
Aney Niger **100** D3
Angara *r.* Rus. Fed. **94** I3
Part of the Yenisey-Angara-Selenga, 3rd longest in Asia.
Angarsk Rus. Fed. **80** C1
Ånge Sweden **46** D3
Ángel de la Guarda, Isla *i.* Mex. **142** A2
Angeles Phil. **76** B2
Ängelholm Sweden **46** C4
Angel, Salto *waterfall* Venez. **
Highest waterfall in the world.*
Ångermanälven *r.* Sweden **46** D3
Angermünde Ger. **54** G1
Angers France **58** B2
Angikuni Lake Can. **126** F1

Anglesey *i.* U.K. **52** A3
Angoche Moz. **106** C1
Angohrān Iran **90** C2
Angola *country* Africa **104** B4
Angola U.S.A. **136** D2
Angoon U.S.A. **126** B2
Angoulême France **58** C2
Angren Uzbek. **88** E2
Anguilla *terr.* West Indies **144** D3
United Kingdom Overseas Territory.
Angul India **86** C2
Anholt *i.* Denmark **46** C4
Anhua China **82** B3
Anhui *prov.* China **82** B2
Anhumas Brazil **154** B1
Anicuns Brazil **154** C1
Aniva, Mys *c.* Rus. Fed. **78** D1
Aniva, Zaliv *b.* Rus. Fed. **78** D1
Anjü N. Korea **76** D2
Ankang China **82** A2
Ankara Turkey **40** C5
Capital of Turkey.
Anlu China **82** B2
Anna Rus. Fed. **42** F3
Annaba Alg. **100** C1
Annaberg-Buchholtz Ger. **54** F2
An Nafūd *des.* Saudi Arabia **90** B2
An Najaf Iraq **92** C2
Annan U.K. **50** C3
Annapolis U.S.A. **136** E3
Capital of Maryland.
Annapurna I *mt.* Nepal **86** C2
Ann Arbor U.S.A. **136** D2
Anna Regina Guyana **150** D2
An Nāşirīyah Iraq **92** C2
Annecy France **58** D2
An Nimāş Saudi Arabia **90** B3
Anning China **74** B1
Anniston U.S.A. **138** C2
Annonay France **58** C2
An Nu'ayrīyah Saudi Arabia **90** B2
Anorontany, Tanjona *hd* Madag. **106**◻ D1
Ano Viannos Greece **64** C3
Anpu China **82** B3
Anqing China **82** B2
Ansan S. Korea **76** D2
Ansbach Ger. **54** E3
Anshan China **82** C1
Anshun China **82** A3
An Sirhān, Wādī *watercourse*
Saudi Arabia **90** A1
Ansongo Mali **100** C3
Antabamba Peru **150** B4
Antakya Turkey **92** B2
Antalaha Madag. **106**◻ E1
Antalya Turkey **92** B2
Antalya Körfezi *g.* Turkey **92** B2
Antananarivo Madag. **106**◻ D1
Capital of Madagascar.
Antarctica **118**
Most southerly and coldest continent, and the continent with the highest average elevation.
Antarctic Peninsula Antarctica **118** N3
An Teallach *mt.* U.K. **50** B2
Antequera Spain **60** C2
Anthony U.S.A. **140** C2
Anti Atlas *mts* Morocco **100** B2
Antibes France **58** D3
Anticosti, Île d' *i.* Can. **128** D2
Antigonish Can. **128** D2
Antigua *i.* Antigua **144** D3
Antigua and Barbuda *country*
West Indies **144** D3
Antiguo-Morelos Mex. **142** C2
Antikythira *i.* Greece **64** B3
Antipodes Islands N.Z. **110**
Antofagasta Chile **152** A3
Antonina Brazil **154** C3
Antrim U.K. **50** G1
Antrim Hills U.K. **50** G1

Antsalova Madag. **106**◻ D1
Antsirabe Madag. **106**◻ D1
Antsirañana Madag. **106**◻ D1
Antsohihy Madag. **106**◻ D1
Antwerp Belgium **54** B2
Anupgarh India **86** B2
Anuradhapura Sri Lanka **84** C4
Anxi China **80** C2
Anyang China **82** B2
Anzio Italy **62** E2
Aomori Japan **78** D2
Aosta Italy **62** A1
Aoukâr *reg.* Mali/Maur. **96**
Apalachee Bay U.S.A. **138** D3
Apaporis *r.* Col. **150** C3
Aparecida do Tabuado Brazil **154** B2
Aparri Phil. **76** B2
Apatity Rus. Fed. **40** C2
Apatzingán Mex. **142** B3
Apeldoorn Neth. **54** B1
Apen Ger. **54** C1
Apennines *mts* Italy **62** A2
Apia Samoa **112**
Capital of Samoa.
Apiaí Brazil **154** C2
Apo, Mount *vol.* Phil. **76** B3
Apolda Ger. **54** E2
Apollo Bay Austr. **116** C3
Apopka, Lake U.S.A. **138** D3
Aporé Brazil **154** B1
Aporé *r.* Brazil **154** B1
Apostolos Andreas, Cape Cyprus **92** B2
Appalachian Mountains U.S.A. **130** E3
Appin Austr. **116** E2
Appleton U.S.A. **136** C2
Aprilia Italy **62** E2
Apsheronsk Rus. Fed. **44** E3
Apucarana Brazil **154** B2
Apucarana, Serra da *hills* Brazil **154** B2
Aqaba, Gulf of Asia **90** A2
Aqqikkol Hu *salt l.* China **86** C1
Aquidauana Brazil **154** A2
Aquidauana *r.* Brazil **154** A1
Ara India **86** C2
Arab, Bahr el *watercourse* Sudan **102** A4
Arabian Peninsula Asia **102** C5
Arabian Sea Indian Ocean **160** G4
Aracaju Brazil **150** F4
Aracati Brazil **150** F3
Araçatuba Brazil **154** B2
Aracruz Brazil **154** D1
Araçuaí Brazil **154** D1
Arad Romania **44** B2
Arada Chad **100** E3
Arafura Sea Austr./Indon. **70** C3
Aragarças Brazil **154** B1
Aragón *r.* Spain **60** C1
Araguaia *r.* Brazil **150** E3
Araguaína Brazil **150** E3
Araguari Brazil **154** C1
Arai Japan **78** C3
Arak Alg. **100** C2
Arāk Iran **92** C2
Arakan Yoma *mts* Myanmar **74** A1
Arak's *r.* Armenia **92** C1
Aral Sea *salt l.* Kazakh./Uzbek. **88** D2
2nd largest lake in Asia, and 6th in the world.
Aral'sk Kazakh. **88** D2
Aranda de Duero Spain **60** C1
Arandelovac S.M. **62** I2
Aran Islands Rep. of Ireland **50** F2
Aranjuez Spain **60** C1
Aranos Namibia **108** A1
Aransas Pass U.S.A. **140** E3
Arao Japan **78** B4
Araouane Mali **100** C3
Arapiraca Brazil **150** F3
Arapongas Brazil **154** B2
Araquari Brazil **154** C3

Atacama Desert Chile 152 B3
Driest place in the world.
Atakpamé Togo 100 C4
Atalanti Greece 64 B3
Atalaya Peru 150 B4
Atamyrat Turkm. 88 D3
'Ataq Yemen 90 B3
Atâr Maur. 100 A2
Atascadero U.S.A. 132 B3
Atasu Kazakh. 88 E2
Atbara Sudan 102 B3
Atbara r. Sudan 102 B3
Atbasar Kazakh. 88 D1
Atchison U.S.A. 134 D3
Aterno r. Italy 62 B2
Atessa Italy 62 B2
Ath Belgium 54 A2
Athabasca Can. 126 D2
Athabasca r. Can. 126 D2
Athabasca, Lake Can. 126 E2
Athens Greece 64 B3
Capital of Greece.
Athens GA U.S.A. 138 D2
Athens OH U.S.A. 136 D3
Athens TN U.S.A. 138 D1
Athens TX U.S.A. 140 E2
Athies France 54 A3
Athina Greece see Athens
Athlone Rep. of Ireland 50 G2
Athos mt. Greece 64 B2
Athy Rep. of Ireland 50 G2
Ati Chad 100 D3
Atikokan Can. 128 A2
Atiu i. Cook Is 110
Atkarsk Rus. Fed. 40 D3
Atlanta U.S.A. 138 D2
Capital of Georgia.
Atlantic U.S.A. 134 D2
Atlantic City U.S.A. 136 F3
Atlantic Ocean 160
2nd largest ocean in the world.
Atlantis S. Africa 108 A3
Atlas Mountains Africa 100 B1
Atlas Saharien mts Alg. 100 C1
Atlin Can. 126 B2
Atlin Lake Can. 126 B2
Atmore U.S.A. 138 C2
Atoka U.S.A. 140 E2
Atrai r. India 86 C2
Aṭ Ṭā'if Saudi Arabia 90 B2
Attapu Laos 74 B2
Attavyros mt. Greece 64 C3
Attawapiskat Can. 128 B1
Attawapiskat r. Can. 128 B1
Attawapiskat Lake Can. 128 B1
Attendorn Ger. 54 C2
Aṭ Ṭūr Egypt 102 B2
At Turbah Yemen 90 B3
Atyrau Kazakh. 88 D2
Aubenas France 58 C3
Auboué France 54 B3
Auburn AL U.S.A. 138 C2
Auburn CA U.S.A. 132 B3
Auburn NE U.S.A. 134 D2
Auburn NY U.S.A. 136 E2
Aubusson France 58 C2
Auch France 58 C3
Auckland N.Z. 118 B2
5th most populous city in Oceania.
Auckland Islands N.Z. 110
Audo Range mts Eth. 104 E2
Aue Ger. 54 F2
Augsburg Ger. 56 C3
Augusta Italy 62 C3
Augusta GA U.S.A. 138 D2
Augusta KS U.S.A. 134 D3
Augusta ME U.S.A. 136 G2
Capital of Maine.
Augustus, Mount Austr. 114 A2
Aulnoye-Aymeries France 54 A2

Auob watercourse Namibia/S. Africa
108 B2
Aurangabad India 86 B3
Aurich Ger. 54 C1
Aurilândia Brazil 154 B1
Aurillac France 58 C3
Aurora CO U.S.A. 134 C3
Aurora IL U.S.A. 136 C2
Aurora NE U.S.A. 134 D2
Aus Namibia 108 A2
Austin MN U.S.A. 134 E2
Austin NV U.S.A. 132 C3
Austin TX U.S.A. 140 E2
Capital of Texas.
Australes, Îles is Fr. Polynesia see
Tubuai Islands
Australia country Oceania 114
Largest and most populous country in
Oceania, and 6th largest in the world.
Australian Capital Territory admin. div.
Austr. 116 D3
Austria country Europe 56 C3
Autlán Mex. 142 B3
Autun France 58 C2
Auxerre France 58 C2
Auxonne France 58 D2
Avallon France 58 C2
Avalon Peninsula Can. 128 E2
Avaré Brazil 154 C2
Avarua Cook Is 112
Capital of the Cook Islands, on Rarotonga.
Avdiyivka Ukr. 44 E2
Aveiro Port. 60 B1
Avellino Italy 62 B2
Avesnes-sur-Helpe France 54 A2
Avesta Sweden 46 D3
Avezzano Italy 62 B2
Aviemore U.K. 50 C2
Avignon France 58 C3
Ávila Spain 60 C1
Avilés Spain 60 B1
Avola Italy 62 C3
Avon r. England U.K. 52 B3
Avon r. England U.K. 52 C4
Avranches France 58 B2
Awanui N.Z. 118 B2
Âwash Eth. 102 C4
Âwash r. Eth. 102 C3
Awbārī Libya 100 D2
Aw Dheegle Somalia 102 C4
Awe, Loch l. U.K. 50 B2
Aweil Sudan 102 A4
Awka Nigeria 100 A2
Axel Heiberg Island Can. 124 F1
Axim Ghana 100 B4
Ay France 54 B3
Ayacucho Peru 150 B4
Ayagoz Kazakh. 88 F2
Ayakkum Hu salt l. China 80 B2
Ayamonte Spain 60 B2
Ayan Rus. Fed. 94 L3
Ayaviri Peru 150 B4
Âybak Afgh. 86 A1
Aybas Kazakh. 88 B2
Aydar r. Ukr. 44 E2
Aydarko'l ko'li l. Uzbek. 88 D2
Aydın Turkey 64 C3
Ayeat, Gora h. Kazakh. 88 D2
Ayers Rock h. Austr. see Uluṟu
Aylesbury U.K. 52 C4
Ayllón Spain 60 C1
Aylmer Lake Can. 126 E1
Ayod Sudan 102 B4
Ayon, Ostrov i. Rus. Fed. 94 N2
'Ayoûn el 'Atroûs Maur. 100 B3
Ayr Austr. 114 D1
Ayr U.K. 50 B3
Ayre, Point of pt Isle of Man 52 A2
Ayteke Bi Kazakh. 88 D2
Aytos Bulg. 64 C2
Ayutla Mex. 142 C3

Ayutthaya Thai. 74 B2
Ayvacık Turkey 64 C3
Ayvalık Turkey 64 C3
Azaouagh, Vallée de watercourse
Mali/Niger 100 C3
Azerbaijan country Asia 92 C1
Azopol'ye Rus. Fed. 40 D2
Azores aut. reg. Port. 38
Autonomous Region of Portugal.
Azov Rus. Fed. 44 E2
Azov, Sea of Rus. Fed./Ukr. 44 E2
Azraq, Bahr el r. Eth./Sudan see
Blue Nile
Azuaga Spain 60 D2
Azuero, Península de pen. Panama
144 B4
Azul Arg. 152 C4
Az Zaqāzīq Egypt 92 B2
Az Zarqā' Jordan 92 B2
Az Zaydīyah Yemen 90 B3
Azzel Matti, Sebkha salt pan Alg. 100 C2
Az Zilfī Saudi Arabia 90 B2
Az Zuqur i. Yemen 90 B3

B

Baardheere Somalia 102 C4
Bābā, Kūh-e mts Afgh. 86 A1
Babadag Romania 44 C3
Babaeski Turkey 64 C2
Bāb al Mandab str. Africa/Asia 90 B3
Babana Indon. 72 C2
Babar i. Indon. 70 C3
Babati Tanz. 104 D3
Babayevo Rus. Fed. 42 E2
Babine r. Can. 126 C2
Babine Lake Can. 126 C2
Babo Indon. 70 C3
Bābol Iran 92 D2
Baboon Point pt S. Africa 108 A3
Babruysk Belarus 42 C3
Babuyan i. Phil. 76 B2
Babuyan Islands Phil. 76 B2
Bacabal Brazil 150 E3
Bacan i. Indon. 70 C3
Bacău Romania 44 C2
Bacchus Marsh Austr. 116 C3
Bachu China 88 E3
Back r. Can. 126 F1
Bačka Palanka S.M. 64 A1
Bac Lac Vietnam 74 B1
Bac Liêu Vietnam 74 B3
Bacolod Phil. 76 B2
Bacqueville, Lac l. Can. 128 C1
Badajoz Spain 60 B2
Badarpur India 74 A1
Bad Berka Ger. 54 D2
Bad Berleburg Ger. 54 D2
Bad Bevensen Ger. 54 E1
Bad Ems Ger. 54 C2
Baden Austria 56 D3
Baden-Baden Ger. 56 B3
Bad Freienwalde Ger. 54 G1
Bad Harzburg Ger. 54 E2
Bad Hersfeld Ger. 54 D2
Bad Hofgastein Austria 56 C3
Bad Homburg vor der Höhe Ger. 54 D2
Badin Pak. 86 A2
Bad Ischl Austria 58 E2
Bādiyat ash Shām des. Asia see
Syrian Desert
Bad Kissingen Ger. 54 E2
Bad Kreuznach Ger. 54 C3
Bad Lauterberg im Harz Ger. 54 E2
Bad Liebenwerda Ger. 54 F2
Bad Lippspringe Ger. 54 D2
Bad Mergentheim Ger. 54 D3
Bad Nauheim Ger. 54 D2
Bad Neuenahr-Ahrweiler Ger. 54 C2
Bad Neustadt an der Saale Ger. 54 E2

Bangor U.S.A. **136** G2
Bang Saphan Yai Thai. **74** A2
Bangued Phil. **76** B2
Bangui C.A.R. **104** B2
Capital of the Central African Republic.
Bangweulu, Lake Zambia **106** B1
Ban Huai Khon Thai. **74** B2
Banī Mazār Egypt **92** B3
Banī Suwayf Egypt **102** B2
Banī Walīd Libya **100** D1
Bāniyās Syria **92** B2
Banja Luka Bos.-Herz. **62** C2
Banjarmasin Indon. **72** C2
Banjul Gambia **100** A3
Capital of The Gambia.
Banks Island *B.C.* Can. **126** B2
Banks Island *N.W.T.* Can. **124** D2
Banks Islands Vanuatu **110**
Banks Lake Can. **126** F1
Banks Peninsula N.Z. **118** B3
Bankura India **86** C2
Banmauk Myanmar **74** A1
Ban Mouang Laos **74** B2
Bann *r.* U.K. **50** G1
Ban Napè Laos **74** B2
Ban Na San Thai. **74** A3
Bannerman Town Bahamas **138** E4
Bannu Pak. **86** B1
Banswara India **86** B2
Ban Tha Kham Thai. **74** A3
Ban Tha Song Yang Thai. **74** A2
Ban Tôp Laos **74** B2
Bantry Rep. of Ireland **50** F3
Bantry Bay Rep. of Ireland **50** F3
Banyo Cameroon **104** B2
Banyoles Spain **60** D1
Banyuwangi Indon. **72** C2
Baochang China **82** B1
Baoding China **82** B2
Baoji China **82** A2
Bao Lôc Vietnam **74** B2
Baoqing China **78** B1
Baoshan China **74** A1
Baotou China **82** B1
Baotou Shan *mt.* China/N. Korea **76** D1
Bapaume France **54** A2
Ba'qūbah Iraq **92** C2
Bar S.M. **64** A2
Baraawe Somalia **102** C4
Baracoa Cuba **144** C2
Baradine Austr. **116** D2
Barahona Dom. Rep. **144** C3
Baraka *watercourse* Eritrea/Sudan **102** B3
Baram *r.* Malaysia **72** C1
Baranîs Egypt **90** A2
Baranivka Ukr. **44** C1
Barankul Kazakh. **88** C2
Baranof Island U.S.A. **126** B2
Barat Daya, Kepulauan *is* Indon. **70** C3
Barbacena Brazil **154** D2
Barbados *country* West Indies **144** E3
Barbastro Spain **60** D1
Barbezieux-St-Hilaire France **58** B2
Barcaldine Austr. **114** D2
Barcelona Spain **60** D1
Barcelona Venez. **150** C1
Barcelonnette France **58** D3
Barcelos Brazil **150** C3
Barcs Hungary **56** D3
Barddhaman India **86** C2
Bardejov Slovakia **56** E3
Bardsīr Iran **90** C2
Bareilly India **86** B2
Barentin France **52** D5
Barents Sea Arctic Ocean **40** D1
Barentu Eritrea **90** A3
Barfleur, Pointe de *pt* France **52** C5
Barh India **86** C2
Bar Harbor U.S.A. **136** G2
Bari Italy **62** C2

Barika Alg. **60** E2
Barikot Afgh. **86** B1
Barinas Venez. **150** B2
Baripada India **86** C2
Barisal Bangl. **86** D2
Barisan, Pegunungan *mts* Indon.
    72 B2
Barito *r.* Indon. **72** C2
Barkā Oman **90** C2
Barkava Latvia **42** C2
Barkly Tableland *reg.* Austr. **114** C1
Barkol China **80** C2
Bârlad Romania **44** C2
Bar-le-Duc France **58** D2
Barlee, Lake *salt flat* Austr. **114** A2
Barletta Italy **62** C2
Barmedman Austr. **116** D2
Barmer India **86** B2
Barmouth U.K. **52** A3
Barmstedt Ger. **54** D1
Barnard Castle U.K. **52** C2
Barnato Austr. **116** C2
Barnaul Rus. Fed. **88** F1
Barneveld Neth. **54** B1
Barneville-Carteret France **52** C5
Barnsley U.K. **52** C3
Barnstaple U.K. **52** A4
Barnwell U.S.A. **138** D2
Barquisimeto Venez. **150** C1
Barra *i.* U.K. **50** A2
Barraba Austr. **116** E2
Barra do Corda Brazil **150** E3
Barra do Garças Brazil **154** B1
Barra do São Manuel Brazil **150** D3
Barranca *Lima* Peru **150** B4
Barranca *Loreto* Peru **150** B3
Barranqueras Arg. **152** C3
Barranquilla Col. **150** B1
Barreiras Brazil **150** E4
Barretos Brazil **154** C2
Barrie Can. **128** C2
Barrière Can. **126** C2
Barrier Range *hills* Austr. **116** C2
Barrington, Mount Austr. **116** E2
Barrington Lake Can. **126** E2
Barringun Austr. **116** D1
Barrow *r.* Rep. of Ireland **50** G2
Barrow U.S.A. **124** B2
Barrow, Point *pt* U.S.A. **124** B2
Barrow Creek Austr. **114** C2
Barrow-in-Furness U.K. **52** B2
Barrow Island Austr. **114** A2
Barrow Strait Can. **124** F2
Barry U.K. **52** B4
Barrys Bay Can. **128** C2
Barsalpur India **86** B2
Barstow U.S.A. **132** C4
Bar-sur-Aube France **58** C2
Bartın Turkey **92** B1
Bartle Frere, Mount Austr. **114** D1
Bartlesville U.S.A. **140** E1
Bartoszyce Pol. **56** E2
Barung *i.* Indon. **72** C2
Baruun-Urt Mongolia **80** D1
Barvinkove Ukr. **44** E2
Barwon *r.* Austr. **116** D2
Barysaw Belarus **42** C3
Basarabi Romania **44** C3
Basel Switz. **58** D2
Bashtanka Ukr. **44** D2
Basilan *i.* Phil. **76** B3
Basildon U.K. **52** D4
Basingstoke U.K. **52** C4
Başkale Turkey **92** C2
Baskatong, Réservoir *resr* Can. **128** C2
Basle Switz. *see* Basel
Basoko Dem. Rep. Congo **104** C2
Basra Iraq **92** C2
Bassano Can. **126** D2
Bassar Togo **100** C4
Bassein Myanmar **74** A2

Basse-Terre Guadeloupe **144** D3
Capital of Guadeloupe.
Basseterre St Kitts and Nevis **144** D3
Capital of St Kitts and Nevis.
Bassikounou Maur. **100** B3
Bass Strait Austr. **114** D3
Bastak Iran **90** C2
Bastheim Ger. **54** E2
Basti India **86** C2
Bastia France **58** D3
Bastogne Belgium **54** B2
Bastrop U.S.A. **138** B2
Bata Equat. Guinea **104** A2
Batagay Rus. Fed. **94** K2
Bataguassu Brazil **154** B2
Batalha Port. **60** B2
Batan *i.* Phil. **76** B1
Batangafo C.A.R. **104** B2
Batangas Phil. **76** B2
Batanghari *r.* Indon. **72** B2
Batan Islands Phil. **76** B1
Batavia U.S.A. **136** E2
Bataysk Rus. Fed. **44** E2
Batchawana Mountain *h.* Can. **128** B2
Batchelor Austr. **114** C1
Bătdâmbâng Cambodia **74** B2
Batemans Bay Austr. **116** E3
Batesville U.S.A. **138** B1
Batetskiy Rus. Fed. **42** D2
Bath U.K. **52** B4
Bathinda India **86** B1
Bathurst Austr. **116** D2
Bathurst Can. **124** H3
Bathurst Inlet Can. **124** E2
Bathurst Inlet *inlet* Can. **124** E2
Bathurst Island Austr. **114** C1
Bathurst Island Can. **124** F1
Bāţin, Wādī al *watercourse* Asia **90** B1
Batman Turkey **92** C2
Batna Alg. **100** C1
Baton Rouge U.S.A. **138** B2
Capital of Louisiana.
Batopilas Mex. **142** B2
Batouri Cameroon **104** B2
Batovi Brazil **154** B1
Båtsfjord Norway **46** F1
Batticaloa Sri Lanka **84** C4
Battipaglia Italy **62** B2
Battle *r.* Can. **126** E2
Battle Creek U.S.A. **136** C2
Battle Mountain U.S.A. **132** C2
Batu *mt.* Eth. **102** B4
Batu, Pulau-pulau *is* Indon. **72** A2
Batudaka *i.* Indon. **72** D2
Bat'umi Georgia **92** C1
Batu Pahat Malaysia **72** B1
Baubau Indon. **72** D2
Bauchi Nigeria **100** C3
Baugé France **58** B2
Baume-les-Dames France **58** D2
Bauru Brazil **154** C2
Baús Brazil **154** B1
Bauska Latvia **42** B2
Bautzen Ger. **56** C2
Bavispe *r.* Mex. **142** B2
Bavly Rus. Fed. **40** E3
Bawdwin Myanmar **74** A1
Bawean *i.* Indon. **72** C2
Bawku Ghana **100** B3
Bayamo Cuba **144** C2
Bayanhongor Mongolia **80** C1
Bayan Hot China **82** A2
Bayan Obo Kuangqu China **82** A1
Bayan Ul Hot China **82** B1
Bayawan Phil. **76** B3
Bayburt Turkey **92** C1
Bay City *MI* U.S.A. **136** D2
Bay City *TX* U.S.A. **140** E3
Baydaratskaya Guba Rus. Fed. **40** F2
Baydhabo Somalia **102** C4
Bayeux France **52** C5

Bergen op Zoom Neth. **54** B2
Bergerac France **58** C3
Bergheim (Erft) Ger. **54** C2
Bergisch Gladbach Ger. **54** C2
Bergland Namibia **108** A1
Bergsviken Sweden **46** E2
Bergues France **54** A2
Beringen Belgium **54** B2
Bering Sea N. Pacific Ocean **94** N3
Bering Strait Rus. Fed./U.S.A. **94** O2
Berkeley U.S.A. **132** B3
Berkhout Neth. **54** B1
Berkner Island Antarctica **118** D2
Berkovitsa Bulg. **64** B2
Berlevåg Norway **46** F1
Berlin Ger. **54** F1
    Capital of Germany.
Berlin U.S.A. **136** F2
Berlingerode Ger. **54** E2
Bermagui Austr. **116** E3
Bermejillo Mex. **142** B2
Bermejo Bol. **152** B3
Bermen, Lac *l.* Can. **128** D1
Bermuda *terr.* N. Atlantic Ocean **160** B3
    United Kingdom Overseas Territory.
Bern Switz. **58** D2
    Capital of Switzerland.
Bernau Ger. **54** F1
Bernburg (Saale) Ger. **54** E2
Bernkastel-Kues Ger. **54** C3
Beroroha Madag. **106**□ D2
Berounka *r.* Czech Rep. **54** G3
Berri Austr. **116** C2
Berrouaghia Alg. **60** D2
Berry Islands Bahamas **144** C2
Bersenbrück Ger. **54** C1
Bershad' Ukr. **44** C2
Berté, Lac *l.* Can. **128** D1
Bertoua Cameroon **104** B2
Beru *atoll* Kiribati **110**
Beruri Brazil **150** C3
Berwick-upon-Tweed U.K. **52** B2
Beryslav Ukr. **44** D2
Besalampy Madag. **106**□ D1
Besançon France **58** D2
Besnard Lake Can. **126** E2
Bessemer U.S.A. **138** C2
Besshoky, Gora *h.* Kazakh. **88** C2
Betanzos Spain **60** B1
Bétaré Oya Cameroon **104** B2
Bethanie Namibia **108** A2
Bethlehem S. Africa **108** C2
Bethlehem U.S.A. **136** E2
Béthune France **54** A2
Betioky Madag. **106**□ D2
Betpak-Dala *plain* Kazakh. **88** E2
Betroka Madag. **106**□ D2
Betsiamites Can. **128** D2
Betsiboka *r.* Madag. **106**□ D1
Bettendorf U.S.A. **134** F2
Bettiah India **86** C2
Betul India **86** B2
Betwa *r.* India **86** B2
Betws-y-coed U.K. **52** B3
Beverley U.K. **52** C3
Beverungen Ger. **54** D2
Beverwijk Neth. **54** B1
Bexhill U.K. **52** D4
Beykoz Turkey **64** C2
Beyla Guinea **100** B4
Beyneu Kazakh. **88** C2
Beypazarı Turkey **92** B1
Beyrouth Lebanon *see* Beirut
Beyşehir Turkey **92** B2
Beyşehir Gölü *l.* Turkey **92** B2
Beysug *r.* Rus. Fed. **44** E2
Bezhanitsy Rus. Fed. **42** C2
Bezhetsk Rus. Fed. **42** E2
Béziers France **58** C3
Bhadrak India **86** C2
Bhadravati India **84** B3

Bhagalpur India **86** C2
Bhairi Hol *mt.* Pak. **86** A2
Bhakkar Pak. **86** B1
Bhamo Myanmar **74** A1
Bhanjanagar India **86** C3
Bharatpur India **86** B2
Bharuch India **86** B2
Bhavnagar India **86** B2
Bhawanipatna India **86** C3
Bhekuzulu S. Africa **108** D2
Bhilwara India **86** B2
Bhima *r.* India **84** B3
Bhiwani India **86** B2
Bhongweni S. Africa **108** C3
Bhopal India **86** B2
Bhubaneshwar India **86** C2
Bhuj India **86** A2
Bhumiphol Dam Thai. **74** A2
Bhusawal India **86** B2
Bhutan *country* Asia **86** D2
Bia, Phou *mt.* Laos **74** B2
Biak Indon. **70** D3
Biak *i.* Indon. **70** D3
Biała Podlaska Pol. **56** E2
Białogard Pol. **56** D2
Białystok Pol. **56** E2
Bianco Italy **62** C3
Biarritz France **58** B3
Biasca Switz. **58** D2
Bibai Japan **78** D2
Bibala Angola **106** A1
Biberach an der Riß Ger. **56** B3
Bida Nigeria **100** C4
Biddeford U.S.A. **136** F2
Bideford U.K. **52** A4
Bideford Bay U.K. **52** A4
Biedenkopf Ger. **54** D2
Biel Switz. **58** D2
Bielefeld Ger. **54** D1
Biella Italy **62** A1
Bielsko-Biała Pol. **56** D3
Biên Hoa Vietnam **74** B2
Bienville, Lac *l.* Can. **128** C1
Bièvre Belgium **54** B3
Bifoun Gabon **104** B3
Biga Turkey **64** C2
Big Bend Swaziland **108** D2
Biggar Can. **124** E3
Biggar U.K. **50** C3
Big Hole *r.* U.S.A. **132** D1
Bighorn *r.* U.S.A. **134** B1
Bighorn Mountains U.S.A. **134** B2
Big Lake U.S.A. **140** D2
Big Rapids U.S.A. **136** C2
Big River Can. **126** E2
Big Sand Lake Can. **126** F2
Big Sioux *r.* U.S.A. **134** D2
Big Spring U.S.A. **140** D2
Big Timber U.S.A. **132** E1
Big Trout Lake Can. **128** B1
Big Trout Lake *l.* Can. **128** A1
Bihać Bos.-Herz. **62** C2
Bihar Sharif India **86** C2
Bihor, Vârful *mt.* Romania **44** B2
Bijagós, Arquipélago dos *is*
    Guinea-Bissau **100** A3
Bījār Iran **92** C2
Bijeljina Bos.-Herz. **62** C2
Bijelo Polje S.M. **64** A2
Bijie China **82** A3
Bikaner India **86** B2
Bikin Rus. Fed. **78** B1
Bikin *r.* Rus. Fed. **78** B1
Bikoro Dem. Rep. Congo **104** B3
Bilād Banī Bū 'Alī Oman **90** C2
Bilaspur India **86** C2
Bila Tserkva Ukr. **44** D2
Bilauktaung Range *mts* Myanmar/Thai.
    74 A2
Bilbao Spain **60** C1
Bilecik Turkey **64** C2

Biłgoraj Pol. **56** E2
Bilhorod-Dnistrovs'kyy Ukr. **44** D2
Bili Dem. Rep. Congo **104** C2
Bilibino Rus. Fed. **94** N2
Billings U.S.A. **132** E1
Bill of Portland *hd* U.K. **52** B4
Bilma Niger **100** D3
Biloela Austr. **114** E2
Bilohirs'k Ukr. **44** D2
Bilohir''ya Ukr. **44** C1
Bilopillya Ukr. **44** D1
Bilovods'k Ukr. **44** E2
Biloxi U.S.A. **138** C2
Bilpa Morea Claypan *salt flat* Austr.
    114 C2
Bilshausen Ger. **54** E2
Biltine Chad **100** E3
Bilyayivka Ukr. **44** D2
Bimini Islands Bahamas **138** E3
Bina-Etawa India **86** B2
Binaija, Gunung *mt.* Indon. **70** C3
Bindu Dem. Rep. Congo **104** B3
Bindura Zimbabwe **106** C1
Binefar Spain **60** D1
Bingara Austr. **116** E1
Bingen am Rhein Ger. **54** C3
Bingham U.S.A. **136** G1
Binghamton U.S.A. **136** E2
Bingöl Turkey **92** C2
Binjai Indon. **72** A1
Bintuhan Indon. **72** B2
Bintulu Malaysia **72** C1
Binzhou China **82** B2
Bioco *i.* Equat. Guinea **104** A2
Biograd na Moru Croatia **62** C2
Birao C.A.R. **104** C1
Biratnagar Nepal **86** C2
Birch Mountains Can. **126** D2
Birdsville Austr. **114** C2
Birecik Turkey **92** B2
Bireun Indon. **72** A1
Birganj Nepal **86** C2
Birhan *mt.* Eth. **102** B3
Birigüi Brazil **154** B2
Bīrjand Iran **88** C3
Birkenhead U.K. **52** B3
Birmingham U.K. **52** C3
Birmingham U.S.A. **138** C2
Bîr Mogreïn Maur. **100** A2
Birnin-Kebbi Nigeria **100** C3
Birnin Konni Niger **100** C3
Birobidzhan Rus. Fed. **80** E1
Birr Rep. of Ireland **50** G2
Birsay U.K. **50** C1
Bi'r Shalatayn Egypt **90** A2
Biržai Lith. **42** B2
Bisalpur India **86** B2
Bisbee U.S.A. **140** C2
Biscay, Bay of *sea* France/Spain **58** A2
Bischofshofen Austria **56** C3
Biscotasi Lake Can. **128** B2
Bishkek Kyrg. **88** E2
    Capital of Kyrgyzstan.
Bisho S. Africa **108** C3
Bishop U.S.A. **132** C3
Bishui China **80** E1
Bisinaca Col. **150** C2
Biskra Alg. **100** C1
Bismarck U.S.A. **134** C1
    Capital of North Dakota.
Bismarck Archipelago *is* P.N.G. **70** D3
Bismarck Sea P.N.G. **110**
Bissa, Djebel *mt.* Alg. **60** D2
Bissamcuttak India **84** C3
Bissau Guinea-Bissau **100** A3
    Capital of Guinea-Bissau.
Bissett Can. **126** F2
Bistcho Lake Can. **126** D2
Bistriţa Romania **44** B2
Bistriţa *r.* Romania **44** C2
Bitburg Ger. **54** C3

Bontoc Phil. **76** B2
Bontosunggu Indon. **72** C2
Bontrug S. Africa **108** C3
Booligal Austr. **116** C2
Boomi Austr. **116** D1
Boonah Austr. **116** E1
Boone *IA* U.S.A. **134** E2
Boone *NC* U.S.A. **136** D3
Booneville U.S.A. **138** C2
Boonville U.S.A. **134** E3
Boorowa Austr. **116** D2
Boothia, Gulf of Can. **124** G2
Boothia Peninsula Can. **124** F2
Boppard Ger. **54** C2
Boquilla, Presa de la *resr* Mex. **142** B2
Bor S.M. **64** B2
Bor Sudan **102** B4
Bor Turkey **92** B2
Boraha, Nosy *i.* Madag. **106**□ E1
Borås Sweden **46** C4
Borāzjān Iran **92** D3
Borba Brazil **150** D3
Bordeaux France **58** B3
Bordertown Austr. **116** C3
Bordj Bou Arréridj Alg. **60** D2
Bordj Bounama Alg. **60** D2
Bordj Messaouda Alg. **100** C1
Bordj Omer Driss Alg. **100** C2
Borðoy *i.* Faroe Is **48** B1
Borgarnes Iceland **46**□
Borgosesia Italy **62** A1
Borisoglebsk Rus. Fed. **44** F1
Borisoglebskiy Rus. Fed. **42** E2
Borisovka Rus. Fed. **44** E1
Borisovo-Sudskoye Rus. Fed. **42** E2
Borken Ger. **54** C2
Borkenes Norway **46** D2
Borkum Ger. **54** C1
Borkum *i.* Ger. **54** C1
Borlänge Sweden **46** D3
Borna Ger. **54** F2
Borneo *i.* Asia **72** C1
   Largest island in Asia, and 3rd in the world.
Bornholm *i.* Denmark **46** C4
Bornova Turkey **64** C3
Borodyanka Ukr. **44** C1
Borovichi Rus. Fed. **42** D2
Borovsk Rus. Fed. **42** E2
Borroloola Austr. **114** C1
Borşa Romania **44** B2
Borshchiv Ukr. **44** C2
Borshchovochnyy Khrebet *mts*
   Rus. Fed. **80** D1
Börßum Ger. **54** E1
Borūjerd Iran **92** C2
Boryslav Ukr. **44** B2
Boryspil' Ukr. **44** D1
Borzna Ukr. **44** D1
Borzya Rus. Fed. **80** D1
Bosanska Dubica Bos.-Herz. **62** C1
Bosanska Gradiška Bos.-Herz. **62** C1
Bosanska Krupa Bos.-Herz. **62** C2
Bosanski Novi Bos.-Herz. **62** C1
Bosansko Grahovo Bos.-Herz. **62** C2
Bose China **82** A3
Boshof S. Africa **108** C2
Bosnia-Herzegovina *country* Europe
   62 C2
Bosobolo Dem. Rep. Congo **104** B2
Bosporus *str.* Turkey **64** C2
Bossangoa C.A.R. **104** B2
Bossembélé C.A.R. **104** B2
Bosten Hu *l.* China **88** F2
Boston U.K. **52** C3
Boston U.S.A. **136** F2
   Capital of Massachusetts.
Boston Mountains U.S.A. **138** B1
Botany Bay Austr. **116** E2
Botev *mt.* Bulg. **64** B2
Botevgrad Bulg. **92** A1
Bothnia, Gulf of Fin./Sweden **46** D3

Botoşani Romania **44** C2
Botshabelo S. Africa **108** C2
Botswana *country* Africa **106** B2
Botte Donato, Monte *mt.* Italy **62** C3
Bottineau U.S.A. **134** C1
Bottrop Ger. **54** C2
Botucatu Brazil **154** C2
Bouaké Côte d'Ivoire **100** B4
Bouar C.A.R. **104** B2
Bouârfa Morocco **100** B1
Bouctouche Can. **128** D2
Bougaa Alg. **60** E2
Bougainville Island P.N.G. **110**
Bougaroûn, Cap *c.* Alg. **60** E2
Bougouni Mali **100** B3
Bouillon Belgium **54** B3
Bouira Alg. **60** D2
Boujdour Western Sahara **100** A2
Boulder U.S.A. **134** B2
Boulder City U.S.A. **132** D3
Boulia Austr. **114** C2
Boulogne-Billancourt France **58** C2
Boulogne-sur-Mer France **52** D4
Boumango Gabon **104** B3
Boumba *r.* Cameroon **104** B2
Boumerdes Alg. **60** D2
Bouna Côte d'Ivoire **100** B4
Boundiali Côte d'Ivoire **100** B4
Bountiful U.S.A. **132** D2
Bourem Mali **100** B3
Bourganeuf France **58** C2
Bourg-en-Bresse France **58** D2
Bourges France **58** C2
Bourke Austr. **116** D2
Bournemouth U.K. **52** C4
Bou Saâda Alg. **100** C1
Bousso Chad **100** D3
Boutilimit Maur. **100** A3
Bouy France **54** B3
Bow *r.* Can. **126** D3
Bowen Austr. **114** D2
Bow Island Can. **126** D3
Bowling Green *KY* U.S.A. **136** C3
Bowling Green *OH* U.S.A. **136** D2
Bowman U.S.A. **134** C1
Boxberg Ger. **54** D3
Boxtel Neth. **54** B2
Boyabat Turkey **92** B1
Boyang China **82** B3
Boyle Rep. of Ireland **50** F2
Boyne *r.* Rep. of Ireland **50** G2
Boysen Reservoir U.S.A. **134** B2
Boyuibe Bol. **152** B3
Bozburun Turkey **64** C3
Bozcaada *i.* Turkey **64** C3
   Most westerly point of Asia.
Bozdağ *mt.* Turkey **64** C3
Boz Dağları *mts* Turkey **64** C3
Bozdoğan Turkey **64** C3
Bozeman U.S.A. **132** D1
Bozoum C.A.R. **104** B2
Bozüyük Turkey **64** D3
Brač *i.* Croatia **62** C2
Bracebridge Can. **128** C2
Brachet, Lac au *l.* Can. **128** D2
Bracknell U.K. **52** C4
Bradano *r.* Italy **62** C2
Bradenton U.S.A. **138** D3
Bradford U.K. **52** C3
Bradford U.S.A. **136** E2
Brady U.S.A. **140** E2
Braemar U.K. **50** F2
Braga Port. **60** B1
Bragança Brazil **150** E3
Bragança Port. **60** B1
Brahin Belarus **42** D3
Brahmanbaria Bangl. **74** A1
Brahmapur India **84** C3
Brahmaputra *r.* China/India **74** A1
Brăila Romania **44** C2

Brainerd U.S.A. **134** E1
Braintree U.K. **52** D4
Braives Belgium **54** B2
Brake (Unterweser) Ger. **54** D1
Brakwater Namibia **108** A1
Bramsche Ger. **54** D1
Branco *r.* Brazil **150** C3
Brandenburg Ger. **54** F1
Brandon Can. **126** F3
Brandon Mountain *h.* Rep. of Ireland
   50 E2
Brandvlei S. Africa **108** B3
Braniewo Pol. **56** D2
Brantford Can. **128** B2
Bras d'Or Lake Can. **128** D2
Brasil, Planalto do *plat.* Brazil **154** D1
Brasilândia Brazil **154** C1
Brasília Brazil **154** C1
   Capital of Brazil.
Brasília de Minas Brazil **154** D1
Braslaw Belarus **42** C2
Braşov Romania **44** C2
Bratislava Slovakia **56** D3
   Capital of Slovakia.
Bratsk Rus. Fed. **94** I3
Braunau am Inn Austria **56** C3
Braunschweig Ger. **54** E1
Brautarholt Iceland **46**□
Bråviken *inlet* Sweden **42** A2
Bravo del Norte, Río *r.* Mex./U.S.A. *see*
   Rio Grande
Brawley U.S.A. **132** C4
Bray Rep. of Ireland **50** G2
Brazil *country* S. America **150** D3
   *Largest and most populous country in
   South America, and 5th largest and most
   populous in the world.*
Brazilian Highlands *mts* Brazil **146**
Brazos *r.* U.S.A. **140** E3
Brazzaville Congo **104** B3
   Capital of Congo.
Brčko Bos.-Herz. **62** C2
Brechin U.K. **50** C2
Brecht Belgium **54** B2
Breckenridge U.S.A. **140** E2
Břeclav Czech Rep. **56** D3
Brecon U.K. **52** B4
Brecon Beacons *reg.* U.K. **52** B4
Breda Neth. **54** B2
Bredasdorp S. Africa **108** B3
Bregenz Austria **56** B3
Breivikbotn Norway **46** E1
Brekstad Norway **46** B3
Bremen Ger. **54** D1
Bremerhaven Ger. **54** D1
Bremerton U.S.A. **132** B1
Bremervörde Ger. **54** D1
Brenham U.S.A. **140** E2
Brennero Italy **56** C3
Brenner Pass Austria/Italy **56** C3
Brentwood U.K. **52** D4
Brescia Italy **62** B1
Bressanone Italy **62** B1
Bressay *i.* U.K. **50**□
Bressuire France **58** B2
Brest Belarus **42** B3
Brest France **58** B2
Breton Sound *b.* U.S.A. **138** C3
Breves Brazil **150** D3
Brewarrina Austr. **116** D1
Brewster U.S.A. **132** C1
Breytovo Rus. Fed. **42** E2
Brezovo Polje *plain* Croatia **62** C1
Bria C.A.R. **104** C2
Briançon France **58** D3
Briceni Moldova **44** C2
Bridgend U.K. **52** B4
Bridgeport *CT* U.S.A. **136** F2
Bridgeport *NE* U.S.A. **134** C2
Bridgetown Barbados **144** E3
   Capital of Barbados.

Butte U.S.A. **132** D1
Butterworth Malaysia **72** B1
Butt of Lewis *hd* U.K. **50** A1
Button Bay Can. **126** F2
Butuan Phil. **76** B3
Buturlinovka Rus. Fed. **42** F3
Butwal Nepal **86** C2
Butzbach Ger. **54** D2
Buulobarde Somalia **102** C4
Buur Gaabo Somalia **102** C5
Buurhabaka Somalia **102** C4
Buxoro Uzbek. **88** D3
Buxtehude Ger. **54** D1
Buy Rus. Fed. **42** F2
Buynaksk Rus. Fed. **40** D4
Büyükmenderes *r.* Turkey **64** C3
Buzai Gumbad Afgh. **86** B1
Buzău Romania **44** C2
Búzi Moz. **106** C1
Buzuluk Rus. Fed. **40** E3
Byala Bulg. **64** C2
Byalynichy Belarus **42** C3
Byarezina *r.* Belarus **42** D3
Byaroza Belarus **42** B3
Bydgoszcz Pol. **56** D2
Byerazino Belarus **42** C3
Byeshankovichy Belarus **42** C2
Bykhaw Belarus **42** D3
Bylot Island Can. **124** G2
Byrkjelo Norway **48** E1
Byrock Austr. **116** D2
Byron Bay Austr. **116** E1
Bytantay *r.* Rus. Fed. **94** K2
Bytom Pol. **56** D2
Bytów Pol. **56** D2

C

Caaguazú, Cordillera de *hills* Para. **154** A3
Caarapó Brazil **154** B2
Caazapá Para. **154** A3
Cabanatuan Phil. **76** B2
Cabdul Qaadir Somalia **102** C3
Cabeceira Rio Manso Brazil **154** A1
Cabeza del Buey Spain **60** B2
Cabezas Bol. **152** B2
Cabimas Venez. **150** B1
Cabinda Angola **104** B3
Cabinda *prov.* Angola **104** B3
Cabo Frio Brazil **154** D2
Cabo Frio, Ilha do *i.* Brazil **154** D2
Cabonga, Réservoir *resr* Can. **128** C2
Caboolture Austr. **116** E1
Cabo Pantoja Peru **150** B3
Cabora Bassa, Lake *resr* Moz. **106** C1
Caborca Mex. **142** A1
Cabot Strait Can. **128** C2
Cabral, Serra do *mts* Brazil **154** D1
Cabrera *i.* Spain **60** D2
Cabrera, Sierra de la *mts* Spain **60** B1
Cabri Can. **126** E2
Cabriel *r.* Spain **60** C2
Caçador Brazil **154** B3
Čačak S.M. **64** B2
Caccia, Capo *c.* Italy **62** A2
Cáceres Brazil **150** D4
Cáceres Spain **60** B2
Cache Creek Can. **126** C2
Cacheu Guinea-Bissau **100** A3
Cachimbo, Serra do *hills* Brazil **150** D3
Cachoeira Alta Brazil **154** B1
Cachoeiro de Itapemirim Brazil **154** D2
Cacine Guinea-Bissau **100** A3
Cacolo Angola **104** B4
Caçu Brazil **154** B1
Čadca Slovakia **56** D3
Cadenberge Ger. **54** D1
Cadereyta Mex. **142** B2
Cadillac U.S.A. **136** C2

Cádiz Spain **60** B2
Cádiz, Golfo de *g.* Spain **60** B2
Cadotte Lake Can. **126** D2
Caen France **58** B2
Caernarfon U.K. **52** A3
Caernarfon Bay U.K. **52** A3
Cafayate Arg. **152** B3
Cagayan de Oro Phil. **76** B3
Cagli Italy **62** B2
Cagliari Italy **62** A3
Cagliari, Golfo di *b.* Italy **62** A3
Caha Mountains Rep. of Ireland **50** F3
Cahermore Rep. of Ireland **50** E3
Cahersiveen Rep. of Ireland **50** E3
Cahir Rep. of Ireland **50** G2
Cahore Point *pt* Rep. of Ireland **50** G2
Cahors France **58** C3
Cahul Moldova **44** C2
Caia Moz. **106** C1
Caiabis, Serra dos *hills* Brazil **150** D4
Caianda Angola **106** B1
Caiapó, Serra do *mts* Brazil **154** B1
Caiapônia Brazil **154** B1
Caicos Islands Turks and Caicos Is **144** C2
Cairngorm Mountains U.K. **50** C2
Cairnryan U.K. **50** B3
Cairns Austr. **114** D1
Cairo Egypt **102** B1
Capital of Egypt, and most populous city in Africa.
Caistor U.K. **52** C3
Caiundo Angola **106** A1
Cajamarca Peru **150** B3
Čakovec Croatia **62** C1
Cala S. Africa **108** C3
Calabar Nigeria **104** A2
Calabozo Venez. **150** C2
Calafat Romania **44** B3
Calafate Arg. **152** A6
Calahorra Spain **60** C1
Calais France **58** C1
Calais U.S.A. **136** G1
Calama Chile **152** B3
Calamian Group *is* Phil. **76** A2
Calamocha Spain **60** C1
Calandula Angola **104** B3
Calang Indon. **72** A1
Calanscio Sand Sea *des.* Libya **100** E1
Calapan Phil. **76** B2
Călăraşi Romania **44** C2
Calatayud Spain **60** C1
Calau Ger. **54** F2
Calayan *i.* Phil. **76** B2
Calbayog Phil. **76** B2
Calcanhar, Ponta do *pt* Brazil **150** F3
Calçoene Brazil **150** D2
Calcutta India *see* Kolkata
Caldas da Rainha Port. **60** B2
Caldas Novas Brazil **154** C1
Caldera Chile **152** A3
Caldwell U.S.A. **132** C2
Caledon *r.* Lesotho/S. Africa **108** C3
Caledon S. Africa **108** A3
Caleta Olivia Arg. **152** B5
Calf of Man *i.* Isle of Man **52** A2
Calgary Can. **126** D2
Cali Col. **150** B2
Calicut India **84** B3
Caliente U.S.A. **132** D3
California *state* U.S.A. **132** B2
California, Gulf of Mex. **132** D4
California Aqueduct *canal* U.S.A. **132** B3
Calitzdorp S. Africa **108** B3
Calkiní Mex. **142** C2
Callabonna, Lake *salt flat* Austr. **116** C1
Callander U.K. **50** B2
Callao Peru **150** B4
Caltagirone Italy **62** B3
Caltanissetta Italy **62** B3
Caluquembe Angola **106** A1

Caluula Somalia **102** D3
Calvi France **58** D3
Calvià Spain **60** D2
Calvillo Mex. **142** B2
Calvinia S. Africa **108** A3
Calvo, Monte *mt.* Italy **62** C2
Camacho Mex. **142** B2
Camacupa Angola **106** A1
Camagüey Cuba **144** C2
Camana Peru **150** B4
Camapuã Brazil **154** B1
Camargo Mex. **142** C2
Ca Mau Vietnam **74** B3
Ca Mau, Mui *c.* Vietnam **74** B3
Cambodia *country* Asia **74** B2
Camborne U.K. **52** A4
Cambrai France **58** C1
Cambrian Mountains U.K. **52** B3
Cambridge N.Z. **118** C2
Cambridge U.K. **52** D3
Cambridge *MA* U.S.A. **136** F2
Cambridge *MD* U.S.A. **136** E3
Cambridge *MN* U.S.A. **134** E1
Cambridge *OH* U.S.A. **136** D2
Cambrien, Lac *l.* Can. **128** D1
Camden Austr. **116** E2
Camden *AR* U.S.A. **138** B2
Camden *ME* U.S.A. **136** G2
Cameroon *country* Africa **104** B2
Cameroun, Mont *vol.* Cameroon **96**
Cametá Brazil **150** E3
Camiguin *i.* Phil. **76** B2
Camiri Bol. **152** B3
Camocim Brazil **150** E3
Camooweal Austr. **114** C1
Camorta *i.* India **74** A3
Campana, Isla *i.* Chile **152** A5
Campbell S. Africa **108** B2
Campbell, Cape N.Z. **118** B3
Campbell Island N.Z. **110**
Campbell River Can. **126** C2
Campbellsville U.S.A. **136** C3
Campbellton Can. **136** G1
Campbeltown U.K. **50** B3
Campeche Mex. **142** C3
Campeche, Bahía de *g.* Mex. **142** C3
Camperdown Austr. **116** C3
Câmpina Romania **44** C2
Campina Grande Brazil **150** F3
Campinas Brazil **154** C2
Campina Verde Brazil **154** C1
Campobasso Italy **62** B2
Campo Belo Brazil **154** C2
Campo Florido Brazil **154** C1
Campo Gallo Arg. **152** B3
Campo Grande Brazil **154** B2
Campo Maior Brazil **150** E3
Campo Maior Port. **60** B2
Campo Mourão Brazil **154** B2
Campos Brazil **154** D2
Campos Altos Brazil **154** C1
Campos do Jordão Brazil **154** C2
Câmpulung Romania **44** C2
Camp Verde U.S.A. **140** B2
Cam Ranh Vietnam **74** B2
Camrose Can. **126** D2
Camsell Portage Can. **126** D2
Çan Turkey **64** C2
Canada *country* N. America **124** D2
2nd largest country in the world, and 3rd most populous in North America.
Canadian U.S.A. **140** D1
Canadian *r.* U.S.A. **140** E1
Canadian Shield *reg.* Can. **120**
Çanakkale Turkey **64** C2
Cananea Mex. **142** A1
Cananéia Brazil **154** C2
Canary Islands *terr.* N. Atlantic Ocean **100** A2
Autonomous Community of Spain.
Canastra, Serra da *mts* Brazil **154** C1

Catherine, Mount Egypt *see* Kātrīnā, Jabal
Cat Island Bahamas 144 C2
Cat Lake Can. 128 A1
Catoche, Cabo *c.* Mex. 142 D2
Catskill Mountains U.S.A. 136 F2
Cauayan Phil. 76 B3
Caubvick, Mount Can. 128 D1
Cauca *r.* Col. 150 B2
Caucaia Brazil 150 F3
Caucasus *mts* Asia/Europe 92 C1
Caudry France 54 A2
Caulonia Italy 62 C3
Causapscal Can. 128 D2
Cavaillon France 58 D3
Cavalcante Brazil 150 E4
Cavan Rep. of Ireland 50 G2
Cavernoso, Serra do *mts* Brazil 154 B3
Caxias Brazil 150 E3
Caxias do Sul Brazil 152 C3
Caxito Angola 104 B3
Cayenne Fr. Guiana 150 D2
  Capital of French Guiana.
Cayman Islands *terr.* West Indies 144 B3
  United Kingdom Overseas Territory.
Caynabo Somalia 102 C4
Cazombo Angola 106 B1
Ceballos Mex. 142 B2
Cebu Phil. 76 B2
Cebu *i.* Phil. 76 B2
Cecil Plains Austr. 116 E1
Cecina Italy 62 B2
Cedar *r.* U.S.A. 136 D2
Cedar City U.S.A. 132 D3
Cedar Falls U.S.A. 134 E2
Cedar Lake Can. 126 E2
Cedar Rapids U.S.A. 134 E2
Cedros, Isla *i.* Mex. 142 A2
Ceduna Austr. 114 C3
Ceeldheere Somalia 102 C4
Ceerigaabo Somalia 102 C3
Cefalù Italy 62 B3
Celaya Mex. 142 B2
Celebes *i.* Indon. 72 D2
  4th largest island in Asia.
Celebes Sea Indon./Phil. 70 C2
Celestún Mex. 142 C2
Celle Ger. 54 E1
Celtic Sea Rep. of Ireland/U.K. 48 B3
Cenderawasih, Teluk *b.* Indon. 70 D3
Central, Cordillera *mts* Col. 150 B2
Central, Cordillera *mts* Peru 150 B4
Central, Cordillera *mts* Phil. 76 B2
Central African Republic *country* Africa 104 C2
Central Brahui Range *mts* Pak. 86 A2
Central City U.S.A. 134 D2
Centralia *IL* U.S.A. 136 C4
Centralia *WA* U.S.A. 132 B1
Central Makran Range *mts* Pak. 86 A2
Central Range *mts* P.N.G. 70 D3
Central Russian Upland *hills* Rus. Fed. 42 E3
Central Siberian Plateau Rus. Fed. 94 J2
Cephalonia *i.* Greece 64 B3
Ceram Sea Indon. *see* Seram, Laut
Ceres Arg. 152 B3
Ceres S. Africa 108 A3
Céret France 58 C3
Cerezo de Abajo Spain 60 C1
Cerignola Italy 62 C2
Cernavodă Romania 44 C3
Cerralvo Mex. 142 C2
Cerralvo, Isla *i.* Mex. 142 B2
Cerritos Mex. 142 B2
Cerro Azul Brazil 154 C2
Cerro Azul Mex. 142 C2
Cerro de Pasco Peru 150 B4
Cervione France 58 B3
Cervo Spain 60 B1
Cesena Italy 62 B2

Cēsis Latvia 42 C2
České Budějovice Czech Rep. 56 C3
Český Les *mts* Czech Rep./Ger. 54 F3
Çeşme Turkey 64 C3
Cessnock Austr. 116 E2
Cetinje S.M. 64 A2
Cetraro Italy 62 C3
Ceuta N. Africa 60 B2
  Autonomous Community of Spain.
Cévennes *mts* France 58 C3
Chābahār Iran 90 D2
Chabyêr Caka *salt l.* China 86 C1
Chachapoyas Peru 150 B3
Chachersk Belarus 42 D3
Chachoengsao Thai. 74 B2
Chad *country* Africa 100 D3
  5th largest country in Africa.
Chad, Lake Africa 100 D3
  4th largest lake in Africa.
Chadaasan Mongolia 80 C1
Chadan Rus. Fed. 88 G1
Chadibe Botswana 108 C1
Chadron U.S.A. 134 C2
Chaeryŏng N. Korea 76 D2
Chagai Pak. 86 A2
Chaghcharān Afgh. 86 A1
Chagny France 56 A3
Chagoda Rus. Fed. 42 E2
Chagos Archipelago *is* B.I.O.T. 66
Chagyl Turkm. 88 C2
Chaibasa India 86 C2
Chainat Thai. 74 B2
Chaiyaphum Thai. 74 B2
Chajarí Arg. 152 C4
Chakonipau, Lac *l.* Can. 128 D1
Chala Peru 150 B4
Chalap Dalan *mts* Afgh. 86 A1
Chaleur Bay *inlet* Can. 128 D2
Chalisgaon India 86 B2
Chalki *i.* Greece 64 C3
Chalkida Greece 64 B3
Challans France 58 B2
Challenger Deep *sea feature* N. Pacific Ocean 158 C4
  Deepest point in the world (Mariana Trench).
Challis U.S.A. 132 D2
Châlons-en-Champagne France 58 C2
Chalon-sur-Saône France 58 C2
Cham Ger. 54 F3
Chama U.S.A. 140 C1
Chama Zambia 106 C1
Chaman Pak. 86 A1
Chamba India 86 B1
Chambal *r.* India 86 B2
Chamberlain U.S.A. 134 D2
Chambersburg U.S.A. 136 E3
Chambéry France 58 D2
Chambeshi Zambia 106 C1
Champaign U.S.A. 136 C3
Champlain, Lake Can./U.S.A. 128 C2
Champotón Mex. 142 C3
Chañaral Chile 152 A3
Chandalar *r.* U.S.A. 124 C2
Chandeleur Islands U.S.A. 138 C3
Chandigarh India 86 B1
Chandler U.S.A. 140 B2
Chandrapur India 86 B3
Chang, Ko *i.* Thai. 74 B2
Changane *r.* Moz. 106 C2
Changara Moz. 106 C1
Changbai China 76 D1
Changbai Shan *mts* China/N. Korea 76 D1
Changchun China 76 D1
Changde China 82 B3
Ch'angdo N. Korea 76 D2
Changhua Taiwan 82 C3
Changhŭng S. Korea 76 D3
Chang Jiang *r.* China *see* Yangtze
Changjin N. Korea 76 D1
Changjin-gang *r.* N. Korea 76 D1

Changsha China 82 B3
Changsŏng S. Korea 76 D2
Changting China 82 B3
Ch'angwŏn S. Korea 76 D2
Changyuan China 82 B2
Changzhi China 82 B2
Changzhou China 82 B2
Chania Greece 64 B3
Channel Islands English Chan. 52 B5
Channel Islands U.S.A. 132 C4
Channel-Port-aux-Basques Can. 128 E2
Chanthaburi Thai. 74 B2
Chantilly France 58 C2
Chanute U.S.A. 134 E4
Chany, Ozero *salt l.* Rus. Fed. 88 E1
Chaouèn Morocco 60 B2
Chaoyang Guangdong China 82 B3
Chaoyang Liaoning China 82 C1
Chaozhou China 82 B3
Chapala, Laguna de *l.* Mex. 142 B2
Chapayev Kazakh. 88 C1
Chapecó Brazil 154 B3
Chapel Hill U.S.A. 138 E1
Chapleau Can. 128 B2
Chaplygin Rus. Fed. 42 E3
Chaplynka Ukr. 44 D2
Charcas Mex. 142 B2
Chard U.K. 52 B4
Chardzhev Turkm. *see* Turkmenabat
Charente *r.* France 58 B2
Chārīkār Afgh. 86 A1
Charkayuvom Rus. Fed. 40 E2
Charleroi Belgium 54 B2
Charles, Cape U.S.A. 136 E3
Charles City U.S.A. 134 E2
Charleston *IL* U.S.A. 136 C3
Charleston *SC* U.S.A. 138 E2
Charleston *WV* U.S.A. 136 D3
  Capital of West Virginia.
Charleston Peak U.S.A. 132 C3
Charleville Austr. 114 C2
Charleville-Mézières France 58 C2
Charlotte U.S.A. 138 D1
Charlotte Amalie Virgin Is (U.S.A.) 144 D3
  Capital of the U.S. Virgin Islands.
Charlotte Harbor *b.* U.S.A. 138 D3
Charlottesville U.S.A. 136 E3
Charlottetown Can. 128 D2
  Capital of Prince Edward Island.
Charlton Austr. 116 C3
Charlton Island Can. 128 C1
Charozero Rus. Fed. 42 E1
Charters Towers Austr. 114 D2
Chartres France 58 C2
Chase Can. 126 D2
Chashniki Belarus 42 C3
Chasŏng N. Korea 76 D1
Chassiron, Pointe de *pt* France 58 B2
Châteaubriant France 58 B2
Château-du-Loir France 58 B2
Châteaudun France 58 C2
Châteaulin France 58 B2
Châteauneuf-les-Martigues France 58 D3
Châteauneuf-sur-Loire France 58 C2
Château-Thierry France 58 C2
Chateh Can. 126 D2
Châtelet Belgium 54 B2
Châtellerault France 58 C2
Chatham Can. 136 D2
Chatham Islands N.Z. 110
Châtillon-sur-Seine France 58 C2
Chattahoochee *r.* U.S.A. 138 D2
Chattanooga U.S.A. 138 C1
Châu Đôc Vietnam 74 B2
Chauk Myanmar 74 A1
Chaumont France 58 D2
Chauny France 58 C2
Chaves Brazil 150 E3
Chaves Port. 60 B1
Chavigny, Lac *l.* Can. 128 C1

INDEX

180

Chukotskiy Poluostrov *pen.* Rus. Fed. 94 O2
Chula Vista U.S.A. 132 C4
Chulym Rus. Fed. 94 H3
Chumbicha Arg. 152 B3
Chumikan Rus. Fed. 94 L3
Chumphon Thai. 74 A2
Ch'unch'ŏn S. Korea 76 D2
Chungking China *see* Chongqing
Chunya *r.* Rus. Fed. 94 I2
Chuquibamba Peru 150 B4
Chuquicamata Chile 152 B3
Chur Switz. 58 D2
Churachandpur India 74 A1
Churchill Can. 126 F2
Churchill *r.* Man. Can. 126 F2
Churchill *r.* Nfld. and Lab. Can. 128 D1
Churchill, Cape Can. 126 F2
Churchill Falls Can. 128 D1
Churchill Lake Can. 126 E2
Churu India 86 B2
Chute-des-Passes Can. 128 C2
Chuuk *is* Micronesia 110
Chuxiong China 74 B1
Ciadîr-Lunga Moldova 44 C2
Ciamis Indon. 72 B2
Cianjur Indon. 72 B2
Cianorte Brazil 154 B2
Ciechanów Pol. 56 E2
Ciego de Ávila Cuba 144 C2
Cienfuegos Cuba 144 B2
Cieza Spain 60 C2
Cigüela *r.* Spain 60 C2
Cihanbeyli Turkey 92 B2
Cihuatlán Mex. 142 B3
Cijara, Embalse de *resr* Spain 60 C2
Cilacap Indon. 72 B2
Cimarron *r.* U.S.A. 140 E1
Cimişlia Moldova 44 C2
Cimone, Monte *mt.* Italy 62 B2
Cincinnati U.S.A. 136 D3
Çine Turkey 64 C3
Ciney Belgium 54 B2
Cintalapa Mex. 142 C3
Circle *AK* U.S.A. 124 C2
Circle *MT* U.S.A. 134 B1
Cirebon Indon. 72 B2
Cirencester U.K. 52 C4
Ciriè Italy 62 A1
Cirò Marina Italy 62 C3
Čitluk Bos.-Herz. 62 C2
Citrusdal S. Africa 108 A3
Città di Castello Italy 58 E3
Ciudad Acuña Mex. 142 B2
Ciudad Altamirano Mex. 142 B3
Ciudad Bolívar Venez. 150 C2
Ciudad Camargo Mex. 142 B2
Ciudad Constitución Mex. 142 A2
Ciudad del Carmen Mex. 142 C3
Ciudad Delicias Mex. 142 B2
Ciudad de Valles Mex. 142 C2
Ciudad Guayana Venez. 150 C2
Ciudad Guerrero Mex. 140 C3
Ciudad Guzmán Mex. 142 B3
Ciudad Hidalgo Mex. 142 C3
Ciudad Ixtepec Mex. 142 C3
Ciudad Juárez Mex. 142 B1
Ciudad Mante Mex. 142 C2
Ciudad Mier Mex. 142 C2
Ciudad Obregón Mex. 142 B2
Ciudad Real Spain 60 C2
Ciudad Río Bravo Mex. 142 C2
Ciudad Rodrigo Spain 60 B1
Ciudad Victoria Mex. 142 C2
Ciutadella de Menorca Spain 60 D1
Cıvan Dağ *mt.* Turkey 64 C3
Cividale del Friuli Italy 62 B1
Civitanova Marche Italy 62 B2
Civitavecchia Italy 62 B2
Civray France 58 C2
Çivril Turkey 64 C3

Cixi China 82 C2
Clacton-on-Sea U.K. 52 D4
Claire, Lake Can. 126 D2
Clamecy France 58 C2
Clanwilliam S. Africa 108 A3
Clare Austr. 116 B2
Clare Island Rep. of Ireland 50 E2
Claremont U.S.A. 136 F2
Claremorris Rep. of Ireland 50 F2
Clarence N.Z. 118 B3
Clarenville Can. 128 E2
Claresholm Can. 126 D2
Clarinda U.S.A. 134 D2
Clarión, Isla *i.* Mex. 142 A3
Clarkebury S. Africa 108 C3
Clark Fork *r.* U.S.A. 132 C1
Clark Hill Reservoir U.S.A. 138 D2
Clarksburg U.S.A. 136 D3
Clarksdale U.S.A. 138 B2
Clarksville *AR* U.S.A. 138 B1
Clarksville *TN* U.S.A. 138 C1
Claro *r.* Brazil 154 B1
Clayton U.S.A. 140 D1
Clear, Cape Rep. of Ireland 50 F3
Cleare, Cape U.S.A. 124 C3
Clear Lake U.S.A. 134 E2
Clear Lake *l.* U.S.A. 132 B3
Clearwater Can. 126 D2
Clearwater *r.* Can. 126 D2
Clearwater U.S.A. 138 D3
Clearwater *r.* U.S.A. 132 C1
Cleburne U.S.A. 140 E2
Clermont Austr. 114 D2
Clermont-en-Argonne France 54 B3
Clermont-Ferrand France 58 C2
Cleve Austr. 116 B2
Cleveland *MS* U.S.A. 138 B2
Cleveland *OH* U.S.A. 136 D2
Cleveland *TN* U.S.A. 138 D1
Cleveland, Mount U.S.A. 132 D1
Clewiston U.S.A. 138 D3
Clifden Rep. of Ireland 50 E2
Clifton Austr. 116 E1
Clifton U.S.A. 140 C2
Clinton Can. 126 C2
Clinton *IA* U.S.A. 134 E2
Clinton *MO* U.S.A. 134 E3
Clinton *OK* U.S.A. 140 E1
Clisham *h.* U.K. 50 A2
Clitheroe U.K. 52 B3
Clonakilty Rep. of Ireland 50 F3
Cloncurry Austr. 114 D2
Clones Rep. of Ireland 50 G1
Clonmel Rep. of Ireland 50 G2
Cloppenburg Ger. 54 D1
Cloud Peak U.S.A. 134 B2
Clovis U.S.A. 140 D2
Cluff Lake Mine Can. 126 E2
Cluj-Napoca Romania 44 B2
Cluny Austr. 114 C2
Cluses France 58 D2
Clutha *r.* N.Z. 118 A4
Clyde *r.* U.K. 50 B3
Clyde, Firth of *est.* U.K. 50 B3
Clydebank U.K. 50 B3
Clyde River Can. 124 H2
Coalcomán Mex. 142 B3
Coaldale U.S.A. 132 C3
Coal River Can. 126 C2
Coari Brazil 150 C3
Coari *r.* Brazil 150 C3
Coastal Plain U.S.A. 138 B2
Coast Mountains Can. 126 C2
Coast Ranges *mts* U.S.A. 132 B2
Coatbridge U.K. 50 B3
Coats Island Can. 126 G1
Coats Land *reg.* Antarctica 118 D2
Coatzacoalcos Mex. 142 C3
Cobán Guat. 144 A3
Cobar Austr. 116 D2
Cóbh Rep. of Ireland 50 F3

Cobija Bol. 152 B2
Cobourg Can. 136 E2
Cobourg Peninsula Austr. 114 C1
Cobram Austr. 116 D3
Coburg Ger. 54 E2
Cochabamba Bol. 152 B2
Cochem Ger. 54 C2
Cochin India 84 B4
Cochrane Can. 128 D2
Cochrane Chile 152 A5
Cockburn Austr. 116 C2
Cockburn Town Turks and Caicos Is *see* Grand Turk
Cockermouth U.K. 52 B2
Cockscomb *mt.* S. Africa 108 B3
Coco *r.* Hond./Nic. 144 B3
Cocos Islands *terr.* Indian Ocean 70 A3
Australian External Territory.
Cocula Mex. 142 B2
Cocuy, Sierra Nevada del *mt.* Col. 150 B2
Cod, Cape U.S.A. 136 F2
Codigoro Italy 62 B2
Cod Island Can. 128 D1
Codó Brazil 150 E3
Cody U.S.A. 134 B2
Coen Austr. 114 D1
Coesfeld Ger. 54 C2
Coeur d'Alene U.S.A. 132 C1
Coffee Bay S. Africa 108 C3
Coffeyville U.S.A. 134 D3
Coffs Harbour Austr. 116 E2
Cognac France 58 B2
Cogo Equat. Guinea 104 A2
Cohuna Austr. 116 C3
Coiba, Isla de *i.* Panama 144 B4
Coihaique Chile 152 A5
Coimbatore India 84 B3
Coimbra Port. 60 B1
Colac Austr. 116 C3
Colatina Brazil 154 D1
Colby U.S.A. 134 C3
Colchester U.K. 52 D4
Cold Lake Can. 126 D2
Coldstream U.K. 50 C3
Coleman U.S.A. 140 E2
Coleraine Austr. 116 C3
Coleraine U.K. 50 F1
Coles, Punta de *pt* Peru 146
Colesberg S. Africa 108 C3
Colima Mex. 142 B3
Colima, Nevado de *vol.* Mex. 142 B3
Coll *i.* U.K. 50 A2
Collarenebri Austr. 116 D1
Collier Bay Austr. 114 B1
Collingwood N.Z. 118 B3
Collo Alg. 60 C2
Collooney Rep. of Ireland 50 F1
Colmar France 58 D2
Cologne Ger. 54 C2
Colômbia Brazil 154 C2
Colombia *country* S. America 150 B2
2nd most populous and 4th largest country in South America.
Colombo Sri Lanka 84 B4
Former capital of Sri Lanka.
Colomiers France 58 C3
Colón Arg. 152 C4
Colón Panama 144 C4
Colonna, Capo *c.* Italy 62 C3
Colonsay *i.* U.K. 50 A2
Colorado *r.* Arg. 152 B4
Colorado *r.* Mex./U.S.A. 140 A2
Colorado *r.* U.S.A. 140 E3
Colorado *state* U.S.A. 134 B3
Colorado Plateau U.S.A. 134 B3
Colorado Springs U.S.A. 134 C3
Colotlán Mex. 142 B2
Cölpin Ger. 54 F1
Colstrip U.S.A. 134 B1
Columbia *MO* U.S.A. 134 E3

Columbia *SC* U.S.A. **138** D2
Capital of South Carolina.
Columbia *TN* U.S.A. **138** C1
Columbia *r.* U.S.A. **132** B1
Columbia, Mount Can. **126** D2
Columbia Falls U.S.A. **132** D1
Columbia Mountains Can. **126** C2
Columbia Plateau U.S.A. **132** C1
Columbus *GA* U.S.A. **138** D2
Columbus *IN* U.S.A. **136** C3
Columbus *MS* U.S.A. **138** C2
Columbus *NE* U.S.A. **134** D2
Columbus *NM* U.S.A. **140** C2
Columbus *OH* U.S.A. **136** D3
Capital of Ohio.
Colville U.S.A. **132** C1
Colville *r.* U.S.A. **124** B2
Colville Lake Can. **124** D2
Colwyn Bay U.K. **52** B3
Comacchio Italy **62** B2
Comalcalco Mex. **142** C3
Comăneşti Romania **44** C2
Combles France **54** A2
Comencho, Lac *l.* Can. **128** C1
Comeragh Mountains Rep. of Ireland
50 G2
Comilla Bangl. **86** D2
Comines Belgium **54** A2
Comino, Capo *c.* Italy **62** A2
Comitán de Domínguez Mex. **142** C3
Commentry France **58** C2
Commerce U.S.A. **140** E2
Como Italy **62** A1
Como, Lake Italy **62** A1
Comodoro Rivadavia Arg. **152** B5
Comorin, Cape India **66**
Comoro Islands Africa **96**
Comoros *country* Africa **106** D1
Compiègne France **58** C2
Compostela Mex. **142** B2
Comrat Moldova **44** C2
Conakry Guinea **100** A4
Capital of Guinea.
Conceição da Barra Brazil **154** E1
Conceição do Araguaia Brazil **150** E3
Conceição do Mato Dentro Brazil
154 D1
Concepción Arg. **152** B3
Concepción Chile **152** A4
Concepción Mex. **142** B2
Conception, Point *pt* U.S.A. **132** B4
Conchas Brazil **154** C2
Conchas Lake U.S.A. **140** D1
Conchos *r.* Nuevo León/Tamaulipas Mex.
142 C2
Conchos *r.* Mex. **142** B2
Concord *CA* U.S.A. **132** B3
Concord *NH* U.S.A. **136** F2
Capital of New Hampshire.
Concordia Arg. **152** C4
Concordia S. Africa **108** A2
Concordia U.S.A. **134** D3
Condobolin Austr. **116** D2
Condom France **58** C3
Condon U.S.A. **132** B1
Conegliano Italy **62** B1
Conflict Group *is* P.N.G. **114** E1
Confolens France **58** C2
Congdü China **86** C2
Congo *country* Africa **104** B3
Congo *r.* Congo/Dem. Rep. Congo **96**
*2nd longest river in Africa, and 8th in the
world.*
Congo, Democratic Republic of
country Africa **104** C3
*3rd largest and 4th most populous
country in Africa.*
Congo Basin Dem. Rep. Congo **96**
Conklin Can. **126** D2
Conn, Lough *l.* Rep. of Ireland **50** F1
Connaught *reg.* Rep. of Ireland **50** F2

Connecticut *r.* U.S.A. **136** F2
Connecticut *state* U.S.A. **136** F2
Connemara *reg.* Rep. of Ireland **50** F2
Conrad U.S.A. **132** D1
Conroe U.S.A. **140** E2
Conselheiro Lafaiete Brazil **154** D2
Conselheiro Pena Brazil **154** D1
Consett U.K. **52** C2
Côn Son *i.* Vietnam **74** B3
Constanţa Romania **44** C3
Constantina Spain **60** B2
Constantine Alg. **100** C1
Contact U.S.A. **132** D2
Contamana Peru **150** B3
Contreras, Isla *i.* Chile **152** A6
Contwoyto Lake Can. **126** D1
Conway *AR* U.S.A. **138** B1
Conway *NH* U.S.A. **136** F2
Coober Pedy Austr. **116** A1
Cook, Mount N.Z. **118** B3
Highest mountain in New Zealand.
Cookeville U.S.A. **138** C1
Cook Inlet *sea chan.* U.S.A. **124** B2
Cook Islands S. Pacific Ocean **110**
Self-governing New Zealand territory.
Cook Islands *terr.* S. Pacific Ocean **112**
Cook's Harbour Can. **128** E1
Cookstown U.K. **50** G1
Cook Strait N.Z. **118** B3
Cooktown Austr. **114** D1
Coolabah Austr. **116** D2
Coolamon Austr. **116** D2
Coolangatta Austr. **116** E1
Coolgardie Austr. **114** B3
Cooma Austr. **116** D3
Coombah Austr. **116** C2
Coonabarabran Austr. **116** D2
Coonalpyn Austr. **116** B3
Coonamble Austr. **116** D2
Cooper Creek *watercourse* Austr. **116** B1
Coos Bay U.S.A. **132** B2
Cootamundra Austr. **116** D2
Copainalá Mex. **142** C3
Copala Mex. **142** C3
Copenhagen Denmark **46** C4
Capital of Denmark.
Copertino Italy **62** C2
Copiapó Chile **152** A3
Copper Harbor U.S.A. **136** C1
Coppermine Can. *see* Kugluktuk
Coppermine *r.* Can. **124** E2
Copperton S. Africa **108** B2
Coquimbo Chile **152** A3
Corabia Romania **44** B3
Coração de Jesus Brazil **154** D1
Coracora Peru **150** B4
Coraki Austr. **116** E1
Coral Bay Austr. **114** A2
Coral Harbour Can. **124** G2
Coral Sea S. Pacific Ocean **114** E1
Coral Sea Islands Territory *terr.* Austr.
112
Australian External Territory.
Corangamite, Lake Austr. **116** C3
Corby U.K. **52** C3
Corcovado, Golfo de *sea chan.* Chile
152 A5
Cordele U.S.A. **138** D2
Cordilleras Range *mts* Phil. **76** B2
Córdoba Arg. **152** B4
Córdoba Mex. **142** C3
Córdoba Spain **60** C2
Córdoba, Sierras de *mts* Arg. **152** B4
Cordova U.S.A. **126** A1
Corfu *i.* Greece **64** A3
Coria Spain **60** B2
Corinth Greece **64** B3
Corinth U.S.A. **138** C2
Corinth, Gulf of *sea chan.* Greece
64 B3
Corinto Brazil **154** D1

Cork Rep. of Ireland **50** F3
Çorlu Turkey **64** C2
Cornélio Procópio Brazil **154** B2
Corner Brook Can. **128** E2
Corner Inlet *b.* Austr. **116** D3
Corning *CA* U.S.A. **132** B3
Corning *NY* U.S.A. **136** E2
Corno, Monte *mt.* Italy **62** B2
Cornwall Can. **128** C2
Cornwallis Island Can. **124** F1
Coro Venez. **150** C1
Coromandel Brazil **154** C1
Coromandel Peninsula N.Z. **118** C2
Coronation Can. **126** D2
Coronation Gulf Can. **124** E2
Coronel Oviedo Para. **152** C3
Coronel Suárez Arg. **152** B4
Çorovodë Albania **64** B2
Corozal Belize **142** C3
Corpus Christi U.S.A. **140** E3
Corque Bol. **152** B2
Corrente Brazil **150** E4
Correntes Brazil **154** B1
Correntina Brazil **150** E4
Corrib, Lough *l.* Rep. of Ireland **50** F2
Corrientes Arg. **152** C3
Corrientes, Cabo *c.* Arg. **146**
Corrientes, Cabo *c.* Mex. **142** B2
Corryong Austr. **116** D3
Corse *i.* France *see* Corsica
Corse, Cap *c.* France **58** D3
Corsica *i.* France **58** D3
Corsicana U.S.A. **140** E2
Corte France **58** D3
Cortegana Spain **60** B2
Cortez U.S.A. **134** B3
Cortina d'Ampezzo Italy **62** B1
Cortland U.S.A. **136** E2
Cortona Italy **62** B2
Coruche Port. **60** B2
Çoruh Turkey *see* Artvin
Çorum Turkey **92** B1
Corumbá Brazil **152** C2
Corumbá *r.* Brazil **154** C1
Corvallis U.S.A. **132** B2
Corwen U.K. **52** B3
Cosalá Mex. **142** B2
Cosamaloapan Mex. **142** C3
Cosenza Italy **62** C3
Cosne-Cours-sur-Loire France **58** C2
Costa Blanca *coastal area* Spain **60** C2
Costa Brava *coastal area* Spain **60** D1
Costa del Sol *coastal area* Spain **60** B2
Costa de Mosquitos *coastal area* Nic.
144 B3
Costa Rica Brazil **154** B1
Costa Rica *country* Central America
144 B3
Costa Rica Mex. **142** B2
Costeşti Romania **44** B3
Cotabato Phil. **76** B3
Côte d'Ivoire *country* Africa **100** B4
Cotopaxi, Volcán *vol.* Ecuador **150** B3
Cotswold Hills U.K. **52** B4
Cottage Grove U.S.A. **132** B2
Cottbus Ger. **56** C2
Coubre, Pointe de la *pt* France **58** B2
Coüedic, Cape de Austr. **116** B3
Council Bluffs U.S.A. **134** D2
Courland Lagoon *b.* Lith./Rus. Fed. **42** B2
Courtenay Can. **126** C3
Coutances France **58** B2
Coutras France **58** B2
Couvin Belgium **54** B2
Coventry U.K. **52** C3
Covington U.S.A. **136** D3
Cowan, Lake *salt flat* Austr. **114** B3
Cowdenbeath U.K. **50** C2
Cowes Austr. **116** D3
Cowlitz *r.* U.S.A. **132** B1
Cowra Austr. **116** D2

Coxim Brazil **154** B1
Cox's Bazar Bangl. **86** D2
Coyuca de Benitez Mex. **142** B3
Cozumel Mex. **142** D2
Cozumel, Isla de *i.* Mex. **142** D2
Cradock S. Africa **108** C3
Craig U.S.A. **134** B2
Crailsheim Ger. **54** E3
Craiova Romania **44** B3
Cranberry Portage Can. **126** E2
Cranbourne Austr. **116** D3
Cranbrook Can. **126** D3
Crateús Brazil **150** E3
Crato Brazil **150** F3
Crawford U.S.A. **134** C2
Crawfordsville U.S.A. **136** C2
Crawley U.K. **52** C4
Crazy Mountains U.S.A. **132** D1
Cree *r.* Can. **126** E2
Creel Mex. **142** B2
Cree Lake Can. **126** E2
Creil Neth. **54** B1
Crema Italy **58** D2
Cremona Italy **62** B1
Crépy-en-Valois France **54** A3
Cres *i.* Croatia **62** B2
Crescent City U.S.A. **132** B2
Creston Can. **126** D3
Creston U.S.A. **134** E2
Crestview U.S.A. **138** C2
Crete *i.* Greece **64** B3
Creus, Cap de *c.* Spain **60** D1
Creutzwald France **54** C3
Crewe U.K. **52** E2
Crianlarich U.K. **50** B2
Criciúma Brazil **152** D3
Crieff U.K. **50** C2
Crikvenica Croatia **62** B1
Crimea *pen.* Ukr. **44** D2
Crimmitschau Ger. **54** F2
Cristalina Brazil **154** C1
Crivitz Ger. **54** E1
Crna Gora *aut. rep.* S.M. **64** A2
Črnomelj Slovenia **62** C1
Croagh Patrick *h.* Rep. of Ireland **50** F2
Croatia *country* Europe **62** C1
Crocker, Banjaran *mts* Malaysia **72** C1
Crockett U.S.A. **140** E2
Croker Island Austr. **70** C3
Cromer U.K. **52** D3
Cromwell N.Z. **118** A4
Crookston U.S.A. **134** D1
Crookwell Austr. **116** D2
Crosby U.S.A. **134** C1
Cross City U.S.A. **138** D3
Crossett U.S.A. **138** B2
Cross Fell *h.* U.K. **52** B2
Cross Lake Can. **126** F2
Crossville U.S.A. **138** C1
Crotone Italy **62** C3
Crowborough U.K. **52** D4
Crowley U.S.A. **138** B2
Crowsnest Pass Can. **126** D3
Cruz, Cabo *c.* Cuba **144** C3
Cruz Alta Brazil **152** C3
Cruz del Eje Arg. **152** B4
Cruzeiro Brazil **154** D2
Cruzeiro do Sul Brazil **150** B3
Crystal Brook Austr. **116** B2
Crystal City U.S.A. **140** E3
Crystal Falls U.S.A. **136** C1
Csongrád Hungary **56** E3
Cuando *r.* Angola/Zambia **106** B1
Cuangar Angola **106** A1
Cuango *r.* Angola/Dem. Rep. Congo **104** B3
Cuanza *r.* Angola **104** B3
Cuatro Ciénegas Mex. **140** D3
Cuauhtémoc Mex. **142** B2
Cuautla Mex. **142** C3

Cuba *country* West Indies **144** B2
5th largest island and 5th most populous country in North America.
Cubal Angola **106** A1
Cubango *r.* Angola/Namibia **106** B1
Cúcuta Col. **150** B2
Cuddalore India **84** B3
Cuddapah India **84** B3
Cuéllar Spain **60** C1
Cuemba Angola **106** A1
Cuenca Ecuador **150** B3
Cuenca Spain **60** C1
Cuenca, Serranía de *mts* Spain **60** C1
Cuernavaca Mex. **142** C3
Cuero U.S.A. **140** E3
Cuiabá Brazil **154** A1
Cuiabá *r.* Brazil **150** D4
Cuillin Sound *sea chan.* U.K. **50** A2
Cuilo Angola **104** B3
Cuito *r.* Angola **106** B1
Cuito Cuanavale Angola **106** A1
Cukai Malaysia **72** B1
Culcairn Austr. **116** D3
Culgoa *r.* Austr. **116** D1
Culiacán Mex. **142** B2
Culion *i.* Phil. **76** A2
Cullera Spain **60** C2
Cullman U.S.A. **138** C2
Cullybackey U.K. **50** G1
Culuene *r.* Brazil **150** D4
Cumaná Venez. **150** C1
Cumberland U.S.A. **136** E3
Cumberland *r.* U.S.A. **136** C3
Cumberland Lake Can. **126** E2
Cumberland Peninsula Can. **124** H2
Cumberland Plateau U.S.A. **138** C1
Cumberland Sound *sea chan.* Can. **124** H2
Cumbernauld U.K. **50** C3
Cummings U.S.A. **132** B3
Cumnock U.K. **50** B3
Cumpas Mex. **142** B1
Cunduacán Mex. **142** C3
Cunene *r.* Angola **106** A1
Cuneo Italy **62** A2
Cuorgnè Italy **62** A1
Cupar U.K. **50** C2
Curaçao *i.* Neth. Antilles **144** D3
Curaray *r.* Ecuador **150** B3
Curicó Chile **152** A4
Curitiba Brazil **154** C3
Curitibanos Brazil **154** B3
Curnamona Austr. **116** B2
Currie Austr. **114** D3
Curtis Island Austr. **114** E2
Curuá *r.* Brazil **150** D3
Curup Indon. **72** B2
Cururupu Brazil **150** E3
Curvelo Brazil **154** D1
Cusco Peru **150** B4
Cushing U.S.A. **140** E1
Cut Bank U.S.A. **132** D1
Cuttack India **86** C2
Cuxhaven Ger. **54** D1
Cuyo Islands Phil. **76** B2
Cuzco Peru *see* Cusco
Cyangugu Rwanda **104** C3
Cyclades *is* Greece **64** B3
Cypress Hills Can. **126** D3
Cyprus *country* Asia **102** B1
Cyprus *i.* Asia **92** B2
Czech Republic *country* Europe **56** C3
Czersk Pol. **56** D2
Częstochowa Pol. **56** D2

D

Daban China **82** B1
Dabola Guinea **100** A3

Dacca Bangl. *see* Dhaka
Dachau Ger. **56** C3
Dadu Pak. **86** A2
Daegu S. Korea *see* Taegu
Daet Phil. **76** B2
Dagana Senegal **100** A3
Dagupan Phil. **76** B2
Dahanu India **86** B3
Da Hinggan Ling *mts* China **82** B1
Dahlak Archipelago *is* Eritrea **102** C3
Dahlem Ger. **54** C2
Dahm, Ramlat *des.* Saudi Arabia/Yemen **90** B3
Dahme Ger. **54** F2
Dahn Ger. **54** C3
Daik Indon. **72** B2
Daimiel Spain **60** C2
Dajarra Austr. **114** C2
Dakar Senegal **100** A3
Capital of Senegal.
Daketa Shet' *watercourse* Eth. **104** E2
Dākhilah, Wāḩāt al *oasis* Egypt **102** A2
Dakhla Oasis Egypt *see* Dākhilah, Wāḩāt al
Dakoank India **74** A3
Dakol'ka *r.* Belarus **42** C3
Đakovica S.M. **64** B2
Đakovo Croatia **62** C1
Dala Angola **106** B1
Dalain Hob China **80** C2
Dalälven *r.* Sweden **46** D3
Dalaman Turkey **64** C3
Dalaman *r.* Turkey **64** C3
Dalandzadgad Mongolia **80** C2
Đa Lat Vietnam **74** B2
Dalbandin Pak. **86** A2
Dalbeattie U.K. **50** C3
Dalby Austr. **116** E1
Dale *Hordaland* Norway **48** E1
Dale *Sogn og Fjordane* Norway **48** E1
Dale Hollow Lake U.S.A. **138** C1
Dalgety Austr. **116** D3
Dalhart U.S.A. **140** D1
Dalhousie Can. **136** G1
Dali China **74** B1
Dalian China **82** C2
Dalkeith U.K. **50** C3
Dallas U.S.A. **140** E2
Dall Island U.S.A. **126** B2
Dalmatia *reg.* Bos.-Herz./Croatia **62** C2
Dal'negorsk Rus. Fed. **78** C2
Dal'nerechensk Rus. Fed. **78** B1
Daloa Côte d'Ivoire **100** B4
Dalrymple, Mount Austr. **114** D2
Dalsmynni Iceland **46**□
Daltenganj India **86** C2
Dalton U.S.A. **138** D2
Daludalu Indon. **72** B1
Dalvík Iceland **46**□
Daly *r.* Austr. **114** C1
Daly Waters Austr. **114** C1
Daman India **86** B2
Damanhūr Egypt **92** B2
Damar *i.* Indon. **70** C3
Damascus Syria **92** B2
Capital of Syria.
Damaturu Nigeria **100** D3
Damghan Iran **92** D2
Dammam Saudi Arabia **90** C2
Damme Ger. **54** D1
Damoh India **86** B2
Damongo Ghana **100** B4
Dampir, Selat *sea chan.* Indon. **70** C3
Damroh India **74** A1
Damxung China **86** D1
Danané Côte d'Ivoire **100** B4
Đa Nẵng Vietnam **74** B2
Danbury U.S.A. **136** F2
Dandong China **82** C1
Dangriga Belize **144** B3
Dangshan China **82** B2

Danilov Rus. Fed. **42** F2
Danilovskaya Vozvyshennost' *hills*
Rus. Fed. **42** F2
Danjiangkou China **82** B2
Dankov Rus. Fed. **42** E3
Danlí Hond. **144** B3
Dannenberg (Elbe) Ger. **54** E1
Dannevirke N.Z. **118** C3
Dan Sai Thai. **74** B2
Dantu China **82** B2
Danube r. Austria/Ger. **56** D3
Danube r. Bulg./Croatia/S.M. **64** C2
Danube r. Hungary **56** D3
   2nd longest river in Europe.
Danube r. Romania **44** C2
Danube Delta Romania/Ukr. **44** C2
Danville *IL* U.S.A. **136** C2
Danville *KY* U.S.A. **136** D3
Danville *VA* U.S.A. **136** E3
Danzhou China **82** A4
Daoxian China **82** B3
Dapaong Togo **100** C3
Da Qaidam Zhen China **80** C2
Daqing China **80** E1
Dar'ā Syria **92** B2
Dārāb Iran **92** D3
Daraj Libya **100** D1
Dārān Iran **92** D2
Đa Răng, Sông r. Vietnam **74** B2
Darbhanga India **86** C2
Dardanelles *str.* Turkey **64** C2
Dar es Salaam Tanz. **104** D3
   Former capital of Tanzania.
Darfur *reg.* Sudan **102** A3
Dargai Pak. **86** B1
Dargaville N.Z. **118** B2
Dargo Austr. **116** D3
Darhan Mongolia **80** D1
Darién, Golfo del g. Col. **150** B2
Darjiling India **86** C2
Darlag China **80** C2
Darling r. Austr. **116** C2
   2nd longest river in Oceania, and a major
   part of the longest (Murray-Darling)
Darling Downs *hills* Austr. **116** D1
Darling Range *hills* Austr. **114** A3
Darlington U.K. **52** C2
Darlington Point Austr. **116** D2
Darłowo Pol. **56** D2
Darmstadt Ger. **54** D3
Darnah Libya **100** E1
Darnick Austr. **116** C2
Daroca Spain **60** C1
Dartford U.K. **52** D4
Dartmoor *hills* U.K. **52** A4
Dartmouth Can. **128** D2
Dartmouth U.K. **52** B4
Daru P.N.G. **70** D3
Darvaza Turkm. **88** C2
Darwin Austr. **114** C1
   Capital of Northern Territory.
Dashoguz Turkm. **88** C2
Dasht r. Pak. **86** A2
Datadian Indon. **72** C1
Datça Turkey **64** C3
Datong China **82** B1
Datu Piang Phil. **76** B3
Daud Khel Pak. **86** B1
Daugava r. Latvia **42** B2
Daugavpils Latvia **42** C2
Daun Ger. **54** C2
Dauphin Can. **126** E2
Dauphin Lake Can. **126** F2
Davangere India **84** B3
Davao Phil. **76** B3
Davao Gulf Phil. **76** B3
Davenport U.S.A. **134** E2
Daventry U.K. **52** C3
Daveyton S. Africa **108** C2
David Panama **144** B4
Davidson Can. **126** E2

Davis U.S.A. **132** B3
Davis Inlet Can. **128** D1
Davis Sea Antarctica **118** I3
Davis Strait Can./Greenland **124** I2
Davos Switz. **58** D2
Dawqah Oman **90** C3
Dawson Can. **126** B1
Dawson U.S.A. **138** C2
Dawson Creek Can. **126** C2
Dawsons Landing Can. **126** C2
Dawu China **80** C2
Dax France **58** B3
Da Xueshan *mts* China **80** C2
Dayr az Zawr Syria **92** C2
Dayton U.S.A. **136** D3
Daytona Beach U.S.A. **138** D3
Da Yunhe *canal* China **82** B2
Dazhou China **82** A2
De Aar S. Africa **108** B3
Dead Sea *salt l.* Asia **92** B2
   Lowest point in the world and in Asia.
De'an China **82** B3
Deán Funes Arg. **152** B4
Dease Lake Can. **126** C2
Death Valley *depr.* U.S.A. **132** C3
   Lowest point in the Americas.
Deauville France **58** C2
Debak Malaysia **72** C1
Debar Macedonia **64** B2
Debrecen Hungary **56** E3
Debre Markos Eth. **102** B3
Debre Tabor Eth. **102** B3
Debre Zeyit Eth. **102** B4
Decatur *AL* U.S.A. **138** C2
Decatur *IL* U.S.A. **136** C3
Deccan *plat.* India **84** B3
   Plateau making up most of southern and
   central India.
Děčín Czech Rep. **56** C2
Decorah U.S.A. **134** E2
Dedovichi Rus. Fed. **42** D2
Dedza Malawi **106** C1
Dee r. England/Wales U.K. **52** B3
Dee r. Scotland U.K. **50** C2
Deepwater Austr. **116** E1
Deer Lake Can. **128** E2
Deer Lodge U.S.A. **132** D1
Defiance U.S.A. **136** D2
Dêgê China **80** C2
Degeh Bur Eth. **102** C4
Deggendorf Ger. **56** C3
Degtevo Rus. Fed. **44** F2
Dehra Dun India **86** B1
Dehri India **86** C2
Dehui China **80** E2
Deinze Belgium **54** A2
Dej Romania **44** B2
De Kalb U.S.A. **136** C2
Dekemhare Eritrea **90** A3
Dekese Dem. Rep. Congo **104** C3
Delano U.S.A. **132** C3
Delano Peak U.S.A. **132** D3
Delap-Uliga-Djarrit Marshall Is **112**
   Capital of the Marshall Islands, on Majuro
   atoll.
Delārām Afgh. **86** A1
Delareyville S. Africa **108** C2
Delaronde Lake Can. **126** E2
Delaware U.S.A. **136** D2
Delaware r. U.S.A. **136** E3
Delaware *state* U.S.A. **136** E3
Delaware Bay U.S.A. **136** E3
Delegate Austr. **116** D3
Delémont Switz. **58** D2
Delft Neth. **54** B1
Delfzijl Neth. **54** C1
Delgado, Cabo c. Moz. **104** E4
Delhi India **86** B2
Deli i. Indon. **72** B2
Déljne Can. **126** C1
Delitzsch Ger. **54** F2

Dellys Alg. **60** D2
Delmenhorst Ger. **54** D1
Delnice Croatia **62** B1
De-Longa, Ostrova *is* Rus. Fed. **94** M1
Deloraine Can. **126** E3
Delphi *tourist site* Greece **64** B3
Del Rio U.S.A. **140** D3
Delta *CO* U.S.A. **134** B3
Delta *UT* U.S.A. **132** D3
Delta Junction U.S.A. **124** C2
Delvinë Albania **64** B3
Demanda, Sierra de la *mts* Spain **60** C1
Demba Dem. Rep. Congo **104** C3
Dembī Dolo Eth. **102** B4
Demidov Rus. Fed. **42** D2
Deming U.S.A. **140** C2
Demirci Turkey **64** C3
Demirköy Turkey **64** C2
Demmin Ger. **56** C2
Demopolis U.S.A. **138** C2
Dempo, Gunung *vol.* Indon. **72** B2
Demyansk Rus. Fed. **42** D2
De Naawte S. Africa **108** B3
Denakil *reg.* Eritrea/Eth. **102** C3
Den Burg Neth. **54** B1
Dendermonde Belgium **54** B2
Dengkou China **82** A1
Dengzhou China **82** B2
Den Haag Neth. *see* The Hague
Denham Austr. **114** A2
Den Helder Neth. **54** B1
Deniliquin Austr. **116** C3
Denio U.S.A. **132** C2
Denison *IA* U.S.A. **134** D2
Denison *TX* U.S.A. **140** E2
Denizli Turkey **64** C3
Denman Austr. **116** E2
Denmark Austr. **114** A3
Denmark *country* Europe **46** C4
Denmark Strait Greenland/Iceland
   124 K2
Denpasar Indon. **72** C2
Denton U.S.A. **140** E2
D'Entrecasteaux, Point *pt* Austr. **114** A3
Denver U.S.A. **134** B3
   Capital of Colorado.
Deogarh *Orissa* India **86** C2
Deogarh *Rajasthan* India **86** B2
Deoghar India **86** C2
Deputatskiy Rus. Fed. **94** L2
Dêqên China **74** A1
De Queen U.S.A. **138** B2
Dera Bugti Pak. **86** A2
Dera Ghazi Khan Pak. **86** B1
Dera Ismail Khan Pak. **86** B1
Derbent Rus. Fed. **40** D4
Derby Austr. **114** B1
Derby U.K. **52** C3
Dereham U.K. **52** D3
Derg, Lough l. Rep. of Ireland **50** F2
Derhachi Ukr. **44** E2
De Ridder U.S.A. **138** B2
Derkul r. Rus. Fed./Ukr. **44** E2
Dêrub China **86** B1
Derudeb Sudan **102** B3
De Rust S. Africa **108** B3
Derventa Bos.-Herz. **62** C2
Derwent r. U.K. **52** C3
Derwent Water l. U.K. **52** B2
Derzhavinsk Kazakh. **88** D1
Desaguadero r. Bol. **152** B2
Désappointement, Îles du *is*
   Fr. Polynesia **110**
Deschambault Lake Can. **126** E2
Deschutes r. U.S.A. **132** B1
Desē Eth. **102** B3
Deseado Arg. **152** B5
Deseado r. Arg. **152** B5
Des Moines U.S.A. **134** E2
   Capital of Iowa.
Des Moines r. U.S.A. **134** E2

Desna r. Rus. Fed./Ukr. **44** D1
Desnogorsk Rus. Fed. **42** D3
Dessau Ger. **54** F2
Destruction Bay Can. **126** B1
Desventurados, Islas de los is
  S. Pacific Ocean **148**
Detah Can. **126** D1
Detmold Ger. **54** D2
Detroit U.S.A. **136** D2
Detroit Lakes U.S.A. **134** D1
Deurne Neth. **54** B2
Deva Romania **44** B2
Deventer Neth. **54** C1
Deveron r. U.K. **50** C2
Devét Skal h. Czech Rep. **56** D3
Devil's Lake U.S.A. **134** D1
Devil's Paw mt. U.S.A. **126** B2
Devizes U.K. **52** C4
Devli India **86** B2
Devnya Bulg. **64** C2
Devon Can. **126** D2
Devon Island Can. **124** F1
Devonport Austr. **114** D4
Dewas India **86** B2
Dexter U.S.A. **134** F3
Deyang China **82** A2
Deyong, Tanjung pt Indon. **70** D3
Dezfül Iran **92** C2
Dezhou China **82** B2
Dhahran Saudi Arabia **90** C2
Dhaka Bangl. **86** D2
  Capital of Bangladesh, and 7th most
  populous city in Asia.
Dhamār Yemen **90** B3
Dhamtari India **86** C2
Dhanbad India **86** C2
Dhankuta Nepal **86** C2
Dharmanagar India **74** A1
Dharmjaygarh India **86** C2
Dharwad India **84** B3
Dhasa India **86** B2
Dhubāb Yemen **90** B3
Dhule India **86** B2
Diablo, Picacho del mt. Mex. **142** A1
Diamantina watercourse Austr. **114** C2
Diamantina Brazil **154** D1
Diamantina, Chapada plat. Brazil **150** E4
Diamantino Brazil **150** D4
Dianbai China **82** B3
Dianópolis Brazil **150** E4
Dianra Côte d'Ivoire **100** B4
Diapaga Burkina **100** C3
Dibā al Ḥiṣn U.A.E. **90** C2
Dibaya Dem. Rep. Congo **104** C3
Dibrugarh India **84** D2
Dickinson U.S.A. **134** C1
Dickson U.S.A. **138** C1
Dicle r. Turkey see Tigris
Die France **58** D3
Diefenbaker, Lake Can. **126** E2
Diéma Mali **100** B3
Diên Châu Vietnam **74** B2
Diepholz Ger. **54** D1
Dieppe France **58** C2
Diffa Niger **100** D3
Digby Can. **128** D2
Digne-les-Bains France **58** D3
Digoin France **58** C2
Digos Phil. **76** B3
Digul r. Indon. **70** D3
Dijlah, Nahr r. Iraq/Syria **66**
Dijon France **58** D2
Dikhil Djibouti **102** C3
Dikili Turkey **64** C3
Diksmuide Belgium **54** A2
Dikwa Nigeria **100** D3
Dīla Eth. **102** B4
Dili East Timor **70** C3
  Capital of East Timor.
Dillenburg Ger. **54** D2
Dillon U.S.A. **132** D1

Dilolo Dem. Rep. Congo **104** C4
Dimapur India **74** A1
Dimashq Syria see Damascus
Dimboola Austr. **116** C3
Dimitrovgrad Bulg. **64** C2
Dimitrovgrad Rus. Fed. **40** D3
Dinagat i. Phil. **76** B2
Dinan France **58** B2
Dinant Belgium **54** B2
Dinar Turkey **92** B2
Dīnār, Kūh-e mt. Iran **92** D2
Dinaric Alps mts Bos.-Herz./Croatia **36**
Dindigul India **84** B3
Dindiza Moz. **108** D1
Dingelstädt Ger. **54** E2
Dingle Rep. of Ireland **50** E2
Dingle Bay Rep. of Ireland **50** E2
Dingwall U.K. **50** B2
Dingxi China **82** A2
Dinkelsbühl Ger. **54** E3
Dinngyê China **86** C2
Dionísio Cerqueira Brazil **154** B3
Diourbel Senegal **100** A3
Dipolog Phil. **76** B3
Dir Pak. **86** B1
Direction, Cape Austr. **114** D1
Dirē Dawa Eth. **102** C4
Dirico Angola **106** B1
Dirk Hartog Island Austr. **114** A2
Dirranbandi Austr. **116** D1
Ḍirs Saudi Arabia **90** B3
Disappointment, Cape S. Georgia
  152 E6
Disappointment, Lake salt flat Austr.
  114 B2
Discovery Bay Austr. **116** C3
Dismal Swamp U.S.A. **136** E3
Diss U.K. **52** D3
Dittaino r. Italy **62** C3
Diu India **86** B2
Divinópolis Brazil **154** D2
Divnoye Rus. Fed. **40** D4
Divo Côte d'Ivoire **100** B4
Divriği Turkey **92** B2
Dixon U.S.A. **136** C2
Dixon Entrance sea chan. Can./U.S.A.
  126 B2
Diyarbakır Turkey **92** C2
Diz Pak. **86** A2
Djado Niger **100** D2
Djado, Plateau du Niger **100** D2
Djambala Congo **104** B3
Djanet Alg. **100** C2
Djelfa Alg. **100** C1
Djéma C.A.R. **104** C2
Djenné Mali **100** B3
Djibo Burkina **100** B3
Djibouti country Africa **102** C3
Djibouti Djibouti **102** C3
  Capital of Djibouti.
Djougou Benin **100** C4
Djúpivogur Iceland **46**□
Dmitriyevka Rus. Fed. **42** F3
Dmitriyev-L'govskiy Rus. Fed. **42** E3
Dmitrov Rus. Fed. **42** E2
Dnepr r. Rus. Fed. see Dnieper
Dnieper r. Rus. Fed. **42** D3
Dnieper r. Ukr. **44** D2
  3rd longest river in Europe.
Dniester r. Ukr. **44** C2
Dnipro r. Ukr. see Dnieper
Dniprodzerzhyns'k Ukr. **44** D2
Dnipropetrovs'k Ukr. **44** E2
Dniprorudne Ukr. **44** D2
Dnister r. Ukr. see Dniester
Dno Rus. Fed. **42** C2
Doba Chad **100** D4
Dobele Latvia **42** C1
Döbeln Ger. **54** F2
Doberai, Jazirah pen. Indon. **70** C3
Dobo Indon. **70** C3

Doboj Bos.-Herz. **62** C2
Dobrich Bulg. **64** C2
Dobrinka Rus. Fed. **42** F3
Dobroye Rus. Fed. **42** E3
Dobrush Belarus **42** D3
Doce r. Brazil **154** E1
Doctor Arroyo Mex. **142** B2
Doctor Belisario Domínguez Mex.
  142 B2
Dodecanese is Greece **64** C3
Dodekanisos is Greece see Dodecanese
Dodge City U.S.A. **134** C3
Dodoma Tanz. **104** D3
  Capital of Tanzania.
Doetinchem Neth. **54** C2
Dofa Indon. **70** C3
Dogai Coring salt l. China **86** C1
Dog Creek Can. **126** C2
Dōgo i. Japan **78** B3
Dogondoutchi Niger **100** C3
Doğubeyazıt Turkey **92** C2
Doha Qatar **90** C2
  Capital of Qatar.
Doi Saket Thai. **74** A2
Dokkum Neth. **54** B1
Dokshytsy Belarus **42** C3
Dokuchayevs'k Ukr. **44** E2
Dolak, Pulau i. Indon. **70** D3
Dolbeau Can. **128** C2
Dol-de-Bretagne France **58** B2
Dole France **58** D2
Dolgellau U.K. **52** B3
Dolgorukovo Rus. Fed. **42** E3
Dolgoye Rus. Fed. **42** E3
Dolinsk Rus. Fed. **80** F1
Dolisie Congo see Loubomo
Dolomites mts Italy **62** B1
Dolo Odo Eth. **102** C4
Dolyna Ukr. **44** B2
Domažlice Czech Rep. **56** C3
Dombås Norway **46** B3
Dombóvár Hungary **56** D3
Dome Creek Can. **126** C2
Dominica country West Indies **144** D3
Dominican Republic country
  West Indies **144** C3
Domodedovo Rus. Fed. **42** E2
Domokos Greece **64** B3
Dompu Indon. **72** C2
Don r. Rus. Fed. **42** E3
  5th longest river in Europe.
Don r. U.K. **50** C2
Donaghadee U.K. **50** H1
Donald Austr. **116** C3
Donau r. Austria/Ger. see Danube
Donauwörth Ger. **56** C3
Don Benito Spain **60** B2
Doncaster U.K. **52** C3
Dondo Angola **104** B3
Dondo Moz. **106** C1
Dondra Head hd Sri Lanka **84** C4
Donegal Rep. of Ireland **50** F1
Donegal Bay Rep. of Ireland **50** F1
Donets'k Ukr. **44** E2
Donets'kyy Kryazh hills Rus. Fed./Ukr.
  44 E2
Dongara Austr. **114** A2
Dongchuan China **82** A3
Dongfang China **82** A4
Dongfanghong China **78** B1
Donggala Indon. **72** C2
Donggang China **76** C2
Dongguan China **82** B3
Đông Ha Vietnam **74** B2
Đông Hôi Vietnam **74** B2
Dongou Congo **104** C2
Dongshan China **82** B3
Dongsheng China see Ordos
Dongtai China **82** C2
Dongting Hu l. China **82** B3
Dongying China **82** B2

Eagle Cap *mt.* U.S.A. **132** C1
Eagle Lake Can. **128** A2
Eagle Lake U.S.A. **132** B2
Eagle Pass U.S.A. **140** D3
Eagle Plain Can. **124** C2
Ear Falls Can. **128** A1
East Antarctica *reg.* Antarctica **118** I2
Eastbourne U.K. **52** D4
East China Sea N. Pacific Ocean **80** E2
East Coast Bays N.Z. **118** B2
Eastend Can. **132** E1
Easter Island *i.* S. Pacific Ocean **158** G6
  Part of Chile.
Eastern Cape *prov.* S. Africa **108** C3
Eastern Desert Egypt **102** B2
Eastern Ghats *mts* India **84** B3
Easterville Can. **126** F2
East Falkland *i.* Falkland Is **152** C6
East Frisian Islands Ger. **54** C1
East Kilbride U.K. **50** B3
Eastleigh U.K. **52** C4
East Liverpool U.S.A. **136** D2
East London S. Africa **108** C3
Eastmain Can. **128** C1
Eastmain *r.* Can. **128** C1
Eastman U.S.A. **138** D2
East Sea N. Pacific Ocean *see*
  Japan, Sea of
East Siberian Sea Rus. Fed. **94** L2
East St Louis U.S.A. **136** B3
East Timor *country* Asia **68**
  The world's newest independent country.
  Gained independence from Indonesia in
  2002.
Eau Claire U.S.A. **136** B2
Eau Claire, Lac à l' *l.* Can. **128** C1
Eauripik *atoll* Micronesia **70** D2
Ebano Mex. **142** C2
Ebbw Vale U.K. **52** B4
Eberswalde-Finow Ger. **54** F1
Eboli Italy **62** C2
Ebolowa Cameroon **104** B2
Ebro *r.* Spain **60** D1
Ech Chélif Alg. **100** C1
Echeverria, Pico *mt.* Mex. **142** A2
Echoing *r.* Can. **126** F2
Echternach Lux. **54** C3
Echuca Austr. **116** C3
Écija Spain **60** B2
Eckernförde Ger. **56** B2
Ecuador *country* S. America **150** B3
Ed Eritrea **102** C3
Ed Da'ein Sudan **102** A3
Ed Damazin Sudan **102** B3
Ed Damer Sudan **102** B3
Ed Debba Sudan **102** B3
Ed Dueim Sudan **102** B3
Eddystone Point *pt* Austr. **114** D4
Ede Neth. **54** B1
Edéa Cameroon **104** B2
Edéia Brazil **154** C1
Eden Austr. **116** D3
Eden *r.* U.K. **52** B2
Edenburg S. Africa **108** C2
Edenderry Rep. of Ireland **50** G2
Edenhope Austr. **116** C3
Edessa Greece **64** B2
Edgeøya *i.* Svalbard **94** D1
Edinburg U.S.A. **140** D3
Edinburgh U.K. **50** C3
  Capital of Scotland.
Edirne Turkey **64** C2
Edmonton Can. **126** D2
  Capital of Alberta.
Edmundston Can. **136** G1
Edremit Turkey **64** C3
Edremit Körfezi *b.* Turkey **64** C3
Edson Can. **126** D2
Edward, Lake
  Dem. Rep. Congo/Uganda **104** C3
Edward's Creek Austr. **116** B1

Edwards Plateau U.S.A. **140** D2
Eenrum Neth. **54** C1
Éfaté *i.* Vanuatu **110**
Effingham U.S.A. **136** C3
Egan Range *mts* U.S.A. **132** D3
Eger Hungary **56** E3
Egersund Norway **46** B4
Egilsstaðir Iceland **46**☐
Eğirdir Turkey **92** B2
Eğirdir Gölü *l.* Turkey **92** B2
Égletons France **58** C2
Egvekinot Rus. Fed. **94** O2
Egypt *country* Africa **102** A2
  2nd most populous country in Africa.
Ehen Hudag China **82** A2
Eibergen Neth. **54** C2
Eifel *hills* Ger. **54** C2
Eigg *i.* U.K. **50** A2
Eight Degree Channel India/Maldives
  84 B4
Eighty Mile Beach Austr. **114** B1
Eilat Israel **92** B3
Eilenburg Ger. **54** F2
Einbeck Ger. **54** D2
Eindhoven Neth. **54** B2
Eirunepé Brazil **150** C3
Eiseb *watercourse* Namibia **106** B1
Eisenach Ger. **54** E2
Eisenhüttenstadt Ger. **56** C2
Eisenstadt Austria **56** D3
Eisleben Lutherstadt Ger. **54** E2
Eivissa Spain **60** D2
Eivissa *i.* Spain *see* Ibiza
Ejea de los Caballeros Spain **60** C1
Ejeda Madag. **106**☐ D2
Ekenäs Fin. **46** E4
Ekibastuz Kazakh. **88** E1
Ekostrovskaya Imandra, Ozero *l.*
  Rus. Fed. **46** G2
Eksjö Sweden **46** C4
Eksteenfontein S. Africa **108** A2
Ekwan *r.* Can. **128** B1
Ela Myanmar **74** A2
Elandsdoorn S. Africa **108** C2
Elassona Greece **64** B3
Elazığ Turkey **92** B2
Elba, Isola d' *i.* Italy **62** B2
El Banco Col. **150** B2
Elbasan Albania **64** B2
El Baúl Venez. **150** C2
El Bayadh Alg. **100** C1
Elbe *r.* Ger. **54** D1
Elbert, Mount U.S.A. **134** B3
Elberton U.S.A. **138** D2
Elbeuf France **58** C2
Elbistan Turkey **92** B2
Elbląg Pol. **56** D2
El'brus *mt.* Rus. Fed. **92** C1
  Highest mountain in Europe.
Elburz Mountains Iran **92** C2
El Callao Venez. **150** C2
El Campo U.S.A. **140** E3
El Centro U.S.A. **132** C4
El Cerro Bol. **152** B2
Elche-Elx Spain **60** C2
Elda Spain **60** C2
Eldon U.S.A. **134** E3
Eldorado Arg. **154** B3
El Dorado Mex. **142** B2
El Dorado *AR* U.S.A. **138** B2
El Dorado *KS* U.S.A. **134** D3
El Eglab *plat.* Alg. **100** B2
El Ejido Spain **60** C2
Elektrostal' Rus. Fed. **42** E2
El Encanto Col. **150** B3
El Eulma Alg. **60** E2
Eleuthera *i.* Bahamas **144** C2
El Fasher Sudan **102** A3
El Fuerte Mex. **142** B2
El Geneina Sudan **102** A3
El Geteina Sudan **102** B3

Elgin U.K. **50** C2
Elgin U.S.A. **136** C2
El Goléa Alg. **100** C1
El Golfo de Santa Clara Mex. **142** A1
Elgon, Mount Uganda **104** D2
El Ḥammâmi *reg.* Maur. **100** A2
El Hierro *i.* Canary Is **100** A2
El Higo Mex. **142** C2
El Homr Alg. **100** C2
Elim U.S.A. **124** B2
Elista Rus. Fed. **40** D4
Elizabeth U.S.A. **136** F2
Elizabeth City U.S.A. **138** E1
Elizabethtown U.S.A. **136** C3
El Jadida Morocco **100** B1
Ełk Pol. **56** E2
Elk City U.S.A. **140** E1
Elkford Can. **126** D2
Elkhart U.S.A. **136** C2
Elkhovo Bulg. **64** C2
Elkins U.S.A. **136** E3
Elko Can. **126** D3
Elko U.S.A. **132** C2
Elk Point Can. **126** D2
Ellef Ringnes Island Can. **124** F1
Ellendale U.S.A. **134** D1
Ellensburg U.S.A. **132** B1
Ellesmere, Lake N.Z. **118** B3
Ellesmere Island Can. **124** G1
  4th largest island in North America, and
  10th in the world.
Ellesmere Port U.K. **52** B3
Ellice *r.* Can. **124** F2
Elliotdale S. Africa **108** C3
Ellon U.K. **50** C2
Ellsworth U.S.A. **136** G2
Ellsworth Mountains Antarctica **118** N2
Elmalı Turkey **64** C3
El Meghaïer Alg. **100** C1
El Milia Alg. **60** E2
Elmira U.S.A. **136** E2
El Moral Spain **60** C2
Elmshorn Ger. **54** D1
El Muglad Sudan **102** A3
El Nido Phil. **76** A2
El Obeid Sudan **102** B3
El Oro Mex. **142** B2
El Oued Alg. **100** C1
Eloy U.S.A. **140** B2
El Paso U.S.A. **140** C2
El Porvenir Mex. **142** B1
El Prat de Llobregat Spain **60** D1
El Progreso Hond. **142** D3
El Reno U.S.A. **140** E1
Elsa Can. **126** B1
El Salado Mex. **142** B2
El Salto Mex. **142** B2
El Salvador *country* Central America
  144 B3
El Salvador Mex. **142** B2
El Sauz Mex. **140** C3
El Socorro Mex. **142** A1
Elsterwerda Ger. **54** F2
El Temascal Mex. **142** C2
El Tigre Venez. **150** C2
El Tocuyo Venez. **144** D4
Elva Estonia **42** C2
Elvas Port. **60** B2
Elverum Norway **46** C3
El Wak Kenya **104** E2
Ely U.K. **52** D3
Ely *MN* U.S.A. **134** E1
Ely *NV* U.S.A. **132** D3
Emāmrūd Iran **92** D2
Emån *r.* Sweden **46** D4
Emba Kazakh. **88** C2
Emba *r.* Kazakh. **88** C2
Embalenhle S. Africa **108** C2
Emborção, Represa de *resr* Brazil
  154 C1
Embu Kenya **104** D3

Ezhva Rus. Fed. **40** E2
Ezine Turkey **64** C3

F

Fabens U.S.A. **140** C2
Fåborg Denmark **56** C1
Fabriano Italy **62** B2
Fachi Niger **100** D3
Fada-N'Gourma Burkina **100** C3
Faenza Italy **62** B2
Fafanlap Indon. **70** C3
Făgăraş Romania **44** B2
Fagatogo American Samoa **112**
Capital of American Samoa.
Fagernes Norway **46** B3
Fagersta Sweden **46** D4
Fagnano, Lago *l.* Arg./Chile **152** B6
Faguibine, Lac *l.* Mali **100** B3
Fagurhólsmýri Iceland **46**□
Fairbanks U.S.A. **124** C2
Fairbury U.S.A. **134** D2
Fairfield U.S.A. **132** B3
Fair Isle *i.* U.K. **50**□
Fairmont *MN* U.S.A. **134** E2
Fairmont *WV* U.S.A. **136** D3
Fairview Can. **126** D2
Fairweather, Mount Can./U.S.A. **126** B2
Fais *i.* Micronesia **70** D2
Faisalabad Pak. **86** B1
Faith U.S.A. **134** C1
Faizabad India **86** C2
Fakarava *atoll* Fr. Polynesia **110**
Fakfak Indon. **70** C3
Faku China **76** C1
Falaba Sierra Leone **100** A4
Falcon Lake Mex./U.S.A. **140** E3
Falfurrias U.S.A. **140** E3
Falher Can. **126** D2
Falkenberg Ger. **54** F2
Falkenberg Sweden **46** C4
Falkensee Ger. **54** F1
Falkirk U.K. **50** C3
Falkland Islands *terr.* S. Atlantic Ocean **152** C6
United Kingdom Overseas Territory.
Falköping Sweden **46** C4
Fallon U.S.A. **132** C3
Fall River U.S.A. **136** F2
Falls City U.S.A. **134** D2
Falmouth U.K. **52** A4
False Bay S. Africa **108** A3
Falso, Cabo *c.* Mex. **120**
Falster *i.* Denmark **46** C5
Fălticeni Romania **44** C2
Falun Sweden **46** D3
Fameck France **54** C3
Fangchenggang China **82** A3
Fangshan Taiwan **82** C3
Fangzheng China **80** E1
Fano Italy **62** B2
Fan Si Pan *mt.* Vietnam **74** B1
Faradje Dem. Rep. Congo **104** C2
Farafangana Madag. **106**□ D2
Farāfirah, Wāḥāt al *oasis* Egypt **102** A2
Farāh Afgh. **86** A1
Farah Rūd *watercourse* Afgh. **86** A1
Faranah Guinea **100** A3
Farasān, Jazā'ir *is* Saudi Arabia **90** B3
Farewell, Cape Greenland **124** J2
Farewell, Cape N.Z. **118** B3
Fargo U.S.A. **134** D1
Farg'ona Uzbek. **88** E2
Faribault U.S.A. **134** E2
Faribault, Lac *l.* Can. **128** C1
Farmington *ME* U.S.A. **136** F2
Farmington *NM* U.S.A. **140** C1
Farmville U.S.A. **136** E3
Farnborough U.K. **52** C4
Farnham, Mount Can. **126** D2

Faro Can. **126** B1
Faro Port. **60** B2
Fårö *i.* Sweden **42** A2
Faroe Islands *terr.* N. Atlantic Ocean **48** B1
Self-governing Danish territory.
Farrāshband Iran **92** D3
Farwell U.S.A. **140** D2
Fāryāb Iran **90** C2
Fasā Iran **92** D3
Fasano Italy **62** C2
Fastiv Ukr. **44** C1
Fatehgarh India **86** B2
Fatehpur India **86** C2
Faulquemont France **54** C3
Fauske Norway **46** D2
Faxaflói *b.* Iceland **46**□
Faxälven *r.* Sweden **46** D3
Faya Chad **100** D3
Fayetteville *AR* U.S.A. **138** B1
Fayetteville *NC* U.S.A. **138** E1
Fayetteville *TN* U.S.A. **138** C1
Fazilka India **86** B1
Fdérik Maur. **100** A2
Fear, Cape U.S.A. **138** E2
Featherston N.Z. **118** C3
Fécamp France **58** C2
Fehmarn *i.* Ger. **56** C2
Fehrbellin Ger. **54** F1
Feia, Lagoa *lag.* Brazil **154** D2
Feijó Brazil **150** B3
Feilding N.Z. **118** C3
Feira de Santana Brazil **150** F4
Felanitx Spain **60** D2
Feldberg Ger. **54** F1
Felipe C. Puerto Mex. **142** D3
Felixlândia Brazil **154** D1
Felixstowe U.K. **52** D4
Felsberg Ger. **54** D2
Feltre Italy **62** B1
Femunden *l.* Norway **46** C3
Fengcheng *Jiangxi* China **82** B3
Fengcheng *Liaoning* China **76** C1
Fengqing China **74** A1
Fengxian China **82** B2
Fengyüan Taiwan **82** C3
Fengzhen China **82** B1
Feno, Capo di *c.* France **58** D3
Fenoarivo Atsinanana Madag. **106**□ D1
Feodosiya Ukr. **44** E2
Fer, Cap de *c.* Alg. **62** A3
Fergus Falls U.S.A. **134** D1
Ferkessédougou Côte d'Ivoire **100** B4
Fermo Italy **62** B2
Fermont Can. **128** D1
Fermoselle Spain **60** B1
Fermoy Rep. of Ireland **50** F2
Fernandina Beach U.S.A. **138** D2
Fernandópolis Brazil **154** B2
Fernie Can. **126** D3
Ferrara Italy **62** B2
Ferreiros Brazil **154** B2
Ferro, Capo *c.* Italy **62** A2
Ferrol Spain **60** B1
Ferwert Neth. **54** B1
Fès Morocco **100** B1
Feshi Dem. Rep. Congo **104** B3
Festus U.S.A. **134** E3
Fethiye Turkey **64** C3
Fetlar *i.* U.K. **50**□
Feucht Ger. **54** E3
Feuilles, Rivière aux *r.* Can. **128** C1
Feyzābād Afgh. **86** B1
Fez Morocco *see* Fès
Fianarantsoa Madag. **106**□ D2
Fichē Eth. **102** B4
Fier Albania **64** A2
Fife Ness *pt* U.K. **50** C2
Figeac France **58** C3
Figueira da Foz Port. **60** B1
Figueres Spain **60** D1

Figuig Morocco **100** B1
Fiji *country* S. Pacific Ocean **112**
4th most populous and 5th largest country in Oceania.
Fīk' Eth. **104** E2
Filadelfia Para. **152** B3
Filchner Ice Shelf Antarctica **118** D2
Filey U.K. **52** C2
Filippiada Greece **64** B3
Filipstad Sweden **46** C4
Findhorn *r.* U.K. **50** C2
Findlay U.S.A. **136** D2
Fingal Austr. **114** D4
Finger Lakes U.S.A. **136** E2
Finisterre, Cape Spain **60** B1
Finland *country* Europe **46** F3
Finland, Gulf of Europe **46** E4
Finlay *r.* Can. **126** C2
Finley Austr. **116** C3
Finne *ridge* Ger. **54** E2
Finnmarksvidda *reg.* Norway **46** E2
Finnsnes Norway **46** D2
Finspång Sweden **46** D4
Finsterwalde Ger. **54** F2
Fionnphort U.K. **50** A2
Firenze Italy *see* Florence
Firminy France **58** C2
Firozabad India **86** B2
Firozpur India **86** B1
Firūzābād Iran **92** D3
Fish *watercourse* Namibia **108** A2
Fish *r.* S. Africa **108** B3
Fisher Strait Can. **126** G1
Fishguard U.K. **52** A4
Fismes France **58** C2
Fisterra, Cabo *c.* Spain *see* Finisterre, Cape
Fitchburg U.S.A. **136** F2
Fitzgerald Can. **126** D2
Fitzroy Crossing Austr. **114** B1
Fivizzano Italy **62** B2
Fizi Dem. Rep. Congo **104** C3
Fjällsjöälven *r.* Sweden **46** D3
Flagstaff S. Africa **108** C3
Flagstaff U.S.A. **140** B1
Flaherty Island Can. **128** C1
Flamborough Head *hd* U.K. **52** C2
Fläming *hills* Ger. **54** F1
Flaming Gorge Reservoir U.S.A. **134** B2
Flathead *r.* U.S.A. **132** D1
Flathead Lake U.S.A. **132** D1
Flattery, Cape Austr. **114** D1
Flattery, Cape U.S.A. **132** B1
Fleetwood U.K. **52** B3
Flekkefjord Norway **46** B4
Flen Sweden **42** A2
Flensburg Ger. **56** B2
Flers France **58** B2
Flinders *r.* Austr. **114** D1
Flinders Bay Austr. **114** A3
Flinders Island Austr. **114** D3
Flinders Ranges *mts* Austr. **116** B2
Flin Flon Can. **126** E2
Flint U.S.A. **136** D2
Florac France **60** D1
Florence Italy **62** B2
Florence *AL* U.S.A. **138** C2
Florence *AZ* U.S.A. **140** B2
Florence *OR* U.S.A. **132** B2
Florence *SC* U.S.A. **138** E2
Florencia Col. **150** B2
Flores Guat. **144** B3
Flores *i.* Indon. **72** D2
Flores, Laut *sea* Indon. *see* Flores, Laut
Flores Sea Indon. *see* Flores, Laut
Floresta Brazil **150** F3
Floresville U.S.A. **140** E3
Floriano Brazil **150** E3
Florianópolis Brazil **154** C3
Florida Uru. **152** C4
Florida *state* U.S.A. **138** D2

Fumay France 58 C2
Funafuti *atoll* Tuvalu 110
Funchal Madeira 100 A1
Capital of Madeira.
Fundão Port. 60 B1
Fundy, Bay of *g.* Can. 128 D2
Funhalouro Moz. 108 D1
Funing *Jiangsu* China 82 B2
Funing *Yunnan* China 82 A3
Funtua Nigeria 100 C3
Fürgun, Küh-e *mt.* Iran 90 C2
Furmanov Rus. Fed. 42 F2
Furnas, Represa *resr* Brazil 154 C2
Furneaux Group *is* Austr. 114 D4
Fürstenau Ger. 54 C1
Fürstenwalde Ger. 54 G1
Fürth Ger. 54 E3
Furth im Wald Ger. 54 F3
Furukawa Japan 78 D3
Fushun China 82 C1
Fusong China 76 D1
Fuwayriṭ Qatar 90 C2
Fuxin China 82 C1
Fuyang China 82 B2
Fuyu China 80 E1
Fuyun China 88 F2
Fuzhou *Fujian* China 82 B3
Fuzhou *Jiangxi* China 82 B3
Fyn *i.* Denmark 46 C4

G

Gaalkacyo Somalia 102 C4
Gabela Angola 106 A1
Gabès Tunisia 100 D1
Gabès, Golfe de *g.* Tunisia 100 D1
Gabgaba, Wadi *watercourse* Sudan 90 A2
Gabon *country* Africa 104 B3
Gaborone Botswana 108 C1
Capital of Botswana.
Gabrovo Bulg. 64 C2
Gabú Guinea-Bissau 100 A3
Gadag India 84 B3
Gadchiroli India 86 C2
Gadebusch Ger. 54 E1
Gadsden U.S.A. 138 C2
Găeşti Romania 44 C3
Gaeta Italy 62 B2
Gaferut *i.* Micronesia 110
Gaffney U.S.A. 138 D1
Gafsa Tunisia 100 C1
Gagarin Rus. Fed. 42 E2
Gagnoa Côte d'Ivoire 100 B4
Gagnon Can. 128 D1
Gagra Georgia 92 C1
Gaiab *watercourse* Namibia 108 A2
Gaillac France 58 C3
Gainesville *FL* U.S.A. 138 D3
Gainesville *GA* U.S.A. 138 D2
Gainesville *TX* U.S.A. 140 E2
Gainsborough U.K. 52 C3
Gairdner, Lake *salt flat* Austr. 116 B2
Gairloch U.K. 50 B2
Galana *r.* Kenya 104 E3
Galanta Slovakia 56 D3
Galapagos Islands Ecuador 148
Part of Ecuador.Most westerly point of
South America.
Galashiels U.K. 50 C3
Galaţi Romania 44 C2
Galdhøpiggen *mt.* Norway 46 B3
Galeana Mex. 142 B2
Galena Bay Can. 126 D2
Galera, Punta *pt* Chile 146
Galesburg U.S.A. 136 B2
Galich Rus. Fed. 42 F2
Galichskaya Vozvyshennost' *hills*
Rus. Fed. 42 F2
Galicia *aut. comm.* Spain 60 B1

Galilee, Sea of *l.* Israel 92 B2
Gallatin U.S.A. 138 C1
Galle Sri Lanka 84 C4
Gallinas, Punta *pt* Col. 150 B1
Most northerly point of South America.
Gallipoli Italy 62 C2
Gallipoli Turkey 64 C2
Gällivare Sweden 46 E2
Gallup U.S.A. 140 C1
Galtat Zemmour Western Sahara 100 A2
Galtymore *h.* Rep. of Ireland 50 F2
Galveston U.S.A. 140 F3
Galveston Bay U.S.A. 140 F3
Galway Rep. of Ireland 50 F2
Galway Bay Rep. of Ireland 50 F2
Gamá Brazil 154 C1
Gamalakhe S. Africa 108 D3
Gambia, The *country* Africa 100 A3
Gambier, Îles *is* Fr. Polynesia 110
Gambier Islands Austr. 116 B3
Gambo Can. 128 E2
Gamboma Congo 104 B3
Ganado U.S.A. 140 C1
Ganāveh Iran 90 D3
Gäncä Azer. 92 C1
Gandadiwata, Bukit *mt.* Indon. 72 C2
Gandajika Dem. Rep. Congo 104 C3
Gander Can. 128 E2
Gander *r.* Can. 128 E2
Ganderkesee Ger. 54 D1
Gandesa Spain 60 D1
Gandhidham India 86 B2
Gandhinagar India 86 B2
Gandhi Sagar *resr* India 86 B2
Gandía Spain 60 C2
Ganga *r.* Bangl./India 86 D2
Gangán Arg. 152 B5
Ganganagar India 86 B2
Gangca China 80 C2
Gangdisê Shan *mts* China 86 C1
Ganges France 58 C3
Ganges, Mouths of the Bangl./India
86 C2
Gangtok India 86 C2
Gannat France 58 C2
Gannett Peak U.S.A. 134 B2
Gansbaai S. Africa 108 A3
Gansu *prov.* China 82 A2
Ganzhou China 82 B3
Gao Mali 100 B3
Gaoual Guinea 100 A3
Gaoyou China 82 B2
Gaoyou Hu *l.* China 82 B2
Gap France 58 D3
Gap Carbon *hd* Alg. 60 C2
Gar China 86 C1
Garah Austr. 116 D1
Garanhuns Brazil 150 F3
Garbaharrey Somalia 104 E2
Garberville U.S.A. 132 B2
Garbsen Ger. 54 D1
Garça Brazil 154 C2
Garda, Lake Italy 62 B1
Gardelegen Ger. 54 E1
Garden City U.S.A. 134 C3
Garden Hill Can. 126 F2
Gardēz Afgh. 86 A1
Gariep Dam *resr* S. Africa 108 C3
Garies S. Africa 108 A3
Garissa Kenya 104 D3
Garmisch-Partenkirchen Ger. 56 C3
Garnpung Lake *imp. l.* Austr. 116 C2
Garonne *r.* France 58 B3
Garoowe Somalia 102 C4
Garoth India 86 B2
Garoua Cameroon 104 B2
Garry *r.* U.K. 50 B2
Garry Lake Can. 126 E1
Garsen Kenya 104 E3
Garut Indon. 72 B2

Gary U.S.A. 136 C2
Garza García Mex. 142 B2
Garzê China 80 C2
Gascony, Gulf of France 58 B3
Gascoyne *r.* Austr. 114 A2
Gashua Nigeria 100 D3
Gaspé Can. 128 D2
Gaspé, Péninsule de *pen.* Can.
128 D2
Gaston, Lake U.S.A. 138 E1
Gastonia U.S.A. 138 D1
Gata, Cabo de *c.* Spain 60 C2
Gatchina Rus. Fed. 42 D2
Gateshead U.K. 52 C2
Gatesville U.S.A. 140 E2
Gatineau *r.* Can. 128 C2
Gatton Austr. 116 E1
Gauer Lake Can. 126 F2
Gausta *mt.* Norway 46 B4
Gauteng *prov.* S. Africa 108 C2
Gāvbandī Iran 90 C2
Gavdos *i.* Greece 64 B4
Most southerly point of Europe.
Gävle Sweden 46 D3
Gavrilov Posad Rus. Fed. 42 F2
Gavrilov-Yam Rus. Fed. 42 E2
Gawai Myanmar 74 A1
Gawler Austr. 116 B2
Gawler Ranges *hills* Austr. 116 B2
Gaya India 86 C2
Gaya Niger 100 C3
Gaylord U.S.A. 136 D1
Gayny Rus. Fed. 40 E2
Gaza *terr.* Asia 92 B2
Semi-autonomous region.
Gaz-Achak Turkm. 88 D2
Gazandzhyk Turkm. 88 C3
Gaziantep Turkey 102 B1
Gbarnga Liberia 100 B4
Gdańsk Pol. 56 D2
Gdańsk, Gulf of Pol./Rus. Fed. 56 D2
Gdov Rus. Fed. 42 C2
Gdynia Pol. 56 D2
Gedaref Sudan 102 B3
Gedern Ger. 54 D2
Gediz *r.* Turkey 64 C3
Gedser Denmark 56 C2
Geel Belgium 54 B2
Geelong Austr. 116 C3
Geesthacht Ger. 54 E1
Gê'gyai China 86 C1
Geikie *r.* Can. 124 F3
Geilo Norway 46 B3
Gejiu China 82 A3
Gela Italy 62 B3
Gelendzhik Rus. Fed. 44 E3
Gelibolu Turkey *see* Gallipoli
Gelsenkirchen Ger. 54 C2
Gemena Dem. Rep. Congo 104 B2
Gemlik Turkey 64 C2
Gemona del Friuli Italy 58 E2
Genalē Wenz *r.* Eth. 102 C4
General Acha Arg. 152 B4
General Alvear Arg. 152 B4
General Belgrano Arg. 152 C4
General Cepeda Mex. 142 B2
General Pico Arg. 152 B4
General Roca Arg. 152 B4
General Santos Phil. 76 B3
Genesee *r.* U.S.A. 136 E2
Geneseo U.S.A. 136 E2
Geneva Switz. 58 D2
Geneva U.S.A. 136 E2
Geneva, Lake France/Switz. 58 D2
Genève Switz. *see* Geneva
Genil *r.* Spain 60 D2
Genk Belgium 54 B2
Genoa Italy 62 A2
Genova Italy *see* Genoa
Gent Belgium *see* Ghent
Genthin Ger. 54 F1

Gorokhovets Rus. Fed. **42** F2
Gorom Gorom Burkina **100** B3
Gorontalo Indon. **72** D1
Gorshechnoye Rus. Fed. **42** E3
Gorumna Island Rep. of Ireland **50** F2
Goryachiy Klyuch Rus. Fed. **44** E3
Gorzów Wielkopolski Pol. **56** D2
Gosford Austr. **116** E2
Goshogawara Japan **78** D2
Goslar Ger. **54** E2
Gospić Croatia **62** C2
Gosport U.K. **52** C4
Gostivar Macedonia **64** B2
Göteborg Sweden *see* Gothenburg
Gotha Ger. **54** E2
Gothenburg Sweden **46** C4
Gothenburg U.S.A. **134** C2
Gotland *i.* Sweden **46** D4
Gotse Delchev Bulg. **64** B2
Gotska Sandön *i.* Sweden **46** D4
Gōtsu Japan **78** B4
Göttingen Ger. **54** D2
Gott Peak Can. **126** C2
Gouda Neth. **54** B1
Goudiri Senegal **100** A3
Goudoumaria Niger **100** D3
Gouin, Réservoir *resr* Can. **128** C2
Goulburn Austr. **116** D2
Goulburn *r.* N.S.W. Austr. **116** C3
Goulburn *r.* Vic. Austr. **116** C3
Goundam Mali **100** B3
Gouraya Alg. **60** D2
Gourdon France **58** C3
Gouré Niger **100** D3
Gourits *r.* S. Africa **108** B3
Gourma-Rharous Mali **100** B3
Gourock Range *mts* Austr. **116** D3
Governador Valadares Brazil **154** D1
Governor's Harbour Bahamas **138** E3
Govĭ Altayn Nuruu *mts* Mongolia **80** C2
Govind Ballash Pant Sagar *resr* India **86** C2
Gower *pen.* U.K. **52** A4
Goya Arg. **152** C3
Göyçay Azer. **92** C1
Gozha Co *salt l.* China **86** C1
Graaf-Reinet S. Africa **108** B3
Grabow Ger. **54** E1
Gračac Croatia **62** C2
Grachevka Rus. Fed. **40** E3
Gräfenhainichen Ger. **54** F2
Grafton Austr. **116** E1
Grafton U.S.A. **134** D1
Graham U.S.A. **140** E2
Graham Island Can. **126** B2
Graham Land *reg.* Antarctica **118** N3
Grahamstown S. Africa **108** C3
Grajaú Brazil **150** B3
Grammos *mt.* Greece **64** B2
Grampian Mountains U.K. **50** B2
Granada Nic. **144** B3
Granada Spain **60** C2
Granby Can. **136** F1
Gran Canaria *i.* Canary Is **100** A2
Gran Chaco *reg.* Arg./Para. **152** B3
Grand *r.* U.S.A. **134** C2
Grand Bahama *i.* Bahamas **144** C2
Grand Bank Can. **128** E2
Grand Canal China *see* Da Yunhe
Grand Canyon U.S.A. **140** B1
Grand Canyon *gorge* U.S.A. **140** B1
Grand Cayman *i.* Cayman Is **144** C2
Grand Centre Can. **126** D2
Grand Coulee U.S.A. **132** C1
Grande *r.* Bol. **152** B2
Grande *r.* Brazil **154** B2
Grande, Bahía *b.* Arg. **152** B6
Grande, Ilha *i.* Brazil **154** D2
Grande Cache Can. **126** D2
Grande Comore *i.* Comoros *see* Njazidja

Grande Prairie Can. **126** D2
Grand Erg de Bilma *des.* Niger **100** D3
Grand Erg Occidental *des.* Alg. **100** B1
Grand Erg Oriental *des.* Alg. **100** C2
Grande-Rivière Can. **128** D2
Grandes, Salinas *salt marsh* Arg. **152** B4
Grand Falls *N.B.* Can. **136** G1
Grand Falls Nfld. and Lab. Can. **128** E2
Grand Forks Can. **126** D3
Grand Forks U.S.A. **134** D1
Grandin, Lac *l.* Can. **126** D1
Grand Island U.S.A. **134** D2
Grand Isle U.S.A. **138** B3
Grand Junction U.S.A. **134** B3
Grand-Lahou Côte d'Ivoire **100** B4
Grand Lake *N.B.* Can. **128** D2
Grand Lake Nfld. and Lab. Can. **128** E2
Grand Marais U.S.A. **134** E1
Grândola Port. **60** B2
Grand Rapids Can. **126** F2
Grand Rapids *MI* U.S.A. **136** C2
Grand Rapids *MN* U.S.A. **134** E1
Grand Teton *mt.* U.S.A. **134** A2
Grand Turk Turks and Caicos Is **144** C2
Capital of the Turks and Caicos Islands.
Grangeville U.S.A. **132** C1
Granisle Can. **126** C2
Granite Peak U.S.A. **132** E1
Granitola, Capo *c.* Italy **62** B3
Gränna Sweden **46** C4
Gransee Ger. **54** F1
Grantham U.K. **52** C3
Grantown-on-Spey U.K. **50** C2
Grants U.S.A. **140** C1
Grants Pass U.S.A. **132** B2
Granville France **58** B2
Granville Lake Can. **126** E2
Grão Mogol Brazil **154** D1
Grarem Alg. **60** E2
Graskop S. Africa **108** D1
Grasse France **58** D3
Graus Spain **60** D1
Gravdal Norway **46** C2
Grave, Pointe de *pt* France **58** B2
Gravelbourg Can. **126** E3
Gravenhurst Can. **128** C2
Gravesend Austr. **116** E1
Gravesend U.K. **52** D4
Gray France **58** D2
Graz Austria **56** D3
Great Abaco *i.* Bahamas **144** C2
Great Australian Bight *g.* Austr. **114** B3
Great Barrier Island N.Z. **118** C2
Great Barrier Reef Austr. **114** D1
Great Basin U.S.A. **132** C3
Great Bear Lake Can. **126** D1
3rd largest lake in North America, and 8th in the world.
Great Belt *sea chan.* Denmark **46** C4
Great Bend U.S.A. **134** D3
Great Coco Island Cocos Is **74** A2
Great Dividing Range *mts* Austr. **116** C3
Greater Antilles *is* Caribbean Sea **144** B2
Great Falls U.S.A. **132** D1
Great Fish *r.* S. Africa **108** C3
Great Fish Point *pt* S. Africa **108** C3
Great Inagua *i.* Bahamas **144** C2
Great Karoo *plat.* S. Africa **108** B3
Great Kei *r.* S. Africa **108** C3
Great Malvern U.K. **52** B3
Great Namaqualand *reg.* Namibia **108** A2
Great Nicobar *i.* India **74** A3
Great Ouse *r.* U.K. **52** D3
Great Plains *reg.* U.S.A. **120**
Great Rift Valley Africa **104** D3
Great Ruaha *r.* Tanz. **104** D3
Great Salt Lake U.S.A. **132** D2
Great Salt Lake Desert U.S.A. **132** D2
Great Sand Sea *des.* Egypt/Libya **102** A2
Great Sandy Desert Austr. **114** B2

Great Slave Lake Can. **126** D1
Deepest and 5th largest lake in North America.
Great Smoky Mountains U.S.A. **138** D1
Great Victoria Desert Austr. **114** B2
Great Yarmouth U.K. **52** D3
Gredos, Sierra de *mts* Spain **60** B1
Greece country Europe **64** B3
Greeley U.S.A. **134** C2
Greem-Bell, Ostrov *i.* Rus. Fed. **94** G1
Green *r.* Can. **136** G1
Green *r.* KY U.S.A. **138** C1
Green *r.* WY U.S.A. **134** B3
Green Bay U.S.A. **136** C2
Green Bay *b.* U.S.A. **136** C1
Greenbrier *r.* U.S.A. **136** D3
Greencastle U.S.A. **136** C3
Greeneville U.S.A. **138** D1
Greenfield U.S.A. **136** F2
Green Lake Can. **126** E2
Greenland *terr.* N. America **124** J2
Greenland Sea Greenland/Svalbard **94** B1
Greenock U.K. **50** B3
Green River UT U.S.A. **132** D3
Green River WY U.S.A. **134** B2
Greensburg IN U.S.A. **136** C3
Greensburg PA U.S.A. **136** E2
Green Swamp U.S.A. **138** E2
Green Valley U.S.A. **140** B2
Greenville Liberia **100** B4
Greenville AL U.S.A. **138** C2
Greenville MS U.S.A. **138** B2
Greenville NC U.S.A. **138** E1
Greenville SC U.S.A. **138** D2
Greenville TX U.S.A. **140** E2
Greenwell Point Austr. **116** E2
Greenwood U.S.A. **138** C2
Gregory, Lake *salt flat* Austr. **114** B2
Gregory Range *hills* Austr. **114** D1
Greifswald Ger. **56** C2
Greiz Ger. **54** F2
Grená Denmark **46** C4
Grenada U.S.A. **138** C2
Grenada country West Indies **144** D3
Grenade France **58** C3
Grenfell Austr. **116** D2
Grenfell Can. **126** E2
Grenoble France **58** D2
Grenville, Cape Austr. **114** D1
Gresham U.S.A. **132** B1
Greven Ger. **54** C1
Grevena Greece **64** B2
Grevenbroich Ger. **54** C2
Greybull U.S.A. **134** B2
Grey Hunter Peak Can. **126** B1
Grey Islands Can. **128** E1
Greymouth N.Z. **118** B3
Grey Range *hills* Austr. **116** C1
Greystones Rep. of Ireland **50** G2
Gribanovskiy Rus. Fed. **44** F1
Griffin U.S.A. **138** C2
Griffith Austr. **116** D2
Grimma Ger. **54** F2
Grimmen Ger. **56** C2
Grimsby U.K. **52** C3
Grimshaw Can. **126** D2
Grímsstaðir Iceland **46**□
Grimstad Norway **46** B4
Grinnell U.S.A. **134** E2
Griqualand East *reg.* S. Africa **108** C3
Griqualand West *reg.* S. Africa **108** B2
Grise Fiord Can. **124** G1
Gritley U.K. **50** C1
Groblersdal S. Africa **108** C2
Groblershoop S. Africa **108** B2
Groix, Île de *i.* France **58** B2
Gronau (Westfalen) Ger. **54** C1
Grong Norway **46** C3
Groningen Neth. **54** C1
Grootdrink S. Africa **108** B2

Haicheng China **76** C1
Hai Dương Vietnam **74** B1
Haifa Israel **92** B2
Haifeng China **82** B3
Haikou China **82** B3
Ḩā'il Saudi Arabia **90** B2
Hailar China *see* Hulun Buir
Hailuoto *i.* Fin. **46** E2
Hainan *i.* China **80** D3
Hainan *prov.* China **82** A4
Haines U.S.A. **126** B2
Haines Junction Can. **126** B1
Hainich *ridge* Ger. **54** E2
Hainleite *ridge* Ger. **54** E2
Hai Phong Vietnam **74** B1
Haiti *country* West Indies **144** C3
Haiya Sudan **102** B3
Hajdúböszörmény Hungary **56** E3
Ḩajhir *mt.* Yemen **90** C3
Ḩajjah Yemen **90** B3
Ḩājjīābād Iran **92** D3
Hajmā' Oman **90** C3
Haka Myanmar **74** A1
Hakkâri Turkey **92** C2
Hakodate Japan **78** D2
Ḩalab Syria *see* Aleppo
Halabān Saudi Arabia **90** B2
Halabja Iraq **92** C2
Halaib Sudan **102** B2
Ḩalāniyāt, Juzur al *is* Oman **90** C3
Ḩālat 'Ammār Saudi Arabia **90** A2
Halban Mongolia **80** C1
Halberstadt Ger. **54** E2
Halcon, Mount Phil. **76** B2
Halden Norway **46** C4
Haldensleben Ger. **54** E1
Haldwani India **86** B2
Hāleh Iran **90** C2
Halfmoon Bay N.Z. **118** A4
Halifax Can. **128** D2
Capital of Nova Scotia.
Halifax U.K. **52** C3
Halifax U.S.A. **136** E3
Halla-san *mt.* S. Korea **76** D3
Hall Beach Can. **124** G2
Halle Belgium **54** B2
Hallein Austria **56** C3
Halle (Saale) Ger. **54** E2
Hallock U.S.A. **134** D1
Halls Creek Austr. **114** B1
Halmahera *i.* Indon. **70** C2
Halmstad Sweden **46** C4
Ham France **54** A3
Hamada Japan **78** B4
Hamadān Iran **92** C2
Ḩamāh Syria **92** B2
Hamamatsu Japan **78** C4
Hamar Norway **46** C3
Ḩamāṭah, Jabal *mt.* Egypt **102** B2
Hambantota Sri Lanka **84** C4
Hamburg Ger. **54** D1
Ḩamḍ, Wādī al *watercourse*
  Saudi Arabia **90** A2
Ḩamḍah Saudi Arabia **90** B3
Hämeenlinna Fin. **46** E3
Hameln Ger. **54** D1
Hamersley Range *mts* Austr. **114** A2
Hamhŭng N. Korea **76** D2
Hami China **80** C2
Hamid Sudan **102** B2
Hamilton Austr. **116** C3
Hamilton Can. **128** C2
Hamilton N.Z. **118** C2
Hamilton U.K. **50** B3
Hamilton *AL* U.S.A. **138** C2
Hamilton *MT* U.S.A. **132** D1
Hamilton *OH* U.S.A. **136** D3
Hamina Fin. **46** F3
Hamm Ger. **54** C2
Hammada du Drâa *plat.* Alg. **100** B2
Ḩammār, Hawr al *imp. l.* Iraq **92** C2

Hammelburg Ger. **54** D2
Hammerdal Sweden **46** D3
Hammerfest Norway **46** E1
Hammond U.S.A. **138** B2
Hammonton U.S.A. **136** F3
Hāmūn-e Jaz Mūrīān *salt marsh* Iran
  90 C2
Hamun-i-Lora *dry lake* Afgh./Pak. **86** A2
Hāmūn-i Mashkel *salt flat* Iran **90** C2
Hamun-i-Mashkel *salt flat* Pak. **86** A2
Ḩanak Saudi Arabia **90** A2
Hanamaki Japan **78** D3
Hanau Ger. **54** D2
Hancheng China **82** B2
Hancock U.S.A. **136** C1
Handan China **82** B2
Hanford U.S.A. **132** C3
Hangayn Nuruu *mts* Mongolia **80** C1
Hangzhou China **82** C2
Hangzhou Wan *b.* China **82** C2
Hanko Fin. **46** E4
Hanksville U.S.A. **132** D3
Hanmer Springs N.Z. **118** B3
Hanna Can. **126** D2
Hannibal U.S.A. **134** E3
Hannover Ger. **54** D1
Hannoversch Münden Ger. **54** D2
Hanöbukten *b.* Sweden **46** C4
Ha Nôi Vietnam **74** B1
Capital of Vietnam.
Hanoi Vietnam *see* Ha Nôi
Hanover Can. **128** B2
Hanover S. Africa **108** B3
Hanstholm Denmark **46** B4
Hantsavichy Belarus **42** C3
Hanumana India **86** C2
Hanumangarh India **86** B2
Hanzhong China **82** A2
Hao *atoll* Fr. Polynesia **110**
Haparanda Sweden **46** E2
Hapert Neth. **54** B2
Happy Valley - Goose Bay Can. **128** D1
Ḩaql Saudi Arabia **90** A2
Ḩaraḍh Saudi Arabia **90** B2
Haradok Belarus **42** C2
Ḩarajā Saudi Arabia **90** B3
Harare Zimbabwe **106** C1
Capital of Zimbabwe.
Ḩarāsīs, Jiddat al *des.* Oman **90** C3
Har-Ayrag Mongolia **80** D1
Harbin China **80** E1
Harbour Breton Can. **128** E2
Harda India **86** B2
Hardangerfjorden *sea chan.* Norway
  46 B4
Hardenberg Neth. **54** C1
Harderwijk Neth. **54** B1
Hardeveld *mts* S. Africa **108** A3
Hardin U.S.A. **132** E1
Hardisty Lake Can. **126** D1
Haren (Ems) Ger. **54** C1
Hārer Eth. **102** C4
Hargeysa Somalia **102** C4
Harghita-Mădăraș, Vârful *mt.* Romania
  44 C2
Haripur Pak. **86** B1
Hari Rūd *r.* Afgh./Iran **86** A1
Harlingen Neth. **54** B1
Harlingen U.S.A. **140** E3
Harlow U.K. **52** D4
Harlowton U.S.A. **132** E1
Harnes France **54** A2
Harney Basin U.S.A. **132** C2
Harney Lake U.S.A. **132** C2
Härnösand Sweden **46** D3
Har Nur China **80** E1
Har Nuur *l.* Mongolia **80** C1
Harper Liberia **100** B4
Harpstedt Ger. **54** D1
Harricanaw *r.* Can. **128** C1

Harrington Austr. **116** E2
Harrington Harbour Can. **128** E1
Harris *pen.* U.K. **50** A2
Harris, Lake *salt flat* Austr. **116** B2
Harris, Sound of *sea chan.* U.K. **50** A2
Harrisburg *IL* U.S.A. **136** C3
Harrisburg *PA* U.S.A. **136** E2
Capital of Pennsylvania.
Harrismith S. Africa **108** C2
Harrison U.S.A. **138** B1
Harrison, Cape Can. **128** E1
Harrison Bay U.S.A. **124** B2
Harrisonburg U.S.A. **136** E3
Harrisonville U.S.A. **134** E3
Harrogate U.K. **52** C3
Hârşova Romania **44** C3
Harstad Norway **46** D2
Hartbees *watercourse* S. Africa **108** B2
Hartberg Austria **56** D3
Hartford U.S.A. **136** F2
Capital of Connecticut.
Hartland Point *pt* U.K. **52** A4
Hartlepool U.K. **52** C2
Hartley Bay Can. **126** C2
Harts *r.* S. Africa **108** B2
Hartwell Reservoir U.S.A. **138** D2
Har Us Nuur *l.* Mongolia **80** C1
Harvey U.S.A. **134** C1
Harwich U.K. **52** D4
Harz *hills* Ger. **54** E2
Hassan India **84** B3
Hasselt Belgium **54** B2
Hassi Messaoud Alg. **100** C1
Hässleholm Sweden **46** C4
Hastière-Lavaux Belgium **54** B2
Hastings Austr. **116** D3
Hastings N.Z. **118** C2
Hastings U.K. **52** D4
Hastings *MN* U.S.A. **134** E2
Hastings *NE* U.S.A. **134** D2
Hatay Turkey *see* Antakya
Hatchet Lake Can. **126** E2
Hatfield Austr. **116** C2
Hatgal Mongolia **80** C1
Ha Tinh Vietnam **74** B2
Hatteras, Cape U.S.A. **138** E1
Hattiesburg U.S.A. **138** C2
Hattingen Ger. **54** C2
Hat Yai Thai. **74** B3
Haud *reg.* Eth. **102** C4
Haugesund Norway **46** B4
Haukeligrend Norway **46** B4
Haukipudas Fin. **46** F2
Hauraki Gulf N.Z. **118** C2
Haut Atlas *mts* Morocco **100** B1
Hauterive Can. **128** D2
Hauts Plateaux Alg. **100** B1
Havana Cuba **144** B2
Capital of Cuba.
Havant U.K. **52** C4
Havel *r.* Ger. **54** E1
Havelberg Ger. **54** F1
Havelock N.Z. **118** B3
Havelock North N.Z. **118** C2
Haverfordwest U.K. **52** A4
Havlíčkův Brod Czech Rep. **56** D3
Havøysund Norway **46** E1
Havran Turkey **64** C3
Havre U.S.A. **132** E1
Havre Aubert Can. **128** D2
Havre-St-Pierre Can. **128** D1
Hawaii *i.* U.S.A. **120**
Hawaiian Islands N. Pacific Ocean
  158 E3
Hawarden U.K. **52** B3
Hawea, Lake N.Z. **118** A3
Hawera N.Z. **118** B2
Hawes U.K. **52** C2
Hawick U.K. **50** C3
Hawke Bay N.Z. **118** C2
Hawker Austr. **116** B2

Holyoke U.S.A. **134** C2
Holzminden Ger. **54** D2
Homalin Myanmar **74** A1
Homberg (Efze) Ger. **54** D2
Hombori Mali **100** B3
Homburg Ger. **54** C3
Home Bay Can. **124** H2
Homestead U.S.A. **138** D3
Hommelvik Norway **46** C3
Homs Syria **92** B2
Homyel' Belarus **42** D3
Honolulu U.S.A. **122**
  Capital of Hawaii.
Hondeklipbaai S. Africa **108** A3
Hondo *r.* Belize/Mex. **142** D3
Hondo U.S.A. **140** E3
Honduras *country* Central America **144** B3
Hønefoss Norway **46** C3
Honey Lake *salt l.* U.S.A. **132** B2
Honfleur France **58** C2
Hông Gai Vietnam **74** B1
Honghu China **82** B3
Hongjiang China **82** A3
Hong Kong China **82** B3
Hong Kong *aut. reg.* China **82** B3
Hongwŏn N. Korea **76** D1
Hongze Hu *l.* China **82** B2
Honiara Solomon Is **112**
  Capital of the Solomon Islands.
Honjō Japan **78** D3
Honningsvåg Norway **46** F1
Honshū *i.* Japan **78** B3
  Largest island in Japan, 3rd largest in Asia and 7th in the world.
Hood, Mount *vol.* U.S.A. **132** B1
Hood Point *pt* Austr. **114** A3
Hood River U.S.A. **132** B1
Hoogeveen Neth. **54** C1
Hoogezand-Sappemeer Neth. **54** C1
Hoog-Keppel Neth. **54** C2
Hook of Holland Neth. **54** B2
Hoonah U.S.A. **126** B2
Hoorn Neth. **54** B1
Hoorn, Îles de *is* Wallis and Futuna Is **110**
Hope Can. **126** C3
Hope U.S.A. **138** B2
Hope, Point *pt* U.S.A. **94** O2
Hopedale Can. **128** D1
Hope Mountains Can. **128** D1
Hopetoun Austr. **116** C3
Hopetown S. Africa **108** B2
Hopewell U.S.A. **136** E3
Hopewell Islands Can. **128** C1
Hopkins, Lake *salt flat* Austr. **114** B2
Hopkinsville U.S.A. **136** C3
Hoquiam U.S.A. **132** B1
Horasan Turkey **92** C1
Horažďovice Czech Rep. **54** F3
Hörby Sweden **46** C4
Horki Belarus **42** D3
Horlivka Ukr. **44** E2
Hormak Iran **90** D2
Hormuz, Strait of Iran/Oman **90** C2
Horn Austria **56** D3
Horn *c.* Iceland **46**□
Horn, Cape Chile **152** B6
  Most southerly point of South America.
Hornell U.S.A. **136** E2
Hornepayne Can. **128** E2
Hornsea U.K. **52** C3
Horodenka Ukr. **44** C2
Horodnya Ukr. **44** D1
Horodok *Khmel'nyts'ka Oblast'* Ukr. **44** C2
Horodok *L'vivs'ka Oblast'* Ukr. **44** B2
Horokhiv Ukr. **44** B1
Horse Islands Can. **128** E1
Horsham Austr. **116** C3
Horton *r.* Can. **124** D2
Hosa'ina Eth. **102** B4
Hoshab Pak. **86** A2

Hoshiarpur India **86** B1
Hotan China **86** C1
Hotazel S. Africa **108** B2
Hot Springs *AR* U.S.A. **138** B2
Hot Springs *SD* U.S.A. **134** C2
Hottah Lake Can. **126** D1
Houffalize Belgium **54** B2
Houma China **82** B2
Houma U.S.A. **138** B3
Houston Can. **126** C2
Houston U.S.A. **140** E3
Houwater S. Africa **108** B3
Hovd Mongolia **80** C1
Hove U.K. **52** C4
Hövsgöl Nuur *l.* Mongolia **80** C1
Hövüün Mongolia **80** C2
Howar, Wadi *watercourse* Sudan **102** A3
Howe, Cape Austr. **116** D3
Howland Island *terr.* N. Pacific Ocean **112**
  United States Unincorporated Territory.
Howlong Austr. **116** D3
Höxter Ger. **54** D2
Hoy *i.* U.K. **50** C1
Høyanger Norway **46** B3
Hoyerswerda Ger. **56** C2
Hpapun Myanmar **74** A2
Hradec Králové Czech Rep. **56** D2
Hrasnica Bos.-Herz. **62** C2
Hrebinka Ukr. **44** D1
Hrodna Belarus **42** B3
Hsi-hseng Myanmar **74** A1
Hsinchu Taiwan **82** C3
Hsinying Taiwan **82** C3
Hsipaw Myanmar **74** A1
Huachi China **82** A2
Huacho Peru **150** B4
Huade China **82** B1
Huadian China **76** D1
Huai'an China **82** B2
Huaibei China **82** B2
Huaihua China **82** A3
Huainan China **82** B2
Huaiyang China **82** B2
Huaiyin China *see* Huai'an
Huajuápan de León Mex. **142** C3
Huaki Indon. **70** C3
Hualien Taiwan **82** C3
Huallaga *r.* Peru **150** B3
Huambo Angola **106** A1
Huancavelica Peru **150** B4
Huancayo Peru **150** B4
Huangchuan China **82** B2
Huang Hai *sea* N. Pacific Ocean *see* Yellow Sea
Huang He *r.* China *see* Yellow River
Huangliu China **82** A4
Huangnihe China **76** D1
Huangshan China **82** B3
Huangshi China **82** B2
Huangtu Gaoyuan *plat.* China **82** A2
Huangyan China **82** C3
Huanren China **76** D1
Huánuco Peru **150** B3
Huanuni Bol. **152** B2
Huaráz Peru **150** B3
Huarmey Peru **150** B4
Huascarán, Nevado de *mt.* Peru **146**
Huasco Chile **152** A3
Huasco *r.* Chile **152** A3
Huatabampo Mex. **142** B2
Huatusco Mex. **142** C3
Huayuan China **82** A3
Huayxay Laos **74** B1
Hubei *prov.* China **82** B2
Hubli India **84** B3
Hückelhoven Ger. **54** C2
Hucknall U.K. **52** C3
Huddersfield U.K. **52** C3
Hudiksvall Sweden **46** D3
Hudson *r.* U.S.A. **136** F2

Hudson Bay Can. **126** E2
Hudson Bay *sea* Can. **124** G3
Hudson's Hope Can. **126** C2
Hudson Strait Can. **124** H2
Huê Vietnam **74** B2
Huehuetenango Guat. **144** A3
Huehueto, Cerro *mt.* Mex. **142** B2
Huejutla Mex. **142** C2
Huelva Spain **60** B2
Huércal-Overa Spain **60** C2
Huesca Spain **60** C1
Huéscar Spain **60** C2
Hughes Austr. **114** B3
Hugo U.S.A. **140** E2
Huhudi S. Africa **108** B2
Huib-Hoch Plateau Namibia **108** A2
Huichang China **82** B3
Huich'ŏn N. Korea **76** D1
Huilai China **82** B3
Huila Plateau Angola **106** A1
Huili China **74** B1
Huinan China **76** D1
Huittinen Fin. **46** E3
Huixtla Mex. **142** C3
Huize China **82** A3
Huizhou China **82** B3
Hujirt Mongolia **80** C1
Hujr Saudi Arabia **90** B2
Hukuntsi Botswana **108** B1
Ḩulayfah Saudi Arabia **90** B2
Hulin China **78** B1
Hull Can. **128** C2
Hulun Buir China **80** D1
Hulun Nur *l.* China **80** D1
Hulyaypole Ukr. **44** E2
Huma China **80** E1
Humaitá Brazil **150** C3
Humansdorp S. Africa **108** B3
Humber *est.* U.K. **52** C3
Humboldt Can. **124** E3
Humboldt U.S.A. **138** C1
Humboldt *r.* U.S.A. **132** C2
Humenné Slovakia **56** E3
Hume Reservoir Austr. **116** D3
Humphreys Peak U.S.A. **140** B1
Húnaflói *b.* Iceland **46**□
Hunan *prov.* China **82** B3
Hunchun China **76** E1
Hunedoara Romania **44** B2
Hünfeld Ger. **54** D2
Hungary *country* Europe **56** D3
Hungerford Austr. **116** C1
Hüngnam N. Korea **76** D2
Hun He *r.* China **76** C1
Hunstanton U.K. **52** D3
Hunte *r.* Ger. **54** D1
Hunter Island S. Pacific Ocean **110**
Hunter Islands Austr. **114** D4
Huntingdon U.K. **52** C3
Huntington *IN* U.S.A. **136** C2
Huntington *WV* U.S.A. **136** D3
Huntly N.Z. **118** C2
Huntly U.K. **50** C2
Huntsville Can. **128** C2
Huntsville *AL* U.S.A. **138** C2
Huntsville *TX* U.S.A. **140** E2
Huon Peninsula P.N.G. **70** D3
Huozhou China **82** B2
Huron U.S.A. **134** D2
Huron, Lake Can./U.S.A. **136** D2
  2nd largest lake in North America, and 3rd in the world.
Hurricane U.S.A. **132** D3
Húsavík Iceland **46**□
Huşi Romania **44** C2
Huslia U.S.A. **124** B2
Ḩuşn Āl 'Abr Yemen **90** B3
Husnes Norway **48** E2
Husum Ger. **56** B2
Hutag Mongolia **80** C1
Hutanopan Indon. **72** A1

Ipswich Austr. **116** E1
Ipswich U.K. **52** D3
Iqaluit Can. **124** H2
Capital of Nunavut.
Iquique Chile **152** A3
Iquitos Peru **150** B3
Irai Brazil **154** B3
Irakleio Greece *see* Iraklion
Iraklion Greece **64** C3
Iran *country* Asia **92** D2
Iran, Pegunungan *mts* Indon. **72** C1
Īrānshahr Iran **90** D2
Irapuato Mex. **142** B2
Iraq *country* Asia **92** C2
Irati Brazil **154** B3
Irbid Jordan **92** B2
Irbit Rus. Fed. **40** F3
Irecê Brazil **150** E4
Ireland *i.* Rep. of Ireland/U.K. **36**
Ireland, Republic of *country* Europe **50** F2
Irema Dem. Rep. Congo **104** C3
Irgiz Kazakh. **88** D2
Irîgui *reg.* Mali/Maur. **100** B3
Iringa Tanz. **104** D3
Iriri *r.* Brazil **150** D3
Irish Sea Rep. of Ireland/U.K. **48** B3
Irkutsk Rus. Fed. **80** C1
Iron Knob Austr. **116** B2
Iron Mountain U.S.A. **136** C1
Ironwood U.S.A. **136** B1
Irosin Phil. **76** B2
Irō-zaki *pt* Japan **78** C4
Irpin' Ukr. **44** D1
Irrawaddy *r.* Myanmar **74** A2
Irrawaddy, Mouths of the Myanmar **74** A2
Irtysh *r.* Kazakh./Rus. Fed. **88** E1
Irún Spain **60** C1
Irvine U.K. **50** B3
Isabela Phil. **76** B3
Isabela, Cordillera *mts* Nic. **144** B3
Ísafjörður Iceland **46**□
Isahaya Japan **78** B4
Isar *r.* Ger. **58** E2
Isbister U.K. **50**□
Ischia, Isola d' *i.* Italy **62** B2
Ise Japan **78** C4
Isengi Dem. Rep. Congo **104** C2
Isère, Pointe *pt* Fr. Guiana **146**
Iserlohn Ger. **54** C2
Isernhagen Ger. **54** D1
Ise-wan *b.* Japan **78** C4
Iseyin Nigeria **100** C4
Ishikari-wan *b.* Japan **78** D2
Ishim *r.* Kazakh./Rus. Fed. **88** E1
Ishinomaki Japan **78** D3
Ishioka Japan **78** D3
Ishpeming U.S.A. **136** C1
Işıklar Dağı *mts* Turkey **64** C2
Işıklı Turkey **64** C3
Isil'kul' Rus. Fed. **88** E1
Isipingo S. Africa **108** D2
Isiro Dem. Rep. Congo **104** C2
İskenderun Turkey **92** B2
Iskitim Rus. Fed. **94** H3
Iskûr *r.* Bulg. **64** B2
Iskut *r.* Can. **126** B2
Islamabad Pak. **86** B1
Capital of Pakistan.
Island Lagoon *salt flat* Austr. **116** B2
Island Lake Can. **126** F2
Islands, Bay of N.Z. **118** B2
Islay *i.* U.K. **50** A3
Isle of Man *i.* Irish Sea **52** A2
United Kingdom Crown Dependency.
Ismoili Somoní, Qullai *mt.* Tajik. **88** E3
Isna Egypt **90** A2
Isola di Capo Rizzuto Italy **62** C3
Isperikh Bulg. **64** C2
Israel *country* Asia **92** B2

Issoire France **58** C2
İstanbul Turkey **64** C2
İstanbul Boğazı *str.* Turkey *see* Bosporus
Istiaia Greece **64** B3
Istres France **58** C3
Istria *pen.* Croatia **62** B1
Itaberaba Brazil **150** E4
Itabira Brazil **154** D1
Itabirito Brazil **154** D2
Itabuna Brazil **150** F4
Itacoatiara Brazil **150** D3
Itaguajé Brazil **154** B2
Itaí Brazil **154** C2
Itaipu, Represa de *resr* Brazil **154** B3
Itaituba Brazil **150** D3
Itajaí Brazil **154** C3
Itajubá Brazil **154** C2
Italy *country* Europe **62** B2
5th most populous country in Europe.
Itamarandiba Brazil **154** D1
Itambacuri Brazil **154** D1
Itambé, Pico de *mt.* Brazil **154** D1
Itanagar India **74** A1
Itanhaém Brazil **154** C2
Itanhém Brazil **154** D1
Itaobím Brazil **154** D1
Itapajipe Brazil **154** C1
Itapebi Brazil **154** E1
Itapemirim Brazil **154** D2
Itaperuna Brazil **154** D2
Itapetinga Brazil **150** E4
Itapetininga Brazil **154** C2
Itapeva Brazil **154** C2
Itapicuru *r.* Brazil **150** F4
Itapicuru Mirim Brazil **150** E3
Itapuranga Brazil **154** C1
Itararé Brazil **154** C2
Itarsi India **86** B2
Itarumã Brazil **154** B1
Itaúna Brazil **154** D2
Itbayat *i.* Phil. **76** B1
Ithaca U.S.A. **136** E2
Ith Hils *ridge* Ger. **54** D1
Itimbiri *r.* Dem. Rep. Congo **104** C2
Itinga Brazil **154** D1
Itiquira Brazil **154** B1
Itiquira *r.* Brazil **154** A1
Itō Japan **78** C4
Ittoqqortoormiit Greenland **124** K2
Itu Brazil **154** C2
Ituí *r.* Brazil **150** B3
Ituiutaba Brazil **154** C1
Itula Dem. Rep. Congo **104** C3
Itumbiara Brazil **154** C1
Iturama Brazil **154** B1
Itzehoe Ger. **56** B2
Iul'tin Rus. Fed. **94** O2
Ivaí *r.* Brazil **154** B2
Ivalo Fin. **46** F2
Ivanava Belarus **42** C3
Ivanhoe Austr. **116** C2
Ivankiv Ukr. **44** C1
Ivano-Frankivs'k Ukr. **44** B2
Ivanovo Rus. Fed. **42** F2
Ivatsevichy Belarus **42** C3
Ivaylovgrad Bulg. **64** C2
Ivdel' Rus. Fed. **40** F2
Ivinheima Brazil **154** B2
Ivinheima *r.* Brazil **154** B2
Ivrea Italy **62** A1
İvrindi Turkey **64** C3
Ivujivik Can. **124** G2
Iwaki Japan **78** D3
Iwakuni Japan **78** B4
Iwamizawa Japan **78** D2
Iwanai Japan **78** D2
Iwye Belarus **42** C3
Ixopo S. Africa **108** D3
Ixtlán Mex. **142** B2

Izabal, Lago de *l.* Guat. **142** D3
Izamal Mex. **142** D2
Izberbash Rus. Fed. **92** C1
Izhevsk Rus. Fed. **40** E3
Izhma Rus. Fed. **40** E2
Izmalkovo Rus. Fed. **42** E3
Izmayil Ukr. **44** C2
İzmir Turkey **64** C3
İznik Gölü *l.* Turkey **64** C2
Izumo Japan **78** B3
Izyaslav Ukr. **44** C1
Izyum Ukr. **44** E2

J

Jabalón *r.* Spain **60** C2
Jabalpur India **86** B2
Jabiru Austr. **114** C1
Jablanica Bos.-Herz. **62** C2
Jaboatão Brazil **150** F4
Jaboticabal Brazil **154** C2
Jaca Spain **60** C1
Jacala Mex. **142** C2
Jacareacanga Brazil **150** D3
Jacareí Brazil **154** C2
Jacinto Brazil **154** D1
Jackman U.S.A. **136** F1
Jackson *AL* U.S.A. **138** C2
Jackson *MI* U.S.A. **136** D2
Jackson *MS* U.S.A. **138** B2
Capital of Mississippi.
Jackson *TN* U.S.A. **138** C1
Jackson *WY* U.S.A. **134** A2
Jackson Head *hd* N.Z. **118** A3
Jacksonville *AR* U.S.A. **138** B2
Jacksonville *FL* U.S.A. **138** D2
Jacksonville *IL* U.S.A. **136** B3
Jacksonville *NC* U.S.A. **138** E2
Jacksonville *TX* U.S.A. **140** E2
Jacmel Haiti **144** C3
Jacobabad Pak. **86** A2
Jacobina Brazil **150** E4
Jacques Cartier, Mont *mt.* Can. **128** D2
Jacunda Brazil **150** E3
Jacupiranga Brazil **154** C2
Jadovnik *mt.* Bos.-Herz. **62** C2
Jaén Peru **150** B3
Jaén Spain **60** C2
Jaffa, Cape Austr. **116** B3
Jaffna Sri Lanka **84** B4
Jagdalpur India **84** C3
Jagersfontein S. Africa **108** C2
Jaghīn Iran **90** C2
Jaguariaíva Brazil **154** C2
Jahrom Iran **92** D3
Jaipur India **86** B2
Jaisalmer India **86** B2
Jajarkot Nepal **86** C2
Jajce Bos.-Herz. **62** C2
Jakarta Indon. **72** B2
Capital of Indonesia.
Jakes Corner Can. **126** B1
Jäkkvik Sweden **46** D2
Jakobstad Fin. **46** E3
Jalālābād Afgh. **86** B1
Jalal-Abad Kyrg. **88** E2
Jalandhar India **86** B1
Jalapa Mex. **142** C3
Jales Brazil **154** B2
Jalgaon India **86** B2
Jalingo Nigeria **100** D4
Jalna India **86** B3
Jalpa Mex. **142** B2
Jalpaiguri India **86** C2
Jalpan Mex. **142** C2
Jālū Libya **100** E2
Jamaica *country* West Indies **144** C3
Jamalpur Bangl. **86** C2
Jambi Indon. **72** B2

Joutseno Fin. **46** F3
Juan de Fuca Strait Can./U.S.A. **132** B1
Juan Fernández, Archipiélago *is*
   S. Pacific Ocean **148**
Juaréz Mex. **142** B2
Juàzeiro Brazil **150** E3
Juàzeiro do Norte Brazil **150** F3
Juba Sudan **102** B4
Jubba *r.* Somalia **102** C5
Jubbah Saudi Arabia **90** B2
Júcar *r.* Spain **60** C2
Juchitán Mex. **142** C3
Judenburg Austria **56** C3
Jühnde Ger. **54** D2
Juigalpa Nic. **144** B3
Juist *i.* Ger. **54** C1
Juiz de Fora Brazil **154** D2
Juliaca Peru **150** B4
Jumla Nepal **86** C2
Junagadh India **86** B2
Junction U.S.A. **140** E2
Junction City U.S.A. **134** D3
Jundiaí Brazil **154** C2
Juneau U.S.A. **126** B2
   Capital of Alaska.
Junee Austr. **116** D2
Jungfrau *mt.* Switz. **58** D2
Juniata *r.* U.S.A. **136** E2
Junsele Sweden **46** D3
Juntura U.S.A. **132** C2
Juquiá Brazil **154** C2
Jur *r.* Sudan **102** A4
Jura *mts* France/Switz. **58** D2
Jura *i.* U.K. **50** B2
Jura, Sound of *sea chan.* U.K. **50** B3
Jurbarkas Lith. **42** B2
Jūrmala Latvia **42** B2
Juruá *r.* Brazil **150** C3
Juruena *r.* Brazil **150** D3
Jutaí *r.* Brazil **150** C3
Jüterbog Ger. **54** F2
Jutland *pen.* Denmark **36**
Juventud, Isla de la *i.* Cuba **144** B2
Juxian China **82** B2
Jūyom Iran **92** D3
Jwaneng Botswana **108** B1
Jyväskylä Fin. **46** F3

K

K2 *mt.* China/Jammu and Kashmir **86** B1
   *2nd highest mountain in the world and in
   Asia.*
Kaarina Fin. **42** B1
Kabaena *i.* Indon. **72** D2
Kabalo Dem. Rep. Congo **104** C3
Kabare Dem. Rep. Congo **104** C3
Kabinakagami Lake Can. **128** B2
Kabinda Dem. Rep. Congo **104** C3
Kabo C.A.R. **104** B2
Kabompo Zambia **106** B1
Kabongo Dem. Rep. Congo **104** C3
Kābul Afgh. **86** A1
   Capital of Afghanistan.
Kaburuang *i.* Indon. **76** B3
Kabwe Zambia **106** B1
Kachchh, Gulf of India **86** A2
Kachchh, Rann of *marsh* India **86** B2
Kachug Rus. Fed. **94** J3
Kaçkar Daği *mt.* Turkey **92** C1
Kadavu *i.* Fiji **110**
Kadıköy Turkey **64** C2
Kadiolo Mali **100** B3
Kadmat *atoll* India **84** B3
Kadom Rus. Fed. **42** F3
Kadoma Zimbabwe **106** B1
Kadonkani Myanmar **74** A2
Kaduna Nigeria **100** C3
Kaduy Rus. Fed. **42** E2

Kadzherom Rus. Fed. **40** E2
Kaédi Maur. **100** A3
Kaélé Cameroon **104** B1
Kaesŏng N. Korea **76** D2
Kaffrine Senegal **100** A3
Kafireas, Akra *pt* Greece **64** B3
Kafue Zambia **106** B1
Kafue *r.* Zambia **106** B1
Kaga Bandoro C.A.R. **104** B2
Kagal'nitskaya Rus. Fed. **44** F2
Kagoshima Japan **78** B4
Kaharlyk Ukr. **44** D2
Kahayan *r.* Indon. **72** C2
Kahemba Dem. Rep. Congo **104** B3
Kahla Ger. **54** E2
Kahnūj Iran **90** C2
Kahperusvaarat *mts* Fin. **46** E2
Kahramanmaraş Turkey **92** B2
Kahūrak Iran **90** C2
Kai, Kepulauan *is* Indon. **70** C3
Kaiama Nigeria **100** C4
Kaiapoi N.Z. **118** B3
Kai Besar *i.* Indon. **70** C3
Kaifeng China **82** B2
Kaiingveld *reg.* S. Africa **108** B2
Kai Kecil *i.* Indon. **70** C3
Kaikoura N.Z. **118** B3
Kailahun Sierra Leone **100** A4
Kaili China **82** A3
Kaimana Indon. **70** C3
Kaimanawa Mountains N.Z. **118** C2
Kainan Japan **78** C4
Kainji Reservoir Nigeria **100** C3
Kaipara Harbour N.Z. **118** B2
Kairana India **86** B2
Kairouan Tunisia **100** D1
Kaitaia N.Z. **118** B2
Kaitawa N.Z. **118** C2
Kaiwatu Indon. **70** C3
Kaiyuan *Liaoning* China **76** C1
Kaiyuan *Yunnan* China **82** A3
Kajaani Fin. **46** F3
Kajabbi Austr. **114** D2
Kakamas S. Africa **108** B2
Kakamega Kenya **104** D2
Kakhovka Ukr. **44** D2
Kakhovs'ke Vodoskhovyshche *resr*
   Ukr. **44** D2
Kakinada India **84** C3
Kakisa Can. **126** D1
Kakoswa Dem. Rep. Congo **104** C3
Kaktovik U.S.A. **124** C2
Kalabahi Indon. **70** C3
Kalabo Zambia **106** B1
Kalach Rus. Fed. **44** F1
Kalacha Dida Kenya **104** D2
Kaladan *r.* India/Myanmar **74** A1
Kalahari Desert Africa **106** C3
Kalajoki Fin. **46** E3
Kalamare Botswana **108** C1
Kalamaria Greece **64** B2
Kalamata Greece **64** B3
Kalamazoo U.S.A. **136** C2
Kalampaka Greece **64** B3
Kalanchak Ukr. **44** D2
Kalao *i.* Indon. **72** D2
Kalaotoa *i.* Indon. **72** D2
Kalasin Thai. **74** B2
Kalāt Afgh. **86** A1
Kalāt Iran **90** C2
Kalat Pak. **86** A2
Kalbarri Austr. **114** A2
Kale Turkey **64** C3
Kalecik Turkey **92** B1
Kalema Dem. Rep. Congo **104** C3
Kalemie Dem. Rep. Congo **104** C3
Kalemyo Myanmar **74** A1
Kalevala Rus. Fed. **46** G2
Kalgoorlie Austr. **114** B3
Kali Croatia **62** C2
Kaliakra, Nos *pt* Bulg. **64** C2

Kalima Dem. Rep. Congo **104** C3
Kalimantan *reg.* Indon. **72** C2
Kaliningrad Rus. Fed. **42** B3
Kalininskaya Rus. Fed. **44** E2
Kalispell U.S.A. **132** D1
Kalisz Pol. **56** D2
Kalitva *r.* Rus. Fed. **44** F2
Kalix Sweden **46** E2
Kalixälven *r.* Sweden **46** E2
Kalkan Turkey **64** C3
Kalkfeld Namibia **106** A2
Kallavesi *l.* Fin. **46** F3
Kallsjön *l.* Sweden **46** C3
Kalmar Sweden **46** D4
Kalmarsund *sea chan.* Sweden **46** D4
Kalomo Zambia **106** B1
Kalone Peak Can. **126** C2
Kalpa India **86** B1
Kalpeni *atoll* India **84** B3
Kalpi India **86** B2
Kaltag U.S.A. **124** B2
Kaltenkirchen Ger. **54** D1
Kaluga Rus. Fed. **42** E3
Kalundborg Denmark **46** C4
Kalush Ukr. **44** B2
Kalyazin Rus. Fed. **42** E2
Kalymnos *i.* Greece **64** C3
Kama Dem. Rep. Congo **104** C3
Kama Myanmar **74** A2
Kama *r.* Rus. Fed. **40** E3
   4th longest river in Europe.
Kamaishi Japan **78** D3
Kaman Turkey **92** B2
Kamanjab Namibia **106** A1
Kamarān *i.* Yemen **90** B3
Kamarod Pak. **86** A2
Kambalda Austr. **114** B3
Kambove Dem. Rep. Congo **104** C4
Kamchatka Peninsula *mts* Rus. Fed.
   94 M3
Kamchiya *r.* Bulg. **64** C2
Kamenitsa *mt.* Bulg. **64** B2
Kamenjak, Rt *pt* Croatia **62** B2
Kamenka Kazakh. **88** C1
Kamenka Rus. Fed. **44** E1
Kamen'-na-Obi Rus. Fed. **88** F1
Kamennomostskiy Rus. Fed. **44** F3
Kamenolomni Rus. Fed. **44** F2
Kamenskoye Rus. Fed. **94** N2
Kamensk-Shakhtinskiy Rus. Fed. **44** F2
Kamensk-Ural'skiy Rus. Fed. **40** F3
Kamiesberge *mts* S. Africa **108** A3
Kamieskroon S. Africa **108** A3
Kamilukuak Lake Can. **126** E1
Kamina Dem. Rep. Congo **104** C3
Kaminak Lake Can. **126** F1
Kamin'-Kashyrs'kyy Ukr. **44** B1
Kamloops Can. **126** C2
Kamonia Dem. Rep. Congo **104** C3
Kampala Uganda **104** D2
   Capital of Uganda.
Kampar *r.* Indon. **72** B1
Kampar Malaysia **72** B1
Kampen Neth. **54** B1
Kampene Dem. Rep. Congo **104** C3
Kamphaeng Phet Thai. **74** A2
Kâmpóng Cham Cambodia **74** B2
Kâmpóng Chhnăng Cambodia **74** B2
Kâmpóng Spœ Cambodia **74** B2
Kâmpôt Cambodia **74** B2
Kamsack Can. **126** E2
Kamskoye Vodokhranilishche *resr*
   Rus. Fed. **40** E3
Kam"yanets'-Podil's'kyy Ukr. **44** C2
Kam"yanka-Buz'ka Ukr. **44** B1
Kamyanyets Belarus **42** B3
Kamyshevatskaya Rus. Fed. **44** E2
Kamyshin Rus. Fed. **40** D3
Kanab U.S.A. **132** D3

Kluczbork Pol. 56 D2
Klukwan U.S.A. 126 B2
Klupro Pak. 86 A2
Klyaz'ma r. Rus. Fed. 42 F2
Klyetsk Belarus 42 C3
Knaresborough U.K. 52 C2
Knästen h. Sweden 46 C3
Knee Lake Can. 126 F2
Knesebeck Ger. 54 E1
Knetzgau Ger. 54 E3
Knin Croatia 62 C2
Knittelfeld Austria 56 C3
Knjaževac S.M. 64 B2
Knokke-Heist Belgium 54 A2
Knoxville U.S.A. 138 D1
Knysna S. Africa 108 B3
Kōbe Japan 78 C4
København Denmark see Copenhagen
Koblenz Ger. 54 C2
Kobroör i. Indon. 70 C3
Kobryn Belarus 42 B3
Kočani Macedonia 64 B2
Kocasu r. Turkey 64 C2
Koch Bihar India 86 C2
Kōchi Japan 78 B4
Kochubey Rus. Fed. 40 D4
Kodarma India 86 C2
Kodiak Island U.S.A. 124 B3
Kodok Sudan 102 B4
Kodyma Ukr. 44 C2
Kodzhaele mt. Bulg./Greece 64 C2
Koës Namibia 108 A2
Koffiefontein S. Africa 108 C2
Koforidua Ghana 100 B4
Kōfu Japan 78 C3
Kogaluk r. Can. 128 D1
Kohat Pak. 86 B1
Kohima India 74 A1
Kohtla-Järve Estonia 42 C2
Kokand Uzbek. see Qo'qon
Kokkola Fin. 46 E3
Kokomo U.S.A. 136 C2
Kokpekti Kazakh. 88 F2
Kokshetau Kazakh. 88 D1
Koksoak r. Can. 128 D1
Kokstad S. Africa 108 C3
Koktokay China see Fuyun
Kolaka Indon. 72 D2
Kola Peninsula Rus. Fed. 40 C2
Kolari Fin. 46 E2
Kolda Senegal 100 A3
Kolding Denmark 46 B4
Koléa Alg. 60 D2
Kolguyev, Ostrov i. Rus. Fed. 40 D2
Kolhapur India 84 B3
Kolkasrags pt Latvia 42 B2
Kolkata India 86 C2
  4th most populous city in Asia, and 7th in
  the world.
Kolmanskop Namibia 108 A2
Köln Ger. see Cologne
Kołobrzeg Pol. 56 D2
Kolokani Mali 100 B3
Kolomna Rus. Fed. 42 E2
Kolomyya Ukr. 44 C2
Kolonedale Indon. 72 D2
Kolonkwaneng Botswana 108 B2
Kolpashevo Rus. Fed. 94 H3
Kolpny Rus. Fed. 42 E3
Kol'skiy Poluostrov pen. Rus. Fed. see
  Kola Peninsula
Koluli Eritrea 90 B3
Kolwezi Dem. Rep. Congo 104 C4
Kolyma r. Rus. Fed. 94 M2
Kolymskaya Nizmennost' lowland
  Rus. Fed. 94 M2
Kolymskiy, Khrebet mts Rus. Fed. 94 N2
Komaki Japan 78 C3
Komandorskiye Ostrova is Rus. Fed.
  94 N3
Komárno Slovakia 56 D3

Komati r. Swaziland 108 D2
Komatsu Japan 78 C3
Kombe Dem. Rep. Congo 104 C3
Kominternivs'ke Ukr. 44 D2
Komiža Croatia 62 C2
Komló Hungary 56 D3
Komono Congo 104 B3
Komotini Greece 64 C2
Komsberg mts S. Africa 108 B3
Komsomolets, Ostrov i. Rus. Fed. 94 I1
Komsomol'sk Rus. Fed. 42 F2
Komsomol's'k Ukr. 44 D2
Komsomol'skiy Rus. Fed. 40 D4
Komsomol'sk-na-Amure Rus. Fed. 80 F1
Konakovo Rus. Fed. 42 E2
Kondagaon India 86 C3
Kondinskoye Rus. Fed. 40 F2
Kondoa Tanz. 104 D3
Kondopoga Rus. Fed. 40 C2
Kondrovo Rus. Fed. 42 E3
Kong Christian IX Land reg. Greenland
  124 J2
Kong Frederik VI Kyst coastal area
  Greenland 124 J2
Kongju S. Korea 76 D2
Kongolo Dem. Rep. Congo 104 C3
Kongsberg Norway 46 B4
Kongsvinger Norway 46 C3
Kongur Shan mt. China 88 E3
Königswinter Ger. 54 C2
Königs Wusterhausen Ger. 54 F1
Konin Pol. 56 D2
Konjic Bos.-Herz. 62 C2
Konkiep watercourse Namibia 108 A2
Konotop Ukr. 44 D1
Konstantinovsk Rus. Fed. 44 F2
Konstanz Ger. 56 B3
Kontagora Nigeria 100 C3
Kon Tum Vietnam 74 B2
Kon Tum, Cao Nguyên plat. Vietnam
  74 B2
Konya Turkey 92 B2
Konz Ger. 54 C3
Konzhakovskiy Kamen', Gora mt.
  Rus. Fed. 40 E3
Kooskia U.S.A. 132 C1
Kootenay Lake Can. 126 D3
Kootjieskolk S. Africa 108 B3
Kópasker Iceland 46□
Koper Slovenia 62 B1
Kopparberg Sweden 46 D4
Koprivnica Croatia 62 C1
Korablino Rus. Fed. 42 F3
Koraput India 84 C3
Korbach Ger. 54 D2
Korçë Albania 64 B2
Korčula Croatia 62 C2
Korčula i. Croatia 62 C2
Korea, North country Asia 76 D1
Korea, South country Asia 76 D2
Korea Bay g. China/N. Korea 76 C2
Korea Strait Japan/S. Korea 76 D3
Korenovsk Rus. Fed. 44 E2
Korets' Ukr. 44 C1
Körfez Turkey 64 C2
Korhogo Côte d'Ivoire 100 B4
Korinthos Greece see Corinth
Kőris-hegy h. Hungary 56 D3
Koritnik mt. Albania 64 B2
Kōriyama Japan 78 D3
Korkuteli Turkey 92 B2
Korla China 88 C2
Körmend Hungary 56 D3
Koro Mali 100 B3
Koroc r. Can. 128 D2
Korocha Rus. Fed. 44 E1
Korogwe Tanz. 104 D3
Koror Palau 70 C2
  Capital of Palau.
Korosten' Ukr. 44 C1
Korostyshiv Ukr. 44 C1

Koro Toro Chad 100 D3
Korsakov Rus. Fed. 78 D1
Korsør Denmark 56 C1
Korsun'-Shevchenkivs'kyy Ukr. 44 D2
Korsze Pol. 56 E2
Kortrijk Belgium 54 A2
Koryakskaya, Sopka vol. Rus. Fed.
  94 M3
Koryakskiy Khrebet mts Rus. Fed. 94 N2
Koryazhma Rus. Fed. 40 D2
Koryŏng S. Korea 76 D2
Koryukivka Ukr. 44 D1
Kos Greece 64 C3
Kos i. Greece 64 C3
Kosan N. Korea 76 D2
Kościan Pol. 56 D2
Kosciuszko, Mount Austr. 116 D3
Kosh-Agach Rus. Fed. 88 F2
Košice Slovakia 56 E3
Koskullskulle Sweden 46 E2
Kosŏng N. Korea 76 D2
Kosovo prov. S.M. 64 B2
Kosovska Mitrovica S.M. 64 B2
Kosrae atoll Micronesia 110
Kossou, Lac de l. Côte d'Ivoire 100 B4
Kostanay Kazakh. 88 D1
Kostenets Bulg. 64 B2
Koster S. Africa 108 C2
Kosti Sudan 102 B3
Kostomuksha Rus. Fed. 46 G3
Kostopil' Ukr. 44 C1
Kostroma Rus. Fed. 42 F2
Kostroma r. Rus. Fed. 42 F2
Kostrzyn Pol. 56 C2
Koszalin Pol. 56 D2
Kőszeg Hungary 56 D3
Kota India 86 B2
Kotaagung Indon. 72 B2
Kotabaru Indon. 72 C2
Kota Belud Malaysia 72 C1
Kota Bharu Malaysia 72 B1
Kotabumi Indon. 72 B2
Kota Kinabalu Malaysia 72 C1
Kota Samarahan Malaysia 72 C1
Kotel'nich Rus. Fed. 40 D3
Kotel'nikovo Rus. Fed. 40 D4
Kotel'nyy, Ostrov i. Rus. Fed. 94 L1
Köthen (Anhalt) Ger. 54 E2
Kotka Fin. 46 F3
Kotlas Rus. Fed. 40 D2
Kotlik U.S.A. 124 B2
Kotor Varoš Bos.-Herz. 62 C2
Kotovo Rus. Fed. 40 D3
Kotovsk Rus. Fed. 42 F3
Kotovs'k Ukr. 44 C2
Kotuy r. Rus. Fed. 94 I2
Kotzebue U.S.A. 124 B2
Kotzebue Sound sea chan. U.S.A. 124 B2
Kötzting Ger. 54 F3
Koudekerke Neth. 54 A2
Koudougou Burkina 100 B3
Kougaberge mts S. Africa 108 B3
Koulamoutou Gabon 104 B3
Koulikoro Mali 100 B3
Koundâra Guinea 100 A3
Kourou Fr. Guiana 150 D2
Kouroussa Guinea 100 B3
Kousséri Cameroon 104 B1
Koutiala Mali 100 B3
Kouvola Fin. 46 F3
Kovdor Rus. Fed. 46 G2
Kovel' Ukr. 44 B1
Kovrov Rus. Fed. 42 F2
Kowhitirangi N.Z. 118 B3
Köyceğiz Turkey 64 C2
Koyda Rus. Fed. 40 D2
Koyukuk r. U.S.A. 124 C2
Kozani Greece 64 B2
Kozelets' Ukr. 44 D1
Kozel'sk Rus. Fed. 42 E3
Kozyatyn Ukr. 44 C2

Lubao Dem. Rep. Congo **104** C3
Lubartów Pol. **56** E2
Lübbecke Ger. **54** D1
Lübben Ger. **54** F2
Lübbenau Ger. **54** F2
Lubbock U.S.A. **140** D2
Lübeck Ger. **54** E1
Lubei China **82** C1
Lubenka Kazakh. **88** C1
Lubin Pol. **56** D2
Lublin Pol. **56** E2
Lubny Ukr. **44** D1
Lubok Antu Malaysia **72** C1
Lübtheen Ger. **54** E1
Lubudi Dem. Rep. Congo **104** C3
Lubuklinggau Indon. **72** B2
Lubumbashi Dem. Rep. Congo **104** C4
Lubungu Zambia **106** B1
Lubutu Dem. Rep. Congo **104** C3
Lucala Angola **104** B3
Lucan Rep. of Ireland **50** G2
Lucapa Angola **104** C3
Luce Bay U.K. **50** B3
Lucélia Brazil **154** B2
Lucena Phil. **76** B2
Lucena Spain **60** C2
Lučenec Slovakia **56** D3
Lucera Italy **62** C2
Lucerne Switz. **58** D2
Lüchow Ger. **54** E1
Lucira Angola **106** A1
Luckau Ger. **54** F2
Luckenwalde Ger. **54** F1
Luckhoff S. Africa **108** B2
Lucknow India **86** C2
Lucusse Angola **106** B1
Lüdenscheid Ger. **54** C2
Lüder Ger. **54** E1
Lüderitz Namibia **108** A2
Ludhiana India **86** B1
Ludington U.S.A. **136** C2
Ludlow U.K. **52** E3
Ludlow U.S.A. **132** C4
Ludogorie reg. Bulg. **64** C2
Ludvika Sweden **46** D3
Ludwigsburg Ger. **56** B3
Ludwigsfelde Ger. **54** F2
Ludwigshafen am Rhein Ger. **54** D3
Ludwigslust Ger. **54** E1
Ludza Latvia **42** C2
Luebo Dem. Rep. Congo **104** C3
Luena Angola **106** A1
Lüeyang China **82** A2
Lufeng China **82** B3
Lufkin U.S.A. **140** F2
Luga Rus. Fed. **42** C2
Luga r. Rus. Fed. **42** C2
Lugano Switz. **58** D2
Lugenda r. Moz. **106** C1
Lugo Spain **60** B1
Lugoj Romania **44** B2
Luhans'k Ukr. **44** E2
Luhombero Tanz. **104** D3
Luhyny Ukr. **44** C1
Luiana Angola **106** B1
Luilaka r. Dem. Rep. Congo **104** C3
Luino Italy **56** B3
Luiro r. Fin. **46** F2
Luiza Dem. Rep. Congo **104** C3
Lujiang China **82** B2
Lukavac Bos.-Herz. **62** C2
Lukenie r. Dem. Rep. Congo **104** B3
Lukeville U.S.A. **140** B2
Lukh r. Rus. Fed. **42** F2
Lukhovitsy Rus. Fed. **42** E3
Łuków Pol. **56** E2
Lukulu Zambia **106** B1
Luleå Sweden **46** E2
Luleälven r. Sweden **46** E2
Lüleburgaz Turkey **64** C2
Lüliang Shan mts China **82** B2

Lumajang Indon. **72** C2
Lumajangdong Co salt l. China **86** C1
Lumbala Kaquengue Angola **106** B1
Lumbala N'guimbo Angola **106** B1
Lumberton U.S.A. **138** E2
Lumbis Indon. **72** C1
Lumbrales Spain **60** B1
Lumphăt Cambodia **74** B2
Lumsden Can. **126** E2
Lumsden N.Z. **118** A4
Lund Sweden **46** C4
Lundazi Zambia **106** C1
Lundy i. U.K. **52** A4
Lüneburg Ger. **54** E1
Lüneburger Heide reg. Ger. **54** E1
Lünen Ger. **54** C2
Lunéville France **58** D2
Lunga r. Zambia **106** B1
Lungi Sierra Leone **100** A4
Lunglei India **74** A1
Lungnaquilla Mountain h.
    Rep. of Ireland **50** G2
Lungwebungu r. Zambia **106** B1
Luni r. India **86** B2
Luninyets Belarus **42** C3
Lunsar Sierra Leone **100** A4
Luntai China **88** F2
Luodian China **82** A3
Luoding China **82** B3
Luohe China **82** B2
Luoyang China **82** B2
Lupane Zimbabwe **106** B1
Lupanshui China **82** A3
Lupeni Romania **44** B2
Lupilichi Moz. **106** C1
Luppa Ger. **54** F2
Lúrio Moz. **106** D1
Lurio r. Moz. **106** D1
Lusaka Zambia **106** B1
    Capital of Zambia.
Lusambo Dem. Rep. Congo **104** C3
Lushnjë Albania **64** A2
Lusk U.S.A. **134** C2
Lut, Dasht-e des. Iran **88** C3
Lutherstadt Wittenberg Ger. **54** F2
Luton U.K. **52** C4
Lutong Malaysia **72** C1
Łutselk'e Can. **126** D1
Luts'k Ukr. **44** C1
Lutzputs S. Africa **108** B2
Lutzville S. Africa **108** A3
Luuq Somalia **102** C4
Luverne U.S.A. **134** D2
Luvua r. Dem. Rep. Congo **104** C3
Luvuvhu r. S. Africa **108** D1
Luwero Uganda **104** D2
Luwuk Indon. **72** D2
Luxembourg country Europe **54** C3
Luxembourg Lux. **54** C3
    Capital of Luxembourg.
Luxeuil-les-Bains France **58** D2
Luxolweni S. Africa **108** C3
Luxor Egypt **102** B2
Luyksgestel Neth. **54** B2
Luza Rus. Fed. **40** D2
Luzern Switz. see Lucerne
Luzhou China **82** A3
Luziânia Brazil **154** C1
Luzilândia Brazil **150** E3
Luzon i. Phil. **76** B2
Luzon Strait Phil. **76** B1
L'viv Ukr. **44** B2
L'vov Ukr. see L'viv
Lyakhavichy Belarus **42** C3
Lycksele Sweden **46** D3
Lydenburg S. Africa **108** D2
Lyel'chytsy Belarus **42** C3
Lyepyel' Belarus **42** C3
Lyme Bay U.K. **52** B4
Lynchburg U.S.A. **136** E3
Lynn Lake Can. **126** E2

Lynx Lake Can. **126** E1
Lyon France **58** C2
Lyozna Belarus **42** D2
Lys'va Rus. Fed. **40** E3
Lysychans'k Ukr. **44** E2
Lytham St Anne's U.K. **52** B3
Lyuban' Belarus **42** C3
Lyubertsy Rus. Fed. **42** E2
Lyubeshiv Ukr. **44** C1
Lyubim Rus. Fed. **42** F2
Lyubotyn Ukr. **44** E2
Lyubytino Rus. Fed. **42** D2
Lyudinovo Rus. Fed. **42** D3

M

Ma'ān Jordan **92** B2
Maardu Estonia **42** C2
Maas r. Neth. **54** B2
Maaseik Belgium **54** B2
Maasin Phil. **76** B2
Maastricht Neth. **54** B2
Mabalane Moz. **106** C2
Mabaruma Guyana **150** D2
Mabote Moz. **106** C2
Mabule Botswana **108** B2
Mabutsane Botswana **108** B1
Macaé Brazil **154** D2
Macaloge Moz. **106** C1
Macapá Brazil **150** D2
Macará Ecuador **150** B3
Macarani Brazil **154** D1
Macassar Strait Indon. see
    Makassar, Selat
Macau China **80** D3
Macau aut. reg. China **82** B3
Maccaretane Moz. **108** D1
Macclesfield U.K. **52** B3
Macdonald, Lake salt flat Austr.
    114 B2
Macdonnell Ranges mts Austr. **114** C2
MacDowell Lake Can. **128** A1
Macedo de Cavaleiros Port. **60** B1
Macedon mt. Austr. **116** C3
Macedonia country Europe **64** B2
Maceió Brazil **150** F3
Macerata Italy **62** B2
Macfarlane, Lake salt flat Austr. **116** B2
Macgillycuddy's Reeks mts
    Rep. of Ireland **50** F3
Mach Pak. **86** A2
Machado Brazil **154** C2
Machaila Moz. **106** C2
Machakos Kenya **104** D3
Machala Ecuador **150** B3
Machanga Moz. **106** C2
Machault France **54** B3
Macheng China **82** B2
Machias U.S.A. **136** G2
Machiques Venez. **150** B1
Machu Picchu tourist site Peru **150** B4
Macia Moz. **106** C2
Mãcin Romania **44** C2
Macintyre r. Austr. **116** E1
Mackay Austr. **114** D2
Mackay, Lake salt flat Austr. **114** B2
MacKay Lake Can. **126** D1
Mackenzie Can. **126** C2
Mackenzie r. Can. **126** B1
Mackenzie Bay Can. **124** C2
Mackenzie King Island Can. **124** E1
Mackenzie Mountains Can. **126** B1
Macklin Can. **126** D2
Macksville Austr. **116** E2
Maclean Austr. **116** E1
MacLeod, Lake imp. l. Austr. **114** A2
Macomb U.S.A. **136** B2
Macomer Italy **62** A2
Mâcon France **58** C2
Macon GA U.S.A. **138** D2

Manakara Madag. **106**◻ D2
Manākhah Yemen **90** B3
Manama Bahrain **90** C2
Capital of Bahrain.
Manam Island P.N.G. **70** D3
Mananara *r.* Madag. **106**◻ D2
Mananara Avaratra Madag. **106**◻ D1
Mananjary Madag. **106**◻ D2
Manantali, Lac de *l.* Mali **100** A3
Manas Hu *l.* China **88** F2
Manatuto East Timor **70** C3
Man-aung Kyun *i.* Myanmar **74** A2
Manaus Brazil **150** C3
Manavgat Turkey **92** B2
Manchester U.K. **52** B3
Manchester U.S.A. **136** F2
Mandabe Madag. **106**◻ D2
Mandal Norway **46** B4
Mandala, Puncak *mt.* Indon. **70** D3
3rd highest mountain in Oceania.
Mandalay Myanmar **74** A1
Mandalgovï Mongolia **80** D1
Mandan U.S.A. **134** C1
Mandara Mountains Cameroon/Nigeria
104 B1
Mandas Italy **62** A3
Manderscheid Ger. **54** C2
Mandi India **86** B1
Mandiana Guinea **100** B3
Mandi Burewala Pak. **86** B1
Mandla India **86** C2
Mandritsara Madag. **106**◻ D1
Mandsaur India **86** B2
Mandurah Austr. **114** A3
Mandya India **84** B3
Manerbio Italy **62** B1
Manevychi Ukr. **44** C1
Manfredonia Italy **62** C2
Manga Burkina **100** B3
Mangai Dem. Rep. Congo **104** B3
Mangalia Romania **44** C3
Mangakino N.Z. **118** C2
Mangalore India **84** B3
Manguang S. Africa **108** C2
Manggar Indon. **72** B2
Mangnai China **80** C2
Mangochi Malawi **106** C1
Mangole *i.* Indon. **70** C3
Mangueirinha Brazil **154** B3
Mangui China **80** E1
Mangystau Kazakh. **88** C2
Manhattan U.S.A. **134** D3
Manhica Moz. **106** C2
Manhuaçu Brazil **154** D2
Mania *r.* Madag. **106**◻ D1
Maniago Italy **62** B1
Manicoré Brazil **150** C3
Manicouagan *r.* Can. **128** D2
Manicouagan, Petit Lac *l.* Can. **128** D1
Manicouagan, Réservoir *resr* Can.
128 D1
Manīfah Saudi Arabia **90** B2
Manihiki *atoll* Cook Is **110**
Manila Phil. **76** B2
Capital of the Philippines.
Manilla Austr. **116** E2
Manisa Turkey **64** C3
Manistee U.S.A. **136** C2
Manitoba *prov.* Can. **126** F2
Manitoba, Lake Can. **126** F2
Manitou Islands U.S.A. **136** C1
Manitoulin Island Can. **128** B2
Manitowoc U.S.A. **136** C2
Maniwaki Can. **128** C2
Manizales Col. **150** B2
Mankato U.S.A. **134** E2
Mankono Côte d'Ivoire **100** B4
Mankota Can. **132** E1
Mankulam Sri Lanka **84** C4
Manmad India **86** B2
Mannar, Gulf of India/Sri Lanka **84** B4

Mannheim Ger. **54** D3
Manning Can. **126** D2
Mannum Austr. **116** B2
Mannville Can. **126** D2
Manokwari Indon. **70** C3
Manono Dem. Rep. Congo **104** C3
Manoron Myanmar **74** A2
Manosque France **58** D3
Manouane, Lac *l.* Can. **128** C1
Manresa Spain **60** D1
Mansa Zambia **106** B1
Mansel Island Can. **124** G2
Mansel'kya *ridge* Fin./Rus. Fed. **46** F2
Mansfield Austr. **116** D3
Mansfield U.K. **52** C3
Mansfield *LA* U.S.A. **138** B2
Mansfield *OH* U.S.A. **136** D2
Mansfield *PA* U.S.A. **136** E2
Manta Ecuador **150** A3
Manteo U.S.A. **138** E1
Mantes-la-Jolie France **58** C2
Mantiqueira, Serra da *mts* Brazil **154** C2
Mantova Italy *see* Mantua
Mantua Italy **62** B1
Manuelzinho Brazil **150** D3
Manui *i.* Indon. **72** D2
Manukau N.Z. **118** B2
Manus Island P.N.G. **70** D3
Many U.S.A. **138** B2
Manych-Gudilo, Ozero *l.* Rus. Fed. **40** D4
Manyoni Tanz. **104** D3
Manzanares Spain **60** C2
Manzanillo Mex. **142** B3
Manzhouli China **80** D1
Manzini Swaziland **108** D2
Mao Chad **100** D3
Maoke, Pegunungan *mts* Indon. **70** D3
Maokeng S. Africa **108** C2
Maokui Shan *mt.* China **76** C1
Maoming China **82** B3
Mapai Moz. **106** C2
Mapam Yumco *l.* China **86** C1
Mapane Indon. **72** D2
Mapastepec Mex. **142** C3
Mapimí Mex. **142** B2
Mapimí, Bolsón de *des.* Mex. **142** B2
Mapin *i.* Phil. **76** A3
Mapinhane Moz. **106** C2
Maple Creek Can. **126** E3
Maputo Moz. **106** C2
Capital of Mozambique.
Maputo *r.* Moz./S. Africa **108** D2
Maquan He *r.* China **86** C2
Maquela do Zombo Angola **104** B3
Maquinchao Arg. **152** B5
Maquoketa U.S.A. **134** E2
Mar, Serra do *mts* Brazil **146**
Maraã Brazil **150** C3
Maraba Brazil **150** E3
Maracá, Ilha de *i.* Brazil **150** D2
Maracaibo Venez. **150** B1
Maracaibo, Lake Venez. **150** B2
Maracaju Brazil **154** A2
Maracajú, Serra de *hills* Brazil **154** A2
Maracay Venez. **150** C1
Marādah Libya **100** D2
Maradi Niger **100** C3
Marāgheh Iran **92** C2
Marajó, Baía de *est.* Brazil **150** E3
Marajó, Ilha de *i.* Brazil **150** D3
Marākī Iran **90** C2
Maralal Kenya **104** D2
Maralinga Austr. **114** C3
Marand Iran **92** C2
Maranoa *r.* Austr. **116** D1
Marañón *r.* Peru **150** B3
Marathon Can. **128** B2
Marathon U.S.A. **138** D4
Marbella Spain **60** C2
Marble Bar Austr. **114** A2
Marble Hall S. Africa **108** C1

Marburg S. Africa **108** D3
Marburg an der Lahn Ger. **54** D2
March U.K. **52** D3
Marche-en-Famenne Belgium **54** B2
Marchena Spain **60** B2
Mar Chiquita, Lago *l.* Arg. **152** B4
Marchtrenk Austria **58** E2
Marcoing France **54** A2
Marcy, Mount U.S.A. **136** F2
Mardan Pak. **86** B1
Mar del Plata Arg. **152** C4
Mardin Turkey **92** C2
Maree, Loch *l.* U.K. **50** B2
Marettimo, Isola *i.* Italy **62** B3
Marevo Rus. Fed. **42** D2
Marfa U.S.A. **140** D2
Margaret River Austr. **114** A3
Margarita, Isla de *i.* Venez. **144** D3
Margate S. Africa **108** D3
Margate U.K. **52** D4
Margherita Peak
Dem. Rep. Congo/Uganda **104** C2
3rd highest mountain in Africa.
Mārgow, Dasht-e *des.* Afgh. **86** A1
Marhanets' Ukr. **44** D2
Mari Myanmar **74** A1
María Elena Chile **152** B3
Mariana Trench *sea feature*
N. Pacific Ocean **158** C4
Deepest trench in the world.
Marianna *AR* U.S.A. **138** B2
Marianna *FL* U.S.A. **138** C2
Mariánské Lázně Czech Rep. **56** C3
Marías, Islas *is* Mex. **142** B2
Mariato, Punta *pt* Panama **150** A2
Most southerly point of North America.
Ma'rib Yemen **90** B3
Maribor Slovenia **62** C1
Maridi *watercourse* Sudan **102** A4
Marie Byrd Land *reg.* Antarctica **118** L2
Marie-Galante *i.* Guadeloupe **144** D3
Mariehamn Fin. **46** D3
Mariental Namibia **108** A1
Mariestad Sweden **46** C4
Marietta *GA* U.S.A. **138** D2
Marietta *OH* U.S.A. **136** D3
Marignane France **58** D3
Marii, Mys *pt* Rus. Fed. **94** L3
Marijampolė Lith. **42** B3
Marília Brazil **154** C2
Marín Spain **60** B1
Marina di Gioiosa Ionica Italy **62** C3
Mar"ina Horka Belarus **42** C3
Marinette U.S.A. **136** C1
Maringá Brazil **154** B2
Marinha Grande Port. **60** B2
Marion *IN* U.S.A. **136** C2
Marion *OH* U.S.A. **136** D2
Marion *SC* U.S.A. **138** E2
Marion *VA* U.S.A. **136** D3
Marion, Lake U.S.A. **138** D2
Marion Bay Austr. **116** B3
Mariscal Estigarribia Para. **152** B3
Maritsa *r.* Bulg. **64** C2
Mariupol' Ukr. **44** E2
Marka Somalia **102** C4
Marken S. Africa **108** C1
Markermeer *l.* Neth. **54** B1
Markha *r.* Rus. Fed. **94** J2
Markivka Ukr. **44** E2
Marksville U.S.A. **138** B2
Marktheidenfeld Ger. **54** D3
Marktredwitz Ger. **54** F2
Marle France **54** A3
Marlin U.S.A. **140** E2
Marmande France **58** C3
Marmara, Sea of *g.* Turkey **64** C2
Marmara Denizi *g.* Turkey *see*
Marmara, Sea of
Marmaris Turkey **64** C3
Marne *r.* France **54** A3

Mealhada Port. **60** B1
Mealy Mountains Can. **128** E1
Meander River Can. **126** D2
Meaux France **54** A3
Mecca Saudi Arabia **90** A2
Mechelen Belgium **54** B2
Mechelen Neth. **54** B2
Mechernich Ger. **54** C2
Meckenheim Ger. **54** C2
Mecklenburger Bucht *b.* Ger. **46** C5
Meda Port. **60** B1
Medan Indon. **72** A1
Medanosa, Punta *pt* Arg. **152** B5
Medawachchiya Sri Lanka **84** C4
Médéa Alg. **60** D2
Medellín Col. **150** B2
Medenine Tunisia **100** D1
Medford U.S.A. **132** B2
Medgidia Romania **44** C3
Mediaş Romania **44** B2
Medicine Bow Mountains U.S.A. **134** B2
Medicine Bow Peak U.S.A. **134** B2
Medicine Hat Can. **126** D2
Medicine Lodge U.S.A. **134** D3
Medina Brazil **154** D1
Medina Saudi Arabia **90** A2
Medinaceli Spain **60** C1
Medina del Campo Spain **60** C1
Medina de Rioseco Spain **60** B1
Mediterranean Sea **60** C2
Medjedel Alg. **60** D2
Medley Can. **126** D2
Mednogorsk Rus. Fed. **40** E3
Medvezh'i, Ostrova *is* Rus. Fed. **94** M2
Medvezh'yegorsk Rus. Fed. **40** C2
Meekatharra Austr. **114** A2
Meeker U.S.A. **134** B2
Meerut India **86** B2
Meetkerke Belgium **54** A2
Megalopoli Greece **64** B3
Meghasani *mt.* India **86** C2
Megisti *i.* Greece **64** C3
Mehamn Norway **46** F1
Meharry, Mount Austr. **114** A2
Mehrān *watercourse* Iran **90** C2
Meia Ponte *r.* Brazil **154** C1
Meiganga Cameroon **104** B2
Meihekou China **76** D1
Meiktila Myanmar **74** A1
Meiningen Ger. **54** E2
Meißen Ger. **54** F2
Meizhou China **82** B3
Mejicana *mt.* Arg. **152** B3
Mejillones Chile **152** A3
Mek'elē Eth. **102** B3
Mekerrhane, Sebkha *salt pan* Alg. **100** C2
Meknès Morocco **100** B1
Mekong *r.* Asia **74** B2
Mekong *r.* China **74** B1
Mekong, Mouths of the Vietnam **74** B3
Melaka Malaysia **72** B1
Melanesia *is* Pacific Ocean **158** D5
Melbourne Austr. **116** C3
Capital of Victoria. 2nd most populous city in Oceania.
Melbourne U.S.A. **138** D3
Mele, Capo *c.* Italy **62** A2
Melenki Rus. Fed. **42** F2
Mélèzes, Rivière aux *r.* Can. **128** C1
Mélfi Chad **100** D3
Melfi Italy **62** C2
Melfort Can. **126** E2
Melhus Norway **46** C3
Melide Spain **60** B1
Melilla N. Africa **60** C2
Autonomous Community of Spain.
Melitopol' Ukr. **44** E2
Melle Ger. **54** D1
Mellerud Sweden **46** C4
Mellrichstadt Ger. **54** E2

Mellum *i.* Ger. **54** D1
Melo Uru. **152** C4
Melrhir, Chott *salt l.* Alg. **100** C1
Melton Mowbray U.K. **52** C3
Melun France **58** C2
Melville Can. **124** F3
Melville, Cape Austr. **114** D1
Melville, Lake Can. **128** E1
Melville Island Austr. **114** C1
Melville Island Can. **124** E1
Melville Peninsula Can. **124** G2
Memboro Indon. **72** C2
Memmingen Ger. **56** C3
Mempawah Indon. **72** B1
Memphis *tourist site* Egypt **92** B3
Memphis *TN* U.S.A. **138** B1
Memphis *TX* U.S.A. **140** D2
Mena Ukr. **44** D1
Mena U.S.A. **138** B2
Ménaka Mali **100** C3
Mènam Khong *r.* Asia *see* Mekong
Mende France **58** C3
Mendefera Eritrea **102** B3
Méndez Mex. **142** C2
Mendī Eth. **104** D2
Mendi P.N.G. **70** D3
Mendip Hills U.K. **52** B4
Mendoza Arg. **152** B4
Menemen Turkey **64** C3
Menggala Indon. **72** B2
Mengzi China **82** A3
Menihek Can. **128** D1
Menindee Austr. **116** C2
Menindee, Lake Austr. **116** C2
Meningie Austr. **116** B3
Mennecy France **58** C2
Menominee U.S.A. **136** C1
Menongue Angola **106** A1
Menorca *i.* Spain *see* Minorca
Mentawai, Kepulauan *is* Indon. **72** A2
Mentok Indon. **72** B2
Menzies Austr. **114** B2
Meppel Neth. **54** C1
Meppen Ger. **54** C1
Mepuze Moz. **108** D1
Meqheleng S. Africa **108** C2
Merano Italy **62** B1
Merauke Indon. **70** D3
Merbein Austr. **116** C2
Merced U.S.A. **132** B3
Mercedes Arg. **152** C3
Mercy, Cape Can. **124** H2
Meredith, Lake U.S.A. **140** D1
Merefa Ukr. **44** E2
Merga Oasis Sudan **102** A3
Mergui Archipelago *is* Myanmar **74** A2
Meriç *r.* Greece/Turkey **64** C2
Mérida Mex. **142** D2
Mérida Spain **60** B2
Mérida Venez. **150** B2
Meridian U.S.A. **138** C2
Mérignac France **58** B3
Merimbula Austr. **116** D3
Mérouana Alg. **60** E2
Merowe Sudan **102** B3
Merredin Austr. **114** A3
Merrick *h.* U.K. **50** B3
Merrill U.S.A. **136** C1
Merrillville U.S.A. **136** C2
Merritt Can. **126** C2
Merrygoen Austr. **116** D2
Mersa Fatma Eritrea **102** C3
Mersch Lux. **54** C3
Merseburg (Saale) Ger. **54** E2
Mersey *r.* U.K. **52** B3
Mersin Turkey **92** B2
Mersing Malaysia **72** B1
Mers-les-Bains France **52** D4
Merta India **86** B2
Merthyr Tydfil U.K. **52** B4
Mértola Port. **60** B2

Mertvyy Kultuk, Sor *dry lake* Kazakh. **88** C2
Meru *vol.* Tanz. **104** D3
4th highest mountain in Africa.
Merzig Ger. **54** C3
Mesa U.S.A. **140** B2
Mesagne Italy **62** C2
Meschede Ger. **54** D2
Meshchovsk Rus. Fed. **42** E3
Meshkovskaya Rus. Fed. **44** F2
Mesimeri Greece **64** B2
Mesolongi Greece **64** B3
Messalo *r.* Moz. **106** D1
Messina Italy **62** C3
Messina, Stretta di *str.* Italy **62** C3
Messiniakos Kolpos *b.* Greece **64** B3
Mesta *r.* Bulg. **64** B2
Meta *r.* Col./Venez. **150** C2
Metán Arg. **152** B3
Methoni Greece **64** B3
Metković Croatia **62** C2
Metro Indon. **72** B2
Metu Eth. **102** B4
Metz France **58** D2
Meuse *r.* Belgium/France **54** B2
Mexia U.S.A. **140** E2
Mexicali Mex. **142** A1
Mexico *country* Central America **142** B2
2nd most populous and 4th largest country in North America.
Mexico U.S.A. **134** E3
Mexico, Gulf of Mex./U.S.A. **144** A2
Mexico City Mex. **142** C3
Capital of Mexico. Most populous city in North America, and 2nd in the world
Meyenburg Ger. **54** F1
Meymaneh Afgh. **86** A1
Mezen' Rus. Fed. **40** D2
Mezen' *r.* Rus. Fed. **40** D2
Mezhdusharskiy, Ostrov *i.* Rus. Fed. **40** E1
Mezőtúr Hungary **56** E3
Mezquitic Mex. **142** B2
Mežvidi Latvia **42** C2
Mfuwe Zambia **106** C1
Mhlume Swaziland **108** D2
Mhow India **86** B2
Miahuatlán Mex. **142** C3
Miajadas Spain **60** B2
Miami *FL* U.S.A. **138** D3
Miami *OK* U.S.A. **140** F1
Miami Beach U.S.A. **138** D3
Miandowāb Iran **92** C2
Miandrivazo Madag. **106**□ D1
Mīāneh Iran **92** C2
Mianwali Pak. **86** B1
Mianyang China **82** A2
Miarinarivo Madag. **106**□ D1
Miass Rus. Fed. **40** F3
Mica Creek Can. **126** D2
Michalovce Slovakia **56** E3
Michigan *state* U.S.A. **136** C1
Michigan, Lake U.S.A. **136** C2
3rd largest lake in North America, and 5th in the world.
Michigan City U.S.A. **136** C2
Michipicoten Island Can. **128** B2
Michipicoten River Can. **128** B2
Michurinsk Rus. Fed. **42** F3
Micronesia *is* Pacific Ocean **158** D4
Micronesia, Federated States of *country* N. Pacific Ocean **70** D2
Middelburg Neth. **54** A2
Middelburg *E. Cape* S. Africa **108** C3
Middelburg *Mpumalanga* S. Africa **108** C2
Middelharnis Neth. **54** B2
Middle Alkali Lake U.S.A. **132** B2
Middle Andaman *i.* India **74** A2
Middle Loup *r.* U.S.A. **134** D2
Middlesboro U.S.A. **136** D3

Muzaffarpur India **86** C2
Muzamane Moz. **108** D1
Múzquiz Mex. **142** B2
Muztag *mt.* China **86** C1
Muz Tag *mt.* China **86** C1
Mwanza Dem. Rep. Congo **104** C3
Mwanza Tanz. **104** D3
Mweka Dem. Rep. Congo **104** C3
Mwenda Zambia **104** C4
Mwene-Ditu Dem. Rep. Congo **104** C3
Mwenezi Zimbabwe **106** C2
Mweru, Lake Dem. Rep. Congo/Zambia **104** C3
Mwimba Dem. Rep. Congo **104** C3
Mwinilunga Zambia **106** B1
Myadzyel Belarus **42** C3
Myanaung Myanmar **74** A2
Myanmar *country* Asia **74** A1
Myaungmya Myanmar **74** A2
Myeik Myanmar **74** A2
Myingyan Myanmar **74** A1
Myitkyina Myanmar **74** A1
Mykolayiv Ukr. **44** D2
Mykonos Greece **64** C3
Mykonos *i.* Greece **64** C3
Myla Rus. Fed. **40** E2
Mymensingh Bangl. **86** D2
Myŏnggan N. Korea **76** D1
Myory Belarus **42** C2
Mýrdalsjökull *ice cap* Iceland **46**□
Myrhorod Ukr. **44** D2
Myronivka Ukr. **44** D2
Myrtle Beach U.S.A. **138** E2
Myrtleford Austr. **116** D3
Myrtle Point U.S.A. **132** B2
Myshkin Rus. Fed. **42** E2
Myślibórz Pol. **56** C2
Mysore India **84** B3
Mys Shmidta Rus. Fed. **94** O2
My Tho Vietnam **74** B2
Mytilini Greece **64** C3
Mytishchi Rus. Fed. **42** E2
Mzamomhle S. Africa **108** C3
Mzimba Malawi **106** C1
Mzuzu Malawi **106** C1

N

Naas Rep. of Ireland **50** G2
Nababeep S. Africa **108** A2
Naberezhnyye Chelny Rus. Fed. **40** E3
Nabire Indon. **70** D3
Nāblus West Bank **92** B2
Naboomspruit S. Africa **108** C1
Nacala Moz. **106** D1
Nachuge India **74** A2
Nacogdoches U.S.A. **140** F2
Nacozari de García Mex. **142** B1
Nadiad India **86** B2
Nador Morocco **60** C2
Nadvirna Ukr. **44** B2
Nadvoitsy Rus. Fed. **40** C2
Nadym Rus. Fed. **40** G2
Næstved Denmark **46** C4
Nafpaktos Greece **64** B3
Nafplio Greece **64** B3
Nafy Saudi Arabia **90** B2
Naga Phil. **76** B2
Nagagami *r.* Can. **128** B1
Nagano Japan **78** C3
Nagaoka Japan **78** C3
Nagaon India **86** D2
Nagar India **86** B1
Nagar Parkar Pak. **86** B2
Nagasaki Japan **78** A4
Nagato Japan **78** B4
Nagaur India **86** B2
Nagercoil India **84** B4
Nagha Kalat Pak. **86** A2
Nag' Ḥammādī Egypt **90** A2

Nagina India **86** B2
Nagoya Japan **78** C3
Nagpur India **86** B2
Nagqu China **86** D1
Nagyatád Hungary **56** D3
Nagykanizsa Hungary **56** D3
Nahanni Butte Can. **126** C1
Nahāvand Iran **92** C2
Nahrendorf Ger. **54** E1
Nahuel Huapí, Lago *l.* Arg. **152** A5
Nain Can. **128** D1
Nā'īn Iran **92** D2
Nairn U.K. **50** C2
Nairobi Kenya **104** D3
Capital of Kenya.
Naivasha Kenya **104** D3
Najafābād Iran **92** D2
Najd *reg.* Saudi Arabia **90** B2
Nájera Spain **60** C1
Najin N. Korea **76** E1
Najrān Saudi Arabia **90** B3
Nakatsugawa Japan **78** C3
Nakfa Eritrea **90** A3
Nakhodka Rus. Fed. **78** B2
Nakhon Pathom Thai. **74** B2
Nakhon Ratchasima Thai. **74** B2
Nakhon Sawan Thai. **74** B2
Nakhon Si Thammarat Thai. **74** A3
Nakina Can. **128** B1
Nakonde Zambia **104** D3
Nakskov Denmark **46** C5
Nakuru Kenya **104** D3
Nakusp Can. **126** D2
Nalbari India **86** D2
Nal'chik Rus. Fed. **40** D4
Nālūt Libya **100** D1
Namahadi S. Africa **108** C2
Namakzar-e Shadad *salt flat* Iran **90** C1
Namangan Uzbek. **88** E2
Namaqualand *reg.* S. Africa **108** A2
Nambour Austr. **114** E2
Nambucca Heads Austr. **116** E2
Nam Co *salt l.* China **86** D1
Nam Đinh Vietnam **74** B1
Namib Desert Namibia **106** A2
Namibe Angola **106** A1
Namibia *country* Africa **108** A1
Namjagbarwa Feng *mt.* China **84** D2
Namlea Indon. **70** C3
Namoi *r.* Austr. **116** D2
Nampa U.S.A. **132** C2
Nampala Mali **100** B3
Namp'o N. Korea **76** D2
Nampula Moz. **106** C1
Namrup India **74** A1
Namsang Myanmar **74** A1
Namsos Norway **46** C3
Nam Tok Thai. **74** A2
Namtsy Rus. Fed. **94** K2
Namtu Myanmar **74** A1
Namur Belgium **54** D2
Namwala Zambia **106** B1
Namwŏn S. Korea **76** D2
Namya Ra Myanmar **74** A1
Nan Thai. **74** B2
Nanaimo Can. **126** C3
Nan'an China **82** B3
Nananib Plateau Namibia **108** A1
Nanao Japan **78** C3
Nanchang *Jiangxi* China **82** B3
Nanchang *Jiangxi* China **82** B3
Nanchong China **82** A2
Nancowry *i.* India **74** A3
Nancy France **58** D2
Nanda Devi *mt.* India **86** C1
Nandan China **82** A3
Nanded India **84** B3
Nandurbar India **86** B2
Nandyal India **84** B3
Nanfeng China **82** B3
Nanga Eboko Cameroon **104** B2

Nangahpinoh Indon. **72** C2
Nanga Parbat *mt.* Jammu and Kashmir **86** B1
Nangatayap Indon. **72** C2
Nangong China **82** B2
Nangulangwa Tanz. **104** D3
Nanjing China **82** B2
Nanking China see Nanjing
Nankova Angola **106** A1
Nan Ling *mts* China **82** B3
Nanning China **82** A3
Nanortalik Greenland **124** I2
Nanpan Jiang *r.* China **82** A3
Nanpara India **86** C2
Nanping China **82** B3
Nansei-shotō *is* Japan *see* Ryukyu Islands
Nantes France **58** B2
Nantong China **82** C2
Nantucket Island U.S.A. **136** G2
Nanumea *atoll* Tuvalu **110**
Nanuque Brazil **154** D1
Nanusa, Kepulauan *is* Indon. **76** B3
Nanxiong China **82** B3
Nanyang China **82** B2
Nanzhang China **82** B2
Nao, Cabo de la *c.* Spain **60** D2
Naococane, Lac *l.* Can. **128** C1
Naokot Pak. **86** A2
Napa U.S.A. **132** B3
Napaktulik Lake Can. **126** D1
Napasoq Greenland **124** I2
Napier N.Z. **118** C2
Naples Italy **62** B2
Naples U.S.A. **138** D3
Napo *r.* Ecuador **150** B3
Napoli Italy *see* Naples
Nara Mali **100** B3
Narach Belarus **42** C3
Naracoorte Austr. **116** C3
Naranjos Mex. **142** C2
Narathiwat Thai. **74** B3
Narbonne France **58** C3
Narcondam Island India **74** A2
Nares Strait Can./Greenland **124** H1
Narib Namibia **108** A1
Narimanov Rus. Fed. **40** D4
Narita Japan **78** D3
Narmada *r.* India **86** B2
Narnaul India **86** B2
Narni Italy **62** B2
Narodychi Ukr. **44** C1
Naro-Fominsk Rus. Fed. **42** E2
Narooma Austr. **116** E3
Narrabri Austr. **116** D2
Narrandera Austr. **116** D2
Narromine Austr. **116** D2
Narva Estonia **42** C2
Narva Bay Estonia/Rus. Fed. **42** C2
Narvik Norway **46** F2
Narvskoye Vodokhranilishche *resr* Estonia/Rus. Fed. **42** C2
Nar'yan-Mar Rus. Fed. **40** E2
Naryn Kyrg. **88** E2
Nashik India **86** B2
Nashua U.S.A. **136** F2
Nashville U.S.A. **138** C1
Capital of Tennessee.
Nasir Sudan **102** B4
Nass *r.* Can. **126** C2
Nassau Bahamas **144** C2
Capital of the Bahamas.
Nasser, Lake *resr* Egypt **102** B2
Nässjö Sweden **46** C4
Nastapoca *r.* Can. **128** C1
Nastapoka Islands Can. **128** C1
Nata Botswana **106** B2
Natal Brazil **150** F3
Natal *prov.* S. Africa see Kwazulu-Natal
Natashquan Can. **128** D1

Newtownards U.K. **50** H1
Newtown St Boswells U.K. **50** C3
Newtownstewart U.K. **50** G1
New Ulm U.S.A. **134** E2
New York U.S.A. **136** F2
  2nd most populous city in North America,
  and 3rd in the world.
New York *state* U.S.A. **136** E2
New Zealand *country* Oceania **118**
  3rd largest and 3rd most populated
  country in Oceania.
Neya Rus. Fed. **42** F2
Neya *r.* Rus. Fed. **42** F2
Neyrīz Iran **92** D3
Neyshābūr Iran **88** C3
Nezahualcóyotl Mex. **142** C3
Nezahualcóyotl, Presa *resr* Mex. **142** C3
Ngabang Indon. **72** B1
Ngamring China **86** C2
Nangla Ringco *salt l.* China **86** C1
Nganglong Kangri *mt.* China **86** C1
Nganglong Kangri *mts* China **86** C1
Ngangzê Co *salt l.* China **86** C1
Ngao Thai. **74** A2
Ngaoundéré Cameroon **104** B2
Ngaruawahia N.Z. **118** C2
Ngathainggyaung Myanmar **74** A2
Ngo Congo **104** B3
Ngoc Linh *mt.* Vietnam **74** B2
Ngol Bembo Nigeria **100** D4
Ngoring Hu *l.* China **80** C2
Ngourti Niger **100** D3
Nguigmi Niger **100** D3
Ngulu *atoll* Micronesia **70** D2
Nguru Nigeria **100** D3
Ngwelezana S. Africa **108** D2
Nhamalabué Moz. **106** C1
Nha Trang Vietnam **74** B2
Nhill Austr. **116** C3
Nhlangano Swaziland **108** D2
Nhulunbuy Austr. **114** C1
Niagara Falls Can. **136** E2
Niamey Niger **100** C3
  Capital of Niger.
Niangara Dem. Rep. Congo **104** C2
Niangay, Lac *l.* Mali **100** B3
Nias *i.* Indon. **72** A1
Nicaragua *country* Central America
  144 B3
  5th largest country in North America.
Nicaragua, Lake Nic. **144** B3
Nice France **58** D3
Nicobar Islands India **84** D4
Nicosia Cyprus **92** B2
  Capital of Cyprus.
Nicoya, Golfo de *b.* Costa Rica **144** B4
Nida Lith. **42** B2
Nidzica Pol. **56** E2
Niebüll Ger. **56** B2
Niederaula Ger. **54** D2
Niefang Equat. Guinea **104** B2
Niemegk Ger. **54** F1
Nienburg (Weser) Ger. **54** D1
Nieuwe-Niedorp Neth. **54** B1
Nieuw Nickerie Suriname **150** D2
Nieuwoudtville S. Africa **108** A3
Nieuwpoort Belgium **54** A2
Niğde Turkey **92** B2
Niger *country* Africa **100** D3
Niger *r.* Africa **100** C4
  3rd longest river in Africa.
Niger, Mouths of the Nigeria **100** C4
Nigeria *country* Africa **100** C4
  Most populous country in Africa, and 10th
  in the world.
Nighthawk Lake Can. **128** B2
Nigrita Greece **64** B2
Niigata Japan **78** B3
Niihama Japan **78** B4
Nii-jima *i.* Japan **78** C4
Niitsu Japan **78** C3

Nijmegen Neth. **54** B2
Nijverdal Neth. **54** C1
Nikel' Rus. Fed. **46** G2
Nikol'skoye Rus. Fed. **94** N3
Nikopol' Ukr. **44** D2
Niksar Turkey **92** B1
Nikshahr Iran **90** D2
Nikšić S.M. **64** A2
Nile *r.* Africa **102** B1
  Longest river in the world and in Africa.
Niles U.S.A. **136** C2
Nîmes France **58** C3
Nimmitabel Austr. **116** D3
Nimule Sudan **102** B4
Nindigully Austr. **116** D1
Nine Degree Channel India **84** B4
Ninety Mile Beach Austr. **116** D3
Ninety Mile Beach N.Z. **118** B1
Ningbo China **82** C3
Ningde China **82** B3
Ningdu China **82** B3
Ningguo China **82** B2
Ninghai China **82** C3
Ninging India **74** A1
Ningjing Shan *mts* China **80** C2
Ningxia Huizu Zizhiqu *aut. reg.* China
  82 A2
Ningyang China **82** B2
Ninh Binh Vietnam **74** B1
Ninh Hoa Vietnam **74** B2
Ninohe Japan **78** D2
Niobrara *r.* U.S.A. **134** D2
Niono Mali **100** B3
Nioro Mali **100** B3
Niort France **58** B2
Nipawin Can. **124** F3
Nipigon Can. **128** B2
Nipigon, Lake Can. **128** B2
Nipishish Lake Can. **128** D1
Nipissing, Lake Can. **128** C2
Nipton U.S.A. **132** C3
Niquelândia Brazil **150** E4
Nirmal India **84** B3
Niš S.M. **64** B2
Nišava *r.* S.M. **64** B2
Niscemi Italy **62** B3
Nishino-omote Japan **78** B4
Niterói Brazil **154** D2
Nith *r.* U.K. **50** C3
Nitra Slovakia **56** D3
Niue *terr.* S. Pacific Ocean **112**
  Self-governing New Zealand Overseas
  Territory.
Nivala Fin. **46** E3
Nivelles Belgium **54** B2
Nizamabad India **84** B3
Nizhnekamsk Rus. Fed. **40** E3
Nizhneudinsk Rus. Fed. **94** I3
Nizhnevartovsk Rus. Fed. **94** H2
Nizhniy Kislyay Rus. Fed. **42** F3
Nizhniy Lomov Rus. Fed. **40** D3
Nizhniy Novgorod Rus. Fed. **40** D3
Nizhniy Odes Rus. Fed. **40** E2
Nizhniy Tagil Rus. Fed. **40** E3
Nizhnyaya Tunguska *r.* Rus. Fed. **94** H2
Nizhyn Ukr. **44** D1
Njazidja *i.* Comoros **106** C1
Njinjo Tanz. **104** D3
Njombe Tanz. **104** D3
Nkhotakota Malawi **106** C1
Nkongsamba Cameroon **104** A2
Nkululeko S. Africa **108** C3
Nkwenkwezi S. Africa **108** C3
Nobeoka Japan **78** B4
Noccundra Austr. **116** C1
Nogales Mex. **142** A1
Nogales U.S.A. **140** B2
Nogent-le-Rotrou France **58** C2
Noginsk Rus. Fed. **42** E2
Nohar India **86** B2
Nohfelden Ger. **54** C3

Noirmoutier, Île de *i.* France **58** B2
Noirmoutier-en-l'Île France **58** B2
Noisseville France **54** C3
Nojima-zaki *c.* Japan **78** C4
Nokha India **86** B2
Nokia Fin. **46** E3
Nok Kundi Pak. **86** A2
Nola C.A.R. **104** B2
Nolinsk Rus. Fed. **40** D3
Nomonde S. Africa **108** C3
Nondweni S. Africa **108** D2
Nong Khai Thai. **74** B2
Nonning Austr. **116** B2
Nonoava Mex. **142** B2
Nonsan S. Korea **76** D2
Nonthaburi Thai. **74** B2
Nonzwakazi S. Africa **108** B3
Norak Tajik. **88** D3
Noranda Can. **136** E1
Nordaustlandet *i.* Svalbard **94** D1
Nordegg Can. **126** D2
Norden Ger. **54** C1
Nordenshel'da, Arkhipelag *is* Rus. Fed.
  94 I1
Norderney Ger. **54** C1
Norderney *i.* Ger. **54** C1
Norderstedt Ger. **54** E1
Nordfjordeid Norway **46** B3
Nordhausen Ger. **54** E2
Nordholz Ger. **54** D1
Nordhorn Ger. **54** C1
Nordkapp *c.* Norway *see* **North Cape**
Nordli Norway **46** C3
Nördlingen Ger. **56** C3
Nordmaling Sweden **46** D3
Norðoyar *i.* Faroe Is **48** B1
Nore *r.* Rep. of Ireland **50** G2
Norfolk *NE* U.S.A. **134** D2
Norfolk *VA* U.S.A. **136** E3
Norfolk Island *terr.* S. Pacific Ocean **112**
  Australian External Territory.
Norheimsund Norway **46** B3
Noril'sk Rus. Fed. **94** H2
Norkyung China **86** C2
Norman U.S.A. **140** E1
Normandes, Îles *is* English Chan. *see*
  Channel Islands
Normandy *reg.* France **58** B2
Normanton Austr. **114** D1
Norman Wells Can. **126** C1
Norrköping Sweden **46** D4
Norrtälje Sweden **46** D4
Norseman Austr. **114** B3
Norsjö Sweden **46** D3
Norte, Punta *pt* Arg. **146**
Northallerton U.K. **52** C2
Northampton Austr. **114** A2
Northampton U.K. **52** C3
North Andaman *i.* India **74** A2
North Battleford Can. **124** E3
North Bay Can. **128** C2
North Belcher Islands Can. **128** C1
North Berwick U.K. **50** C2
North Cape Norway **46** F1
North Cape N.Z. **118** B1
North Caribou Lake Can. **128** A1
North Carolina *state* U.S.A. **138** E1
North Channel *lake channel* Can. **128** C2
North Channel U.K. **50** G1
North Cowichan Can. **126** C3
North Dakota *state* U.S.A. **134** C1
North Downs *hills* U.K. **52** C4
Northeim Ger. **54** D2
Northern Cape *prov.* S. Africa **108** A2
Northern Indian Lake Can. **128** F2
Northern Ireland *prov.* U.K. **50** G1
Northern Mariana Islands *terr.*
  N. Pacific Ocean **70** C1
  United States Commonwealth.
Northern Territory *admin. div.* Austr.
  114 C1

Obninsk Rus. Fed. **42** E2
Obo C.A.R. **104** C2
Obock Djibouti **102** C3
Oboyan' Rus. Fed. **42** E3
Obregón, Presa resr Mex. **142** B2
Obrenovac S.M. **64** B2
Obshchiy Syrt hills Rus. Fed. **40** E3
Obskaya Guba sea chan. Rus. Fed. **40** G2
Obuasi Ghana **100** B4
Obukhiv Ukr. **44** D1
Ob"yachevo Rus. Fed. **40** D2
Ocala U.S.A. **138** D3
Ocampo Mex. **142** B2
Ocaña Spain **60** C2
Occidental, Cordillera mts Col. **150** B2
Occidental, Cordillera mts Peru **150** B4
Ocean City U.S.A. **136** E3
Ocean Falls Can. **126** C2
Oceanside U.S.A. **132** C4
Ochakiv Ukr. **44** D2
Ocher Rus. Fed. **40** E3
Ochsenfurt Ger. **54** E3
Oconee r. U.S.A. **138** D2
Ocosingo Mex. **142** C3
Ocussi enclave East Timor **70** C3
Oda, Jebel mt. Sudan **102** B2
Ōdate Japan **78** D2
Odawara Japan **78** C3
Odda Norway **46** B3
Odemira Port. **60** B2
Ödemiş Turkey **64** C3
Odense Denmark **46** C4
Odenwald reg. Ger. **54** D3
Oderbucht b. Ger. **56** C2
Odesa Ukr. **44** D2
Odessa U.S.A. **140** D2
Odienné Côte d'Ivoire **100** B4
Odra r. Ger./Pol. **56** D3
Oeiras Brazil **150** E3
Oelde Ger. **54** D2
Oelrichs U.S.A. **134** C2
Oelsnitz Ger. **54** F2
Oenkerk Neth. **54** B1
Ofanto r. Italy **62** C2
Offenbach am Main Ger. **54** D2
Offenburg Ger. **56** B3
Ogadēn reg. Eth. **102** C2
Oga-hantō pen. Japan **78** C3
Ōgaki Japan **78** C3
Ogallala U.S.A. **134** C2
Ogden U.S.A. **132** D2
Ogdensburg U.S.A. **136** E2
Ogilvie r. Can. **124** C2
Ogilvie Mountains Can. **124** C2
Oglethorpe, Mount U.S.A. **138** D2
Ogoki r. Can. **128** B1
Ogoki Reservoir Can. **128** B1
Ogre Latvia **42** B2
Ogulin Croatia **62** C1
Ohio r. U.S.A. **136** C3
Ohio state U.S.A. **136** D2
Ohrdruf Ger. **54** E2
Ohrid Macedonia **64** B2
Öhringen Ger. **54** D3
Oiapoque Brazil **150** D2
Oil City U.S.A. **136** E2
Oise r. France **54** A3
Ōita Japan **78** B4
Ojinaga Mex. **142** B2
Ojos del Salado, Nevado mt. Arg./Chile **152** B3
 Highest volcano in the world, and 2nd
 highest mountain in South America.
Oka r. Rus. Fed. **42** F2
Okahandja Namibia **106** A2
Okakarara Namibia **106** A2
Okanagan Falls Can. **126** D3
Okanagan Lake Can. **126** D3
Okanogan U.S.A. **132** C1

Okanogan r. U.S.A. **132** C1
Okara Pak. **86** B1
Okavango r. Botswana/Namibia **106** B1
Okavango Delta swamp Botswana **106** B1
 Largest oasis in the world.
Okaya Japan **78** C3
Okayama Japan **78** B4
Okazaki Japan **78** C4
Okeechobee, Lake U.S.A. **138** D3
Okefenokee Swamp U.S.A. **138** D2
Okehampton U.K. **52** A4
Okha India **86** A2
Okha Rus. Fed. **94** L3
Okhaldhunga Nepal **86** C2
Okhotka r. Rus. Fed. **94** L3
Okhotsk Rus. Fed. **94** L3
Okhotsk, Sea of Japan/Rus. Fed. **94** L4
Okhtyrka Ukr. **44** D1
Okinawa i. Japan **80** E3
Oki-shotō is Japan **78** B3
Oklahoma state U.S.A. **140** E1
Oklahoma City U.S.A. **140** E1
 Capital of Oklahoma.
Okmulgee U.S.A. **140** E1
Oko, Wadi watercourse Sudan **90** A2
Okondja Gabon **104** B3
Okotoks Can. **126** D2
Okovskiy Les for. Rus. Fed. **42** D3
Okoyo Congo **104** B3
Øksfjord Norway **46** E1
Oktwin Myanmar **74** A2
Oktyabr'skiy Arkhangel'skaya Oblast' Rus. Fed. **40** D2
Oktyabr'skiy Kamchatskaya Oblast' Rus. Fed. **94** M3
Oktyabr'skiy Respublika Bashkortostan Rus. Fed. **40** E3
Oktyabr'skoye Rus. Fed. **40** F2
Oktyabr'skoy Revolyutsii, Ostrov i. Rus. Fed. **94** I1
Okulovka Rus. Fed. **42** D2
Okushiri-tō i. Japan **78** C2
Ólafsvík Iceland **46**□
Öland i. Sweden **46** D4
Olary Austr. **116** C2
Olavarría Arg. **152** B4
Oława Pol. **56** D2
Olbernhau Ger. **54** F2
Olbia Italy **62** A2
Old Crow Can. **124** C2
Oldenburg Ger. **54** D1
Oldenburg in Holstein Ger. **56** C2
Oldenzaal Neth. **54** C1
Old Head of Kinsale hd Rep. of Ireland **50** F3
Olds Can. **126** D2
Old Wives Lake Can. **126** E2
Olean U.S.A. **136** E2
Olecko Pol. **56** E2
Olekminsk Rus. Fed. **94** K2
Oleksandriya Ukr. **44** D2
Ølen Norway **48** E2
Olenegorsk Rus. Fed. **46** G2
Olenek Rus. Fed. **94** J2
Olenek r. Rus. Fed. **94** J2
Olenino Rus. Fed. **42** D2
Olevs'k Ukr. **44** C1
Olhão Port. **60** B2
Olifants r. Moz./S. Africa **108** D1
Olifants watercourse Namibia **108** A2
Olifants S. Africa **108** D1
Olifants r. S. Africa **108** A3
Olifantshoek S. Africa **108** B2
Olímpia Brazil **154** C2
Olinda Brazil **150** F3
Oliphants Drift S. Africa **108** C1
Oliva Spain **60** C2
Oliveira Brazil **154** D2
Olivenza Spain **60** B2

Ollagüe Chile **152** B3
Olmos Peru **150** B3
Olney U.S.A. **136** C3
Olomouc Czech Rep. **56** D3
Olongapo Phil. **76** B2
Oloron-Ste-Marie France **58** B3
Olot Spain **60** D1
Olovyannaya Rus. Fed. **80** D1
Olpe Ger. **54** C2
Olsztyn Pol. **56** E2
Olt r. Romania **44** B3
Oltu Turkey **92** C1
Olympia tourist site Greece **64** B3
Olympia U.S.A. **132** B1
 Capital of Washington state.
Olympus, Mount Greece **64** B2
Olympus, Mount U.S.A. **132** B1
Olyutorskiy, Mys c. Rus. Fed. **94** N3
Omagh U.K. **50** G1
Omaha U.S.A. **134** D2
Oman country Asia **90** C2
Oman, Gulf of Asia **90** C2
Omaruru Namibia **106** A2
Omatako watercourse Namibia **106** B1
Omdurman Sudan **102** B3
Omeo Austr. **116** D3
Ometepec Mex. **142** C3
Om Hajēr Eritrea **90** A3
Omineca Mountains Can. **126** C2
Ōmiya Japan **78** C3
Ommen Neth. **54** C1
Omolon r. Rus. Fed. **94** M2
Omont France **54** B3
Omsk Rus. Fed. **88** E1
Omsukchan Rus. Fed. **94** M2
Omu, Vârful mt. Romania **44** C2
Ōmura Japan **78** A4
Onancock U.S.A. **136** E3
Onaping Lake Can. **136** D1
Onatchiway, Lac l. Can. **128** C2
Oncócua Angola **106** A1
Onderstedorings S. Africa **108** B3
Ondjiva Angola **106** A1
Onega Rus. Fed. **40** C2
Onega r. Rus. Fed. **40** C2
Onega, Lake Rus. Fed. **40** C2
 2nd largest lake in Europe.
Oneida Lake U.S.A. **136** E2
O'Neill U.S.A. **134** D2
Oneonta U.S.A. **136** E2
Oneşti Romania **44** C2
Onezhskoye Ozero l. Rus. Fed. see Onega, Lake
Ongers watercourse S. Africa **108** B2
Ongjin N. Korea **76** D2
Ongole India **84** C3
Onilahy r. Madag. **106**□
Onitsha Nigeria **100** C4
Onotoa atoll Kiribati **110**
Onseepkans S. Africa **108** A2
Onslow Austr. **114** A2
Onslow Bay U.S.A. **138** E2
Ontario prov. Can. **128** A1
Ontario U.S.A. **132** C2
Ontario, Lake Can./U.S.A. **136** E2
Oodnadatta Austr. **116** B1
Oostende Belgium see Ostend
Oosterhout Neth. **54** B2
Oosterschelde est. Neth. **54** A2
Oost-Vlieland Neth. **54** B1
Ootsa Lake Can. **126** C2
Ootsa Lake l. Can. **126** C2
Opala Dem. Rep. Congo **104** C3
Opataca, Lac l. Can. **128** C1
Opava Czech Rep. **56** D3
Opelika U.S.A. **138** C2
Opelousas U.S.A. **138** B2
Opinaca, Réservoir resr Can. **128** C1
Opiscotéo, Lac l. Can. **128** D1
Opochka Rus. Fed. **42** C2
Opodepe Mex. **142** A2

Pesaro Italy **62** B2
Pescara Italy **62** B2
Pescara r. Italy **62** B2
Peschanokopskoye Rus. Fed. **44** F2
Peshawar Pak. **86** B1
Peshkopi Albania **64** B2
Pesnica Slovenia **62** C1
Pessac France **58** B3
Pestovo Rus. Fed. **42** E2
Pestyaki Rus. Fed. **42** F2
Petatlán Mex. **142** B3
Petenwell Lake U.S.A. **136** C2
Peterborough Austr. **116** B2
Peterborough Can. **128** C2
Peterborough U.K. **52** C3
Peterhead U.K. **50** D2
Petermann Ranges mts Austr. **114** B2
Peter Pond Lake Can. **126** E2
Petersburg AK U.S.A. **126** B2
Petersburg VA U.S.A. **136** E3
Petershagen Ger. **54** D1
Petit Mécatina r. Can. **128** E1
Peto Mex. **142** D2
Petoskey U.S.A. **136** D1
Petra tourist site Jordan **92** B2
Petra Velikogo, Zaliv b. Rus. Fed. **78** B2
Petrich Bulg. **64** B2
Petrolina Brazil **150** E3
Petropavlovsk Kazakh. **88** D1
Petropavlovsk-Kamchatskiy Rus. Fed. **94** M3
Petroşani Romania **44** B2
Petrovskoye Rus. Fed. **42** F3
Petrozavodsk Rus. Fed. **40** C2
Petrusburg S. Africa **108** C2
Petrus Steyn S. Africa **108** C2
Petrusville S. Africa **108** B3
Petukhovo Rus. Fed. **40** F3
Petushki Rus. Fed. **42** E2
Peureula Indon. **72** A1
Pevek Rus. Fed. **94** N2
Pforzheim Ger. **56** B3
Pfunds Austria **56** C3
Pfungstadt Ger. **54** D3
Phahameng S. Africa **108** C2
Phalaborwa S. Africa **108** D1
Phalodi India **86** B2
Phang Hoei, San Khao mts Thai. **74** B2
Phangnga Thai. **74** A3
Phan Rang Vietnam **74** B2
Phan Thiêt Vietnam **74** B2
Phatthalung Thai. **74** B3
Phayao Thai. **74** A2
Phelps Lake Can. **126** E2
Phenix City U.S.A. **138** C2
Phet Buri Thai. **74** A2
Phichit Thai. **74** B2
Philadelphia U.S.A. **136** E3
Philip U.S.A. **134** C2
Philippeville Belgium **54** B2
Philippine Neth. **54** A2
Philippines country Asia **76** B2
Philippine Sea N. Pacific Ocean **70** C1
Philippsburg Ger. **54** D3
Philip Smith Mountains U.S.A. **124** C2
Philipstown S. Africa **108** B3
Phillip Island Austr. **116** D3
Phillipsburg U.S.A. **134** D3
Phiritona S. Africa **108** C2
Phitsanulok Thai. **74** B2
Phnom Penh Cambodia **74** B2
Capital of Cambodia.
Phoenix U.S.A. **140** B2
Capital of Arizona.
Phoenix Islands Kiribati **110**
Phon Thai. **74** B2
Phôngsali Laos **74** B1
Phrae Thai. **74** B2
Phuket Thai. **74** A3
Phumĭ Sâmraông Cambodia **74** B2

Phuthadithjhaba S. Africa **108** C2
Phyu Myanmar **74** A2
Piacenza Italy **62** A1
Pianosa, Isola i. Italy **58** E3
Piatra Neamţ Romania **44** C2
Piauí r. Brazil **150** E3
Piave r. Italy **62** B1
Pibor r. Sudan **102** B4
Pibor Post Sudan **102** B4
Picayune U.S.A. **138** C2
Pichanal Arg. **152** B3
Pichilingue Mex. **142** A2
Pickering U.K. **52** C2
Pickle Lake Can. **128** A1
Picos Brazil **150** E3
Pico Truncado Arg. **152** B5
Picton Austr. **116** E2
Picton N.Z. **118** B3
Piedras Negras Guat. **142** C3
Piedras Negras Mex. **142** B2
Pieksämäki Fin. **46** F3
Pielinen l. Fin. **46** F3
Pierre U.S.A. **134** C2
Capital of South Dakota.
Pierrelatte France **58** C3
Pietermaritzburg S. Africa **108** D2
Pietersburg S. Africa see Polokwane
Pietrosa mt. Romania **44** B2
Pigeon Lake Can. **126** D2
Pigüé Arg. **152** B4
Pihtipudas Fin. **46** F3
Pijijiapan Mex. **142** C3
Pikes Peak U.S.A. **134** C3
Piketberg S. Africa **108** A3
Pikeville U.S.A. **136** D3
Piła Pol. **56** D2
Pilar Arg. **152** C4
Pilar Para. **152** C3
Pilliga Austr. **116** D2
Pilões, Serra dos mts Brazil **154** C1
Pimenta Bueno Brazil **150** C4
Pinamar Arg. **152** C4
Pınarbaşı Turkey **92** B2
Pinar del Río Cuba **144** B2
Pinatubo, Mount Phil. **76** B2
Pindaré r. Brazil **150** E3
Pindos mts Greece see
Pindus Mountains
Pindus Mountains Greece **64** B3
Pine Bluff U.S.A. **138** B2
Pine Creek Austr. **114** C1
Pinedale U.S.A. **134** B2
Pinega Rus. Fed. **40** D2
Pinehouse Lake Can. **126** E2
Pineios r. Greece **64** B3
Pine Point Can. **126** D1
Pine Ridge U.S.A. **134** C2
Pinetown S. Africa **108** D2
Pingdingshan China **82** B2
Pinggu China **82** A3
Pingjiang China **82** B3
Pingliang China **82** A2
P'ingtung Taiwan **82** C3
Pingxiang Guangxi China **82** A3
Pingxiang Jiangxi China **82** B3
Pingyin China **82** B2
Pinheiro Brazil **150** E3
Pinneberg Ger. **54** D1
Pinotepa Nacional Mex. **142** C3
Pinsk Belarus **42** C3
Pioche U.S.A. **132** D3
Piodi Dem. Rep. Congo **104** C3
Pionki Pol. **56** E2
Piotrków Trybunalski Pol. **56** D2
Pipestone U.S.A. **134** D2
Pipmuacan, Réservoir resr Can. **128** C2
Piquiri r. Brazil **154** B2
Piracanjuba Brazil **154** C1
Piracicaba Brazil **154** C2
Piracicaba r. Brazil **154** D1

Piraçununga Brazil **154** C2
Piraeus Greece **64** B3
Piraí do Sul Brazil **154** C2
Pirajuí Brazil **154** C2
Piranhas Brazil **154** B1
Piranhas r. Brazil **150** F3
Pirapora Brazil **154** D1
Pires do Rio Brazil **154** C1
Piripiri Brazil **150** E3
Pirmasens Ger. **54** C3
Pirna Ger. **54** F2
Piru Indon. **70** C3
Pisa Italy **62** B2
Pisagua Chile **152** A2
Pisco Peru **150** B4
Písek Czech Rep. **56** C3
Pīshīn Iran **90** D2
Pisté Mex. **142** D2
Pisticci Italy **62** C2
Pistoia Italy **62** B2
Pisuerga r. Spain **60** C1
Pit r. U.S.A. **132** B2
Pitanga Brazil **154** B2
Pitangui Brazil **154** D1
Pitcairn Island Pitcairn Is **110**
United Kingdom Overseas Territory.
Pitcairn Islands terr. S. Pacific Ocean **112**
Piteå Sweden **46** E2
Piteälven r. Sweden **46** E2
Piteşti Romania **44** B3
Pithoragarh India **86** C2
Pitlochry U.K. **50** C2
Pitt Island Can. **126** C2
Pittsburg U.S.A. **134** E3
Pittsburgh U.S.A. **136** E2
Pittsfield U.S.A. **136** F2
Pittsworth Austr. **116** E1
Piumhi Brazil **154** C2
Piura Peru **150** A3
Pivdennyy Buh r. Ukr. **44** D2
Placentia Can. **128** E2
Placerville U.S.A. **132** B3
Placetas Cuba **144** C2
Plainview U.S.A. **140** D2
Planaltina Brazil **154** C1
Plaquemine U.S.A. **138** B2
Plasencia Spain **60** B1
Plasy Czech Rep. **54** F3
Plato Col. **144** C4
Platte r. U.S.A. **134** D2
Plattsburgh U.S.A. **136** F2
Plau Ger. **54** F1
Plauen Ger. **54** F2
Plauer See l. Ger. **54** F1
Plavsk Rus. Fed. **42** E3
Plây Cu Vietnam **74** B2
Playgreen Lake Can. **126** F2
Plaza Huincul Arg. **152** B4
Pleasanton U.S.A. **140** E3
Pleasant Point N.Z. **118** B3
Pleaux France **58** C2
Pledger Lake Can. **128** B1
Pleinfeld Ger. **54** E3
Plenty, Bay of g. N.Z. **118** C2
Plentywood U.S.A. **134** C1
Plesetsk Rus. Fed. **40** D2
Plétipi, Lac l. Can. **128** C1
Plettenberg Bay S. Africa **108** B3
Pleven Bulg. **64** B2
Pljevlja S.M. **64** A2
Ploče Croatia **62** C2
Płock Pol. **56** D2
Pločno mt. Bos.-Herz. **62** C2
Ploemeur France **58** B2
Ploieşti Romania **44** C3
Ploskoye Rus. Fed. **42** F2
Plouzané France **58** B2
Plovdiv Bulg. **64** B2
Plungė Lith. **42** B2
Plyeshchanitsy Belarus **42** C3

Poshekhon'ye Rus. Fed. 42 E2
Posio Fin. 46 F2
Poso Indon. 72 D2
Posse Brazil 150 E4
Pößneck Ger. 54 E2
Post U.S.A. 140 D2
Poste-de-la-Baleine Can. see
  Kuujjuarapik
Postmasburg S. Africa 108 B2
Posušje Bos.-Herz. 62 C2
Poteau U.S.A. 140 F1
Potenza Italy 62 C2
Poti r. Brazil 150 E3
P'ot'i Georgia 92 C1
Potiskum Nigeria 100 D3
Potomac, South Branch r. U.S.A.
  136 E3
Potosí Bol. 152 B2
Pototan Phil. 76 B2
Potrero del Llano Mex. 140 D3
Potsdam Ger. 54 F1
Potsdam U.S.A. 136 F2
Pottstown U.S.A. 136 E2
Pottsville U.S.A. 136 E2
Pouch Cove Can. 128 E2
Poughkeepsie U.S.A. 136 F2
Poulton-le-Fylde U.K. 52 B3
Pouso Alegre Brazil 154 C2
Poüthïsät Cambodia 74 B2
Považská Bystrica Slovakia 56 D3
Povlen mt. S.M. 64 A2
Póvoa de Varzim Port. 60 B1
Povorino Rus. Fed. 44 F1
Powell U.S.A. 134 B2
Powell, Lake resr U.S.A. 132 D3
Powell River Can. 126 C3
Poxoréu Brazil 154 B1
Poyang Hu l. China 82 B3
Požarevac S.M. 64 B2
Poza Rica Mex. 142 C2
Požega Croatia 62 C1
Požega S.M. 64 B2
Pozm Tïäb Iran 90 D2
Poznań Pol. 56 D2
Pozoblanco Spain 60 C2
Pozzuoli Italy 62 B2
Prabumulih Indon. 72 B2
Prachatice Czech Rep. 56 C3
Prachuap Khiri Khan Thai. 74 A2
Prado Brazil 154 E1
Prague Czech Rep. 56 C2
  Capital of the Czech Republic.
Praha Czech Rep. see Prague
Praia Cape Verde 98
  Capital of Cape Verde.
Prairie Dog Town Fork r. U.S.A. 140 D2
Prairie du Chien U.S.A. 136 B2
Prapat Indon. 72 A1
Prata Brazil 154 C1
Prato Italy 58 E3
Pratt U.S.A. 134 D3
Praya Indon. 72 C2
Preäh Vihear Cambodia 74 B2
Prechistoye Rus. Fed. 42 F2
Preeceville Can. 126 E2
Preiļi Latvia 42 C2
Premer Austr. 116 D2
Prémery France 58 C2
Premnitz Ger. 54 F1
Prenzlau Ger. 54 F1
Preparis Island Cocos Is 74 A2
Preparis North Channel Cocos Is 74 A2
Preparis South Channel Cocos Is 74 A2
Přerov Czech Rep. 56 D3
Prescott U.S.A. 140 B2
Preševo S.M. 64 B2
Presidencia Roque Sáenz Peña Arg.
  152 B3
Presidente Dutra Brazil 150 E3
Presidente Epitácio Brazil 154 B2
Presidente Prudente Brazil 154 B2

Presidio U.S.A. 140 D3
Prešov Slovakia 56 E3
Presque Isle U.S.A. 136 G1
Pressel Ger. 54 F2
Přeštice Czech Rep. 54 F3
Preston U.K. 52 B3
Preston U.S.A. 132 D2
Prestwick U.K. 50 B3
Preto r. Brazil 154 C1
Pretoria S. Africa 108 C2
  Official capital of South Africa.
Preveza Greece 64 B3
Prey Vêng Cambodia 74 B2
Priboj S.M. 64 A2
Price U.S.A. 132 D3
Prienai Lith. 42 B3
Prieska S. Africa 108 B2
Prievidza Slovakia 56 D3
Prijedor Bos.-Herz. 62 C2
Prikaspiyskaya Nizmennost' lowland
  Kazakh./Rus. Fed. see
  Caspian Lowland
Prilep Macedonia 64 B2
Primorsk Rus. Fed. 42 C1
Primorsko-Akhtarsk Rus. Fed. 44 E2
Primrose Lake Can. 126 E2
Prince Albert Can. 124 E3
Prince Albert S. Africa 108 B3
Prince Albert Peninsula Can. 124 E2
Prince Albert Road S. Africa 108 B3
Prince Alfred, Cape Can. 124 D2
Prince Alfred Hamlet S. Africa 108 A3
Prince Charles Island Can. 124 G2
Prince Charles Mountains Antarctica
  118 H2
Prince Edward Island prov. Can. 128 D2
Prince George Can. 126 C2
Prince of Wales Island Can. 124 F2
Prince of Wales Island U.S.A. 126 B2
Prince Patrick Island Can. 124 E1
Prince Regent Inlet sea chan. Can.
  124 F2
Prince Rupert Can. 126 B2
Princess Charlotte Bay Austr. 114 D1
Princess Royal Island Can. 126 C2
Princeton Can. 126 C3
Príncipe i. São Tomé and Príncipe
  104 A2
Prineville U.S.A. 132 B2
Priozersk Rus. Fed. 46 G3
Pripet r. Belarus see Prypyats'
Pripet Marshes Belarus/Ukr. 42 B3
Priština S.M. 64 B2
Pritzwalk Ger. 54 F1
Privlaka Croatia 62 C2
Privolzhsk Rus. Fed. 42 F2
Prizren S.M. 64 B2
Professor van Blommestein Meer resr
  Suriname 150 D2
Progreso Mex. 142 D2
Prokhladnyy Rus. Fed. 92 C1
Prokuplje S.M. 64 B2
Proletarsk Rus. Fed. 44 F2
Prophet r. Can. 124 D3
Prophet River Can. 126 C2
Proserpine Austr. 114 D2
Protvino Rus. Fed. 42 E3
Provadiya Bulg. 64 C2
Provence reg. France 58 D3
Providence U.S.A. 136 F2
  Capital of Rhode Island.
Providencia, Isla de i. Caribbean Sea
  144 B3
Provideniya Rus. Fed. 94 O2
Provo U.S.A. 132 D2
Provost Can. 126 D2
Prudentópolis Brazil 154 B3
Prudhoe Bay U.S.A. 124 C2
Prüm Ger. 54 C2
Prunelli-di-Fiumorbo France 58 D3
Pruszków Pol. 56 E2

Prut r. Europe 44 C2
Pryluky Ukr. 44 D1
Prymors'k Ukr. 44 E2
Pryor U.S.A. 140 E1
Prypyats' r. Belarus 42 C3
Przemyśl Pol. 56 E3
Psara i. Greece 64 C3
Psebay Rus. Fed. 92 C1
Pshekha r. Rus. Fed. 44 E3
Pskov Rus. Fed. 42 C2
Pskov, Lake Estonia/Rus. Fed. 42 C2
Ptolemaïda Greece 64 B2
Ptuj Slovenia 62 C1
Pucallpa Peru 150 B3
Pucheng China 82 B3
Puchezh Rus. Fed. 42 F2
Puch'ŏn S. Korea 76 D2
Puck Pol. 56 D2
Pudasjärvi Fin. 46 F2
Pudong China 82 C2
Pudozh Rus. Fed. 40 C2
Puebla Mex. 142 C3
Pueblo U.S.A. 134 C3
Puelén Arg. 152 B4
Puente-Genil Spain 60 C2
Puerto Aisén Chile 152 A5
Puerto Alegre Bol. 152 B2
Puerto Ángel Mex. 142 C3
Puerto Armuelles Panama 144 B4
Puerto Ayacucho Venez. 150 C2
Puerto Barrios Guat. 142 D3
Puerto Cabezas Nic. 144 B3
Puerto Carreño Venez. 150 C2
Puerto Cisnes Chile 152 A5
Puerto Cortés Mex. 142 A2
Puerto Escondido Mex. 142 C3
Puerto Frey Bol. 152 B2
Puerto Inírida Col. 150 C2
Puerto Isabel Bol. 152 C2
Puerto Leguizamo Col. 150 B3
Puerto Libertad Mex. 142 A2
Puerto Limón Costa Rica 144 B3
Puertollano Spain 60 C2
Puerto Madryn Arg. 152 B5
Puerto Maldonado Peru 150 C4
Puerto Montt Chile 152 A5
Puerto Natales Chile 152 A6
Puerto Nuevo Col. 150 C2
Puerto Peñasco Mex. 142 A1
Puerto Pinasco Para. 152 C3
Puerto Plata Dom. Rep. 144 C3
Puerto Portillo Peru 150 B3
Puerto Princesa Phil. 76 A3
Puerto Rico Arg. 154 A3
Puerto Rico terr. West Indies 144 D3
  United States Commonwealth.
Puerto Rico Trench sea feature
  Caribbean Sea 160 B4
  Deepest trench in the Atlantic Ocean.
Puerto San José Guat. 144 A3
Puerto Santa Cruz Arg. 152 B6
Puerto Vallarta Mex. 142 B2
Pugachev Rus. Fed. 40 D3
Pugal India 86 B2
Pukaki, Lake N.Z. 118 B3
Pukapuka atoll Cook Is 110
Pukatawagan Can. 126 E2
Pukchin N. Korea 76 D1
Pukch'ŏng N. Korea 76 D1
Pukekohe N.Z. 118 B2
Puksubaek-san mt. N. Korea 76 D1
Pula Croatia 62 B2
Pula Italy 62 A3
Pulkkila Fin. 46 F3
Pullman U.S.A. 132 C1
Pulog, Mount Phil. 76 B2
Puná, Isla i. Ecuador 150 A3
Punakaiki N.Z. 118 B3
Punda Maria S. Africa 108 D1
Pune India 84 B3
P'ungsan N. Korea 76 D1

Rahachow Belarus **42** D3
Rahimyar Khan Pak. **86** B2
Raichur India **84** B3
Raigarh India **86** C2
Rainbow Lake Can. **126** D2
Rainier, Mount *vol.* U.S.A. **132** B1
Rainy Lake Can./U.S.A. **126** F3
Rainy River Can. **126** F3
Raipur India **86** C2
Raisio Fin. **46** E3
Rajahmundry India **84** C3
Rajang *r.* Malaysia **72** C1
Rajanpur Pak. **86** B2
Rajapalaiyam India **84** B4
Rajasthan Canal India **86** B2
Rajgarh India **86** B2
Rajkot India **86** B2
Rajpur India **86** B2
Rajshahi Bangl. **86** C2
Rakaia *r.* N.Z. **118** B3
Rakhiv Ukr. **44** B2
Rakitnoye Rus. Fed. **44** E1
Rakke Estonia **42** C2
Rakovník Czech Rep. **54** F2
Rakvere Estonia **42** C2
Raleigh U.S.A. **138** E1
Capital of North Carolina.
Ralik Chain *is* Marshall Is **110**
Rambutyo Island P.N.G. **70** D3
Ramgarh India **86** B2
Râmhormoz Iran **92** C2
Râmnicu Sărat Romania **44** C2
Râmnicu Vâlcea Romania **44** B2
Ramon' Rus. Fed. **42** E3
Ramotswa Botswana **108** C1
Rampur India **86** B2
Ramree Island Myanmar **74** A2
Ramsey Isle of Man **52** A2
Ramsgate U.K. **52** D4
Ramsing India **74** A1
Ranaghat India **86** C2
Ranau Malaysia **72** C1
Rancagua Chile **152** A4
Ranchi India **86** C2
Randers Denmark **46** C4
Rangiora N.Z. **118** B3
Rangitaiki *r.* N.Z. **118** C2
Rangoon Myanmar **74** A2
Capital of Myanmar.
Rangpur Bangl. **86** C2
Rankin Inlet Can. **126** F1
Rankin's Springs Austr. **116** D2
Rannoch Moor *moorland* U.K. **50** B2
Ranong Thai. **74** A3
Ransiki Indon. **70** C3
Rantaupanjang Indon. **72** C2
Rantauprapat Indon. **72** A1
Rantepao Indon. **72** C2
Ranua Fin. **46** F2
Ranyah, Wādī *watercourse* Saudi Arabia **90** B2
Raoul Island Kermadec Is **110**
Rapa *i.* Fr. Polynesia **110**
Rapid City U.S.A. **134** C2
Rapla Estonia **42** B2
Rapur India **86** A2
Rarotonga *i.* Cook Is **110**
Rasa, Punta *pt* Arg. **152** B5
Ra's al Khaymah U.A.E. **90** C2
Ras Dejen *mt.* Eth. **102** B3
5th highest mountain in Africa.
Raseiniai Lith. **42** B2
Ra's Ghārib Egypt **92** B3
Rasht Iran **92** C2
Ras Koh *mt.* Pak. **86** A2
Rasony Belarus **42** C2
Rasskazovo Rus. Fed. **42** F3
Ras Tannūrah Saudi Arabia **90** C2
Rastede Ger. **54** D1
Ratak Chain *is* Marshall Is **110**
Rätan Sweden **46** C3

Ratangarh India **86** B2
Rat Buri Thai. **74** A2
Rathedaung Myanmar **74** A1
Rathenow Ger. **54** F1
Rathlin Island U.K. **50** G1
Ratlam India **86** B2
Ratnagiri India **84** B3
Ratnapura Sri Lanka **84** C4
Ratne Ukr. **44** B1
Raton U.S.A. **140** D1
Rattray Head *hd* U.K. **50** D2
Ratzeburg Ger. **54** E1
Raufarhöfn Iceland **46**□
Raukumara Range *mts* N.Z. **118** C2
Rauma Fin. **46** E3
Raung, Gunung *vol.* Indon. **72** C2
Raurkela India **86** C2
Ravalli U.S.A. **132** D1
Ravānsar Iran **92** C2
Ravenna Italy **62** B2
Ravensburg Ger. **56** B3
Ravi *r.* Pak. **86** B1
Rawalpindi Pak. **86** B1
Rawicz Pol. **56** D2
Rawlinna Austr. **114** B3
Rawlins U.S.A. **134** B2
Rawson Arg. **152** B5
Rayagada India **84** C3
Raychikhinsk Rus. Fed. **80** E1
Raydah Yemen **90** B3
Rayevskiy Rus. Fed. **40** E3
Raymond Can. **132** D1
Raymond U.S.A. **132** B1
Raymond Terrace Austr. **116** E2
Raymondville U.S.A. **140** E3
Rayón Mex. **142** C2
Rayong Thai. **74** B2
Rayyis Saudi Arabia **90** A2
Raz, Pointe du *pt* France **58** B2
Razāzah, Buḩayrat ar *l.* Iraq **92** C2
Razgrad Bulg. **64** C2
Razim, Lacul *lag.* Romania **44** C3
Razlog Bulg. **64** B2
Ré, Île de *i.* France **58** B2
Reading U.K. **52** C4
Reading U.S.A. **136** E2
Rebiana Sand Sea *des.* Libya **100** E2
Rebun-tō *i.* Japan **78** D1
Recherche, Archipelago of the *is* Austr. **114** B3
Rechytsa Belarus **42** D3
Recife Brazil **150** F3
Recife, Cape S. Africa **108** C3
Recklinghausen Ger. **54** C2
Reconquista Arg. **152** C3
Red *r.* U.S.A. **140** F2
Red Bay Can. **128** E1
Red Bluff U.S.A. **132** B2
Redcar U.K. **52** C2
Redcliff Can. **126** D2
Red Cliffs Austr. **116** C2
Red Deer Can. **126** D2
Red Deer *r.* Can. **124** E3
Red Deer Lake Can. **126** E2
Redding U.S.A. **132** B2
Redditch U.K. **52** C3
Redfield U.S.A. **134** D2
Red Lake Can. **128** A1
Red Lakes U.S.A. **134** E1
Red Lodge U.S.A. **132** E1
Redmond U.S.A. **132** B2
Red Oak U.S.A. **134** D2
Redondo Port. **60** B2
Red Sea Africa/Asia **90** A2
Redstone *r.* Can. **126** C1
Reduzum Neth. **54** B1
Red Wing U.S.A. **134** E2
Redwood Falls U.S.A. **134** D2
Ree, Lough *l.* Rep. of Ireland **50** G2
Reedsport U.S.A. **132** B2
Reefton N.Z. **118** B3

Regen Ger. **54** F3
Regência Brazil **154** E1
Regensburg Ger. **54** F3
Regenstauf Ger. **54** F3
Reggane Alg. **100** C2
Reggio di Calabria Italy **62** C3
Reggio nell'Emilia Italy **62** B2
Reghin Romania **44** B2
Regina Can. **124** F3
Capital of Saskatchewan.
Rehoboth Namibia **108** A1
Reichenbach Ger. **54** F2
Reidsville U.S.A. **138** E1
Reigate U.K. **52** C4
Reims France **58** C2
Reina Adelaida, Archipiélago de la *is* Chile **152** A6
Reinbek Ger. **54** E1
Reindeer *r.* Can. **126** E2
Reindeer Island Can. **126** F2
Reindeer Lake Can. **126** E2
Reine Norway **46** C2
Reinsfeld Ger. **54** C3
Reitz S. Africa **108** C2
Reivilo S. Africa **108** B2
Reliance Can. **126** E1
Relizane Alg. **60** D2
Remeshk Iran **90** C2
Remiremont France **58** D2
Remscheid Ger. **54** C2
Rendsburg Ger. **56** B2
Renfrew Can. **136** E1
Rengat Indon. **72** B2
Reni Ukr. **44** C2
Renmark Austr. **116** C2
Rennell *i.* Solomon Is **110**
Rennerod Ger. **54** D2
Rennes France **58** B2
Rennie Lake Can. **126** E1
Reno *r.* Italy **62** B2
Reno U.S.A. **132** C3
Renshou China **82** A3
Rensselaer U.S.A. **136** C2
Renukut India **86** C2
Renwick N.Z. **118** B3
Reo Indon. **72** D2
Republican *r.* U.S.A. **134** D3
Repulse Bay Can. **124** G2
Requena Peru **150** B3
Requena Spain **60** C2
Reserva Brazil **154** B2
Resistencia Arg. **152** C3
Reşiţa Romania **44** B2
Resolute Can. **124** F2
Resolution Island Can. **124** H2
Rethel France **58** C2
Rethymno Greece **64** B3
Réunion *terr.* Indian Ocean **98**
French Overseas Department.
Reus Spain **60** D1
Reutlingen Ger. **56** B3
Revelstoke Can. **126** D2
Revillagigedo, Islas *is* Mex. **142** A3
Revillagigedo Island U.S.A. **126** B2
Rewa India **86** B2
Rexburg U.S.A. **132** D2
Reykjanestá *pt* Iceland **46**□
Reykjavík Iceland **46**□
Capital of Iceland.
Reynosa Mex. **142** C2
Rēzekne Latvia **42** C2
Rhein *r.* Ger. *see* Rhine
Rheine Ger. **54** C1
Rheinsberg Ger. **54** F1
Rhin *r.* France *see* Rhine
Rhine *r.* France **56** B3
Rhine *r.* Ger. **54** C2
Rhinelander U.S.A. **136** C1
Rhinluch *marsh* Ger. **54** F1
Rhinow Ger. **54** F1
Rhode Island *state* U.S.A. **136** F2

INDEX

Samba Dem. Rep. Congo **104** C3
Sambaliung *mts* Indon. **72** C1
Sambalpur India **86** C2
Sambar, Tanjung *pt* Indon. **72** C2
Sambas Indon. **72** B1
Sambava Madag. **106**□ E1
Sambir Ukr. **44** B2
Samborombón, Bahía *b.* Arg. **152** C4
Samch'ŏk S. Korea **76** D2
Samdi Dag *mt.* Turkey **92** C2
Same Tanz. **104** D3
Samīrah Saudi Arabia **90** B2
Samjiyŏn N. Korea **76** D1
Samoa *country* S. Pacific Ocean **112**
Samoan Islands *is* S. Pacific Ocean **110**
Samobor Croatia **62** C1
Samos *i.* Greece **64** C3
Samothraki Greece **64** C2
Samothraki *i.* Greece **64** C2
Sampit Indon. **72** C2
Sampwe Dem. Rep. Congo **104** C3
Sam Rayburn Reservoir U.S.A. **140** F2
Samsun Turkey **92** B1
Samtredia Georgia **92** C1
Samui, Ko *i.* Thai. **74** B3
Samut Songkhram Thai. **74** B2
San Mali **100** B3
Şan'ā' Yemen **90** B3
    Capital of Yemen.
Sanaga *r.* Cameroon **104** A2
San Ambrosio, Isla *i.* S. Pacific Ocean **148**
Sanandaj Iran **92** C2
San Andrés, Isla de *i.* Caribbean Sea **144** B3
San Andres Mountains U.S.A. **140** C2
San Andrés Tuxtla Mex. **142** C3
San Angelo U.S.A. **140** D2
San Antonio U.S.A. **140** E3
San Antonio, Mount U.S.A. **132** C4
San Antonio Abad Spain **60** D2
San Antonio de los Cobres Arg. **152** B3
San Antonio Oeste Arg. **152** B5
San Benedetto del Tronto Italy **62** B2
San Benedicto, Isla *i.* Mex. **142** A3
San Bernardino U.S.A. **132** C4
San Bernardino Mountains U.S.A. **132** C4
San Blas, Cape U.S.A. **138** C3
San Borja Bol. **152** B2
San Buenaventura Mex. **142** B2
San Carlos Phil. **76** B2
San Carlos Venez. **144** D4
San Carlos de Bariloche Arg. **152** A5
San Carlos del Zulia Venez. **144** C4
San Clemente Island U.S.A. **132** C4
Sancoins France **58** C2
San Cristobal *i.* Solomon Is **110**
San Cristóbal Venez. **150** B2
San Cristóbal de las Casas Mex. **142** C3
Sancti Spíritus Cuba **144** C2
Sand *r.* S. Africa **108** D1
Sandakan Malaysia **72** C1
Sandane Norway **46** B3
Sandanski Bulg. **64** B2
Sanday *i.* U.K. **50** C1
Sanderson U.S.A. **140** D2
Sandia Peru **150** C4
San Diego U.S.A. **132** C4
Sandıklı Turkey **92** B□
Sandnes Norway **46** B4
Sandnessjøen Norway **46** C2
Sandoa Dem. Rep. Congo **104** C3
Sandomierz Pol. **56** E2
Sandovo Rus. Fed. **42** E2
Sandoy *i.* Faroe Is **48** B1
Sandpoint U.S.A. **132** C1
Sandu China **82** B3
Sandur Faroe Is **48** B1
Sandusky U.S.A. **136** D2

Sandveld *mts* S. Africa **108** A3
Sandvika Norway **46** C4
Sandviken Sweden **46** D3
Sandwich Bay Can. **128** E1
Sandy Bay Can. **126** E2
Sandy Cape Austr. **114** E2
Sandy Lake Can. **128** A1
Sandy Lake *l.* Can. **128** A1
San Estanislao Para. **154** A2
San Felipe *Baja California* Mex. **142** A1
San Felipe *Guanajuato* Mex. **142** B2
San Felipe Venez. **150** C1
San Félix Chile **148**
San Fernando *Baja California* Mex. **142** A2
San Fernando *Tamaulipas* Mex. **142** C2
San Fernando Phil. **76** B2
San Fernando Phil. **76** B2
San Fernando Spain **60** B2
San Fernando Trin. and Tob. **144** D3
San Fernando de Apure Venez. **150** C2
Sanford *FL* U.S.A. **138** D3
Sanford *ME* U.S.A. **136** F2
San Francisco Arg. **152** B4
San Francisco U.S.A. **132** B3
San Francisco Javier Spain **60** D2
Sangamner India **86** B3
Sangar Rus. Fed. **94** K2
San Gavino Monreale Italy **62** A3
Sangerhausen Ger. **54** E2
Sanggau Indon. **72** C1
Sangha *r.* Congo **104** B3
San Giovanni in Fiore Italy **62** C3
Sangir *i.* Indon. **76** B3
Sangir, Kepulauan *is* Indon. **70** C2
Sangju S. Korea **76** D2
Sangkulirang Indon. **72** C1
Sangli India **84** B3
Sangmélima Cameroon **104** B2
Sango Zimbabwe **106** C2
Sangre de Cristo Range *mts* U.S.A. **134** B3
Sangsang China **86** C2
San Hipólito, Punta *pt* Mex. **142** A2
San Ignacio Mex. **142** A2
Sanikiluaq Can. **128** C1
Sanjiang China **82** A3
San Joaquin *r.* U.S.A. **132** B3
San Jorge, Golfo de *g.* Arg. **152** B5
San José Costa Rica **144** B4
    Capital of Costa Rica.
San Jose Phil. **76** B2
San Jose Phil. **76** B2
San Jose U.S.A. **132** B3
San José, Isla *i.* Mex. **142** A2
San José de Bavicora Mex. **142** B2
San Jose de Buenavista Phil. **76** B2
San José de Comondú Mex. **142** A2
San José del Cabo Mex. **142** B2
San José del Guaviare Col. **150** B2
San Juan Arg. **152** B4
San Juan *r.* Costa Rica/Nic. **144** B3
San Juan Puerto Rico **144** D3
    Capital of Puerto Rico.
San Juan *r.* U.S.A. **132** D3
San Juan Bautista Spain **60** D2
San Juan Bautista Tuxtepec Mex. **142** C3
San Juan Islands U.S.A. **132** B1
San Juanito Mex. **142** B2
San Juan Mountains U.S.A. **134** B3
San Julián Arg. **152** B5
Sankh *r.* India **86** C2
Sankt Gallen Switz. **58** D2
Sankt Moritz Switz. **58** D2
Sankt-Peterburg Rus. Fed. *see*
    St Petersburg
Sankt Veit an der Glan Austria **56** C3
Sankt Wendel Ger. **54** C3
Şanlıurfa Turkey **92** B2
San Lorenzo Mex. **140** C3

Sanlúcar de Barrameda Spain **60** B2
San Lucas Mex. **142** B2
San Luis Arg. **152** B4
San Luis de la Paz Mex. **142** B2
San Luisito Mex. **140** B2
San Luis Obispo U.S.A. **132** B3
San Luis Potosí Mex. **142** B2
San Luis Río Colorado Mex. **142** A1
San Marcos U.S.A. **140** E3
San Marino *country* Europe **62** B2
San Marino San Marino **62** B2
    Capital of San Marino.
San Martín de Bolaños Mex. **142** B2
San Martín de los Andes Arg. **152** A5
San Matías, Golfo *g.* Arg. **152** B5
Sanmenxia China **82** B2
San Miguel El Salvador **144** B3
San Miguel de Tucumán Arg. **152** B3
San Miguel Sola de Vega Mex. **142** C3
Sanming China **82** B3
San Nicolás de los Arroyos Arg. **152** B4
San Nicolas Island U.S.A. **132** C4
Sannieshof S. Africa **108** C2
Sanok Pol. **56** E3
San Pablo Phil. **76** B2
San Pablo Balleza Mex. **142** B2
San Pedro Arg. **152** B3
San Pedro Bol. **152** B2
San-Pédro Côte d'Ivoire **100** B4
San Pedro Mex. **142** B2
San Pedro *watercourse* U.S.A. **140** B2
San Pedro, Sierra de *mts* Spain **60** B2
San Pedro de las Colonias Mex. **142** B2
San Pedro Sula Hond. **144** B3
San Pietro, Isola di *i.* Italy **62** A3
San Quintín, Cabo *c.* Mex. **142** A1
San Rafael Arg. **152** B4
San Remo Italy **62** A2
San Salvador El Salvador **144** B3
    Capital of El Salvador.
San Salvador de Jujuy Arg. **152** B3
San Severo Italy **62** C2
Sanski Most Bos.-Herz. **62** C2
Santa Ana Bol. **152** B2
Santa Ana El Salvador **144** B3
Santa Ana Mex. **142** A1
Santa Ana U.S.A. **132** C4
Santa Bárbara Mex. **142** B2
Santa Barbara U.S.A. **132** C4
Santa Bárbara, Serra de *hills* Brazil **154** B2
Santa Catalina Chile **152** B3
Santa Clara Col. **150** D3
Santa Clara Cuba **144** C2
Santa Clarita U.S.A. **132** C4
Santa Croce, Capo *c.* Italy **62** C3
Santa Cruz *r.* Arg. **152** B6
Santa Cruz Bol. **152** B2
Santa Cruz Phil. **76** B2
Santa Cruz U.S.A. **132** B3
Santa Cruz Barillas Guat. **142** C3
Santa Cruz Cabrália Brazil **154** E1
Santa Cruz de Moya Spain **60** C2
Santa Cruz de Tenerife Canary Is **100** A2
Santa Cruz Island U.S.A. **132** C4
Santa Cruz Islands Solomon Is **110**
Santa Elena, Punta *pt* Ecuador **146**
Santa Fé Arg. **152** B4
Santa Fe U.S.A. **140** C1
    Capital of New Mexico.
Santa Helena de Goiás Brazil **154** B1
Santa Isabel Arg. **152** B4
Santa Isabel *i.* Solomon Is **110**
Santa Luisa, Serra de *hills* Brazil **154** B1
Santa Maria Brazil **152** C3
Santa Maria *r.* Mex. **142** B1
Santa Maria U.S.A. **132** B4
Santa Maria, Cabo de *c.* Moz. **108** D2
Santa Maria, Cabo de *c.* Port. **60** B2

Schell Creek Range *mts* U.S.A. **132** D3
Schenectady U.S.A. **136** F2
Scheßlitz Ger. **54** E3
Schiermonnikoog *i.* Neth. **54** C1
Schio Italy **62** B1
Schkeuditz Ger. **54** F2
Schladen Ger. **54** E1
Schleiz Ger. **54** E2
Schleswig Ger. **56** B2
Schloss Holte-Stukenbrock Ger. **54** D2
Schlüchtern Ger. **54** D2
Schlüsselfeld Ger. **54** E3
Schmallenberg Ger. **54** D2
Schneverdingen Ger. **54** D1
Schönebeck (Elbe) Ger. **54** E1
Schöningen Ger. **54** E1
Schöntal Ger. **54** D3
Schoonhoven Neth. **54** B2
Schouten Islands P.N.G. **70** D3
Schwabach Ger. **54** E3
Schwäbische Alb *mts* Ger. **56** B3
Schwandorf Ger. **54** F3
Schwaner, Pegunungan *mts* Indon. **72** C2
Schwarzenbek Ger. **54** E1
Schwarzenberg Ger. **54** F2
Schwarzrand *mts* Namibia **108** A2
Schwarzwald *mts* Ger. *see* Black Forest
Schwaz Austria **56** C3
Schwedt an der Oder Ger. **56** C2
Schweinfurt Ger. **54** E2
Schwerin Ger. **54** E1
Schweriner See *l.* Ger. **54** E1
Schwyz Switz. **58** D2
Sciacca Italy **62** B3
Scilly, Isles of U.K. **48** B4
Scioto *r.* U.S.A. **136** D3
Scobey U.S.A. **134** B1
Scone Austr. **116** E2
Scotia Sea S. Atlantic Ocean **118** D4
Scotland *admin. div.* U.K. **50** C2
Scott, Cape Can. **126** C2
Scottburgh S. Africa **108** D3
Scott City U.S.A. **134** C3
Scottsbluff U.S.A. **134** C2
Scottsboro U.S.A. **138** C2
Scourie U.K. **50** B1
Scranton U.S.A. **136** E2
Scunthorpe U.K. **52** C3
Scuol Switz. **58** E2
Seal *r.* Can. **126** F2
Seal, Cape S. Africa **108** B3
Sea Lake Austr. **116** C3
Sealy U.S.A. **140** E3
Searcy U.S.A. **138** B1
Seascale U.K. **52** B2
Seattle U.S.A. **132** B1
Sebago Lake U.S.A. **136** F2
Sebastián Vizcaíno, Bahía *b.* Mex. **142** A2
Sebeş Romania **44** B2
Sebesi *i.* Indon. **72** B2
Sebezh Rus. Fed. **42** C2
Şebinkarahisar Turkey **92** B1
Sebring U.S.A. **138** D3
Sechelt Can. **126** C3
Sechura Peru **150** A3
Secunderabad India **84** B3
Sedalia U.S.A. **134** E3
Sedan France **58** C2
Seddon N.Z. **118** B3
Sedona U.S.A. **140** B2
Seeburg Ger. **54** E2
Seehausen (Altmark) Ger. **54** E1
Seeheim Namibia **108** A2
Sées France **58** C2
Seesen Ger. **54** E2
Seevetal Ger. **54** E1
Sefadu Sierra Leone **100** A4
Sefare Botswana **108** C1
Segamat Malaysia **72** B1

Segezha Rus. Fed. **40** C2
Ségou Mali **100** B3
Segovia Spain **60** C1
Séguédine Niger **100** D2
Séguéla Côte d'Ivoire **100** B4
Seguin U.S.A. **140** E3
Segura *r.* Spain **60** C2
Segura, Sierra de *mts* Spain **60** C2
Sehithwa Botswana **106** B2
Seinäjoki Fin. **46** E3
Seine *r.* France **58** C2
Seine, Baie de *b.* France **58** B2
Sejny Pol. **56** E2
Sekayu Indon. **72** B2
Sekondi Ghana **100** B4
Selaru *i.* Indon. **70** C3
Selatan, Tanjung *pt* Indon. **72** C2
Selawik U.S.A. **124** B2
Selby U.K. **52** C3
Selebi-Phikwe Botswana **106** B2
Selenga *r.* Rus. Fed. **66**
  Part of the Yenisey-Angara-Selenga, 3rd longest in Asia.
Sélestat France **58** D2
Selfoss Iceland **46**□
Sélibabi Maur. **100** A3
Seligman U.S.A. **140** B1
Selîma Oasis Sudan **102** A2
Selimiye Turkey **64** C3
Sélingué, Lac de *l.* Mali **100** B3
Selizharovo Rus. Fed. **42** D2
Seljord Norway **46** B4
Selkirk Can. **126** F2
Selkirk U.K. **50** C3
Selkirk Mountains Can. **126** D2
Selma *AL* U.S.A. **138** C2
Selma *CA* U.S.A. **132** C3
Sel'tso Rus. Fed. **42** D3
Selvas *reg.* Brazil **150** B3
Selway *r.* U.S.A. **132** C1
Selwyn Lake Can. **126** E1
Selwyn Mountains Can. **126** B1
Selwyn Range *hills* Austr. **114** C2
Semangka, Teluk *b.* Indon. **72** B2
Semarang Indon. **72** C2
Sematan Malaysia **72** B1
Sembé Congo **104** B2
Semdinli Turkey **92** C2
Semenivka Ukr. **44** D1
Semeru, Gunung *vol.* Indon. **72** C2
Semikarakorsk Rus. Fed. **44** F2
Semiluki Rus. Fed. **42** E3
Seminoe Reservoir U.S.A. **134** B2
Seminole U.S.A. **140** D2
Seminole, Lake U.S.A. **138** D2
Semipalatinsk Kazakh. **88** F1
Semitau Indon. **72** C1
Semnān Iran **92** D2
Semporna Malaysia **72** C1
Semur-en-Auxois France **58** C2
Sena Madureira Brazil **150** C3
Senanga Zambia **106** B1
Sendai *Kagoshima* Japan **78** B4
Sendai *Miyagi* Japan **78** D3
Senegal *country* Africa **100** A3
Sénégal *r.* Maur./Senegal **100** A3
Senftenberg Ger. **54** G2
Sengerema Tanz. **104** D3
Senhor do Bonfim Brazil **150** E4
Senigallia Italy **62** B2
Senj Croatia **62** B2
Senja *i.* Norway **46** D2
Senlac S. Africa **108** C1
Senlis France **58** C2
Senmonorom Cambodia **74** B2
Sennar Sudan **102** B3
Senneterre Can. **128** C2
Senqu *r.* Lesotho **108** C3
Sens France **58** C2
Senta S.M. **64** B1
Sentinel Peak Can. **126** C2

Seoni India **86** B2
Seoul S. Korea **76** D2
  Capital of South Korea.
Sepetiba, Baía de *b.* Brazil **154** D2
Sepik *r.* P.N.G. **70** D3
Sepinang Indon. **72** C1
Sept-Îles Can. **128** D1
Seram *i.* Indon. **70** C3
Seram, Laut *sea* Indon. **70** C3
Serang Indon. **72** B2
Serbia *aut. rep.* S.M. *see* Srbija
Serbia and Montenegro *country* Europe **64** B2
Serebryannyye Prudy Rus. Fed. **42** E3
Seremban Malaysia **72** B1
Serengeti Plain Tanz. **104** D3
Sergach Rus. Fed. **40** D3
Sergiyev Posad Rus. Fed. **42** E2
Seria Brunei **72** C1
Serian Malaysia **72** C1
Serifos *i.* Greece **64** B3
Serik Turkey **92** B2
Sermata, Kepulauan *is* Indon. **70** C3
Serov Rus. Fed. **40** F3
Serowe Botswana **108** C1
Serpa Port. **60** B2
Serpukhov Rus. Fed. **42** E3
Serra da Mesa, Represa *resr* Brazil **150** E4
Serranópolis Brazil **154** B1
Serre *r.* France **54** A3
Serres Greece **64** B2
Serrinha Brazil **150** F4
Sêrro Brazil **154** D1
Sertãozinho Brazil **154** C2
Sertolovo Rus. Fed. **42** D1
Seruyan *r.* Indon. **72** C2
Sêrxü China **80** C2
Sesfontein Namibia **106** A1
Sessa Aurunca Italy **62** B2
Sestri Levante Italy **62** A2
Sestroretsk Rus. Fed. **42** C1
Sète France **58** C3
Sete Lagoas Brazil **154** D1
Setermoen Norway **46** D2
Setesdal *val.* Norway **46** B4
Sétif Alg. **100** C1
Seto-naikai *sea* Japan **78** B4
Settat Morocco **100** B1
Settle U.K. **52** B2
Setúbal Port. **60** B2
Setúbal, Baía de *b.* Port. **60** B2
Seul, Lac *l.* Can. **128** A1
Sevan Armenia **40** D4
Sevan, Lake Armenia **88** B2
Sevastopol' Ukr. **44** D3
Seven Islands Bay Can. **128** D1
Sévérac-le-Château France **58** C3
Severn *r.* Can. **128** B1
Severn S. Africa **108** B2
Severn *r.* U.K. **52** B4
Severnaya Dvina *r.* Rus. Fed. **40** D2
Severnaya Zemlya *is* Rus. Fed. **94** I1
Severnyy *Nenetskiy Avtonomnyy Okrug* Rus. Fed. **40** D2
Severnyy *Respublika Komi* Rus. Fed. **40** F2
Severodvinsk Rus. Fed. **40** C2
Severomorsk Rus. Fed. **46** G2
Severskaya Rus. Fed. **44** E3
Sevier *r.* U.S.A. **132** D3
Sevier Lake U.S.A. **132** D3
Sevilla Spain *see* Seville
Seville Spain **60** B2
Seward U.S.A. **124** C2
Seward Peninsula U.S.A. **124** B2
Sewell Inlet Can. **126** B2
Sexsmith Can. **126** D2
Sextín *r.* Mex. **142** B2
Seyakha Rus. Fed. **40** G1
Seychelles *country* Indian Ocean **98**

Sierra Leone country Africa 100 A4
Sierra Mojada Mex. 142 B2
Sierra Vista U.S.A. 140 B2
Sierre Switz. 58 D2
Sifnos i. Greece 64 B3
Sig Alg. 60 C2
Sigguup Nunaa pen. Greenland 124 I2
Sighetu Marmaţiei Romania 44 B2
Sighişoara Romania 44 B2
Sigli Indon. 72 A1
Siglufjörður Iceland 46□
Sigmaringen Ger. 56 B3
Signy-l'Abbaye France 54 B3
Sigüenza Spain 60 C1
Siguiri Guinea 100 B3
Sigulda Latvia 42 B2
Sihanoukville Cambodia 74 B2
Siilinjärvi Fin. 46 F3
Siirt Turkey 92 C2
Sijunjung Indon. 72 B2
Sikar India 86 B2
Sikasso Mali 100 B3
Sikeston U.S.A. 134 F3
Sikhote-Alin' mts Rus. Fed. 78 B2
Sikinos i. Greece 64 C3
Silao Mex. 142 B2
Silchar India 74 A1
Siletiteniz, Ozero salt l. Kazakh. 88 E1
Silgarhi Nepal 86 C2
Silifke Turkey 92 B2
Siling Co salt l. China 86 C1
Silistra Bulg. 64 C2
Silivri Turkey 92 A1
Siljan l. Sweden 46 C3
Silkeborg Denmark 46 B4
Sillamäe Estonia 42 C2
Siloam Springs U.S.A. 138 B1
Silobela S. Africa 108 D2
Šilutė Lith. 42 B2
Silvan Turkey 92 C2
Silver City U.S.A. 140 C2
Silverton U.S.A. 134 B3
Simao China 74 B1
Simàrd, Lac l. Can. 128 C2
Simav Turkey 64 C3
Simav Dağları mts Turkey 64 C3
Simba Dem. Rep. Congo 104 C2
Simcoe, Lake Can. 136 E2
Simeulue i. Indon. 72 A1
Simferopol' Ukr. 44 D3
Şimleu Silvaniei Romania 44 B2
Simmern (Hunsrück) Ger. 54 C3
Simonhouse Can. 126 E2
Simpson Desert Austr. 114 C2
Simrishamn Sweden 46 C4
Sinabang Indon. 72 A1
Sinai pen. Egypt 102 B2
Sinan China 82 A3
Sinanju N. Korea 76 D2
Sinbo Myanmar 74 A1
Sincelejo Col. 150 B2
Sındırgı Turkey 64 C3
Sindor Rus. Fed. 40 E2
Sinekçi Turkey 64 C2
Sines Port. 60 B2
Sines, Cabo de c. Port. 60 B2
Singa Sudan 90 A3
Singahi India 86 C2
Singapore Asia 72 B1
    Capital of Singapore.
Singapore country Asia 72 B1
Singaraja Indon. 72 C2
Singida Tanz. 104 D3
Singkaling Hkamti Myanmar 74 A1
Singkang Indon. 72 D2
Singkawang Indon. 72 B1
Singkil Indon. 72 A1
Singleton Austr. 116 E2
Singu Myanmar 74 A1
Siniscola Italy 62 A2
Sinj Croatia 62 C2

Sinjai Indon. 72 D2
Sinkat Sudan 102 B3
Sinkiang aut. reg. China see
    Xinjiang Uygur Zizhiqu
Sinop Turkey 92 B1
Sinp'o N. Korea 76 D1
Sinsheim Ger. 54 D3
Sintang Indon. 72 C1
Sint Anthonis Neth. 54 B2
Sint-Laureins Belgium 54 A2
Sint Maarten i. Neth. Antilles 144 D3
Sint-Niklaas Belgium 54 B2
Sinton U.S.A. 140 E3
Sinüiju N. Korea 76 C1
Siófok Hungary 56 D3
Sion Switz. 58 D2
Sioux Center U.S.A. 134 D2
Sioux City U.S.A. 134 D2
Sioux Falls U.S.A. 134 D2
Sioux Lookout Can. 128 A1
Siping China 76 C1
Sipiwesk Lake Can. 126 F2
Sipura i. Indon. 72 A2
Sira r. Norway 46 B4
Sir Edward Pellew Group is Austr.
    114 C1
Sīrīk Iran 90 C2
Siri Kit Dam Thai. 74 B2
Sir James MacBrien, Mount Can.
    126 C1
Sīrjān Iran 92 D3
Şırnak Turkey 92 C2
Sirohi India 86 B2
Sirsa India 86 B2
Sirte Libya 100 D1
Sirte, Gulf of Libya 100 D1
Širvintos Lith. 42 B2
Sisal Mex. 142 C2
Sishen S. Africa 108 B2
Sisian Armenia 92 C2
Sisipuk Lake Can. 126 E2
Sisŏphŏn Cambodia 74 B2
Sisteron France 58 D3
Sitapur India 86 C2
Siteki Swaziland 108 D2
Sitka U.S.A. 126 B2
Sittard Neth. 54 B2
Sittaung r. Myanmar 74 A2
Sittwe Myanmar 74 A1
Situbondo Indon. 72 C2
Sivas Turkey 92 B2
Sivaslı Turkey 64 C3
Siverek Turkey 92 B2
Sivrihisar Turkey 92 B2
Sīwah Egypt 102 A2
Sīwah, Wāḥāt oasis Egypt 92 A3
Siwalik Range mts India/Nepal 86 B1
Siwa Oasis Egypt see Sīwah, Wāḥāt
Six-Fours-les-Plages France 58 D3
Sixian China 82 B2
Siyabuswa S. Africa 108 C2
Sjenica S.M. 64 B2
Sjøvegan Norway 46 D2
Skadovs'k Ukr. 44 D2
Skagen Denmark 46 C4
Skagerrak str. Denmark/Norway 46 B4
Skagit r. U.S.A. 132 B1
Skagway U.S.A. 126 C3
Skardu Jammu and Kashmir 86 B1
Skarżysko-Kamienna Pol. 56 E2
Skawina Pol. 56 D3
Skeena r. Can. 126 C2
Skeena Mountains Can. 126 C2
Skegness U.K. 52 D3
Skellefteå Sweden 46 E3
Skellefteälven r. Sweden 46 E3
Skerries Rep. of Ireland 50 G2
Skiathos i. Greece 64 B3
Skibbereen Rep. of Ireland 50 F3
Skíðadals-jökull glacier Iceland 46□
Skiddaw h. U.K. 52 B2

Skien Norway 46 B4
Skierniewice Pol. 56 E2
Skikda Alg. 100 C1
Skipton Austr. 116 C3
Skipton U.K. 52 B3
Skive Denmark 46 B4
Skjervøy Norway 46 E1
Skodje Norway 48 E1
Skopelos i. Greece 64 B3
Skopin Rus. Fed. 42 E3
Skopje Macedonia 64 B2
    Capital of Macedonia.
Skövde Sweden 46 C4
Skowhegan U.S.A. 136 G2
Skrunda Latvia 42 B2
Skukum, Mount Can. 126 B1
Skukuza S. Africa 108 D1
Skuodas Lith. 42 B2
Skye i. U.K. 50 A2
Skyros Greece 64 B3
Skyros i. Greece 64 B3
Slagelse Denmark 46 C4
Slaney r. Rep. of Ireland 50 G2
Slantsy Rus. Fed. 42 C2
Slatina Croatia 62 C1
Slatina Romania 44 B3
Slave r. Can. 126 D1
Slave Coast Africa 100 C4
Slave Lake Can. 126 D2
Slavgorod Rus. Fed. 88 C2
Slavonski Brod Croatia 62 C1
Slavuta Ukr. 44 C1
Slavutych Ukr. 44 D1
Slavyanka Rus. Fed. 78 B2
Slavyansk-na-Kubani Rus. Fed. 44 E2
Sławharad Belarus 42 D3
Slawno Pol. 56 D2
Slea Head hd Rep. of Ireland 50 E2
Sleeper Islands Can. 128 C1
Slieve Donard h. U.K. 50 H1
Slieve Gamph hills Rep. of Ireland 50 F2
Sligo Rep. of Ireland 50 F1
Sligo Bay Rep. of Ireland 50 F1
Slite Sweden 46 D4
Sliven Bulg. 64 C2
Slobozia Romania 44 C3
Slocan Can. 126 D3
Slonim Belarus 42 C3
Sloten Neth. 54 B1
Slough U.K. 52 C4
Slovakia country Europe 56 D3
Slovenia country Europe 62 B1
Slov"yans'k Ukr. 44 E2
Sluch r. Ukr. 44 C1
Słupsk Pol. 56 D2
Slutsk Belarus 42 C3
Slyne Head hd Rep. of Ireland 50 E2
Smallwood Reservoir Can. 128 D1
Smalyavichy Belarus 42 C3
Smarhon' Belarus 42 C3
Smeaton Can. 126 E2
Smederevo S.M. 64 B2
Smederevska Palanka S.M. 64 B2
Smila Ukr. 44 D2
Smiltene Latvia 42 C2
Smithers Can. 126 C2
Smithfield U.S.A. 138 E1
Smith Mountain Lake U.S.A. 136 E3
Smiths Falls Can. 128 C2
Smoky Hills U.S.A. 134 C3
Smøla i. Norway 46 B3
Smolensk Rus. Fed. 42 D3
Smolyan Bulg. 64 C2
Smooth Rock Falls Can. 128 B2
Smyrna Turkey see İzmir
Snæfell mt. Iceland 46□
Snaefell h. Isle of Man 52 A2
Snake r. U.S.A. 132 C1
Snake River Plain U.S.A. 132 D2
Sneek Neth. 54 B1
Sneem Rep. of Ireland 50 F3

Spencer U.S.A. **134** D2
Spencer Gulf *est.* Austr. **116** B2
Spennymoor U.K. **52** C2
Spessart *reg.* Ger. **54** D3
Spey *r.* U.K. **50** C2
Speyer Ger. **54** D3
Spiekeroog *i.* Ger. **54** C1
Spijkenisse Neth. **54** B2
Spirit River Can. **126** D2
Spišská Nová Ves Slovakia **56** E3
Spitsbergen *i.* Svalbard **94** D1
  5th largest island in Europe.
Spittal an der Drau Austria **56** C3
Split Croatia **62** C2
Split Lake Can. **126** F2
Split Lake *l.* Can. **126** F2
Spokane U.S.A. **132** C1
Spoleto Italy **58** E3
Spooner U.S.A. **136** B1
Spree *r.* Ger. **56** C2
Springbok S. Africa **108** A2
Springdale Can. **128** E2
Springdale U.S.A. **138** B1
Springe Ger. **54** D1
Springer U.S.A. **140** D1
Springerville U.S.A. **140** C2
Springfield *CO* U.S.A. **134** C3
Springfield *IL* U.S.A. **136** C3
  Capital of Illinois.
Springfield *MA* U.S.A. **136** F2
Springfield *MO* U.S.A. **134** E3
Springfield *OH* U.S.A. **136** D3
Springfield *OR* U.S.A. **132** B2
Springfontein S. Africa **108** C3
Springhill Can. **128** D2
Spring Hill U.S.A. **138** D3
Springs Junction N.Z. **118** B3
Spurn Head *hd* U.K. **52** D3
Squamish Can. **126** C3
Squillace, Golfo di *g.* Italy **62** C3
Srbija *aut. rep.* S.M. **64** B2
Srebrenica Bos.-Herz. **62** C2
Sredets Bulg. **64** C2
Srednekolymsk Rus. Fed. **94** M2
Sredne-Russkaya Vozvyshennost' *hills*
  Rus. Fed. *see* Central Russian Upland
Srednogorie Bulg. **64** B2
Sretensk Rus. Fed. **80** D1
Sri Aman Malaysia **72** C1
Sri Jayewardenepura Kotte Sri Lanka
  84 B4
  Capital of Sri Lanka.
Srikakulam India **84** C3
Sri Lanka *country* Asia **84** C4
Srinagar India **86** B1
Sri Pada *mt.* Sri Lanka **84** C4
Srivardhan India **84** B3
Stade Ger. **54** D1
Stadensen Ger. **54** E1
Stadskanaal Neth. **54** C1
Stadtallendorf Ger. **54** D2
Stadthagen Ger. **54** D1
Staffelstein Ger. **54** E2
Stafford U.K. **52** B3
Staines U.K. **52** C4
Stakhanov Ukr. **44** E2
Stalingrad Rus. Fed. *see* Volgograd
Stalowa Wola Pol. **56** E2
Stamford U.K. **52** C3
Stamford *CT* U.S.A. **136** F2
Stamford *TX* U.S.A. **140** E2
Stampriet Namibia **108** A1
Stamsund Norway **46** C2
Standerton S. Africa **108** C2
Standish U.S.A. **136** D2
Stanger S. Africa **108** D2
Staňkov Czech Rep. **54** F3
Stanley Falkland Is **152** C6
  Capital of the Falkland Islands.
Stanley U.S.A. **134** C1

Stanovoye Nagor'ye *mts* Rus. Fed.
  94 J3
Stanovoy Khrebet *mts* Rus. Fed. **94** K3
Stanthorpe Austr. **116** E1
Starachowice Pol. **56** E2
Stara Planina *mts* Bulg./S.M. *see*
  Balkan Mountains
Staraya Russa Rus. Fed. **42** D2
Staraya Toropa Rus. Fed. **42** D2
Stara Zagora Bulg. **64** C2
Stargard Szczeciński Pol. **56** D2
Starkville U.S.A. **138** C2
Starobil's'k Ukr. **44** E2
Starodub Rus. Fed. **42** D3
Starogard Gdański Pol. **56** D2
Starokostyantyniv Ukr. **44** C2
Starominskaya Rus. Fed. **44** E2
Staroshcherbinovskaya Rus. Fed.
  44 E2
Starotitarovskaya Rus. Fed. **44** E2
Staroyur'yevo Rus. Fed. **42** F3
Start Point *pt* U.K. **52** B4
Staryya Darohi Belarus **42** C3
Staryy Oskol Rus. Fed. **42** E3
Staßfurt Ger. **54** E2
State College U.S.A. **136** E2
Statesboro U.S.A. **138** D2
Statesville U.S.A. **138** D1
Stavanger Norway **46** B4
Stavropol' Rus. Fed. **40** D4
Stavropol'skaya Vozvyshennost' *hills*
  Rus. Fed. **40** D4
Stawell Austr. **116** C3
Steadville S. Africa **108** C2
Steamboat Springs U.S.A. **134** B2
Stedten Ger. **54** E2
Steen River Can. **126** D2
Steens Mountain U.S.A. **132** C2
Steenwijk Neth. **54** C1
Stefansson Island Can. **124** E2
Steigerwald *mts* Ger. **54** E3
Steinbach Can. **126** F3
Steinfurt Ger. **54** C2
Steinhausen Namibia **106** A2
Steinkjer Norway **46** C3
Steinkopf S. Africa **108** A2
Stella S. Africa **108** B2
Stenay France **58** D2
Stendal Ger. **54** E1
Stephenville Can. **128** E2
Stephenville U.S.A. **140** E2
Sterling S. Africa **108** B3
Sterling *CO* U.S.A. **134** C2
Sterling *IL* U.S.A. **136** C2
Sterlitamak Rus. Fed. **40** E3
Sternberg Ger. **54** E1
Stettler Can. **126** D2
Steubenville U.S.A. **136** D2
Stevenage U.K. **52** C4
Stevenson Lake Can. **126** F2
Stevens Village U.S.A. **124** C2
Stewart Can. **126** C2
Stewart *r.* Can. **126** B1
Stewart Island N.Z. **118** A4
Steyr Austria **56** C3
Steytlerville S. Africa **108** B3
Stikine *r.* Can. **126** B2
Stikine Plateau Can. **126** B2
Stilbaai S. Africa **108** B3
Stillwater U.S.A. **140** E1
Štip Macedonia **62** D2
Stirling U.K. **50** C2
Stjørdalshalsen Norway **46** C3
Stockerau Austria **56** D3
Stockholm Sweden **46** D4
  Capital of Sweden.
Stockport U.K. **52** B3
Stockton U.S.A. **132** B3
Stockton-on-Tees U.K. **52** C2
Stod Czech Rep. **54** F3
Stœng Trêng Cambodia **74** B2

Stoer, Point of *pt* U.K. **50** B1
Stoke-on-Trent U.K. **52** B3
Stol *mt.* S.M. **64** B2
Stolac Bos.-Herz. **62** C2
Stolberg (Rheinland) Ger. **54** C2
Stolbovoy Rus. Fed. **40** E1
Stolin Belarus **42** C3
Stollberg Ger. **54** F2
Stolzenau Ger. **54** D1
Stonehaven U.K. **50** C2
Stonewall Can. **126** F2
Stony Rapids Can. **124** E3
Storavan *l.* Sweden **46** D2
Store Bælt *sea chan.* Denmark *see*
  Great Belt
Støren Norway **46** C3
Storforshei Norway **46** C2
Storkerson Peninsula Can. **124** E2
Storm Lake U.S.A. **134** D2
Stornoway U.K. **50** A1
Storozhevsk Rus. Fed. **40** E2
Storozhynets' Ukr. **44** C2
Storsjön *l.* Sweden **46** C3
Storslett Norway **46** E2
Storuman Sweden **46** D2
Stour *r.* England U.K. **52** C3
Stour *r.* England U.K. **52** C4
Stout Lake Can. **128** A1
Stowbtsy Belarus **42** C3
Strabane U.K. **50** G1
Strakonice Czech Rep. **56** C3
Stralsund Ger. **56** C2
Strand S. Africa **108** A3
Stranda Norway **46** B3
Strangford Lough *inlet* U.K. **50** H1
Stranraer U.K. **50** B3
Strasbourg France **58** D2
Strasburg Ger. **54** F1
Stratford Can. **136** D2
Stratford N.Z. **118** B2
Stratford U.S.A. **140** D1
Stratford-upon-Avon U.K. **52** C3
Strathspey *val.* U.K. **50** C2
Straubing Ger. **56** C3
Strausberg Ger. **54** F1
Streaky Bay Austr. **116** A2
Streator U.S.A. **136** C2
Strehaia Romania **44** B3
Stroeder Arg. **152** B5
Ströhen Ger. **54** D1
Stromboli, Isola *i.* Italy **62** C3
Stromness U.K. **50** C1
Strömsund Sweden **46** D3
Stronsay *i.* U.K. **50** C1
Stroud Austr. **116** E2
Stroud U.K. **52** B4
Strücklingen (Saterland) Ger. **54** C1
Struga Macedonia **64** B2
Strugi-Krasnyye Rus. Fed. **42** C2
Struis Bay S. Africa **108** B3
Strumica Macedonia **64** B2
Strydenburg S. Africa **108** B2
Stryy Ukr. **44** B2
Stuart Lake Can. **126** C2
Stull Lake Can. **126** F2
Stupino Rus. Fed. **42** E3
Sturgeon Bay U.S.A. **136** C2
Sturgeon Falls Can. **128** C2
Sturgeon Lake Can. **128** A2
Sturgis *MI* U.S.A. **136** C2
Sturgis *SD* U.S.A. **134** C2
Sturt Creek *watercourse* Austr. **114** B1
Sturt Stony Desert Austr. **116** C1
Stutterheim S. Africa **108** C3
Stuttgart Ger. **56** B3
Stuttgart U.S.A. **138** B2
Stykkishólmur Iceland **46**□
Styr *r.* Belarus/Ukr. **44** C1
Suaçuí Grande *r.* Brazil **154** D1
Suakin Sudan **102** B3
Suara, Mount Eritrea **90** A3

Szentgotthárd Hungary **56** D3
Szigetvár Hungary **56** D3
Szolnok Hungary **56** E3
Szombathely Hungary **56** D3

T

Tābah Saudi Arabia **90** B2
Ţabas Iran **92** D2
Tābask, Küh-e *mt.* Iran **92** D3
Tabatinga Brazil **150** C3
Tabelbala Alg. **100** B2
Taber Can. **126** D3
Tábor Czech Rep. **56** C3
Tabora Tanz. **104** D3
Tabou Côte d'Ivoire **100** B4
Tabrīz Iran **92** C2
Tabūk Saudi Arabia **90** A2
Täby Sweden **42** A2
Tacheng China **88** F2
Tachov Czech Rep. **56** C3
Tacloban Phil. **76** B2
Tacna Peru **150** B4
Tacoma U.S.A. **132** B1
Tacuarembó Uru. **152** C4
Tacupeto Mex. **140** C3
Tadjoura Djibouti **102** C3
Tadmur Syria **92** B2
Tadoule Lake Can. **126** F2
Taegu S. Korea **76** D2
Taejŏn S. Korea **76** D2
Taejŏng S. Korea **76** D3
T'aepaek S. Korea **76** D2
Ta'erqi China **80** E1
Tafalla Spain **60** C1
Tafi Viejo Arg. **152** B3
Taftān, Küh-e *mt.* Iran **90** D2
Taganrog Rus. Fed. **44** E2
Taganrog, Gulf of Rus. Fed./Ukr. **44** E2
Tagaung Myanmar **74** A1
Tagaytay City Phil. **76** B2
Tagbilaran Phil. **76** B3
Tagudin Phil. **76** B2
Tagum Phil. **76** B3
Tagus *r.* Port. **60** B2
Tagus *r.* Spain **60** B2
Tahan, Gunung *mt.* Malaysia **72** B1
Tahat, Mont *mt.* Alg. **100** C2
Tahe China **80** E1
Tahiti *i.* Fr. Polynesia **110**
Tahlequah U.S.A. **140** F1
Tahoe, Lake U.S.A. **132** B3
Tahoe City U.S.A. **132** B3
Tahoua Niger **100** C3
Tahrūd Iran **90** C2
Tahsis Can. **126** C3
Tai'an China **82** B2
T'aichung Taiwan **82** C3
Taihape N.Z. **118** C2
Tai Hu *l.* China **82** C2
Tailem Bend Austr. **116** B3
T'ainan Taiwan **82** C3
Taiobeiras Brazil **154** D1
T'aipei Taiwan **82** C3
Capital of Taiwan.
Taiping Malaysia **72** B1
Taishan China **82** B3
Taitao, Península de *pen.* Chile **152** A5
T'aitung Taiwan **82** C3
Taivalkoski Fin. **46** F2
Taivaskero *h.* Fin. **46** E2
Taiwan *country* Asia **82** C3
Taiwan Strait China/Taiwan **82** B3
Taiyuan China **82** B2
Taizhou *Jiangsu* China **82** B2
Taizhou *Zhejiang* China **82** C3
Ta'izz Yemen **90** B3
Tajamulco, Volcán de *vol.* Guat. **142** C3
Tajikistan *country* Asia **88** E3
Taj Mahal *tourist site* India **86** B2

Tajo *r.* Spain *see* Tagus
Tak Thai. **74** A2
Takaka N.Z. **118** B3
Takamatsu Japan **78** B4
Takaoka Japan **78** C3
Takapuna N.Z. **118** B2
Takasaki Japan **78** C3
Takatokwane Botswana **108** B1
Takatshwaane *Ghanzi* Botswana **108** B1
Takayama Japan **78** C3
Takefu Japan **78** C3
Takengon Indon. **72** A1
Takêv Cambodia **74** B2
Takhemaret Alg. **60** D2
Ta Khmau Cambodia **74** B2
Takikawa Japan **78** D2
Takla Lake Can. **126** C2
Takla Landing Can. **126** C2
Taklimakan Desert China **88** F3
Taklimakan Shamo *des.* China *see*
  Taklimakan Desert
Taku *r.* Can./U.S.A. **126** B2
Takua Pa Thai. **74** A3
Takum Nigeria **100** C4
Talachyn Belarus **42** C3
Talagang Pak. **86** B1
Talara Peru **150** A3
Talaud, Kepulauan *is* Indon. **70** C2
Talavera de la Reina Spain **60** C2
Talca Chile **152** A4
Talcahuano Chile **152** A4
Taldom Rus. Fed. **42** E2
Taldykorgan Kazakh. **88** E2
Talia Austr. **116** A2
Taliabu *i.* Indon. **70** C3
Talisay Phil. **76** B2
Taliwang Indon. **72** C2
Tall 'Afar Iraq **92** C2
Tallahassee U.S.A. **138** D2
  Capital of Florida.
Tallinn Estonia **42** B2
  Capital of Estonia.
Tallulah U.S.A. **138** B2
Talmont-St-Hilaire France **58** B2
Tal'ne Ukr. **44** D2
Talodi Sudan **102** B3
Tāloqān Afgh. **86** A1
Talovaya Rus. Fed. **42** F3
Taloyoak Can. **124** F2
Talsi Latvia **42** B2
Taltal Chile **152** A3
Taltson *r.* Can. **126** D1
Talu Indon. **72** A1
Talwood Austr. **116** D1
Tamala Rus. Fed. **44** F1
Tamale Ghana **100** B4
Tamana *r.* Kenya **104** E3
Tana, Lake Eth. **102** B3
Tanabe Japan **78** C4
Tana Bru Norway **46** F1
Tanahgrogot Indon. **72** C2
Tanahjampea *i.* Indon. **72** D2
Tanami Desert Austr. **114** C1
Tanana U.S.A. **124** B2
Tanaro *r.* Italy **62** A1

Tanch'ŏn N. Korea **76** D1
Tandag Phil. **76** B3
Ţāndārei Romania **44** C3
Ţandil Arg. **152** C4
Tando Adam Pak. **86** A2
Tando Muhammmad Khan Pak. **86** A2
Tanezrouft *reg.* Alg./Mali **100** B2
Tanga Tanz. **104** D3
Tanganyika, Lake Africa **104** C3
  Deepest and 2nd largest lake in Africa,
  and 7th largest in the world.
Tanger Morocco *see* Tangier
Tangermünde Ger. **54** E1
Tanggula Shan *mt.* China **86** D1
Tanggula Shan *mts* China **86** C1
Tangier Morocco **100** B1
Tangra Yumco *salt l.* China **86** C1
Tangshan China **82** B2
Taniantaweng Shan *mts* China **80** C2
Tanimbar, Kepulauan *is* Indon. **70** C3
Tanjay Phil. **76** B3
Tanjungbalai Indon. **72** A1
Tanjungpandan Indon. **72** B2
Tanjungpinang Indon. **72** B1
Tanjungredeb Indon. **72** C1
Tanjungselor Indon. **72** C1
Tank Pak. **86** B1
Tanna *i.* Vanuatu **110**
Tanout Niger **100** C3
Tansen Nepal **86** C2
Ţanţā Egypt **102** B1
Tanzania *country* Africa **104** D3
Taonan China **80** E1
Taos U.S.A. **140** C1
Taoudenni Mali **100** B2
Tapa Estonia **42** C2
Tapachula Mex. **142** C3
Tapajós *r.* Brazil **150** D3
Tapaktuan Indon. **72** A1
Tapanatepec Mex. **142** C3
Tapauá Brazil **150** C3
Tapeta Liberia **100** B4
Tapi *r.* India **86** B2
Tappahannock U.S.A. **136** E3
Tapurucuara Brazil **150** C3
Taquarí *r.* Brazil **154** A1
Taquarí, Pantanal do *marsh* Brazil
  154 A1
Taquarí, Serra do *hills* Brazil **154** B1
Taquaritinga Brazil **154** C2
Taraba *r.* Nigeria **100** D4
Ţarābulus Libya *see* Tripoli
Tarakan Indon. **72** C1
Taran, Mys *pt* Rus. Fed. **42** A3
Taranaki, Mount *vol.* N.Z. **118** B2
Tarancón Spain **60** C1
Taranto Italy **62** C2
Taranto, Golfo di *g.* Italy **62** C2
Tarapoto Peru **150** B3
Tarasovskiy Rus. Fed. **44** F2
Tarauacá Brazil **150** B3
Tarauacá *r.* Brazil **150** C3
Tarawa *atoll* Kiribati **110**
Taraz Kazakh. **88** C2
Tarazona Spain **60** C1
Tarbagatay, Khrebet *mts* Kazakh. **88** F2
Tarbert *Scotland* U.K. **50** A2
Tarbert *Scotland* U.K. **50** B3
Tarbes France **58** C3
Tarbet U.K. **50** B2
Tarcoola Austr. **116** A2
Taree Austr. **116** E2
Târgovişte Romania **44** C3
Targuist Morocco **60** D2
Târgu Jiu Romania **44** B2
Târgu Mureş Romania **44** B2
Târgu Neamţ Romania **44** C2
Tarif U.A.E. **90** C2
Tarija Bol. **152** B3
Tarīm Yemen **90** B3
Tarim Basin China **88** F3

Tremblant, Mont *h*. Can. **128** C2
Tremiti, Isole *is* Italy **62** C2
Tremonton U.S.A. **132** D2
Třemošná Czech Rep. **54** F3
Tremp Spain **60** D1
Trenčín Slovakia **56** D3
Trenque Lauquén Arg. **152** B4
Trent *r*. U.K. **52** C3
Trento Italy **62** B1
Trenton Can. **136** E2
Trenton *MO* U.S.A. **134** E2
Trenton *NJ* U.S.A. **136** F2
Capital of New Jersey.
Trepassey Can. **128** E2
Tres Arroyos Arg. **152** B4
Três Corações Brazil **154** C2
Três Lagoas Brazil **154** B2
Tres Lagos Arg. **152** A5
Três Marias, Represa *resr* Brazil **154** C1
Três Pontas Brazil **154** C2
Tres Puntas, Cabo *c*. Arg. **152** B5
Três Rios Brazil **154** D2
Treuenbrietzen Ger. **54** F1
Treviglio Italy **62** A1
Treviso Italy **62** B1
Trevose Head *hd* U.K. **52** A4
Tricase Italy **62** C3
Trichur India **84** B3
Trida Austr. **116** D2
Trier Ger. **54** C3
Trieste Italy **62** B1
Triglav *mt*. Slovenia **62** B1
Trikora, Puncak *mt*. Indon. **70** D3
2nd highest mountain in Oceania.
Trim Rep. of Ireland **50** G2
Trincomalee Sri Lanka **84** C4
Trindade Brazil **154** C1
Trinidad Bol. **152** B2
Trinidad *i*. Trin. and Tob. **144** D3
Trinidad U.S.A. **134** C4
Trinidad and Tobago *country*
West Indies **144** D3
Trinity Bay Can. **128** E2
Tripoli Greece **64** B3
Tripoli Lebanon **92** B2
Tripoli Libya **100** D1
Capital of Libya.
Tristan da Cunha *i*. S. Atlantic Ocean
160 D8
Dependency of St Helena.
Trivandrum India **84** B4
Trivento Italy **62** B2
Trnava Slovakia **56** D3
Trogir Croatia **62** C2
Troia Italy **62** C2
Troisdorf Ger. **54** C2
Trois Fourches, Cap des *c*. Morocco
60 C2
Trois-Rivières Can. **128** C2
Troitsko-Pechorsk Rus. Fed. **40** E2
Trombetas *r*. Brazil **150** D3
Trompsburg S. Africa **108** C3
Tromsø Norway **46** D4
Trondheim Norway **46** C3
Trout Lake Can. **126** D2
Trout Lake *l. N.W.T.* Can. **126** C1
Trout Lake *l. Ont.* Can. **128** A1
Trowbridge U.K. **52** B4
Troy *AL* U.S.A. **138** C2
Troy *NY* U.S.A. **136** F2
Troyes France **58** C2
Trstenik S.M. **64** B2
Trubchevsk Rus. Fed. **42** D3
Truchas Spain **60** B1
Trucial Coast U.A.E. **90** C2
Trujillo Hond. **144** B3
Trujillo Peru **150** B3
Trujillo Spain **60** B2
Trujillo Venez. **144** C4
Trulben Ger. **54** C3
Trumann U.S.A. **138** B1

Truro Can. **128** D2
Truro U.K. **52** A4
Truth or Consequences U.S.A. **140** C2
Trutnov Czech Rep. **56** D2
Trysil Norway **46** C3
Trzebiatów Pol. **56** D2
Tsagaannuur Mongolia **80** B1
Tsaratanana, Massif du *mts* Madag.
106□ D1
Tsarevo Bulg. **64** C2
Tselina Rus. Fed. **44** F2
Tses Namibia **108** A2
Tsetseng Botswana **108** B1
Tsetserleg Mongolia **80** C1
Tshabong Botswana **108** B2
Tshane Botswana **108** B1
Tshchikskoye Vodokhranilishche *resr*
Rus. Fed. **44** E2
Tshela Dem. Rep. Congo **104** B3
Tshikapa Dem. Rep. Congo **104** C3
Tshikapa *r*. Dem. Rep. Congo **104** C3
Tshipise S. Africa **108** D1
Tshitanzu Dem. Rep. Congo **104** C3
Tshuapa *r*. Dem. Rep. Congo **104** C3
Tshwane S. Africa *see* Pretoria
Tsimlyanskoye Vodokhranilishche *resr*
Rus. Fed. **40** D4
Tsingtao China *see* Qingdao
Tsiroanomandidy Madag. **106**□ D1
Tsna *r*. Rus. Fed. **42** F3
Tsomo S. Africa **108** C3
Tsu Japan **78** C4
Tsuchiura Japan **78** D3
Tsugarū-kaikyō *str*. Japan **78** D2
Tsumeb Namibia **106** A1
Tsumis Park Namibia **108** A1
Tsumkwe Namibia **106** B1
Tsuruga Japan **78** C3
Tsuruoka Japan **78** C3
Tsushima *is* Japan **78** A4
Tsuyama Japan **78** B3
Tswelelang S. Africa **108** C2
Tsyurupyns'k Ukr. **44** D2
Tual Indon. **70** C3
Tuam Rep. of Ireland **50** F2
Tuamotu Archipelago *is* Fr. Polynesia
158 F6
Tuapse Rus. Fed. **44** E3
Tuatapere N.Z. **118** A4
Tuath, Loch a' *b*. U.K. **50** A1
Tuba City U.S.A. **140** B1
Tuban Indon. **72** C2
Tubarão Brazil **152** D3
Tübingen Ger. **56** B3
Tubruq Libya **100** E1
Tubuai Islands Fr. Polynesia **110**
Tubutama Mex. **142** A1
Tucavaca Bol. **152** C2
Tuchitua Can. **126** C1
Tucson U.S.A. **140** B2
Tucumcari U.S.A. **140** D1
Tucupita Venez. **150** C2
Tucurui Brazil **150** E3
Tucuruí, Represa *resr* Brazil **150** E3
Tudela Spain **60** C1
Tuela *r*. Port. **60** B1
Tuensang India **74** C1
Tugela *r*. S. Africa **108** D2
Tuguegarao Phil. **76** B2
Tui Spain **60** B1
Tukangbesi, Kepulauan *is* Indon.
70 C3
Tuktoyaktuk Can. **124** D2
Tukums Latvia **42** B2
Tula Mex. **142** C2
Tula Rus. Fed. **42** E3
Tulancingo Mex. **142** C2
Tulare U.S.A. **132** C3
Tularosa U.S.A. **140** C2
Tulcea Romania **44** C2
Tul'chyn Ukr. **44** C2

Tulemalu Lake Can. **126** F1
Tulia U.S.A. **140** D2
Tulít'a Can. **126** C1
Tullahoma U.S.A. **138** C1
Tullamore Rep. of Ireland **50** G2
Tulle France **58** C2
Tully Austr. **114** D1
Tulsa U.S.A. **140** E1
Tuluksak U.S.A. **124** B2
Tumaco Col. **150** B2
Tumahole S. Africa **108** C2
Tumba Sweden **46** D4
Tumba, Lac *l*. Dem. Rep. Congo **104** B3
Tumbarumba Austr. **116** D3
Tumbes Peru **150** A3
Tumbler Ridge Can. **126** C2
Tumby Bay Austr. **116** B2
Tumen China **76** D1
Tumereng Guyana **150** C2
Tumindao *i*. Phil. **76** A3
Tumkur India **84** B3
Tumnin *r*. Rus. Fed. **80** F1
Tump Pak. **86** A2
Tumucumaque, Serra *hills* Brazil **150** D2
Tumut Austr. **116** D3
Tunbridge Wells, Royal U.K. **52** D4
Tunceli Turkey **92** B2
Tuncurry Austr. **116** E2
Tunduru Tanz. **104** D4
Tundzha *r*. Bulg. **64** C2
Tungsten Can. **126** C1
Tunis Tunisia **100** D1
Capital of Tunisia.
Tunisia *country* Africa **100** C1
Tunja Col. **150** B2
Tunnsjøen *l*. Norway **46** C3
Tupã Brazil **154** B2
Tupaciguara Brazil **154** C1
Tupelo U.S.A. **138** C2
Tupiza Bol. **152** B3
Tura Rus. Fed. **94** I2
Tura *r*. Rus. Fed. **40** F3
Turabah Saudi Arabia **90** B2
Turana, Khrebet *mts* Rus. Fed. **94** K3
Turangi N.Z. **118** C2
Turan Lowland Asia **88** C3
Turayf Saudi Arabia **90** A1
Turba Estonia **42** B2
Turbat Pak. **86** A2
Turbo Col. **150** B2
Turda Romania **44** B1
Turfan China *see* Turpan
Turgay Kazakh. **88** D2
Turgutlu Turkey **64** C3
Turhal Turkey **92** B1
Turia *r*. Spain **60** C2
Turin Italy **62** A1
Turinsk Rus. Fed. **40** F3
Turiys'k Ukr. **44** B1
Turkana, Lake *salt l*. Eth./Kenya **102** B4
Turkestan Kazakh. **88** D2
Turkey *country* Asia/Europe **92** B2
Turkmenabat Turkm. **88** D3
Turkmenbashi Turkm. **88** C2
Turkmenistan *country* Asia **88** C2
Turks and Caicos Islands *terr.*
West Indies **144** D2
United Kingdom Overseas Territory.
Turku Fin. **46** E3
Turlock U.S.A. **132** B3
Turnagain, Cape N.Z. **118** C3
Turneffe Islands *atoll* Belize **142** D3
Turnhout Belgium **54** E3
Turnor Lake Can. **126** E2
Turnu Măgurele Romania **64** B2
Turpan China **88** F2
Turugart Pass China/Kyrg. **88** E2
Tuscaloosa U.S.A. **138** C2
Tuskegee U.S.A. **138** C2
Tuticorin India **84** B4
Tutume Botswana **106** B2

Ussuriysk Rus. Fed. **78** B2
Ust'-Donetskiy Rus. Fed. **44** F2
Ustica, Isola di *i.* Italy **62** B3
Ust'-Ilimsk Rus. Fed. **94** I3
Ust'-Ilych Rus. Fed. **40** E2
Ustka Pol. **56** D2
Ust'-Kamchatsk Rus. Fed. **94** M3
Ust'-Kamenogorsk Kazakh. **88** F2
Ust'-Kara Rus. Fed. **40** F2
Ust'-Kulom Rus. Fed. **40** E2
Ust'-Kut Rus. Fed. **94** J3
Ust'-Labinsk Rus. Fed. **44** E2
Ust'-Luga Rus. Fed. **42** C2
Ust'-Nem Rus. Fed. **40** E2
Ust'-Nera Rus. Fed. **94** L2
Ust'-Omchug Rus. Fed. **94** L2
Ust'-Ordynskiy Rus. Fed. **94** I3
Ust'-Port Rus. Fed. **40** H1
Ust'-Tsil'ma Rus. Fed. **40** E2
Ust'-Ura Rus. Fed. **40** D2
Ustyurt Plateau Kazakh./Uzbek. **88** C2
Ustyuzhna Rus. Fed. **42** E2
Usvyaty Rus. Fed. **42** D2
Utah *state* U.S.A. **132** D3
Utah Lake U.S.A. **132** D2
Utena Lith. **42** C2
Utica U.S.A. **136** E2
Utiel Spain **60** C2
Utikuma Lake Can. **126** D2
Utrecht Neth. **54** B1
Utrera Spain **60** B2
Utsjoki Fin. **46** F2
Utsunomiya Japan **78** C3
Utta Rus. Fed. **40** D4
Uttaradit Thai. **74** B2
Uummannaq Greenland *see* Dundas
Uummannaq Fjord *inlet* Greenland **124** I2
Uusikaupunki Fin. **46** E3
Uvalde U.S.A. **140** E3
Uvarovo Rus. Fed. **44** F1
Uvinza Tanz. **104** D3
Uvs Nuur *salt l.* Mongolia **80** C1
Uwajima Japan **78** B4
'Uwayriḍ, Ḥarrat al *lava field* Saudi Arabia **90** A2
Uweinat, Jebel *mt.* Sudan **102** A2
Uyar Rus. Fed. **94** I3
Uyo Nigeria **100** C4
Uyuni Bol. **152** B3
Uyuni, Salar de *salt flat* Bol. **152** B3
Uzbekistan *country* Asia **88** D2
Uzerche France **58** C2
Uzès France **58** C3
Uzh *r.* Ukr. **44** D1
Uzhhorod Ukr. **44** B2
Užice S.M. **64** A2
Uzlovaya Rus. Fed. **42** E3
Üzümlü Turkey **64** C3
Uzunköprü Turkey **64** C2

V

Vaal *r.* S. Africa **108** B2
Vaal Dam S. Africa **108** C2
Vaalwater S. Africa **108** C1
Vaasa Fin. **46** E3
Vác Hungary **56** D3
Vacaria Brazil **152** C3
Vacaria, Serra *hills* Brazil **154** B2
Vacaville U.S.A. **132** B3
Vacha Rus. Fed. **42** F2
Vadodara India **86** B2
Vadsø Norway **46** F1
Vaduz Liechtenstein **58** D2
Capital of Liechtenstein.
Vágar *i.* Faroe Is **48** B1
Vágur Faroe Is **48** B1
Váh *r.* Slovakia **56** D3

Vaiaku Tuvalu **112**
Capital of Tuvalu, on Funafuti atoll.
Vaida Estonia **42** B2
Vail U.S.A. **134** B3
Vakīlābād Iran **90** C2
Valdagno Italy **62** B1
Valday Rus. Fed. **42** D2
Valdayskaya Vozvyshennost' *hills* Rus. Fed. **42** D2
Valdecañas, Embalse de *resr* Spain **60** B2
Valdemarsvik Sweden **46** D4
Val-de-Meuse France **58** D2
Valdepeñas Spain **60** C2
Val-de-Reuil France **52** D5
Valdés, Península *pen.* Arg. **152** B5
Lowest point in South America.
Valdez U.S.A. **126** A1
Valdivia Chile **152** A4
Val-d'Or Can. **128** C2
Valdosta U.S.A. **138** D2
Valemount Can. **126** D2
Valence France **58** C3
Valencia Spain **60** C2
Valencia Venez. **150** C1
Valencia, Golfo de *g.* Spain **60** D2
Valenciennes France **54** A2
Valentine U.S.A. **134** C2
Valenzuela Phil. **76** B2
Valera Venez. **150** B2
Valjevo S.M. **64** A2
Valka Latvia **42** C2
Valkeakoski Fin. **46** E3
Valkenswaard Neth. **54** B2
Valky Ukr. **44** E2
Valkyrie Dome *ice feature* Antarctica **118** G2
Valladolid Mex. **142** D2
Valladolid Spain **60** C1
Vall de Uxó Spain **60** C2
Valle Norway **46** B4
Vallecillos Mex. **142** C2
Valle de la Pascua Venez. **150** C2
Valledupar Col. **150** B1
Valle Hermoso Mex. **142** C2
Vallejo U.S.A. **132** B3
Vallenar Chile **152** A3
Valletta Malta **100** D1
Capital of Malta.
Valley City U.S.A. **134** D1
Valley Falls U.S.A. **132** B2
Valleyview Can. **126** D2
Valls Spain **60** D1
Val Marie Can. **134** B1
Valmiera Latvia **42** C2
Valognes France **52** C5
Valozhyn Belarus **42** C3
Valparaíso Brazil **154** B2
Valparaíso Chile **152** A4
Valréas France **58** C3
Vals, Tanjung *c.* Indon. **70** D3
Valsad India **86** B2
Valspan S. Africa **108** B2
Valuyki Rus. Fed. **44** E1
Valverde del Camino Spain **60** B2
Van Turkey **92** C2
Van, Lake *salt l.* Turkey **92** C2
Van Buren U.S.A. **136** G1
Vancouver Can. **126** C3
Vancouver U.S.A. **132** B1
Vancouver Island Can. **126** C3
Vandalia U.S.A. **136** C3
Vanderbijlpark S. Africa **108** C2
Vanderhoof Can. **126** C2
Van Diemen Gulf Austr. **70** C3
Vändra Estonia **42** C2
Vänern *l.* Sweden **46** C4
3rd largest lake in Europe.
Vänersborg Sweden **46** C4
Vangaindrano Madag. **106**□ D2
Van Gölü *salt l.* Turkey *see* Van, Lake

Van Horn U.S.A. **140** D2
Vanimo P.N.G. **70** D3
Vanino Rus. Fed. **80** F1
Vannes France **58** B2
Van Rees, Pegunungan *mts* Indon. **70** D3
Vanrhynsdorp S. Africa **108** A3
Vantaa Fin. **46** E3
Vanua Levu *i.* Fiji **158** E6
Vanuatu *country* S. Pacific Ocean **112**
Van Wert U.S.A. **136** D2
Vanwyksvlei S. Africa **108** B3
Van Zylsrus S. Africa **108** B2
Varanasi India **86** C2
Varangerfjorden *sea chan.* Norway **46** F1
Varangerhalvøya *pen.* Norway **46** F1
Varaždin Croatia **62** C1
Varberg Sweden **46** C4
Vardar *r.* Macedonia **64** B2
Varde Denmark **46** B4
Vardø Norway **46** G1
Varel Ger. **54** C1
Varėna Lith. **42** B3
Varese Italy **62** A1
Varginha Brazil **154** C2
Varkaus Fin. **46** F3
Varna Bulg. **64** C2
Värnamo Sweden **46** C4
Várzea da Palma Brazil **154** D1
Varzino Rus. Fed. **40** C2
Vasknarva Estonia **42** C2
Vaslui Romania **44** C2
Västerås Sweden **46** D4
Västerdalälven *r.* Sweden **46** D3
Västerhaninge Sweden **42** A2
Västervik Sweden **46** D4
Vasto Italy **62** B2
Vasyl'kiv Ukr. **44** D1
Vatan France **58** C2
Vatican City Europe **62** B2
Vatnajökull *ice cap* Iceland **46**□
Vatra Dornei Romania **44** C2
Vättern *l.* Sweden **46** C4
Vaughn U.S.A. **140** C2
Vauvert France **58** C3
Vava'u Group *is* Tonga **110**
Vawkavysk Belarus **42** B3
Växjö Sweden **46** C4
Vaygach, Ostrov *i.* Rus. Fed. **40** E1
Vechta Ger. **54** D1
Vedea *r.* Romania **44** C3
Veendam Neth. **54** C1
Veenendaal Neth. **54** B1
Vegreville Can. **126** D2
Vejer de la Frontera Spain **60** B2
Vejle Denmark **46** B4
Velbüzhdki Prokhod *pass* Bulg./Macedonia **64** B2
Veldhoven Neth. **54** B2
Velebit *mts* Croatia **62** B2
Velen Ger. **54** C2
Velenje Slovenia **62** C1
Veles Macedonia **62** B2
Vélez-Málaga Spain **60** C2
Velhas *r.* Brazil **154** D1
Velika Plana S.M. **64** B2
Velikaya *r.* Rus. Fed. **42** C2
Velikiye Luki Rus. Fed. **42** D2
Velikiy Novgorod Rus. Fed. **42** D2
Velikiy Ustyug Rus. Fed. **40** D2
Veliko Tŭrnovo Bulg. **64** C2
Veli Lošinj Croatia **62** B2
Velizh Rus. Fed. **42** D2
Vellberg Ger. **54** D3
Vel'sk Rus. Fed. **40** D2
Velten Ger. **54** F1
Velykyy Burluk Ukr. **44** E1
Venafro Italy **62** B2
Venceslau Bráz Brazil **154** C2
Vendôme France **58** C2
Venev Rus. Fed. **42** E3
Venezia Italy *see* Venice

INDEX

250

INDEX

252

All mapping in this atlas is generated from Collins Bartholomew digital databases. Collins Bartholomew, the UK's leading independent geographical information supplier, can provide a digital, custom, and premium mapping service to a variety of markets. For further information:
Tel: +44 (0) 141 306 3752
e-mail: collinsbartholomew@harpercollins.co.uk

We also offer a choice of books, atlases and maps that can be customized to suit a customer's own requirements. For further information:
Tel: +44 (0) 141 306 3209
e-mail: business.gifts@harpercollins.co.uk

or visit our website at: www.collinsbartholomew.com

INDEX